BEYOND BULLETS AND BOMBS

Recent Titles in
Contemporary Psychology

BEYOND BULLETS AND BOMBS

Grassroots Peacebuilding between Israelis and Palestinians

Edited by Judy Kuriansky, PhD

Contemporary Psychology
Chris E. Stout, Series Editor

Westport, Connecticut
London

5/14/08
Lan
49.95

Library of Congress Cataloging-in-Publication Data

Beyond bullets and bombs : grassroots peacebuilding between Israelis and Palestinians / edited by Judy Kuriansky.

    p. cm. — (Contemporary psychology, ISSN 1546–668X)

Includes index.

  ISBN–13: 978–0–275–99880–6

  ISBN–10: 0–275–99880–0

1. Arab-Israeli conflict—1993—Peace. I. Kuriansky, Judith.

DS119.76.B526 2007

956.9405'4—dc22   2007016059

British Library Cataloguing in Publication Data is available.

Library of Congress Catalog Card Number: 2007016059

ISBN-13: 978–0–275–99880–6

ISBN-10: 0–275–99880–0

ISSN: 1546–668X

First published in 2007

Praeger Publishers, 88 Post Road West, Westport, CT 06881

An imprint of Greenwood Publishing Group, Inc.

www.praeger.com

Printed in the United States of America

The paper used in this book complies with the Permanent Paper Standard issued by the National Information Standards Organization (Z39.48–1984).

10 9 8 7 6 5 4 3 2 1

The publisher has done its best to make sure the instructions and/or recipes in this book are correct. However, users should apply judgment and experience when preparing recipes, especially parents and teachers working with young people. The publisher accepts no responsibility for the outcome of any recipe included in this volume.

*To all the courageous Palestinians and Israelis, Arabs and Jews,
and others from diverse backgrounds and countries around the world,
who are devoting their time, treasure, and talent so that one day all
people will no longer have to live with the threat of bullets and bombs,
but can live together in mutual trust, tolerance, and peace.*

Blessed are the peacemakers, for they shall be called Sons of God.

—*Matthew 5:9*

CONTENTS

FOREWORD

The high-water mark reached by Dr. Kuriansky in her earlier book, *Terror in the Holy Land: Inside the Anguish of the Israeli-Palestinian Conflict* may be eclipsed by this volume, as she takes the dialogue between Israelis and Palestinians to the next level. In doing so, she presents real evidence here that such cooperation between the two peoples can indeed happen. It is such cooperation that is essential in the seemingly intractable conflict.

In the earlier volume, Dr. Kuriansky brought together Israelis and Palestinians who are on the ground in the region, to present issues of the men, women and children suffering on both sides. I have noted that *Terror in the Holy Land* is a truly impressive effort—really the first book of its kind presenting the psychosocial issues behind the conflict by experts from *both* sides in a balanced way. Experts from other cultures also contributed their perspective and experience, including Dr. Kuriansky herself, in what is truly a major contribution to the field of psychology and other disciplines including international relations, political science, culture studies, sociology, and humanitarian interventionism.

Beyond Bullets and Bombs continues where *Terror in the Holy Land* left off. Where *Terror* presented a dialogue through different chapters presenting each side's point of view, *Beyond*, shows how people from both sides are working together, through actual dialogue or cooperative activities. It is the perfect—and essential—follow-up and companion volume. Both are no easy task for even the most heroic of books—as I mentioned in my Foreword for the previous book—as they successfully blend clinical, cultural, historical, religious and anthropological as well as educational perspectives so well together.

In reviewing this book, I am struck with the strength of character and courage of the individuals and groups who are creating cooperative projects despite the overwhelming practical and political blocks. With determination and vision, they are bringing the two sides into engagement with compassion, understanding and action. This effort resonates with me, as it is synchronous with my work with Mari Fitzduff in *The Psychology of Resolving Global Conflicts* (3 volumes, Praeger, 2006) where we explore the challenges and the psychological theories behind endeavors to resolve conflict. In that scholarly tradition, this book examines the principles behind psychological and sociological approaches to the specific conflict, and offers interesting and creative theoretical models to understand the issues and possibilities for resolution. Other chapters show theory in action. Particularly impressive are the efforts of young people, as Palestinian and Israeli youth come together to clean beaches, attend camps, and even produce films to learn about each other, confront the conflict, present their perspective, and forge relationships to turn "enemies" into friends. This is especially heartening in the chapters which describe how youth from other countries—like Japan and Germany—are working hard to create projects—and raise funds to support those efforts—that provide opportunities for Israeli and Palestinian teens to come together. Adults from all walks of life—dentists, real estate developers and housewives—are also devoting valued time and resources to bring people from both sides together in creative ways from the perspective of education, training, and even the arts and entertainment.

For the years that I have known Dr. Kuriansky, I have been continuously impressed with her scholarly approach to research as well as her remarkable sensitivity in her clinical work. While her credentials speak for themselves—with many scientific publications and seminars around the world on cross-cultural and international issues—I have been in professional arenas with her where these qualities, skills, and truly, her humanity, have been evident in her interactions with professionals and people of all cultures.

Most recently, for example, we were both presenting at the Middle East and North African Regional Psychology conference in Amman, Jordan. At this conference, Dr. Kuriansky talked about the topics in this volume, and about her work at the United Nations in bringing psychological issues to the attention of global leaders. Soon thereafter, she went to Geneva to represent the United Nations Committee on Mental Health at the Global Platform for Disaster Risk Reduction, further bringing her skills of advocacy for psychological well-being and peace to global attention. In these arenas, her role resonates with me, given my collaboration with Harvey Langholtz on the book, *The Psychology of Diplomacy (Psychological Dimensions to War and Peace)* where we interviewed psychologists and diplomats to examine their qualities. From that analysis, I would say that Dr. Kuriansky bridges the two disciplines, as a psychologist and a diplomat, being idealistic and egalitarian yet practical when it comes to facilitating between peoples of divergent cultures seeking different outcomes. One might think of her as an "Ambassador of Peace."

As an author of many edited volumes, I know how much work it takes to put together such a project as reflected in this book. For this reason, I am impressed with the range of views of contributors that Dr. Kuriansky has engaged for this book, as well as the sheer number of authors whose work is represented here. It is testimony to her devotion to cross-cultural work and peace in the region and the world. It is further a hopeful reflection of the extensive number and varied types of projects that are going on, despite obstacles, to bring people together from Israeli and Palestinian backgrounds and from Jewish, Arab and Christian cultures. She, and they, are to be credited for bringing their heroic efforts to public attention. All too often, we hear "bad news" about violence in the region and the world. Here, finally, is some "good news."

With the many roles I have held and in the context of international work, I recommend this book to colleagues, policy makers, peace activists, political scientists and students at all levels. I also recommend it to individuals and groups who want to start their own project and are looking for inspiration and models. I further encourage spreading the word about the grassroots efforts presented here. After all, even when governments reach accord, only by seeding and supporting such civilian efforts for peace as presented here, will there be hope for lasting change and peace. Once again, we readers are indebted to Dr. Kuriansky and those whose voices she has brought forth in this wonderful book.

Chris E. Stout
Series editor, Contemporary Psychology

Acknowledgments

This project reflects the ongoing good energy of friends, family, colleagues, and students who supported the intention and realization of this book and the first volume, *Terror in the Holy Land: Inside the Anguish of the Israeli-Palestinian Conflict*. These include the amazing team of Len and Libby Traubman who offered valuable suggestions about important projects to include, who connected me to many people so dedicated to this cause who became good friends, and who inspired me to participate in innumerable activities from conferences to peace camps. I'm also grateful to Tufts graduate Rachel Brandenburg who read through manuscripts with her enthusiastic devotion and familiarity with cooperative projects, and to my student Neil Walsh, who was not only constantly supportive and helpful but always sent me relevant references about contacts and developments on this topic and information on everything else one can think of, in the spirit of what we both like being—a true Renaissance person. Others provided inspiration and support from the start like my Smith College intern, Olivia Moskowitz, Teachers College student Dror Post, professor Salman Elbedour, peace activist Adam Shapiro, my dear time-honored friend Diana Heller, and my cherished former student and friend Deborah Schoenblum who traveled the world with me to places and conferences in Europe and the Middle East that formed the heart of this book. I honor and acknowledge kindred spirit, dear friend and colleague. Evelin Lindner—a true "Citizen of the World," and thank all my friends, including Bircan Unver, who sensitize me to different cultures.

It was truly a wonderful process to have the voice of my dear friend Teri Whitcraft "in my head" as I was writing, and then a gift to have her again apply her expert edit skills and brilliant judgment to this book as she did for the first volume on this important topic. I am also deeply appreciative of the devotion, commitment, enthusiasm and endless hours of tireless work that Tali Elisha spent with me on all aspects of this project. I hold fond memories of times with my former student and dear friend and co-lyricist Russell Daisey, performing our songs of peace around the world including for His Holiness the Dalai Lama and Reverend Desmond Tutu at the Hiroshima Peace Summit, and I deeply appreciate his loving support, perfect processing and brilliant attention to detail, helping me down to the very last minute; indeed proof of his talents and valued friendship. I am most fortunate, too, for the unfailing support of my editor at Praeger/Greenwood Publishing, Deborah Carvalko, who supported the vision of this and the previous volume throughout, and showed her usual excellent judgment and impressive mix of kindness and professionalism. Others I appreciate at Praeger include Karen Holmgren, Laura Mullen and Anthony Chiffolo, as well as the folks at Apex Publishing who cared about this book and worked so hard to make it perfect. Special love and appreciation to my husband Edward—amazing, loving and brilliant human being that he is—and to my mom Sylvia—angel that she is—for her devotion, unconditional love, valuable advice, and endless hours of encouragement, listening, and good advice in this and everything.

My deep gratitude goes particularly to all the authors in this volume, and the people in the organizations and projects they represent, who contributed their expertise and professionalism and shared their personal experiences and vision for peace in the region. Finally, heartfelt appreciation goes to all the people in the region and throughout the world who are working toward—and deserve—trust, understanding, acceptance, security, and peace.

My hope for the future is well expressed in a song from a Jacques Brel revue, that I heard Theodore Bikel sing at a Renaissance Weekend gathering on New Year's Eve, 2005. In the Charleston, South Carolina, Beth Elohim Synagogue—a National Historic Landmark and the country's oldest synagogue in continuous use—Bikel's voice rang out that if we only have love, we can reach people in pain, heal all our wounds, and melt all the guns, and *then give the new world to our daughters and sons.*

INTRODUCTION: A PROFESSIONAL AND PERSONAL ODYSSEY FOR PEACE

Judy Kuriansky

Out beyond ideas of rightdoing and wrongdoing, there is a field. I'll meet you there.

—*Jelaluddin Rumi, thirteenth-century poet, mystic, and scholar*

At a gathering in a New York City apartment in 2004, Aziz, a young Palestinian, and Ya'ara, a young Israeli, shared their stories about losing their brothers as a result of the Intifada. Aziz's brother was shot by an Israeli soldier, imprisoned, and later died. I cried as he recounted how he initially felt hatred and resentment, but as he wrote about these feelings as a journalist, he realized his hatred was only hurting himself. Eventually he quit his journalism job and turned to learning Hebrew—the language of the then-"enemy." Over time, as he met real-life Jews and shared with them the mutual pain of losing loved ones as a result of the violence between Palestinians and Israelis, his hatred turned to compassion. Ya'ara then told about how her beloved brother committed suicide rather than kill others in the conflict, and how she similarly transformed her hatred into compassion. Both Aziz and Ya'ara joined an organization of bereaved families— the Parents Circle-Families Forum—devoted to helping people from both sides of the conflict turn the commonality of their experience into a path to peace.

Aziz and Ya'ara are just two of the many inspiring, heartwarming people I've met, and friendships I've formed, with Arabs and Jews deeply suffering from the conflict but who still believe in working together for mutual understanding and peace. Their stories are recounted in this volume, along with many others I've encountered during meetings in this country and around the world, visits to the region, innumerable conferences like at the Center for Judaic and Middle Eastern Studies supported by my own family foundation (the Kuriansky Foundation), and events I've organized at the United Nations where I represent two international psychological organizations. In the midst of persistent turmoil—and even the recent instability caused by civil war between Hamas and Fatah—brave Palestinians and Israelis continue to create partnerships for peace. Their individual efforts—marching, camping, bicycling, dialoguing—are impressive, and seeing them all together is inspiring.

Peace between Palestinians and Israelis is not only critical for the region but also for the world. Throughout the period of the 2006 Lebanon War and the ongoing Iraq War—during which time this book was being put together— experts and pundits made constant references to how peace cannot be achieved in the Middle East unless the conflict between Israelis and Palestinians is resolved. I heard this posited by many commentators on television shows, by noted speakers at the 2006 Clinton Global Initiative I attended, and by the drafters of the "2006 Iraq Study Group Report: The Way Forward—A New Approach."

While I, like many others, have become frustrated that the goal of peace remains thwarted in political channels, I am heartened that impressive strides are being made in what's called "people-to-people" efforts—civilians working together in grassroots projects. These people "on the ground" are cooperating to dispel fear and mistrust and to foster mutual understanding, cooperation, and coexistence. Their projects take many interesting and creative forms, in fields of education, counseling, and arts and entertainment. Israelis and Palestinians, Jews and Arabs, young and old, male and female, scholars and students, are sailing, cooking, climbing mountains, camping, cleaning beaches, and of course, talking together—for peace. Their efforts are impressively noble and courageous, especially given the obstacles they must overcome, such as pervasive violence, fears of reprisal for "cooperating with the enemy," and insufficient finding.

The collection of contributors in this book is a natural outgrowth from my previous volume, *Terror in the Holy Land: Inside the Anguish of the Israeli-Palestinian Conflict.* That book presented experiences and research by Israelis (Jews and Arabs) and Palestinians (Muslim and Christian), as well as some Americans and experts from other countries, about the psychosocial aspects of the conflict, including issues such as the search for identity and a homeland, the role of humiliation and revenge, and the emotional struggles of women, children, and families on both sides. As the first book of its kind to address the psychosocial perspectives in this conflict—in a balanced way—that volume includes the work of well-respected social scientists, as well as stories of Palestinian female martyrs, struggles of a daughter of a Jihadist raised to hate Jews but now calling for peace with Israelis, and efforts of a team teaching meditation to Palestinians and Israelis to find peace within and with others. Putting together that powerful collection of accounts, research and reflections from each side led to this book as the next logical step: presenting what people from both sides are doing together to build peace. The programs presented here further serve as impressive models for cooperation, coexistence, and peace in other troubled regions.

People are often surprised that I—a psychologist known for dealing with personal relationships for decades, particularly in the media, giving advice on radio and television and in newspaper and magazines—am now addressing the problems in the Middle East. In fact, I have long been involved in this issue. The seeds of my interest in the region dates back to my childhood dream for a more peaceful world and was sparked years later during my first visit to the region in 1969, and my subsequent introduction to the tragic violence characterizing the cultures when I arrived in Munich for the 1972 Olympics on the eve of the massacre of the Israeli athletes. Then, over many decades as a psychologist and relationship counselor doing work around the world, I came to realize how conflict resolution is similar whether applied to the microcosm of individuals, couples and families or to the macrocosm of nations. As I say, inner peace leads to outer peace—between people and even diverse cultures and countries. The Dalai Lama made this same connection when I heard him speak at the First International Hiroshima Peace Summit in November 2006. "We can never obtain peace in the world if we neglect the inner world and don't make peace with ourselves," he said. Even the former U.S. Secretary of Defense Robert McNamara recognized this association between interpersonal relations and global relations when he identified the "empathy imperative"—curiousity and understanding of the other's mindset and putting oneself "inside the other's skin"—as essential in international relations.

My involvement in the region is broad—from spending time there, to participating in innumerable meetings, moderating panels worldwide, teaching peace techniques, doing disaster relief, training local providers, financially supporting projects, and maintaining an extensive and continually expanding network of valued colleagues, students and friends from all perspectives. Many of these people have contributed chapters to this book. Pivotal experiences have intensified my commitment to peace in the region, like finding myself mediating between Israelis and Palestinians at a world conference on psychology during the height of the second Intifada, and also attending the Oseh Shalom~Sanea al-Salaam Palestinian-Jewish Family Peacemakers Camp in the summer of 2006.

As the famed psychologist Abraham Maslow said, "If your instrument in life is a hammer, then everywhere you go, you will find nails." And so it is with my interest in world peace and in the resolution of the Israeli-Palestinian conflict. I find myself constantly associating theoretical psychological frameworks and practical applications of therapeutic techniques to the conflict. Many of these are represented in chapters in this book. In addition, I find myself putting what people say about one situation into the context of the Middle East conflict. For example, in her acceptance of the Humanitarian Award from the Elie Wiesel Foundation at a gala in New York in May 2007, Oprah Winfrey spoke of how she loves her hundreds of pairs of shoes and her private plane, but her work with children in Africa has made her see that the purpose of life lies in contributing to others and making other people's lives' better. "When I leave this earth, I am not going to be asked how many diamonds and square footage of houses I have," she said, "But how did I serve?

What did I do for the powerless? Whose life is better because of me?" On hearing her explain this, I thought about how so many contributors to this book are doing just that—serving others.

Everywhere I go, I meet people who care about the problem in the Middle East, and very often I am asked to speak about the psychosocial issues of the conflict as presented in my previous book *Terror in the Holy Land* and about the grassroots projects for peace in this volume. These occasions include running workshops at annual meetings of the Human Dignity and Humiliation Studies organization, being involved in seminars at the Renaissance Weekend retreats, and making presentations at meetings such as for the Society for the Study of Peace, Conflict, and Violence of the American Psychological Association, and at the 2007 Winter Roundtable on Traditional and Non-Traditional Approaches to Addressing Race and Culture in Psychology and Education at Teachers College in New York, where I teach. At the IV International Congress of Psychic Trauma and Traumatic Stress organized by the Argentine Society for Psychotrauma in Buenos Aires, I even willingly filled in for speakers from the region who unfortunately could not attend—to run a workshop about "Children in Conflict Zones: Psychotherapeutic Techniques to Aid Palestinian and Israeli Children"—lest the chance go by for people to address the issue and exchange ideas. The room was packed with people from South American to the Middle East, including Muslims, Christians, and Jews, all of whom cared about the children, the conflict, and the future of our world.

I have found that opportunities to explore and understand the psychosocial issues and possible solutions to such intractable conflicts are not limited to targeted discussions but can come from perspectives that may seem far afield from traditional views. For example, at the 2007 International Consciousness Conference on Shamanism in Santa Fe, New Mexico, interfaith mystic Andrew Harvey spoke of "sacred activism" through tantra as the only way to confront the apocalypse of the planet from greed, fundamentalism, and glorification of a false self. This resonates with my own decades-long work teaching ancient tantric techniques to harness positive cognitive thought with heart-centeredness. Violence corrupts the collective soul, and the solution proposed by shaman Sandra Ingerman is to refuse to transmit negativity—to oneself or to others. Indeed, the power of positive personal intention is reflected in claims that water can change its consistency when people pray over it while maintaining divine consciousness. And there are lessons to be learned about the conflict in the Middle East from a simple Native American story that Ingerman related, in which a grandfather tells his grandson of the battle between two wolves. One wolf who thrives on anger and the other thrives on love. "Which one of the wolves will win?" asks the boy. "The one I feed," answers the grandfather.

The grassroots projects and people presented in this book feed on the choice of love. It's the answer offered by the co-founder of Search for Common Ground, Susan Collin Marks. Her view on this is described in a chapter in this book.

Occasions not only to speak, but to sing, about peace have also arisen, and fueled my passion for this mission. The importance of music as a tool for peace is evident in many youth groups today which bring Palestinian and Israeli youngsters together. And, in November, 2006, my world music band—headed by my former student and accomplished musician Russell Daisey—performed the songs we had written about healing after the 2001 terrorist attacks on the World Trade Center, at the opening of the First International Peace Summit in Hiroshima, Japan. On stage were the invited guests, Nobel Peace Laureates Archbishop Emeritus Desmond Tutu, Betty Williams (an avid advocate for children in Ireland during conflict in that region in the 1970s) and His Holiness the Dalai Lama.

"Human life is more precious than man-made boundaries," said the exiled Tibetan monk, calling for compassion for all humanity regardless of religious or racial identities. On this occasion, as on others I've attended, Reverend Tutu invoked *Ubuntu*, an African term that means "I am because you are." "We need each other. . . . I need you in order to be me." Elaborating on humanistic philosophy that invokes generosity, sharing, caring, and compassion, the archbishop implored all that "To forgive is not just for you, it is for me. Anger, resentment and desire for revenge are corrosive. We can be free only together. We can be safe only together. There is no such thing as being totally self-sufficient." I've heard the archbishop pray specifically for peace between Palestinians and Israelis on several occasions, including at the opening of the inaugural reception for the Desmond Tutu Education Center at the General Theological Seminary of the Episcopal Church in New York in September 2005, and when accepting the Union Medal for spiritual leadership from the Union Theological Seminary the next Spring.

In the course of putting this volume together—and seemingly every time I turn around—I keep hearing about new ways to stimulate peace. For example, there is even an internet video game where players negotiate Israeli-Palestinian peace. There are also always new opportunities to learn, like I discovered in attending a leadership training in May 2007 on "Islamic Sources of Conflict Resolution" at American University in Washington D.C. coordinated by the Center for Global Peace, the Islamic Society of North American and Salam Institute. And, there are also constantly new opportunities to share ideas and be inspired, like at the conference on Muslim Peacebuilding, Justice and Interfaith Dialogue held the day before the training. It was extremely valuable to hear a consistent theme about peace from professionals from varied disciplines—psychology, religion, international relations and even filmmaking. Further, there are constantly new experiences that affirm the universality of the desire for peace and justice. This was evident to me when attending the second Middle East and North African Psychology Regional Conference in Amman, Jordan in May 2007. Over 150 mental health professionals from 21 countries were present—including Jordan, Qatar, Kuwait, United Arab Emirates, Saudi Arabia, Yemen, Algeria, Palestine, Lebanon, Oman, Israel, Turkey, Australia, England, France, Italy, Greece, Germany, Denmark, Ireland, Singapore, Canada, South Africa and the United States. Jordanian and other Middle Eastern colleagues—spearheaded by Dr. Adnan Farah and Dr. Zuhair Zacharia who impressively stayed up until all hours of the night to draft a document calling for action to promote mental health worldwide. The declaration called for making every possible effort to strengthen human rights, oppose unjust behavior, and establish dignity for all. It was unanimously adopted at the end of the conference, in an impressive showing of widespread support for a high standard of professional behavior, oriented toward peace.

Most importantly, I continually become aware of new projects to promote partnerships between Israelis and Palestinians, Arabs, Christians and Jews, to bring peace to their lives and homeland. Such courageous people persist despite physical barriers (such as the occupation and suicide attacks) and psychological barriers (such as blame and mistrust). Peace educators, human rights activists, health professionals, and ordinary (or rather, extra-ordinary) private citizens remain steadfast in their pursuit of partnership and peace.

The collaborative efforts of these citizen ambassadors highlighted in this volume represent what's called "people-to-people" programs. These are called "bottom-up" as opposed to "top-down," programs that are referred to in academic circles as "track-two diplomacy" (involving unofficial citizens) in contrast to "track-one diplomacy" (involving officials and governments). Their importance is evident when you realize that it is people who have to carry out peace even when governments sign peace treaties. Chapters in Part 1 of this book introduce the concepts of these people-to-people grassroots programs, and consider whether such cooperation can work. Part 2 presents important contemporary approaches to coexistence, including communication skills and the increasingly popular dialogue technique. Highly creative people-to-people cooperative efforts are described in Part 3, including camps for kids, marches, and arts projects where films, music, drama, theatre, television, radio and media are all harnessed for peace. Part 4 focuses on education and mental health projects aimed at healing and mutual understanding—especially for youth—between the two cultures.

The projects are highly diverse and creative. They range from educational endeavors and cultural activities to academic and public forums, art and film-making, interfaith events, dialogue and encounter groups, research and just fun. Some projects are well known and ongoing for years, like Neve Shalom (a unique joint Israeli and Palestinian community), Search for Common Ground, Seeds of Peace, and educational efforts like School for Peace and Hand in Hand. Others are newer but equally ambitious, like a joint textbook project of noted Israeli and Palestinian professors. Some are on a large scale while others are individual efforts, like a mountain climbing team who planted the Israeli and Palestinian flags side by side on the top of Mount Everest, and projects where young people clean beaches in the name of peace. New partnerships are constantly popping up—like art shows of Israeli and Palestinian crafts or friends making documentaries about their shared homeland in the Holy City.

Contributors in these chapters include highly experienced and well-respected leaders in the field of conflict resolution and experts in Israeli-Palestinian relations. And they also include students and young professionals whose dedication and creativity I admire and am pleased to promote, especially rewarding to me in my long-time role as a graduate school professor. A special effort was also made to include programs for young people—who represent the future. In many such projects, young people engage in intense dialoguing as well as fun.

It is an honor to feature them here and elsewhere. For example, at a workshop I developed and moderated at the 2006 United Nations Conference for NGOs (nongovernmental organizations), I included one of the programs in these chapters—Middle East Education through Technology (MEET)—on my panel about "Model Partnerships for Youth: Education, Business and Technology Projects to Further Peace, Well-Being, Community Action and Resilience." A graduate student from Massachusetts Institute of Technology, Shahid Rashid, described how American students, aided by major technology donor companies, teach computer science to Israeli and Palestinian high school students, to help them further their career goals, learn teamwork, and form friendships. Other panelists included a Stamford Business School student who described a program that helps develop personal skills and sustainability for indigenous people in the South American rainforest, and a high school band called Creation that raised money and partnered with the We Are Family Foundation to build a school in Africa. We closed with a prayer flag ceremony by the World Peace Prayer Society where participants present flags of various countries and announce, "May there be partnerships for peace in [fill in a country's name]." Together, the presentations were an impressive showing of partnerships for peace around the world that inspired participants from different regions to explore how programs like these could be adapted to their country and culture.

Opportunities have continually presented themselves to explore partnerships for peace. While putting this volume together, I attended an Open Space Technology training (co-sponsored by Columbia University's International Center for Cooperation and Conflict Resolution and held at Columbia University Teachers College). The format invites participants to convene discussion groups on topics of their interest. I chose "How to facilitate grassroots peace between Israelis and Palestinians." Participants who joined the discussions contributed fascinating ideas. One woman told us about her son's project inviting Arabs on his campus to Jewish ceremonies. A Columbia graduate student described an intriguing model using psychological stages of development to measure steps toward international cooperation, as well as his efforts to establish a youth organization for peace. I enthusiastically invited him to contribute a chapter about that in this book.

The result is that this book is the first comprehensive collection of its kind with academics, thinkers, activists, experts and people of all ages and perspectives addressing the topic of crucial importance today: What is being done to bring Palestinians and Jewish Israelis together to create cooperation and peace? Can these projects survive and make a difference? In the midst of pessimism currently prevailing about the conflict, the answers offer rays of hope.

I'm exceptionally proud of all those Palestinians and Jewish Israelis, and Arabs, Christians and Jews in the region who have contributed their work to this

book which shows clearly the positive efforts being done. And I am also proud of
people and groups from other nationalities who are equally dedicated and active,
like the Oomoto Shinto group who brought Israeli and Palestinian teens to Japan
to engage in dialogue and who sent members of their group to pray for peace at
Mt. Sinai and other places around Israel. I have heard many experts say that
America should take an active role in resolution of the conflict. I remember viv-
idly former U.S. Secretary of State Henry Kissinger making this point at a 2002
luncheon sponsored by *The Week* news magazine. That the United States is considered indispensable in resolving the conflict was reiterated by Rafi Dajani, executive director of the American Task Force on Palestine, reporting on poll results
at a Seminar on "Peace and 'the Street'" in June, 2007 at the New School's Wolfson
Center for National Affairs. But this applies not just to political negotiation. Many
American citizens are rising to this challenge—with grassroots involvement and
action. These include major philanthropists such as Richard Goodwin, Alan
Slivka, and Jerry Hirsch; directors of coalitions of NGOs promoting people-to-
people coexistence between Arabs and Jews, like psychologist Jodi Shams
Prinzivalli of the Alliance for Middle East Peace; educators such as Warren
Spielberg at the New School and Mark Rosenblum at Queens College who give
classes with psychological insights into coexistence; spouses Len and Libby
Traubman, champions of dialogue who maintain an extensive website of resources
about Jewish-Arab peace cooperation projects; Ronit Avni whose team tirelessly
promotes its documentary *Encounter Point* about such cooperation; psychologist
Gary Reiss—who wrote a chapter in my previous volume—who is bringing deep
psychological processing "Worldwork" workshops to the region; and student
activists such as Yaron Prywes at Columbia University Teachers College and
Joseph Gindi at Brandeis University, the MIT students in the MEET program,
and globally conscious young leaders in Americans for Informed Democracy
who try to improve Islamic relations in their "Hope not Hate" campaign. Others
are moved to document the voice of real people in the region, like Cathy Sultan
in her book *Israeli and Palestinian Voices* and Deanna Armbruster in her book
Tears in the Holy Land.

Any ambitious project like achieving peace in a conflict region requires
partnerships between stakeholders from all aspects of society, cultures and countries. Such partnerships are being encouraged by individuals, and by major networks like the Clinton Global Initiative. At the CGI that I attended in 2006, Ron
Pundak, the Director General of the Peres Center for Peace, announced its support of Journeys for Peace, an NGO whose program organizes Mexican students' interviews with leaders such as Reverend Tutu and then-United Nations
Secretary General Kofi Annan to learn lessons about peace. Chair of the CGI
focus area of "mitigating religious and ethnic conflict" Robert Malley—former
Special Assistant to President Clinton for Arab-Israeli Affairs and member of the
U.S. peace team at the Camp David summit—pointed out the importance of
such partnerships, exchange programs involving youth, and harnessing the
media. President Clinton announced a grant to Abraham's Vision—a nonprofit

organization that took Jewish and Palestinian American university students from six campuses known for tensions between Arab, Jewish, and Muslim groups to the past-Olympic-site of Sarajevo. The city—often called a "small Jerusalem" for its religious mix—was chosen so that students could learn to analyze religious conflict in that region and apply those lessons to the troubled Middle East. "We need more projects like this," Clinton said.

Thankfully, more such projects are continually being developed. Even as the deadline for submitting this manuscript approached, I continually became aware of new grassroots efforts for peace—from large organizations starting sports clubs to private individuals sending wheelchairs. Particularly encouraging was the 2006 conference on "Education for Peace and Democracy," convened by the Israel/Palestine Center for Research and Information. The conference brought together more than 100 conflict resolution and activist educators, practitioners, and facilitators in academia, research, and governmental and community organizations from the region and around the world to meet, dialogue, and create cooperation. It is planned to occur annually.

Working on this collection, and the previous volume, was continually inspiring and motivating, but also challenging. At times, I felt in the middle of the conflict itself, impatient for its resolution and frustrated at the impediments to such awesome efforts being pursued by these contributors despite overwhelming odds. I was determined to involve as many people and projects as possible, pushing the limits of the number of pages allowed in a single volume, so I could honor as many projects and people as possible. But the process has not also been without pain. It was painful to learn of an incident where a campus lecture by an author from my previous volume, *Terror in the Holy Land*, was cancelled by the school administration in reaction to protests by a student faction (fortunately, she was later re-invited). And it was painful to hear of death threats to moderates speaking out publicly for cooperation, and fearing for their lives. I was heartened to know I am not the only one who experiences this. At a reception in New York in June 2007, while accepting an award from the Tanenbaum Center for Inter-religious Understanding (an organization dedicated to "give a platform to prominent individuals who inspire the public to make the world safer for religious differences") Archbishop Demetrios of the Greek Orthodox Church of America said, "Whoever has knowledge, has pain, because we see what we have to go through in order to establish a truly coexisting-in-love condition."

Grassroots partnerships, their directors and participants, are inspiring. But even they admit that no one is naïve enough to think that such efforts are sufficient for peace. Citizens should do everything in their personal and collective power to change their lives and societies. But politicians have to play their part to make pacts and change policy. As I have traveled to many danger zones and communities of conflict from Israel to Iran, Belgrade to Batticoloa (where the Tamil Tigers clash to this day with the Sri Lankan government), I have learned that civilians often have far different views from their political leaders. "We want peace," I hear people so often say, "no matter what our leaders do."

Fortunately there are leaders who are working for peace. But moderates, as one of the authors in a chapter in this book laments, have not gotten enough support in the face of extremism. Some, like the late Prime Minister of Israel Yithak Rabin, have even been violently assassinated for their stance on peace with the opposing side. I was profoundly moved at the 10th annual commemoration ceremony in memory of Rabin, by the testimonials of his greatness by TV host Charlie Rose, and the comments by Israel's United Nations Ambassador Dan Gillerman. Gillerman spoke as if addressing Rabin, "Your favorite song means 'friendship,' a bond, a partnership. You taught us to fight for peace, to put an end to the vicious cycle of violence. You left us with a void but a sense of hope."

None of the courageous souls in this book is willing to wait for political solutions; they want to live in coexistence and mutual respect now. For this, they deserve tremendous admiration. It takes great courage to cooperate when working with the "other side" runs the risk of being called a "collaborator" and putting oneself and one's family in danger from militants and extremists. All of these people are willing to put their lives on the line, because they believe that they can make a difference.

I believe they *are* making a difference. The contact hypothesis in social psychology proposes that working together is an effective way to break down barriers between in-groups and out-groups. Working with these peacebuilders who contributed the chapters in this book has been a professionally and personally rewarding and growth-producing experience. In editing and writing chapters here, I have been moved as a psychologist and as a Jewish American to discover the extent of individuals and organizations reaching out to each other across the chasms of misunderstanding and hate to achieve understanding and acceptance. My hope is that the stories, efforts and research described in these volumes will help open readers' hearts and minds to the psychological and social needs as well as peacebuilding skills of the people on both sides and the possibilities for cooperation. I hope that professors will adopt this book as a reader for their classes, that decision-makers, politicians and government officials will use this book to inform policy, and that peace and human rights activists, social scientists, practitioners, health workers, students, and the public around the world will read it and will use it as a reference and an inspiration, to take action, and to initiate and support peacebuilding programs for Israelis and Palestinians, Arabs, Christians and Jews, and people in conflict zones all over the world.

The spirit I feel about this book was evident to me on a trip to the Statue of Liberty and Ellis Island with my friend Sami Adwan, a Palestinian educator who together with Jewish Israeli Dan Bar-On developed programs and pamphlets for sharing narratives that are described in this book. We stood at the large globe in the main hall where thousands of immigrants had passed through. Sami pointed to his homeland and then swept his hand in a circle, saying, "I live there but my hope is for all people in all lands to have the freedom that this place promised."

PART I

THE "NEVER-ENDING" CONFLICT: IS COOPERATION POSSIBLE?

People don't get along because they fear each other. People fear each other because they don't know each other. They don't know each other because they have not properly communicated with each other.

—*Martin Luther King, Jr.*

If you want to make peace with your enemy, you have to work with your enemy. Then he becomes your partner.

—*Nelson Mandela*

In separateness lies the world's great misery; in compassion lies the world's true strength.

—*Buddha*

Can real people make a difference in the face of seemingly never-ending so-called intractable conflict? Can working together really work? Does talking help to ease tensions and foster cooperation and reconciliation? The chapters in this part address those questions. In doing so, they present and evaluate various formats of projects to ease tensions and to further more positive intergroup relations between Palestinians and Arab Israelis and Jewish Israelis. These techniques and approaches are aimed at lessening hostilities and increasing understanding and reconciliation between the two cultures.

A fundamental and useful principle in social psychology—called the "contact hypothesis"—asserts that it is much harder to hate people you really know something about—particularly if you are working together for a common

goal. The projects described in the following chapters are based on this principle and aimed at important goals: cooperation, mutual trust, respect, peaceful coexistence, and conflict transformation—all necessary for peace in this
troubled region. Experts explore why and how these goals can be accomplished.
The models they propose and the efforts they analyze demonstrate real people's courage, commitment, and hope. But along with their success have come
considerable obstacles, which are also explored.

CHAPTER 1

THE INTRACTABLE ISRAELI-PALESTINIAN CONFLICT AND POSSIBLE PATHWAYS TO PEACE

Rafi Nets-Zehngut and Daniel Bar-Tal

The Israeli-Palestinian conflict has lasted for more than a century and has caused enormous bloodshed and suffering to involved societies. The conflict, while caused by multiple factors, is driven by psychological dynamics within and between the societies. In order to psychologically deal with the conflict and its destructive consequences, both societies have developed psychosocial coping strategies. This chapter describes the psychological dynamics of the two societies, and various coping strategies, aimed at overcoming any negative effects of these dynamics in order to promote the well-being of both societies and enable them to reach peace and reconciliation.[1]

The chapter begins with introducing the background and nature of the Israeli-Palestinian conflict as an intractable conflict; then describes the psychological dynamics and coping strategies that have evolved in order to meet the challenges of the conflict; and finally, presents ways to achieve the reconciliation and collective self-healing that are necessary for lasting peace.

Nature of the Israeli-Palestinian Intractable Conflict

The Israeli-Palestinian conflict, which constitutes the core of the Israeli-Arab conflict, began at the beginning of the twentieth century and is centered on contested territory by two national movements: the Palestinian national movement and the Jewish national movement (Zionism). This conflict has had all the characteristics of an intractable conflict in that it is *protracted* (lasting almost a century); *violent* (causing thousands of casualties in both societies); *central* (on the main public agenda); *total* (focused on fundamental goals such as identity and territory); and demanding *extensive psychological and material investments* by the parties, in order to cope with—and win—the conflict.[2] It has also been considered of *zero sum nature* and *irresolvable peacefully* (Bar-Tal & Teichman, 2005; Kriesberg, 1993). As a result, the conflict has inflicted upon both societies threat, stress, pain, exhaustion, and costs, in human and material terms (Abu-Zayyad & Bar-Tal, 2003). Both societies have had to live with this harsh and violent reality, and therefore both have had to psychologically adapt to the ongoing situation.

As is generally prevalent among societies involved in intractable conflicts, this adaptation to this ongoing conflict is necessary on both the individual and collective level (Bar-Tal & Teichman, 2005; Rouhana & Bar-Tal, 1998). With regard to the *individual* level, it is necessary to satisfy basic needs such as needs for mastery, safety, positive identity, and/or for a meaningful understanding of the conflict that can provide a coherent and predictable picture of the situation. With regard to the *collective* level, the parties in the conflict have to be prepared for a long struggle. This requires recruitment of human and material resources such as patriotism, ability to cope with physical and psychological stress, solidarity, and maintenance of the societies' objectives, courage, and endurance. Coping successfully on a psychological level with the challenges posed by intractable conflicts requires that the involved societies develop effective psychosocial strategies (Bar-Tal & Teichman, 2005).

Psychological Dynamics of the Conflict

The psychological dynamics of the individual societies—and of the conflict itself—are formed gradually over time, from the beginning of the conflict, and are based on three interrelated elements: collective memory of the conflict, ethos of the conflict, and collective emotional orientation of the conflict. They help to meet the challenges of the conflict that were noted before.

Collective Memory of Conflict

Collective memory is the collective representations of past events involved in the conflict that are shared by the vast majority of the members of the society, and seen by them as valid accounts (Kansteiner, 2002). Israelis and Palestinians have formed their own collective memories of the conflict, each representing a black-and-white picture that portrays their own society in a positive light and as being the sole victim, while delegitimizing the rival, presenting that party in a very negative light (Nets-Zehngut, 2006; Podeh, 2002; Rouhana & Bar-Tal, 1998).

Ethos of Conflict

Ethos, in general, is defined as the configuration of central shared societal beliefs in a society[3] that provide particular dominant meaning and orientation to a particular society (Bar-Tal, 2000a). The ethos of conflict consists of societal beliefs in a society relating to eight themes: the justness of one's goals; security; patriotism; unity; positive collective in-group images; one's own victimization; delegitimizing the opponent; and peace (Bar-Tal). Both the Israeli and Palestinian societies have developed ethos on all these levels, which also all perpetuate the conflict (Rouhana & Bar-Tal, 1998).

Collective Emotional Orientation of Conflict

Collective emotional orientation, in general, is defined as shared emotions by the members of the society. Both the Israeli and Palestinian societies can be seen as being dominated by fear on a collective level (Bar-Tal, 2001). This fear further stimulates emotions of anger and hatred directed inwardly as well as toward each other.

Negative Consequences of the Psychological Dynamics

Since the described psychological repertoire was functional during the climax of the intractable Israeli-Palestinian conflict, helping to meet its challenges, special attempts were made by the societies to institutionalize it, for example, by transmitting it in cultural products and disseminating it via the educational system (Bar-Tal & Teichman, 2005; Podeh, 2002).

But, the psychological dynamics of the Israelis and Palestinians, as reflected in the previously mentioned three aspects, provided a foundation on which members of each society constructed their respective reality and then have only served to widen the divide between them. The specific positions that result from these dynamics in each society inhibit deescalation of the conflict and peaceful resolution and reconciliation between the parties (Bar-Siman-Tov, 2004; Bar-Tal, 2001), because adhering to each of their respective goals results in the delegitimization, distrust, and hatred of the rival, and therefore does not provide any grounds for the peace process (Rouhana & Bar-Tal, 1998). This situation causes a vicious cycle of intractable or ongoing and irresolvable conflict, and serves as a catalyst for continuation of the conflict. In addition, these dynamics interfere with the well-being of members of society, since living with dynamics as societal beliefs of self-victimization and delegitimization of the other, emotions of fear, hatred, and anger, have negative consequences. These negative consequences include, for example, causing stress in daily life, perpetuating negative images of the other party, and damaging relations with third parties in the conflict (Nets, 2005).

The Need to Improve the Psychological Dynamics in the Conflict

Generally speaking, it is of vital necessity, under the appropriate circumstances, to alter and improve the described psychological dynamics operating in each party in a conflict in order to overcome the previously noted negative consequences.

What are these "appropriate circumstances"? Timing matters, with the best time to intervene effectively being when signs signal prospects for peaceful resolution, for example, when violence is greatly reduced and/or when a negotiation for a peace agreement begins. In the current Israeli-Palestinian conflict, these appropriate circumstances existed after the nomination of Abu Mazen as head of the Palestinian Authority in the end of 2004, at the time of the Israeli disengagement from the Gaza Strip in September 2005, as well as recently when a political reshuffling in Israel was necessitated. These events bring new hope for the possibility to renew the peace process that can be accepted by the Israelis and the Palestinians.

Nature of the Improvement

The three elements of the psychological dynamics of the two societies as described earlier need to be changed and improved for peace to be possible (Bar-Tal, 2000a).

1. Collective Memory

At the most minimal level, it is necessary to recognize that there are two collective memories of the conflict—that of the Israelis and of the Palestinians (Salomon, 2004). But more substantial change demands that through the process of negotiation, each party will critically revise its own past and synchronize it with that of the other party and so a new mutual narrative of the conflict will emerge and substitute the previously dominant and collective memories of both societies. In this new narrative, mutual delegitimization of the other and self-glorification disappears, and both groups can be perceived as victims of the conflict because of their suffering (Kriesberg, 1993).

2. Ethos

The peace process requires major changes in at least four themes of the ethos (Bar-Tal, 2000b): (1) to change the goals of the two societies from ones that caused the conflict to goals that center on maintaining peaceful relations; (2) to change each society's rigid adherence to its own positive image in relation to the other to more objective and self-critical views that acknowledge one's own wrongdoing; (3) to stop delegitimizing the opponent and instead to humanize the members of the rival party; and (4) to incorporate more realistic and multidimensional concepts of peace that outline the costs and benefits, specify conditions and mechanisms for its achievement, and clarify the meaning of living in peace.

3. Collective Emotional Orientation

Change in this dimension requires a reduction of collective fear, anger, and hatred on one hand, and on the other hand, the evolution of collective trust and mutual acceptance and hope for peace (Bar-Tal, 2001).

Two Processes for Change in Intractable Conflict

Two processes—namely, reconciliation and collective self-healing—facilitate positive changes in the psychological dynamics in the societies that experience intractable conflict, as is the case for the Israelis and Palestinians. Both processes depend on changes in the members of the societies as well as in their leaders.

1. Reconciliation Process

Reconciliation requires the formation or restoration of genuine and lasting peaceful relationships between societies that have been involved in an intractable conflict (Bar-Tal, 2000b; Kriesberg, 1998). It consists of establishing mutual recognition and acceptance, investing interests and goals in developing peaceful relations, building mutual trust and positive attitudes, as well as sensitivity and consideration in the other party's needs and interests (Bar-Tal & Bennink, 2004). Reconciliation requires joint efforts of both sides; in other words, both rivals must coordinate and cooperate with each other in order to effect change. Strategies to carry out this process include the following.

Publicized Meetings between Israeli and Palestinian Representatives

Meetings between Israelis and Palestinians can trigger change in the psychological dynamics of each society (Bar-Tal & Bennink, 2004). These meetings provide an example to members of society of how a past enemy should be treated differently in the new peace-oriented climate. Holding such meetings serves to legitimize, equalize, and specifically personalize the rival party members and emphasize their humanity by demonstrating that it is possible to talk with them, to treat them as partners in agreements, and to trust them and consider their needs. Meetings between leaders is especially important in this regard, where they treat each other with respect and trust, since the leaders serve as authority figures to at least some members of the society. For example, the negotiations, meetings, and eventually symbolic handshakes between Israeli Prime Minister Benjamin Netanyahu and PLO Chairman Yasser Arafat in the Wye River Plantation in 1998 had significant positive influence on Israeli supporters of the hawkish parties, increasing their support for the peace process with the Palestinians (Hermann & Yuchtman-Ya'ar, 2002).

Presentations in the Mass Media

Mass media (newspapers, television and radio stations, the Internet) constructs public reality by framing the news and commentaries, thereby presenting a powerful tool for promoting change in the psychological dynamics within and between the conflicting societies (Kriesberg, 1998). As a result, the resources of mass media should be harnessed in early efforts at changing the society's dynamics and strategies with regard to the rival. Media can be used to transmit information to a wide public, including, for example, new peaceful goals, positive aspects of the rival party, and encouragement to develop relations with it. For example, after the Oslo Agreement in 1993, the media played an important role in promoting the theme to "give peace a chance." Also at this time, PLO leaders were interviewed for the first time on Israeli TV, giving the public an opportunity to hear their views, and to personalize them (Wolfsfeld, 1997).

Peace Education

Education constitutes one of the most important methods for promoting reconciliation. This mostly involves using the school system for peace education since this system is often the only institution of which the society can make formal, intentional, and extensive use to change the psychological repertoire of society members. Peace education aims at constructing the students' worldview (i.e., their values, beliefs, attitudes, motivations, skills, and patterns of behavior) in a way that reflects the reality of the peace process and prepares them to live in an era of peace and reconciliation. An attempt to implement peace education was carried in the Israeli schools following Oslo Agreement when the ministry of education declared "peace and coexistence" as a central learning theme in schools for 1994.

Writing a Common History

This method involves jointly recreating a new version of the events of the conflict that can be endorsed by both parties involved in the conflict (Bar-On & Adwan, in press). This process usually involves a joint committee of historians who work together to collect and select materials, and finally negotiate in order to come up with an agreed-upon version of the past events of the conflict. Such work requires exposure of both parties to the untold past of one's own party, which often includes admission of one's own misdeeds, acknowledgment of these unheard pasts, and adhering to agreed-upon facts while rejecting myths and unfounded stories. One effective project of this nature has been accomplished by the Peace Research Institute in the Middle East (PRIME) in which Israelis and Palestinians cooperated to produce booklets presenting Israeli and Palestinian students with two narratives of the history of the conflict (Bar-On & Adwan).

Carrying Out Joint Projects

Joint projects of various content and format in different areas, such as health, media, academia, and tourism, can be carried out by individual members (either professionals or grassroots) or initiated by leaders of both parties, or by nongovernmental organizations (NGOs). These projects can foster links between different levels of society, create interdependence through common goals, and provide benefits for the members of the society. For example, during the period of 1994–1998, 148 joint health projects involving about 4,000 Israeli and Palestinian participants took place. These have made a substantive contribution in changing the dynamics and emotions among members of both parties toward the members of the other party (Barnea & Abdeen, 2002).

Involve NGOs

Nongovernmental organizations (NGOs) can contribute to positive changes in the dynamics of a society by spreading messages about new goals that stress the importance of constructing peaceful relations with the other party and discarding delegitimizing views. Wide-scale cooperation between Israeli and Palestinian NGOs started after the 1993 Oslo agreements, but have been drastically diminished since the 2000 outbreak of the second Intifada (Yes, 2002). Of special importance are NGOs that serve as peace movements, for example, Israeli NGOs Peace Now and Gush Shalom, which propagated ideas of conflict resolution and peace.

Create Cultural Exchanges

Cultural exchanges, such as translations of books, visits of artists, or exchanges of films, television programs, or exhibitions, provide the opportunity for each party to learn about the rival from a cultural perspective that can be neutral, and to contribute to personalize the rival by presenting their needs, aspirations, and concerns in a humane light. People involved in these exchanges find similarities and commonalties with the members of the other party.

In summary, there are various approaches to implement the reconciliation process. No single method is exclusive; what is required is a combination of these methods. The reconciliation process between the Israelis and Palestinians began after the 1993 Oslo agreements, with positive results. But some of these efforts were implemented by only one party, or only partly. The expansion of programs was intensive until the eruption of the Al-Aqsa second Intifada in September 2000, at which time progress was largely diminished. All these methods have been implemented in programs today, with varying success. While some have been scaled back or interrupted because of political tensions and limited funding, fortunately others are flourishing. Stepping up these efforts and developing new programs would be valuable to facilitate reconciliation.

Further, the process of reconciliation requires the establishment of well-defined and unequivocal policies that are supported and implemented by governmental and private sector institutions, as well as by professional and grassroots sectors of the societies. To be effective, the reconciliation process must always proceed top-down and bottom-up simultaneously. This means that the leaders take positions to influence the psychological perceptions and dynamics of the public, on the one hand, and on the other hand, members of civil society can initiate movements and positions that influence the governing bodies and affect policy.

2. The Collective Self-Healing Process

Besides reconciliation, collective self-healing is also necessary to attend to the aftermath of an intractable conflict such as is the case between the Israelis and Palestinians. This is defined as a process by which a party repairs the damage incurred over the course of conflict, independent of the other party in the conflict (Nets-Zehngut, 2006).

Little has been said in the psychological literature about collective self-healing and its role in relation to intractable conflicts (Nets-Zehngut, 2006). Collective self-healing involves two concepts: the concept of "healing" and of the "self." The term *healing* relates to restoring the object of the healing to a sound and healthy condition. From a psychological perspective, healing aims at least partly to reduce pain and suffering caused by the conflict (Frankel, 1998). Collective self-healing refers to healing on the level of the society considered as an entity, and implies that the healing takes place by the party itself, without collaborating with the other party in the conflict—in contrast to reconciliation where the two parties interact.

Both reconciliation and collective self-healing evolve from the same fundamental assumption that peace agreements cannot guarantee genuine peaceful relations between the parties unless the psychological dynamics of the conflict are fully addressed. While reconciliation deals mainly and *directly* with changes in the strategies regarding the other party and with relations between the parties, collective self-healing occurs at a more basic psychological level and can trigger negative psychological conditions, such as posttraumatic stress disorders, learned helplessness symptom, and rage that further fuel the conflict. These consequences must be addressed in order to maintain the well-being of the involved societies and to prevent future outbursts of the conflict. The basic premise of the collective self-healing process is that it is difficult for the parties to heal their relations with each other, while they themselves are not healed. According to this premise, collective self-healing can *directly* improve the well-being of the party that works on this process, as well as *indirectly* facilitate improvement of psychological dynamics among members of the party and consequently their relations with the other party.

Several methods can be used by the Israelis and Palestinians to achieve collective self-healing.

Taking Control over One's Life and Destiny

Generally in conflicts, members of the weaker party especially suffer from syndromes like learned helplessness, which results from losing the sense of control over one's life as the stronger party has power to control many aspects of the weaker party's life (Cemalcilar, Canbeyli, & Sunar, 2003; Herman, 1992). This causes anger and hatred among the weaker party toward the rival party. In the process of collective self-healing, the weaker party reasserts control over its own destiny, allowing for a reduction in anger and hatred that were the outcome of the learned helplessness, and consequently enhancing the likelihood for improvement in collective memory, ethos, and collective emotional orientation.

For example, the Palestinian minority in Israel is becoming more aware and self-critical about their passive behavior in not taking control over their lives and the conditions of their society, and is increasingly recognizing the need to be more active in this regard (Rabinovitch & Abu-Baker, 2002).

Establishing a Network of Psychological Services

Israelis and Palestinians can establish a network of psychological services within each society to help alleviate the traumatic effects of the conflict. Several such projects have already proven successful in various support groups or communities (Lerner, 2003).

Conducting Commemoration Projects

The parties can conduct various commemoration projects for their loved ones who perished as a result of the conflict. Such projects help families and friends of the victims, as well as the society as a whole, to deal more effectively with their losses. For example, the Israelis have been involved in such activities such as monuments, museums, and books (Israeli Ministry of Defense, 2005).

Pilgrimage

Members of society can take organized and purposeful trips to regions that are meaningful in relation to the conflict. Such visits can be a profound experience, allowing the pilgrims to confront their past, release their emotional pain, affirm their identity, and heal themselves. For example, Palestinians living in Israel have visited the ruins of villages where their families lived before the 1948 war (Ben-Zeev, 2003).

Respecting the Influence of Time

Time can have a healing effect on members of a society in several ways. Members of the older generations who were directly involved or harmed by the conflict and who suffer from psychological wounds need time to go through the stages of healing from shock associated with denial, to protest with realization of losses, to despair, accompanied with somatic and emotional upset, to ultimate recovery, marked by increased well-being and acceptance of loss (Stroebe, Schut, & Stroebe, 1998). Also, as time passes, these older generations die, reducing their relatively greater impact on the party in the conflict to which they belong. In addition, as time passes, new generations join the world; these younger generations may not be as in touch with, harmed by, or invested in the conflict, reducing their intention to continue the conflict.

The influence of time is usually relevant in the period after both parties have made some agreements about peace, or better yet, signed a peace agreement.

In summary, successful collective self-healing can be accomplished by a combination of the methods presented. Some can be implemented immediately, even in the current preresolution phase of the Israeli-Palestinian conflict, for example, establishing a network of psychological services and organizing commemoration projects.

Conclusions

The processes of reconciliation and collective self-healing should be attempted by the parties entrenched in an intractable conflict, in order to heal the effects of the conflict and to achieve peace and reconciliation. These processes are complementary, and facilitate each other. In order to achieve substantial positive results, both processes require that the parties involved in a conflict have realistic expectations, implement good planning, and exercise patience as well as persistence. Optimism in the psychological outlook, alterations in the psychological dynamics, and consideration of various strategies are all necessary and helpful in achieving peace and reconciliation. These approaches should be applied in the case of the Israeli-Palestinian conflict for a successful road map to peace.

References

Abu-Zayyad, Z., & Bar-Tal, D. (Eds.). (2003). Two traumatized societies. *Palestine-Israel Journal, 10.*

Bar-On, D., & Adwan, S. (in press). PRIME "Double-Helix" history project: The psychology of a better dialogue between two separate but interdependent narratives. In R. Rotberg (Ed.), *History's double helix: The intertwined narratives of Israel and Palestine.* Bloomington: Indiana University Press.

Bar-Siman-Tov, Y. (Ed.). (2004). *From conflict resolution to reconciliation.* Oxford: Oxford University Press.

Bar-Tal, D. (2000a). *Shared beliefs in a society: Social psychological analysis.* Thousands Oaks, CA: Sage.

Bar-Tal, D. (2000b). From intractable conflict through conflict resolution to reconciliation: Psychological analysis. *Political Psychology, 21,* 351–365.

Bar-Tal, D. (2001). Why does fear override hope in societies engulfed by intractable conflict, as it does in the Israeli society? *Political Psychology, 22,* 601–627.

Bar-Tal, D., & Bennink, G. (2004). The nature of reconciliation as an outcome and as a process. In Y. Bar-Siman-Tov (Ed.), *From conflict resolution to reconciliation* (pp. 11–38). Oxford: Oxford University Press.

Bar-Tal, D., & Teichman, Y. (2005). *Stereotypes and prejudice in conflict: Representations of Arabs in Israeli Jewish society.* Cambridge: Cambridge University Press.

Barnea, T., & Abdeen, Z. (2002). The function of health professionals in advancing Israeli-Palestinian co-existence. In T. Barnea & R. Husseini (Eds.), *The virus does not stop in the checkpoint* (pp. 355–372). Tel Aviv: Am Oved. (In Hebrew)

Ben-Zeev, E. (2003). Homecoming ceremonies of Palestinians to demolished villages. *Alpaim, 25,* 73–88. (In Hebrew)

Cemalcilar, Z., Canbeyli, R., & Sunar, D. (2003). Learned helplessness, therapy and personality traits: An experimental study. *Journal of Social Psychology, 14,* 65–81.

Frankel, E. (1998). Repentance, psychotherapy and healing through a Jewish lens. *The American Behavioral Scientist, 41,* 814–833.

Herman, J. (1992). *Trauma and recovery.* New York: Basic Books.

Hermann, T., & Yuchtman-Ya'ar, E. (2002). Divided yet united: Israeli-Jewish attitudes towards the Oslo process. *Journal of Peace Research, 39*, 597–613.

Israeli Ministry of Defense. (2005). IMOD—Commemoration Wing. Retrieved November 6, 2005, from http://www.mod.gov.il/pages/heritage/machtarotYm.asp.

Kansteiner, W. (2002). Finding meaning in memory: Methodological critique of collective memory studies. *History and Theory, 41*, 179–197.

Kriesberg, L. (1993). Intractable conflicts. *Peace Review, 5*, 417–421.

Kriesberg, L. (1998). Coexistence and the reconciliation of communal conflicts. In E. Weiner (Ed.), *The handbook of interethnic coexistence* (pp. 182–198). New York: Continuum.

Lerner, Y. (2003). Mental health services in the changing Israeli society. *Palestine-Israel Journal, 10*, 42–48.

Nets-Zehngut, R. (2006). *The collective self healing process of the aftermath of intractable conflicts.* Manuscript submitted for publication.

Nets-Zehngut, R. (2006). Refugee tales: 1948 considered—a historical analysis of Israeli attitudes towards the creation of Palestinian refugee problem in 1948. *Yale Israel Journal, 10*, 12–26.

Podeh, E. (2002). *The Arab-Israeli conflict in Israeli history textbooks, 1948–2000.* Westport, CT: Bergin & Garvey.

Rabinovitch, D., & Abu-Baker, K. (2002). *The upright generation.* Jerusalem: Keter. (In Hebrew)

Rouhana, N., & Bar-Tal, D. (1998). Psychological dynamics of intractable conflicts: The Israeli-Palestinian case. *American Psychologist, 53*, 761–770.

Salomon, G. (2004). A narrative-based view of coexistence education. *Journal of Social Issues, 60*, 273–287.

Stroebe, M., Schut, H., & Stroebe, W. (1998). Trauma and grief: A comparative analysis. In J. H. Harvey (Ed.), *Perspectives on loss: A sourcebook.* 81–96. Philadelphia: Taylor & Francis.

Wolfsfeld, G. (1997). *Media and political conflict: News from the Middle East.* Cambridge: Cambridge University Press.

Yes, P. M. (2002). *Years of experience of strategies for peace making: Looking at Israeli-Palestinian people to people activities, 1993–2000.* Jerusalem: Israel-Palestine Center for Research and Information.

CHAPTER 2

HOLDING TWO WORLDS AT THE SAME TIME

Jodi Shams Prinzivalli

We must do the thing we think we cannot do.

—*Eleanor Roosevelt*

Despite the politics of any given moment, there are some of us for whom hope springs eternal. It is easy during particularly violent times to say the effort is not worth it, that things will never change. But we have all witnessed, through the actions of people such as Martin Luther King, Jr. and Mahatma Ghandi, how one person's actions can change the lives of many. Never has this been more evident than in the people-to-people events that continue on the ground in Israel and Palestine, even in this very tumultuous political climate.

As a member of the Alliance for Middle East Peace and president of the U.S. Friends of Interfaith Encounter, I am involved on a regular basis with a multitude of organizations doing the unsung work of coexistence and cross-cultural dialogue using peaceful means. These are not starry-eyed idealists. These are people who truly believe, as do I, that with enough perseverance, resources, and support, a just and healthy peace will prevail in Israel and Palestine. It is merely a matter of time.

Unfortunately, we also live in a society where the media preys on the drama, the death and destruction of the Middle East tragedy. Yes, this is a hot political topic. Yes, there are strong and passionate feelings on every side of the debate. But too much attention is paid to the divisiveness and not enough to the more than 200 groups currently working toward a different way of life, bridging differences. At present, Israel and Palestine have more than double the number of organizations working for reconciliation than any other area in the world. Clearly this one fact in itself is a statement about the will of the people. And in the end, almost everyone

I speak to is growing weary of the situation. There are victims on both sides of the so-called fence, the fence made out of concrete that stands 15 feet high and separates towns, families (sometimes parents from children, siblings from siblings), and often individuals from their place of work and livelihood.

You may conclude by these words that I am pro-Palestinian. This is true. I am also pro-Israeli. I am an American Jew who lived in the Palestinian territories for long periods of time during the 1990s. I grew to know and love the people and their ways. I also love the Jewish people. I feel deeply that Jerusalem is my home, and I long for this homeland to be free of the devastating struggle that has existed for so long. If there is to be change, we must build on the miraculous number of groups who are working on the ground to bring it about. But who even knows about them? It is stunning that with so many coexistence groups actively working in the Middle East, so few Americans know of their work. They only know what they see on the news. The Alliance for Middle East Peace (ALLMEP) is a group that wants to change this unfortunate reality. It is an organization that brings together other organizations working for coexistence. The sole purpose of ALLMEP is to raise awareness and financial support for the work that is already happening on the ground. We want the world to know that the work continues behind the scenes, silently bringing families from opposite sides together, bringing children from opposite sides to the same school, bringing businesspeople from opposite sides into the same business project, and bringing peace-oriented radio programming to homes on both sides. The list could go on for pages. The salient point is that peace is already happening in small ways, in ways that are not glamorous or dramatic, but in ways that real people get to know "the other" as human beings.

Many have given up hope for a just and lasting peace. But this is not a time for despair. This is a time—in fact the most crucial of times—to build on what already exists. It is a time for continuing on, not giving up.

For many, Jerusalem is the heart of the world. Many believe that when peace prevails in Jerusalem, so shall other areas of conflict follow. There are no easy answers, no recipes for peace. Rather, it is more about trying and failing, and then getting back up and trying again with new information from the fall. Falling is not something to fear, but rather something to be seen as a means of learning. Most important, we must learn how to get back up again rather than retreat in despair. The challenge is to join with other like-minded people until there is such a critical mass that peace is inevitable. I personally have no illusions that this will happen rapidly or happen soon. Too much suffering has occurred for too many. It may not happen even in my lifetime. It may require the next generation to continue the work until that inevitable time. But that is not a reason to not do the work. We are preparing the way. We are making the way clear for that inevitable time when a courageous leader will take a chance and lead the region into reconciliation.

Martin Luther King, Jr. became a leader of the civil rights movement after decades of unknown work by others, after many unknown individuals stood up and did the unpopular thing. They paved the way for the life-changing work of

Dr. King. So, too, we are paving the way. The way must be prepared, regardless of when a true peace will prevail.

A wise sage, my father, once told me something I will never forget: most of life is preparation. This is what is happening in Israel and Palestine even as I write these words. Long before my involvement with ALLMEP, I got involved with the Interfaith Encounter Association (IEA). I did so from my true belief that if religion can cause so much hatred and war, it can also be the source of the healing, the place where people come together and forgive, a wellspring from which coexistence and cross-cultural understanding can begin. This goes against the sensibilities of many Americans, for whom church and state must be separated. I often hear people say, "Let's leave religion out of the peace process." But to me this is both impractical and impossible. Religion is where much of the incitement starts. Religion is where much of the misunderstanding and fear of "the other" begins. We must not leave religion out of the equation. Certainly it is not the only avenue, but it also cannot be discounted. The work of the IEA and its founder, Dr. Yehuda Stolov, has been most profound, continuing to hold interfaith gatherings even during the worst of times in the second Intifada. In reality, religion itself is not the problem. It is the human interpretation that creates strife. By bringing Christians and Jews and Muslims into the same room, by studying the teachings and texts of the other, by seeing the humanity of another of a different religious tradition, bridges begin to be built.

At the moment, many people have given up on the possibility of peace between the Palestinians and Israelis. I have often heard it said that if you are working for coexistence, you must be an extreme liberal who is anti-American. This gives me a chuckle, as if peace and security are mutually exclusive. It is also not popular to be a Jew who speaks about the plight of the Palestinians as well as the Israelis. I personally love both sides, and I feel that everyone has been hurt . . . because beyond it all, we are human. Everyone in Israel and Palestine has been traumatized on some level and one individual's pain is no more important than another's. Everyone's pain and suffering is the worst pain and suffering there could be—for that person.

Fear and the need for retribution and power are the real enemies. At some point, the cycle of eye for an eye must be courageously ended. None of us knows who the people will be who will step forward and lead a small majority out of that cycle. But that day will arrive. And when the critical mass has been built, all the work and preparation of these many organizations will be ready and waiting. These currently active groups already know how to support coexistence. They just do not yet have the political will or financial support to move it forward in an impactful and sustainable way.

In the spring of 2000, I was in attendance at a most profound event. The Tariqa Ibrahimiyya, a group of spiritual individuals from the Muslim, Jewish, and Christian faiths, came together at Neve Shalom for a weekend of prayer, music, dancing, and food. A magical moment occurred that night, forever burnt into my memory. It was a model of how things could be. As the sun sank into the desert, the Jewish folks prayed the Kabbalat Shabbat, the prayer for the beginning of *shabbas*, the Jewish sabbath. At the same time, the Muslim folks were praying *Maghrib*, the fourth of the five required daily prayers, and doing *zikr*, or the remembrance of the name of God. And the Christians prayed the rosary. In one unified prayer field, filled with three languages, three religions, three paths, all of which originate from the same father, the Prophet Abraham, everyone prayed for peace. Standing side by side, each in their own tradition, members of the Tariqa Ibrahimiyya called out, cried out to their Beloved Divine One, asking through prayer and *shabbas* dancing, and the rhythm of *zikr* and the drum, for peace to come to the Holy Land that they love; that the bloodshed end in all parts for all people; that the broken hearts everywhere be mended; that a possible just and sustainable peace be discovered.

May that prayer be answered, soon and in our time.

CHAPTER 3

THE PEACEBUILDER'S PARADOX AND THE DYNAMICS OF DIALOGUE: A PSYCHOSOCIAL PORTRAIT OF ISRAELI-PALESTINIAN ENCOUNTERS

Mohammed Abu Nimer and Ned Lazarus

Introduction: The Peacebuilder's Paradox

Inside the encounter, they are all human beings. Outside the encounter, their freedoms, protections, and status—or lack thereof—are determined not by common humanity, but by the different identity cards they are issued by the authorities. Inside the encounter, they face each other armed only with powers of communication. Outside the encounter, lethal violence is an everyday expectation, with machine guns on ubiquitous display in public places. Inside the encounter, ground rules encourage empathy, openness, and respect to foster a "safe space" for all. Outside the encounter, they are divided by barriers erected in the name of security for some. Inside the encounter, discussion leaders mandate equality between participants. Outside the encounter, power structures dictate that they live in separate, unequal societies. Inside the encounter, they may find hope in the discovery that in terms of emotion and psychology, they are mirror images of each other. Yet outside the encounter, reality does not adapt itself to their newfound understanding.

The dissonance between the epiphanies of genuine dialogue and the realities of intractable conflict places a paradox at the heart of efforts to build peaceful relationships between Israelis and Palestinians. In deep-rooted cycles of conflict, making peace means more than negotiating cease-fire agreements between armed forces. Where conflict has stratified the social order and shaped the collective consciousness, making peace requires complementary social and psychological transformation—and you can't have one without working for the other. This is the grassroots peace builder's "Catch-22."

The authors of this essay confront this dilemma as scholars and practitioners of conflict transformation.[1] We came to issues of psychology and social theory seeking ways to understand what we observed in the field. Our advocacy of a psychosocial framework for peacebuilding is grounded in experience—in phenomena we have witnessed recurring in dialogue sessions over 25 turbulent years in the Arab-Israeli conflict, mirrored in dialogues we have facilitated among other groups in conflict.

In this essay, we highlight the interplay of psychological and social factors in the dynamics of Israeli-Palestinian dialogue. Though they have rarely met each other personally before, no Israeli or Palestinian participant begins an encounter as a *tabula rasa*. They must all cross social and often physical barriers in order to participate, and all carry profound psychological "baggage" connected to the other side. In the first section, we explore the "before," describing the experiences and perceptions that participants bring to the encounter. In the next section, we focus on cathartic aspects of dialogue, tracing the process through which participants share emotional burdens they are forced to bear by the conflict. Throughout, we draw on real-world illustrations from our work in Israeli-Palestinian peace building.

Definition of Terms

Approaching this subject from the interdisciplinary field of peace and conflict resolution, we should clarify what we mean by *psychosocial*. *Psychological* connotes for us the unique, subjective, perceptual world of the individual, and the spectrum of shared cognitive and emotional phenomena implied in the idea of common humanity. *Social* connotes the contexts in which individuals are embedded—the webs of relationships, structures, identities, and discourses in which, paraphrasing Max Weber, we are suspended throughout our lives.[2] In a psychosocial paradigm, these fields are not opposite, separate, or mutually exclusive. Instead, like Israeli and Palestinian identities, they are relational, interdependent, and mutually constitutive; each is an integral part of the other. As trauma psychologist Brandon Hamber explains, "the term 'psychosocial' attempts to express the recognition that there is always a close, ongoing, circular interaction between an individual's psychological state and his or her social environment."[3]

That interaction becomes especially salient in cross-conflict encounters, in which the intimate presence of the "enemy" brings to participants' awareness subconscious wells of emotion, in a manner reminiscent of psychotherapy. Indeed, people commonly express reluctance toward dialogue and psychological counseling in similar terms; sensing emotionally loaded territory, many would rather "not go there." That is why it is challenging to bring people to encounters and to effectively facilitate them; it is also why encounters can be catalysts for psychological awareness and social change.

Enemy Images and "Empty Talk"

Deep-rooted conflicts breed apathy toward anything associated with "talk." Enemies often agree about at least one thing—that meetings with "the other side" are futile. Israeli and Palestinian doubters are fond of dismissing diplomatic initiatives and grassroots dialogues with the Arabic phrase *Kalam Fadi*—"empty talk." In our experience, however, Israeli-Palestinian encounters are charged with a complex set of emotions. The simplest exchanges, indeed the act of meeting itself, create profound internal tension for participants. A study of heart rates during cross-conflict discussions would doubtless confirm that this type of talk is the farthest thing from "empty"—and this is likely why many skeptics hesitate to participate.

Many Israelis and Palestinians are aware on a basic level, of course, of pain on both sides of the conflict. They are bombarded with news flashes reporting casualties, violence, and suffering. It takes an elaborate architecture of mutually reinforcing social and psychological barricades to ensure that this information reaches the head, but rarely touches the heart. Each side invokes an extensive repertoire of rationalizations, filing away each episode as a "necessary evil," an "isolated incident," "the result of occupation," "the price of fighting terror," "the will of God," or "they started it"; in each case, the conflict is taken for granted, and its raw emotional impact is repressed. The "enemy image" serves as a key, locking the floodgates of consciousness against confusion, fear, grief, and shame—but also preventing the emergence of empathy.

Competently structured and facilitated encounters can allow Israelis and Palestinians to safely turn the key, inviting psychological transformation by altering a single variable—relationship with the "enemy"—in the social environment of participants. Yet bringing Israelis and Palestinians to dialogue is a complicated endeavor long before discussion begins. Peacebuilders must navigate a complex network of social and psychological "separation barriers": Palestinians must pass through a Kafkaesque maze of Israeli military checkpoints and bureaucratic obstructions, and participants from both sides must overcome fears and taboos, just to get to a meeting.[4] Israelis and Palestinians must go to extraordinary lengths to dialogue, because their societies go to extraordinary lengths to limit relationships with each other.

"Let's Not Go There": The Infrastructure of Avoidance

Avoidance of the other side is ingrained in Israeli and Palestinian social codes, and physically manifested in Israeli state-built infrastructures. Before the Separation Barrier inside the West Bank gave this phenomenon its most prominent incarnation, everyday transportation provided examples. Jewish taxi drivers in Jerusalem and other mixed cities take circuitous routes or refuse passengers to avoid passing through Arab areas. During the 1990s, Israeli governments invested prodigious sums in building "bypass roads," enabling Israeli drivers to circumnavigate Palestinian cities in the Occupied Territories. Since the escalation of violence during the second Intifada (2000–), the Israeli military has barred Palestinian access to the bypass roads with hundreds of checkpoints, ditches, and roadblocks, creating separate (and unequal) transportation systems for Israeli and Palestinian drivers traveling through the same space. Often, bypass roads bear the peculiar distinction of being roads named for places they *don't go*.

Palestinians cannot avoid contact with Israelis in the form of soldiers at checkpoints. Engaging in voluntary social contact with Israelis, however, including dialogue and protest, can be stigmatized as *tatbi'a*. This is commonly translated as "normalization," but its Arabic discursive power far exceeds the banality of the English term.[5] The taboo of *tatbi'a* evokes Palestinian and Arab "enemy images" of Israeli Jews as a monolithic occupying army, and narratives rejecting the integration of Israelis into the Middle East. In the documentary film *Encounter Point*, Palestinian nonviolent resistance advocate Ali Abu Awwad describes *tatbi'a* as a technique of "identity policing" used by opponents of nonviolence: "Meeting with Israelis to call for nonviolence is immediately labeled as 'normalization' . . . [which] refers to someone who sells his principles, who gives in to his enemies and killers."[6]

The effect of these mechanisms of exclusion is that most Israelis and Palestinians remain as socially distant as they are geographically close to each other. In *Encounter Point*, Ali Abu Awwad dialogues with a 31-year-old Israeli, Shlomo Zagman, who admits that Ali is the first Palestinian with whom he's had a meaningful conversation *in his life*. Even among Palestinian and Jewish citizens of Israel, living in neighboring towns or mixed cities, relations beyond the superficial are exceptions to the rule. In workshops involving Jewish and Palestinian educators in Israel, facilitators commonly meet Jewish teachers who have little or no personal experience communicating with Palestinians. Enemy avoidance is embedded in the routines of everyday life to the point that cultivating relationships with people from the other side is seen as anomalous, subversive, or utterly unthinkable. Indeed, in the authors' experience, driving up to checkpoints with a mixed group of Arab and Jewish passengers often elicits incredulous reactions from soldiers. Some are pleasantly surprised; others suspect that the Arabs in the car have kidnapped the Jews.

Enemy Image and the Ethos of Conflict

Elaborate infrastructures of enemy avoidance characterize "intractable conflicts," as defined by Israeli social psychologist Daniel Bar-Tal:

> Intractable conflicts are characterized as protracted, irreconcilable, with vested interests in their continuation, violent, of zero-sum nature, total, and central. They are demanding, stressful, exhausting, and costly both in human and material terms. Societies involved in this type of conflict develop appropriate psychological conditions which enable them to cope successfully with the conflictual situation.[7]

Bar-Tal enumerates a typical set of shared "societal beliefs" about the nature of self, other, and reality that comprise the "psychological infrastructure" of an *ethos of conflict*—a discourse that provides psychological justification for social segregation. This conflict catechism becomes integrated into the reproduction of

the conflict at multiple levels. For individuals, it serves as a psychological survival kit, rationalizing the stresses and sacrifices mandated by the struggle. The
collective comes to depend on the ethos as a source of shared identity, a "social
glue" binding people together. At the systemic level, the ethos functions as en-
abler and an ennobler of conflict, making it seem to well-socialized citizens a
necessary, normal, and dignified way of life.

As Bar-Tal notes, some of these societal beliefs about self and "the other" can
be found in all groups. What distinguishes an ethos of conflict is the *interdependence* of positive self-image and negative enemy image: the justice of one side's
cause is vindicated by the other's alleged crimes; the peacefulness of one side is
predicated on the other's aggressiveness; the innocence of one side is "proven" by
the other's guilt. Each side imagines its own humanity in contrast to the demon-
ized other, in a relationship Kelman calls "negative identity interdependence."[8]

By carefully constructing a context of facilitated communication, equality,
compassion, and respect, the dialogical encounter allows Israelis and Palestinians to experience the mythical "enemy" as a fellow human being. Indeed, one of
the most popular statements of participants who have completed their first encounter is, "We discovered that they are human just like us." This presents a
living contradiction to the "enemy image," and undermines psychological justifications for social realities of segregation and violence. The encounter also creates a time and space for reflection, allowing participants to appreciate and articulate, often for the first time, the psychological toll that life inside the conflict
exacts from them.

The "toll" of the conflict is not equally distributed among the participants, nor
is it only psychological. Israelis and Palestinians live in a reality of asymmetric
power relations, in which most Israelis are born with access to rights, resources,
and opportunities that are denied or severely curtailed for most Palestinians.
Many Palestinian participants struggle during encounters with what they experience as overpsychologizing the relationship, or blurring the differences between
Israeli life in a society enforcing an occupation and Palestinian life under occupation. Psychosocial approaches encourage participants to articulate and recognize
their separate and unequal social realities. Such recognition is an essential step
for participants on both sides to understand each other's distinct, but equally real
and equally human, fears and needs, the different ways in which both groups
perpetuate the dynamics of conflict, and the different ways in which people on
each side pay "the price of no peace."

Empathy between Enemies: The Ideal of Genuine Dialogue

When participants arrive, the peacebuilder's role changes from navigating
"separation barriers" to facilitating dialogue. Yet an echo of the former role
resonates in the latter, as the facilitator guides participants through emotional
minefields that internally mirror the conflict "outside."

Through decades of work, peacebuilding practitioners have developed diverse techniques for "humanizing" perceptions and building relationships between members of enemy groups. Sustained face-to-face dialogue is an essential component of almost all. Scholarly studies document the power of competently orchestrated dialogical encounters to engender empathy between people raised as "enemies," affirming testimonials like this report from a Palestinian graduate of the *Building Bridges for Peace* program:

[Before the program] I didn't know and wasn't willing to hear that the other side was also in pain. I didn't want to listen to that, I didn't want to understand or imagine that. At first I felt like I was being forced to listen to them. . . . I said I didn't want to listen and nothing could make me. I only wanted to be there just to show the world who I was. . . . They insisted that they wanted to talk about their pain and what was hurting them. At last I gave in, not because I wanted to listen but because I became curious. If they wanted to talk, so be it, I didn't have to understand or feel their pain. . . . When they started talking, I realized that they were saying the same things I say, only from a different perspective. The way they talked was different; they were saying the same things I would say.[9]

The ideal path of genuine dialogue is the journey she describes: Beginning with denial and willful ignorance of the other side, confronting psychological defense mechanisms that protect idealized self and dehumanized enemy images, and fostering acknowledgment, empathy, and empowerment as bases for relationships of respect and understanding. Dialogical empathy is not a "product" but a creative process; in communication scholar Benjamin Broome's (1998) terms, it is "the creation of shared meaning":

Though beginning with contrasting perceptions and behaviors, two individuals, through their interaction, create a unique setting for their interaction. In the conjoining of their separate cultures, a third culture, more inclusive than the original ones, is created, which both of them now share. Within that third culture, the two can communicate with each other more effectively. . . . The emergence of this third culture is the essence of relational empathy and is essential for successful conflict resolution.[10]

Thus empathy is not a linear progression toward a finite goal, but a skill, a relationship that must be re-created with each new meeting or topic.

Much of the time, dialogue sessions hardly resemble an idealized portrait of "compassionate listening"; Israeli-Palestinian encounters are marked by interruption, contradiction, and competition to convey each side's narrative of victimhood. This can result in exhaustion, frustration—and sometimes—only *ex post facto* reflection. In the next section, we outline patterns we have repeatedly observed in encounters, and ways that facilitators can guide the process. Given the labyrinths that participants navigate just to arrive, it is no wonder that the course of Israeli-Palestinian dialogue rarely runs smooth.

The Dance of Dialogue: Fearful First Steps

Many participants testify that their first meeting with the other side awakened primal fears. On overnight programs, participants commonly report staying awake or hesitating to share rooms on the first night, fearing what their "enemy" neighbor might do lest they fall asleep. Facilitators can design activities to ease participants through these anxious first impressions:

> It was night when we first arrived at camp. The first thing they [the staff] asked us to do was to feel each other's pulse with our hands. It was the first time I felt the other, I understood, touching them, what the message behind the exercise was. They were girls my age, I never imagined that. It sounds unbelievable but it's true. Just like they imagine that all Palestinians are monsters with weapons, I imagined that it was all a country of soldiers. I was eighteen the first time I [met them], and by touching them and feeling their pulse, I realized that they are not just soldiers with weapons; they are human, just like me. We started to get to know them gradually after that.[11]

Waking up safe the next morning is often experienced as a relief. Many participants describe the initial success of encounters by simply saying, "We made it safely." Overcoming this visceral fear is a first step toward establishing a foundation of interpersonal trust.

Preliminary exercises aim at allowing participants to meet as individuals, to explore similarities and differences, to build social groups and create relationships. Outside structured activities, participants often stick to their own national groups, with only a few daring to voluntarily cross the lines. Inside meetings, facilitators use "ice-breaker" games and humanizing conversations on childhood, culture, family, school, music, films, sport, and other inclusive subjects, in order to build a positive group dynamic. Adult participants may shy away from games at first, but lightly awkward moments usually generate a sense of shared amusement, and spur them to find their own ways to interact informally before delving into difficult issues.

The process is a delicate dance, characterized by nervous laughter and cautious examination of "the other side." Gradually, the focus on cultural and personal similarities can generate feelings of relief and connectedness. It is a quietly myth-shattering experience that often inspires participants to wonder aloud why they cannot coexist peacefully, since they seem to have so much in common. This may be a lighthearted moment, but it is not frivolous; the foundations of trust and experiences of friendliness anchor the group in a sense of basic goodwill when the controversy begins.

Trust-building and informal contact remains important as dialogue heats up. Contemporary programs alternate dialogue sessions with cooperative social activity—sports, art, music, drama, touring, or any kind of shared diversion. These activities do not come at the expense of discussion; they serve a vital, complementary function, granting participants time and space to reinforce personal relationships and group trust, to absorb the emotional shocks of difficult sessions, and to meet again with renewed energy.

Dialogue between Individuals, Dialogue between Identities

In a previous era, facilitators might have been content to successfully "break the ice" between participants. Early Arab-Jewish encounter programs were based upon "harmony models," which steered discussion away from contentious topics. These models were theoretically based upon the "contact hypothesis," a civil rights-era social psychological framework for interracial dialogue in the United States.[12] This framework assumed that the roots of prejudice lay in the lack of normalized intergroup contact caused by residential segregation. The encounter would provide such contact, allowing participants to shed stereotypes by discovering that "the other" is an individual "just like me." In Israel, this model was translated into ministry of education-sponsored Arab-Jewish meetings focused on culture, food, hobbies, or a common project, but ignoring the "elephant in the closet"—the asymmetries of power, the deeply ingrained "enemy images," and the history of intercommunal violence that generate tension between Arab and Jewish collectives regardless of interpersonal relations. In this model, Israeli and Palestinian participants "succeeded" by becoming partners in denial—replacing physical "enemy avoidance" by agreeing to sit together and avoid the subject. This framework often created a veneer of cordial relations, while ultimately vindicating the skeptics' disdain of dialogue as *kalam fadi*, or, in this case, "hummus coexistence."

In the 1990s, a series of trenchant critiques by Israeli and Palestinian scholars and practitioners led to the genesis of new approaches. Facilitators adopted psychosocial paradigms informed by "social identity theory," encouraging participants to represent their collective identities, to openly confront the issues that divide them, and to evoke and express the range of emotions triggered in the process.[13] In this paradigm, "Humanization" and "safe space" become building blocks rather than ends in themselves—preliminary stages of a more ambitious encounter. This "generation gap" is eloquently described by a Palestinian mother in Israel, comparing the coexistence programs of her childhood to her daughter's twenty-first-century encounter experience:

> When I was fifteen years old, the older generation also thought it necessary to initiate meetings for Arab-Jewish reconciliation, and those meetings occurred—although believe me, I couldn't tell you the name of the Jewish school we met with, because the meeting lacked something. Not that we didn't talk—we talked about food, about holidays and customs—but not a single word about the conflict. The adults apparently thought that if we ignore the conflict, it will just disappear . . . we, the Arab students, did not have the courage to talk, and the Jewish students did not have the courage to listen. . . . The youth of Seeds of Peace succeeded where we failed. They played together, ate together, slept together, but also, every day they talked about the conflict. I believe it was difficult for them, but it is right to know what the other side says if you listen to them, and terribly wrong to decide what they think before ever hearing them speak for themselves.[14]

Her daughter's program combined interpersonal contact with intensive "dialogue between identities," the methodology of contemporary psychosocial approaches. The new encounter paradigm incorporates a fundamental tenet of psychotherapy—that healing depends on dissonance and pain being expressed, not repressed.

Coexistence and Catharsis: The Cure Is in the Pain

I remember walking into a coexistence [dialogue] session in which all fourteen participants were sobbing . . . the scene appeared hopeless. I thought I was at a funeral. And yet that moment gave me hope. . . they were not embarrassed to be crying in front of each other. They were unafraid to share one of the most intimate moments of our being as humans. The poison and blood shed in decades of violence seemed to flow in their tears.

—John Wallach, founder of Seeds of Peace[15]

Moving from the "getting-to-know-you" stage to facing the conflict can be a painful process. Participants invariably share stories of suffering—whether direct experiences of humiliation, bereavement, or violence, or secondary absorption of trauma through parents, teachers, and socialization. Skillfully facilitated dialogue empowers Israelis and Palestinians to enact a revolutionary role reversal, in which "enemies," rather than causing each other suffering, transform their relationship into one of mutual support and compassionate listening.

Yet initial discussions of the conflict rarely resemble this therapeutic scenario. Many participants begin by treating the encounter as a trial—an opportunity to establish, once and for all, the guilt of the "enemy." Many choose to present competing narratives of victimhood in a manner reminiscent of a criminal case, each group marshaling facts and objecting loudly to the other side's testimony. The discussion leaps haphazardly across history, but the point-counterpoint dynamic is unshakeable. Both use cultural, ethical, and historical arguments to delegitimize the other. Palestinians describe violent acts of Israeli soldiers and settlers in the Occupied Territories, and Israelis parry by citing Palestinian attacks against Israeli civilians; Palestinians describe the dispossession of Palestinian refugees in the 1948 war, and Israelis counter with Israel's role as a refuge for survivors of the Holocaust and Jews fleeing from persecution in Eastern Europe and the Middle East; Palestinians claim that Jewish identity is limited to its religious aspect, that Israelis have no "authentic" culture or nationality; Israelis claim that Palestinians are simply "Arabs," lacking unique national roots or distinct claims to sovereignty. Both sides talk *past* each other, *at* each other, rather than *to* each other.

This escalating "blame game" is marked by rising tensions and tones of voice. Participants often challenge ground rules of discussion amid mounting frustration. The facilitator's balancing act is to preserve respectful communication, but not to stifle this essential process. Each side will not be deterred from representing its "ethos of conflict"; the process fulfills urgent needs to display loyalty to their respective collectives and solidify internal cohesion. In addition, this "venting" releases pent-up stores of anger, anxiety, and fear—something many participants need to do *first* in order to be able to hear other people at all. In layperson's terms, there is a lot each participant must get off his or her chest in order to listen to others with an open mind and heart. The art of facilitation is guiding these passionate expressions toward acknowledgment, reflection, paraphrasing, validating, and empathizing; to build, rather than damage, the incipient relationship of the group.

These heated exchanges also serve as a recognition of the "peacebuilder's paradox," of the entrenched realities that the encounter in itself cannot change; it lets participants feel that they are "keeping it real." In the absence of any blame game, participants are likely to complain that, "We did not talk about the real issues." While reminding participants of ground rules, and setting standards of active listening by asking them to repeat and clarify each other's statements, facilitators need not panic. A sense of crisis building within the group can become a catalyst, pushing participants beyond their "comfort zones" and deepening the dialogue. As facilitator David Allen Wallach says it, a group often needs "a break*down* in order to have a break*through*."

The blame game typically takes place at a collective level. Each group, in a struggle to justify its version of history, invokes what psychology scholar Vamik Volkan calls "chosen traumas." These are catastrophic events whose painful memories are transmitted from generation to generation, such that mourning for past disasters becomes a collective task, an integral part of the group's shared identity:

> A "chosen trauma," applicable in the subsequent generations after a massive trauma, refers to the "memories," perceptions, expectations, wishes, fears, and other emotions related to shared images of the historical catastrophe and the defenses against these emotions . . . [this] becomes an important identity marker for the affected large group. The term "chosen trauma" accurately reflects a large group's *unconscious* "choice" to add a past generation's mental representation of a shared event to its own identity. While large groups may have experienced any number of traumas caused by "others," only certain ones remain alive over many years—indeed, often over a period of centuries.[16]

Chosen traumas dominate the blame game. Participants invoke them repeatedly in the early stages of the encounter—reciting the histories they have been taught. In the process, participants discover that the other side has its own history, which contradicts the "enemy" narrative. Both groups fight to shift the responsibility for all suffering onto the others, whom they hold responsible for "starting" the cycle of violence.

Faced with disbelief of their collective identities and narratives, participants begin to share personal stories of victimization involving themselves, their families and friends. This begins as another attempt to "win," to prove and disprove. But the authority of personal experience, the notes of genuine pain and fear in speakers' voices, and the safety created by skillful facilitation awaken compassion and begin to break down walls of denial. Soft voices and tears replace the cacophony of the blame game. The move from "chosen" to personal trauma-telling generates cathartic moments, in which participants begin to articulate the emotional effects of violence and oppression, and to mourn together what each has lost.

Whether or not they "believe" the opposing narrative, participants can viscerally feel, often for the first time, the humanity and vulnerability of their "enemies." This is the key to transforming the relationship from mutual denial to mutual recognition, from indifference or hostility to compassion and empathy. It is a continuous process; some will persist in repressing emotions and denying recognition. The facilitator's art is to remain calm, keep faith in the group, allow time and space for personal stories to emerge, model compassionate listening, and elicit supportive responses from the group. The honest expression of pain most often inspires a reciprocal desire to listen, comfort, and heal. When the new dynamic is established, the group may continue this cathartic process for multiple sessions before surfacing from their place of deep reflection.

The power of personal narrative is emphasized by storytelling paradigms such as the TRT (To Reflect and Trust) approach pioneered by social psychologist Dan Bar-On, and the technique of compassionate listening, in which participants may ask clarifying questions, but never comment or interrupt each other's stories. The story itself is not the key—the transformation is inspired by the cross-conflict *relationship* that develops, by the mutual acknowledgment, by the context of empathy between "enemies." Eloquent soliloquies for uninational audiences will not do the trick. As a TRT participant explains, "This healing process can only happen when people from both sides come together. When you are in your own family or in a group where you are all victims, it is so easy to persist with the pain, anger and even the hate you feel and to get used to the victim role."[17]

In contemporary Israel and Palestine, an organization called the Parents Circle Families Forum: Bereaved Families Supporting Peace, Reconciliation and Tolerance exemplifies the way dialogue can transform "the victim role." This is a group with hundreds of Israeli and Palestinian members, all of whom have lost immediate family members in the conflict. They meet together to share their stories and grief, actualizing the vision of cross-conflict dialogue as a healing process. But they do not stop there. Their purpose is both personal and political; in the words of bereaved Israeli mother Robi Damelin, the goal of the Forum is "to stop this killing . . . to find a way to dialogue [in order] to prevent further death."[18] Israeli and Palestinian Forum members speak together publicly throughout the country, broadcasting messages of solidarity with victims on both sides, and opposition to all forms of vengeance and violence.

In *Encounter Point*, a Palestinian skeptic taunts Forum member Ali Abu Awwad, asking, "Are you 'normalizing' relations with Israelis before there is a solution to the conflict?" Yet Ali and his fellow peacebuilders refuse to wait for a solution to appear on its own. The Forum embodies a powerful psychosocial response to the "peace-builder's paradox." Its Israeli and Palestinian activists have all paid, in the words of founding member Aharon Barnea, the ultimate "price of no peace." Yet rather than passively accept a "victim role," they defy the dominant "ethos of conflict" on both sides. Far from acquiescing to the status quo, they contradict the clichés that "normalize" lethal routines of segregation and violence; far from "empty," their "talk" together is fueling a growing grassroots movement for nonviolent social change.

Notes

1. Our field is known by a variety of terms; most prominently, conflict *management, resolution,* or *transformation.* Each term signifies a particular paradigm of theory and practice; when referring to the field as a whole, we use the umbrella term *peacebuilding.* For an overview of the field, see Beyond Intractability, www.beyondintractability.org. For background on "conflict transformation," see Lederach (1997).

2. Max Weber is paraphrased as saying that "man is an animal suspended in webs of significance he himself has spun," in Geertz (1973). An anthropologist, Geertz calls those webs "culture"; we define the webs more broadly as "context," encompassing cultural, economic, political, and social spheres.

3. See Hamber (2004).

4. On military bureaucracy and dialogue, see Pogrund (2003). On checkpoints and travel restrictions in the West Bank, see Conover (2006); see also Hass (2002); also the film *Machsomim* ("Checkpoints"), Yoav Shamir, director, 2004.

5. Salem (2005). See also *Thematic highlights—normalization,* retrieved May 8, 2006 from Just Vision, http://justvision.com/excerpts/?q=Normalization.

6. *Encounter Point,* Ronit Avni and Julia Bacha, directors, Just Vision, 2005.

7. Bar-Tal (1998, p. 22). Bar-Tal characterizes the Middle East, Northern Ireland, Kashmir, and Turkish/Kurdish conflicts as "intractable."

8. Kelman (1999).

9. *Portrait: Inas Radwan,* retrieved May 8, 2006 from Just Vision, http://www.justvision.org/excerpts/inas_radwan.php.

10. Broome (1998, p. 104).

11. *Portrait: Inas Radwan.*

12. Allport (1954).

13. Nimer (1999); see also Halabi (2004).

14. Shehadeh (2001, p. 26).

15. Wallach (2000, p. 115).

16. Volkan.

17. Gruendler (2002).

18. *Encounter Point.*

References

Abu-Nimer, M. (1999). *Dialogue, conflict resolution and change: Arab-Jewish encounters in Israel.* Albany: State University of New York Press.

Abu-Nimer, M. (Ed.). (2001). *Reconciliation, justice, and coexistence: Theory and practice.* New York: Lexington Books.

Allport, G. W. (1954). *The nature of prejudice.* Reading, MA: Addison-Wesley.

Bar-Tal, D. (1998). Societal beliefs in times of intractable conflict: The Israeli case. *International Journal of Conflict Management, 9,* 22–50.

Broome, B. (1998). Managing differences in conflict resolution: The role of relational empathy. In D.J.D. Sandole & H. Van Der Merwe (Eds.), *Conflict resolution theory and practice: Integration and application.* 95–111 Manchester: Manchester University Press.

Conover, T. (2006, March). The checkpoint. *Atlantic Monthly, 297*(2), 72–88.

Fisher, R. J. (1997). *Interactive conflict resolution.* Syracuse, NY: Syracuse University Press.

Fitzduff, M., & Stout, C. E. (Eds.). (2006). *The psychology of resolving global conflicts: From war to peace* (Vols. 1–3). Westport, CT: Praeger.

Geertz, C. (1973). Thick description: Toward an interpretative theory of culture. In *The interpretation of cultures.* p. 5 New York: Basic Books.

Gruendler, E. (2002, February 18). *Dialogue with the enemy: Dan Bar-On develops the TRT process.* HaGalil Online, February 18, 2002, retrieved May 8, 2006 from http://nahost-politik.de/psychologie/bar-on.htm

Halabi, R. (2004). *Israeli and Palestinian identities in dialogue: The School for Peace approach.* Piscataway, NJ: Rutgers University Press.

Hallward, M. C. (2006). *Building space for peace: Challenging the boundaries of Israel/Palestine.* Unpublished doctoral dissertation, American University, Washington, DC.

Hamber, B. (2004). *The impact of trauma: A psychosocial approach.* Keynote address to the A Shared Practice—Victims' Work in Action Conference, April 7–8, Limavady, Northern Ireland. The website of Brandon Hamber. Retrieved December 15, 2005 from http://www.brandonhamber.com/publications/pap-trauma1.htm

Hass, A. (2002, December 6). Long-term sieges. *Haaretz.*

Julius, D. A., Montville, J. V., & Volkan, V. D. (Eds.). 1990. *The psychodynamics of international relationships* (Vols. 1–2). Lexington, MA: Lexington Books.

Kelman, Herbert C. (1999). "The Interdependence of Israeli and Palestinian National Identities: The Role of the Other in Existential Conflicts." *Journal of Social Issues, 55*(3), 581–600.

Landau, Y. (2003). *Healing the Holy Land: Interreligious peace building in Israel/Palestine.* Washington, DC: United States Institute of Peace Press.

Lederach, J. P. (1997). *Building peace: Sustainable reconciliation in divided societies.* Washington, DC: United States Institute of Peace Press.

Maddy-Weitzman, E. (2004). *Waging peace in the Holy Land: A qualitative study of Seeds of Peace 1993–2004.* Unpublished doctoral dissertation, Boston University, Boston, MA.

Pogrund, B. (2003, December 8). How to politely sabotage dialogue. *Haaretz.*

Salem, W. (2005). The anti-normalization discourse in the context of Israeli-Palestinian peacebuilding. *Palestine-Israel Journal of Politics, Economics and Culture, 12*(1), 100–109.

Shehadeh, M. (2001, Fall). Work of a generation. *The Olive Branch, 6*(1), 22–23.

Volkan, V. (2002) *Massively traumatized societies and historical and political processes.* Unpublished paper for commemorative publication in honor of Kurt R. Spillman. University of Virginia, Center for the Study of Mind and Human Interaction.

Volkan, V. D. (1996). *The need to have enemies and allies: From clinical practice to international relationships.* Northvale, NJ: Jason Aronson.

Wallach, J. (2000). *The enemy has a face: The Seeds of Peace experience.* Washington, DC: United States Institute of Peace Press.

Weiner, Y. (Ed.). 1998. *The handbook of interethnic coexistence.* New York: Continuum.

CHAPTER 4

SENSITIVE SUBJECTS AND IDEOLOGICAL DIFFERENCES AFFECTING CIVIL SOCIETY COLLABORATION BETWEEN PALESTINIAN AND ISRAELI PEOPLE

Ronny A. Shtarkshall

For the last 25 years I have been involved in attempts to create collaborations between Arab scientists and professionals, especially Palestinians and Israelis, as part of an effort to develop informal and social routes for peace between these people. My fields—sexuality, sex education, and sexual and reproductive health—are especially problematic when one considers their cultural sensitivity and political ramifications. These efforts have taken many different forms. Some of the most rewarding ones have been my work with Palestinian students studying for their graduate degree at the International MPH (Masters of Public Health) program of the Braun School of Public Health and Community Medicine. Some of my students have chosen topics for their theses that I would not have dared to suggest, such as "The readiness of high school teachers to be involved in the prevention of early marriages among their students" and "Attitudes of Palestinian students toward sex." I would not have proposed such subjects because of their sensitivity and my concern for the welfare of these students, but the results of these theses had shown that there are undercurrents that could be harbingers of change in the areas of sexuality and fertility in the Palestinian society. Progression, although very slow and with a lot of difficulties and frustrations, has also been very rewarding.

The reflections in this paper represent my thoughts about the conceptual frameworks, sociopolitical environment, and organizational culture that I have come to realize are essential for the development of collaborative efforts in the fields of health, education, welfare, and science between Israelis and Palestinians.

I deliberately distinguish between the Israeli and Palestinian political entities and the Israeli and Palestinian people. Although permissions from the former are essential for the collaboration between people or civil society institutions, they are far from sufficient. Political agreements do not create peace. Peace is made between people and therefore needs development far beyond the political arena. I am interested in developing environments that make collaborations possible and that nurture them and allow them to evolve, thus creating the necessary social and cultural understanding that is essential for lasting peace.

The basic assumption is that collaborations will develop between Palestinian and Israeli people whose basic motivation is a stable peace. Both Palestinians and Israelis can dwell amply on past wrongs. They can engage endlessly on issues of guilt, measures of who suffered more, or who started the conflict. Although some people believe that these issues must underlie even the effort for collaboration, my view is that blame, guilt, and comparisons are not only futile but fatal to collaborative efforts.

I posit that the focus of any collaborative effort must be on the future. That means asking, "What are we trying to achieve beyond the particular collaboration?" In order to achieve a stable peace, we have to strive for two main goals: (1) to create an environment in which the socioeconomic conditions among the Palestinians living within their national entity will be higher than the level they are today, to a point beyond that of the average in the Middle East, and that their economy will be self-sustaining and not subjugated to the Israeli economy; and (2) to create an environment in which the social and psychological effects of more than a hundred years of the conflict will be gradually ameliorated to a minimum, which will allow for relationships different from that of political entities living side by side but begrudging each other's existence.

Achieving the second goal requires *true* collaborative projects. Sometimes a collaborative project is a "sanitized" euphemism for aid or investment in a weaker economy or society. This is not a collaborative effort. At best, it may be a true but misguided wish to help from a perspective of superiority; at worst, it can be a self-serving effort disguised as help. True collaboration is one in which all parties have their own interests and all parties will gain from the collaboration. The gain does not have to be equal in terms of funds or achieved results, but if there are two parties in the collaboration, my opinion is that one must have at least one-quarter, and preferably, one-third of the material and intellectual gains in order for the collaboration to be sustained, developed, and continued.

This leads to another essential component of productive collaboration: continuity. If the goals are those stated previously—developing societies that can interact on an equal basis and changing the climate between the two warring societies—then a short-term collaboration can contribute only minimally to those aims while a long-term, ongoing, and continuing collaboration is necessary in order to allow relationships and interests to evolve and results to accumulate. Changes must come gradually, and therefore are dependent on long-term collaborations.

Another important requirement for effective collaboration is to refrain from getting initially involved in issues that are politically and/or culturally sensitive and potentially explosive. Here, one must make very fine distinctions between types of involvement and who initiates them. An example is the issue of fertility and family planning. This is a highly sensitive issue not only because of the involvement of sex and the additional component of premarital contraception, but also because fertility and population growth are part of the political arena of the Israeli-Palestinian conflict. When I was the chairman of the Israeli Family Planning Association (1993–1997), several members tried to initiate collaboration with Palestinian organizations in the field. We were also approached by an outside donor organization. Despite the great temptation, I made a decision to refrain from being involved on the basis of potential damage to the Palestinian organizations (being labeled as collaborators) and to the issue itself. I was glad that I made this decision and that we were not involved when some extremist political elements labeled efforts of reproductive health as a "Zionist Plot." On the other hand, when the Red Crescent organized a course on family planning, and I was asked to conduct five days of workshops on counseling FP issues to professionals, I gladly agreed to do so, as long as I was doing this as an academician and not as the chairman of the Israeli Family Planning Association. The reason for this distinction is that organizations, even NGOs, are perceived to be carriers of political or social policies while people can be perceived as free agents, sometimes acting against official policy. Furthermore, I deliberately refrained from dealing with premarital contraception until the issue was raised toward the end of the workshop by some of the Palestinian participants, and then we had a thorough discussion about the meaning and implications of dealing with these issues.

Another example in the field of sexuality and collaboration is a research project we tried to initiate jointly with Al-Quds School of Public Health. The idea was to qualitatively study families who use contraception and families who do not, sampling families from several important comparable subgroups in both the Israeli and Palestinian societies. Ninety percent of the families would be Palestinian and 10 percent would be Israeli, as a comparison group. The reason for that was, we believed, that most of the funds should be directed to the PA while both parties should benefit from the research. All interviews were to be translated into English and made available to all the researchers. Initial analysis was to be carried by joint protocols under joint supervision of at least one researcher from each of the societies. While academic publication was to be joint, each group could apply the results any way it wanted within its own society.

Unfortunately, donor organizations did not think that this was important enough to be funded. We were told that they were interested in service and application and not in research, despite the fact that such a study is essential for developing programs in subgroups where the total fertility rate is above four, which means that, on the average, women bear at least four children during their fertile years, and can even reach eight, for example, in the Gaza area. Currently, researchers from Al-Quds School of Public Health, The Hebrew University and Hadassah, Braun School of Public Health and Community Medicine, and Rollins School of Public Health, Emory University, are renewing their efforts to realize this study. This attempt relies on a much more elaborate and equal basis, in which the objectives also include the effects of sociopolitical context in mediating religion and religiosity. We hope that donor organizations will not find the subject too sensitive to fund, as all parties believe that understanding fertility decisions and family planning is essential for the future development of the Middle East region in general and the PA and Israel in particular. We seem to touch here on another point that is hard to deal with. Donor organizations meet their own agendas—sometimes against the best interests of the people who receive the donations. Only a strong stand from all those involved can change these policies. For example, it is hard to refuse funds for service applications because there are no funds for proper research when funds are badly needed.

Last but not least, one should not perceive educational, scientific, and social collaboration as having to change one's personal political opinions and/or national identity. In my case, my position is that I support a Palestinian state and a peace agreement, in which each entity will give up some of its aspirations, which stems from my Zionist belief. This belief is based on the assumption that people, in this case the Jewish people, are entitled to their own political entity, and that this is also true for the Palestinians. Other people have very different political opinions. If the condition for collaboration is agreement on a political opinion, the collaboration may be doomed from the start. Instead, it is more constructive to start with the premise that people can maintain their belief and position, that preagreement is not necessary, but that the door is left open for new perspectives to develop out of the collaboration.

CHAPTER 5

CAN TALKING TO EACH OTHER REALLY MAKE A DIFFERENCE? PERSPECTIVES ON RECONCILIATION-AIMED DIALOGUES IN THE CONFLICT BETWEEN ISRAELI-JEWS AND PALESTINIANS

Ifat Maoz, Zvi Bekerman, and Mara Getz Sheftel

Introduction

Avi, an Israeli-Jewish ninth grader from a school in the center of Israel, used to hate Arabs. He heard at home and also understood from the media that they are all evil and want to destroy Israel. When he finally personally encountered Palestinian ninth graders through a facilitated dialogue project his school had participated in, he was surprised to learn that they are actually youth like him, and have dreams and aspirations just like his own. A friendship formed between him and Hassan, a Palestinian youth, that lasted long after the dialogue project had ended. But are facilitated dialogues between groups in conflict usually that effective in changing opinions and attitudes or is this case a single case of change? This chapter probes the perspectives and experiences of facilitators of such reconciliation-aimed dialogues on this issue of: Can talking to each other really make a difference?

Ethnopolitical conflicts tend to be accompanied by psychological phenomena such as mutual prejudice, deligitimization, and dehumanization (Bar-On, 1999; Bar-Tal, 2000). Facilitated, transformative dialogue encounters between groups in conflict have been, in the past few decades, a prevalent psychological device that is used extensively in efforts to improve relations and mutual perceptions (Bar-On & Kassem, 2004; Kelman, 1998; Salomon, 2000). The present study relates to such dialogues aimed at fostering reconciliation and increasing empathy and understanding between Israeli-Jews and Palestinians. It focuses on the motives, experience, and perceptions of those who lead these transformative dialogues, the Jewish and Palestinian group facilitators. Through their perspective, we try to better understand if such dialogues can actually make a difference in relations between the sides, and in what way.

The notion of transformative dialogue is presented in the works of Kenneth Gergen and his colleagues (Gergen, 1999) as a process through which sides deal with disagreement or conflict between them through expressing themselves, listening to the other, and taking in or empathizing with the emotions, experiences, views, and values of the other.

Through such dialogue the sides come to construct themselves and the other differently, extending the boundaries of the self and including parts of the other within the self, and thus including the other within the realm of relational moral responsibility. Perceptions and relations to the other are transformed and greater understanding, acceptance, and connectedness to the experiences and positions of the other are formed (Gergen, 1999).

In the same vein, other scholars also describe transformative relationship-building dialogues as engaging members of conflicting groups in an open and respectful exchange of perspectives where different voices get a chance to express themselves and to be listened to in order to build mutual understanding, trust, and insight. The process focuses on accurate, respectful, two-way communication aimed at bringing each side to understand and appreciate more deeply the subjective reality of the other (Fisher, 1997). In line with Kurt Lewin's (1958) theories of change and "re-education," the group process and the establishment of new group norms (i.e., norms of nonprejudice toward the out-group) are used in these small-group dialogue workshops to transform intergroup perceptions and attitudes (Bar & Bargal, 1995).

Thus, transformative dialogue leading to deeper mutual understanding is seen by many as a desirable, if not ideal, state of affairs. This vision is also inspired by writings by Freire that describe the dialogical encounter as "a practice of freedom in which people critically engage each other in an effort to know more than they currently do. In doing so, they embrace their historical vocation to become more fully human" (Friere, 1970, pp. 81–82).

But can such dialogues actually make a difference? Can they increase awareness, empathy, and psychological understanding of the other? On the one hand, there is the goal of the organizers and even participants of these dialogue encounters to engage in respectful and enriching communication. On the other hand, participants of these dialogues (and often also the organizers) are still members of the groups in conflict, with all the competitive behaviors, power struggles, and negative perceptions that tend to characterize such groups.

In the midst of this is positioned the practitioner—the dialogue-group facilitator with the mission of trying to bridge over or work through this serious gap. The gap between the desired and aimed-for state of mutual empathy, respect, and understanding and between the existing situation of animosity and conflict between the sides.

Past studies have dealt with the effects of dialogues and encounters as measured through changes in participants' attitudes before and after the encounter (e.g., see Bar & Bargal, 1995). Other studies have looked at the processes and dynamics of relations that develop through the dialogue meetings and at discourse around and in the dialogue (Bar-On, 1999; Bar-On & Kassem, 2004; Bekerman, 2000, 2002; Halabi, 2000; Maoz, 2000; Salomon, 2002).

The previously noted research mainly studied participants, directors, and organizers of dialogue-encounters. Although the importance of studying theories of practice in the context of conflict transformation has been emphasized (Ross, 2000), little research attention has been given to those that are situated in the midst of it all—the facilitators of the dialogue group.[1]

Our study investigates perspectives, dilemmas, and psychological motives of Jewish and Palestinian facilitators of reconciliation-aimed dialogue-encounters in the conflict. Through their eyes, we try to understand what brought them to choose this professional/ideological track, their experiences, and difficulties in encounter-facilitation work and, most important, their perspective and theories of practice on whether dialogues can actually make a difference, and in what way (Ross, 2000).

Typically, a dialogue-encounter group includes 8–10 Jewish and 8–10 Palestinian participants and is cofacilitated by one Jewish and one Palestinian facilitator. Dialogue-encounters deal with experiential, affective, and political aspects of the relationship between the sides through the sharing of experience, storytelling (Bar-On & Kassem, 2004), facilitated awareness-increasing discussions (Halabi, 2000), and other psychosocial group work techniques. These range from one-time workshops to a longer process in which the group meets regularly for one year or more.

Our Study

Participants

Some 12 Jewish and 12 Palestinian facilitators were interviewed between October 2004 and May 2005 in a framework of a research on the reassessment of peace education conducted in the Truman Institute for the Advancement of Peace at the Hebrew University of Jerusalem and led by the two first authors. All of the facilitators were involved in dialogue initiatives in major organizations in this field. The research team included the three authors and five advanced students (2 Israeli-Jews, 1 Palestinian, 2 German).[2]

Methodology

Interviews were audio recorded and carefully transcribed. We then analyzed the transcripts for major and repeated themes, categories, and notions that characterize the facilitators' experience and construction of their work.

Findings: Motives, Experiences, and Perceived Effects of Dialogues

We present here interviewee comments, trajectories, notions, and experiences on the three following topics: (1) on becoming a facilitator of transformative dialogues: sources of psychosocial motivation; (2) dialogue facilitation issues: goals and the political discussion dilemma; and (3) does dialogue make a difference? perspectives on effectiveness.

The excerpts presented next might create the impression that the Jewish and Palestinian interviewees experience fully symmetrical realities. Needless to say, given the present sociopolitical situation, this is not true. We are well aware of this fact, and though this study mainly focuses on the similarities that exist in the experiences related to us by facilitators belonging to the two groups, there are also differences in their experiences and points of view that may be further explicated in future research.

1. On Becoming a Facilitator of Transformative Dialogues: Sources of Psychosocial Motivation

The choice to become a facilitator of transformative dialogues in conflict is not a trivial one. Though an interesting work, it is not very well paid. It may also involve some social prices. The facilitator may become identified within his own society as "the one who loves Palestinians" or "the one that loves Jews," or simply, even "the one that believes in Jewish-Palestinian coexistence." These societal categorizations may close certain social circles, options, and contacts for the facilitator who may face rejection and exclusion from those who object to Jewish-Palestinian partnership. In spite of this, our interviewees chose to become involved in facilitation. We try to understand here their psychopolitical motivations to do that.

Psychopolitical Motivations

Both Jewish and Palestinian interviewees described their motivation to become facilitators of intergroup dialogue-encounters as stemming from their sense of responsibility to bring about social change. Younes,[3] a Palestinian male (PM) facilitator noted: "If you want to protect our way of life, if you want to protect our future, I think this [the dialogue workshops] is the main way to do that. And I think that I feel a kind of responsibility to be part of that." In her interview, Theresa, a Palestinian female (PF) facilitator, explained: "Yeah, it is a way of how you deal with the conflict and it's your responsibility, it's my responsibility, this change. If I want to change things, I should begin from *myself*, I have to change myself inside, to be aware to feel responsible to do things and not to wait till the others, or that the leaders will do it." Keren, a Jewish female (JF) facilitator, also expressed her motivation to change the situation, while referring to her own frustration at the way things are: "Suddenly I think maybe I can be useful, maybe I can change things, maybe I can affect people and then maybe I can feel good, because I'm useful, like I can make things different, you know, because I was so frustrated."

In many instances, Palestinian facilitators also saw their work in intergroup encounters as a form of empowerment both for themselves and the dialogue-encounters' participants of the encounters with whom they work. Halil (PM) recounted his first encounter and his own feeling of empowerment: "But at that time I found it so much interesting and exciting to convince Jews that we are human like them, and prove to them that we are no less than them and suddenly they are interested in us." Muhmud (PM) also described a change in the way he related to Jews after participating in an encounter: "I liked the way I [as a participant in a dialogue-encounter] grew out of being *non-persona* in front of a Jew." Thus, while for the most part, both Jewish and Palestinian facilitators began working with dialogue groups as a response to their own feelings of dissatisfaction and frustration with the situation and out of their feeling responsibility for changing it, Palestinian facilitators described an added impetus—to express the voice of the Palestinian people by engaging in encounter-dialogue work.

The different accounts, brought here, seem to reflect or express one basic psychosocial motive—the motive for social change ("to change the situation"). This seems to have brought our interviewees, through different venues and personal trajectories, to their choice to become involved in facilitation of Jewish-Palestinian dialogue-encounters.

2. Dialogue Facilitation: Goals, Cofacilitation, and the Political Discussion Dilemma

Once choosing to become facilitators, our interviewees were faced with the complexity of their work. This complexity of dialogue facilitation in conflict is reflected in the following accounts on Jewish and Palestinian facilitators' goals and on the political discussion dilemma.

Goals of Facilitation

When interviewees explained their main goals in doing dialogue work, they relayed a common theme of creating a critical awareness among the participants running throughout their answers. Thus, some interviewees said that they hoped to give participants the tools to ask questions about the situation they are living in. For example, Khalid (PM) relays that he hopes that after their encounter experience, participants "can *ask* questions, try to re-construct their view of reality, try to think again about what is happening in the encounter . . . and try to look at themselves and learn something and maybe this will open for them the option to change and open their eyes and minds and hearts." Maya (JF) also notes that it is important that participants learn how to ask questions: "A process of learning, of asking questions, I think that is very important."

Also, other interviewees expressed similar goals of creating critical awareness in terms of changing the way participants look at and construct their reality. Theresa (PF) speaks about giving the participants she works with tools to face their reality: "You know, I spoke about giving *tools* and I give, participants, *tools* in order to face their reality and to be *aware* and to do something." Fatima (PF) said that she not only wants to help the dialogue participants look at their own reality but that she also aims to introduce to the participants the realities that the participants from the other group live in: "Like our aim is to help the participants see that there are different realities than those they know in regard to the other, like for the other there is another narrative than the one they know, and for the other there are needs, and there are emotions and there is a background, and there are daily lives that they don't know about."

A number of interviewees also noted that one of their main goals was to create a situation of equity because, outside the encounter, Palestinians and Jews are not equal. Thus, Dafna (JF) said: "So our main work is to allow them to come and to feel equal as much as possible in the encounter and to achieve what they can achieve, because they have a choice and *nothing* can *stop* them." Theresa (PF) agrees with Dafna that creating a feeling of equality is one of the main goals of facilitation. She went further to say that she hopes to teach the participants that the feeling of equality can come from within and that it can also be extended to situations outside the encounter: "Like I said before how to really feel *aware* and responsible to do something for equality, it means, you know, from *inside*, one has to feel it, no matter what is on the outside now, it's like with freedom, even though you are in prison, or whatever, if you feel *free*, you are free, you can *write*, you can think, or whatever. *Express* your feeling, express your situation, your real situation from the *inside* to deal with *outside*."

Some facilitators had more far-reaching ambitions—not only to influence the way the participants relate to their reality and the reality of those around them, but also to make a positive change in society as a whole. For example, Melanie (JF) explained that, "the overall goal is attitudinal change so there'll be a more tolerant society in Israel." Theresa (PF) also noted that by changing the way individuals look at their situation, they can create a positive change in society as a whole: "This is how societies start to, or *nations* start to *change* actually, we are people, but we are one and another, one and another, making a society, making a *nation*." However, Miri (JF) in her interview disagrees with this opi nion and claimed that it is impossible to change society by dialogue-encounters. She commented: "Twenty years ago we would say that it is possible to change [reality]. After that we spoke less positively, seeing that it is impossible to easily overcome [reality]." While interviewees did not agree on whether it is possible to change the sociopolitical reality of the conflict, most of them did think that, in some way, creating a critical awareness among their participants was one of their main goals.

The Political Discussion Dilemma

The political discussion dilemma has been, since the late 1980s, a focal one in dialogue-encounters between Jews and Palestinians (Maoz, 2000; Sonnenschein, Halabi, & Friedman, 1998). Specifically, this dilemma centers on the question of: Should dialogues include in them political discussions on controversial and emotionally loaded issues directly related to the conflict, or concentrate only on interpersonal, professional, or cultural issues that are less loaded and less related to the conflict (Maoz, 2000). Another, softer, version of this dilemma concerns the phase of the dialogue in which political discussion should be introduced. Should it be introduced from the outset of the encounter, or only at a later phase?

This dilemma was also found to be a focal one in facilitators' theories of practice, regarding how an efficient or "good" dialogue should be conducted. A significant number of our interviewees claimed that initially avoiding direct discussion about the political situation was an efficient method of opening the encounter. One method of avoiding political discussions at the outset of the encounter was described as focusing on the less-provocative subject of intercultural or interreligious dialogue. Facilitators agreed that these topics were less controversial, and participants could more easily find common values than when discussing the political situation. Said (PM) recalled a workshop he facilitated in which he and his Jewish cofacilitator started with intercultural dialogue in order to establish a common understanding: "I tried with another friend, Jewish friend, at the beginning, to build up a *cultural* workshop. It means that, first of all, we are getting to know each other on the personal sides: who are you, what are you doing in your daily life, what are your hobbies, what makes you angry, which food do you like, which feasts you have in your culture, dress, music and we try to make this interaction a step-by-step one, to get more and more to culturally know each other. . . . Actually these cultural workshops do a lot for us and for the participants, cause we notice that *after* the cultural workshop we can do the political workshop, or social workshop, I don't know what, and if I know your culture and you already know my culture, *we* have a common place that we can pick up from to discuss a lot of things, like talk about the problem between us, you are the Israeli, I'm the Palestinian." Roy (JM) spoke of the same benefits in starting with interreligious dialogue: "I think, framing discussions in the frame of an interreligious dialogue can help in a few ways, first of all, it helps calm things down, because we begin with personal respect, we explore each other's religious values, we establish some common values, so we build one or two floors of *trust*. . . . I think the interreligious ambience creates a softer framework for a more *heartfelt* discussion, more *genuine* discussion, it lays the ground."

These accounts of the Jewish and Palestinian interviewees regarding their work repeatedly reflect in different ways and emphasis what seems to be the central tension or paradox of their work—the paradox between the outside reality of conflict and the desired state, within the dialogue-group, of mutual understanding and empathy. This tension is also reflected in facilitators' perceptions regarding the effectiveness of dialogue-encounters.

3. Does a Dialogue Really Make a Difference? Perspectives on Effectiveness

One of the major questions regarding dialogue work in intergroup conflict is its effectiveness in actually changing psychological, social, and/or political states. The following facilitators' accounts give a mixed picture that is at once optimistic and pessimistic, one of achievement and hope and of disappointment and despair. This is maybe unsurprising, given the complexity of such reconciliation-aimed dialogue work, the complexity of its goals and dynamics, and its inevitable inherent clash with the political situation of conflict, outside.

Perceived Effectiveness of the Dialogue-Encounter

Both Palestinian and Jewish facilitators said that they perceive their work as successful when they see that the participants have changed after the dialogue-encounter. Many of the facilitators acknowledged that these personal changes may seem small, especially in light of the often stagnant political situation. However, these changes are often easy to see and help people deal with their reality on a personal level. Younes (PM) simply described that he recognizes the success of his group work when participants feel a major influence of the encounter in their personal life: "That the people who were in the group felt that this was a major influence that they have in their own personal life." Galit (JF) explained that a number of the people she has worked with in encounters have even gone on to make dialogue work their professional field. She sees this as a clear sign of success and says: "You see here and there people that adopt a way like this and apply this . . . choose in advance positions where they can influence society and be partners in the doing and, yes, there is one woman that was in an Israeli-Palestinian workshop, that participated, which by the way, was very awesome for her and she created connections with Palestinians, and after that she came to the facilitators course, and after that she went to learn the subject of conflict resolution, she's totally in the field. But there are a lot of examples like this . . . ; there are people who choose this." Effie (JF) acknowledged that sometimes it is hard to see the positive influence of her work when the political situation remains the same, but that she does feel successful when friendships are formed through encounters: "But sometimes you get very depressed when you see that there are so many small (encounter) groups, hundreds [laughs] of small groups are active, but you cannot even make a small, not influence, but even impression on the government that is going God knows where. But . . . the thing, I mean, [is] the friendship that you [develop], and the small circles that you stir, and one more women you get to know."

Thus, while a number of interviewees were indeed skeptical about their ability to change the societal or political reality, a few did note that they felt effective in encouraging the dialogue group participants to ask questions concerning the reality they live in. Maya (JF) related this dichotomy. She said: "I don't believe that if I do a lot of encounters the political situation will change. I think the political situation will change when the political situation will change. But I think it is important . . . to empower people to ask themselves questions. It won't bring the change. It won't bring the political change, but it will somehow help these people." Fatima (PF) agreed that an effective encounter is one that brings its participants to question the reality they live in: "I feel that it's a successful encounter when I move the group to think. Like they begin to think about the other in a different way, it's a successful encounter, too, but much more when they are going back home and asking themselves questions about themselves and about their relations with the other."

Two facilitators, one Jewish and one Palestinian, claimed that they perceive their work as effective when Jewish participants change their point of view as a result of the encounter. Yaron (JM) related such a change to his own experience as a Jew and noted that his own personal goal is to make sure that the participants go through the same process of "enlightenment" regarding the Palestinian situation as he himself went through. He said: "Yeah. I'm mostly interested in the Jewish group so when I say it was a good workshop it means that I felt that the Jewish group that I was working with was able to understand [the right questions], the important, the important thing that I want to do is to help them start the process that I went through. Looking back at their identity, understanding that [I mean to] stop living the way that I lived up until the age of 26. When we could kind of cover up everything. . . . Understanding what it means to be a Palestinian." Furthermore, Mahmud (PM) claimed that he sees his work as successful if the Jewish participants become more sensitive to racism toward Palestinians as a result of the encounter. "*Many, many, many* of the Jews become less tolerant to racism, to discrimination and I have heard others, they come out of this and say: Ok, we know the situation is like this but today there is no alternative." Interestingly, none of the facilitators saw their success in terms of the change or progress of the Palestinian participants.

Disappointment with the Effectiveness of Encounter Work

When referring to the effectiveness of their work, several facilitators also commented on the frustration with their limited ability to change the outside political situation. Ayelet (JF) says frankly that she is very far from reaching her goal of changing society: "If you ask me about achieving goals, and the goal is to change society, well, I am far from reaching it. Well, most of the goals I haven't achieved. . . . We are marginal groups that fight to change the society in Israel." It is interesting that Ayelet still refers to changing society as one of her goals even though she acknowledges how far she is from reaching it. Halil (PF) expresses maybe the strongest disappointment from encounter work: "We lost hope that these encounters will really change reality, or that really it is the most important thing to do for our people." Melanie (JF) agrees that the encounters fail to change the political reality as they have not managed to reach a critical mass of participants. Whether the reason that facilitated dialogue-encounters are unable to effect societal change is due to Melanie's proposition or not, the mere fact that facilitators feel that that they are unable to effect such a change was a source of frustration and disappointment for them.

These accounts indicate that interviewees' perspectives on the effectiveness of dialogue-encounters relates, mainly, to two major aspects. The first aspect is bringing about actual social-political change. In this sense, it seems that most of our interviewees see the dialogue as ineffective. The second aspect is a narrower and more restricted one of changing individual participants. Many of our interviewees did see the dialogue-encounter as effective in this. Thus, it seems from facilitators' accounts that, though the dialogue may succeed to be transformative in regard to some of its own participants, it may not be able to break the "glass wall" and also affect the outside political reality.

Discussion

Intergroup dialogues are becoming increasingly recognized as techniques of psychological group work, intended to foster reconciliation and increase partnership in conflict (Bar-On & Kassem, 2004). Multitudes of such dialogue projects are conducted in different sites of conflict, including the conflict between Israeli-Jews and Palestinians that is the focus of the present study. However, there is scarce information on the psychological issues involved in facilitation of such dialogues and on their perceived impact of effects (Fisher, 1997). In our study we interviewed Jewish-Israeli and Palestinian facilitators of encounter dialogues, in order to learn more from the wisdom of the field and theories of practice (Ross, 2000). The accounts of the women and men involved in this work draw a complex but seemingly realistic picture that is both optimistic and pessimistic, and includes successes and a sense of achievement as well as experiences of disappointment and failure. It seems from these accounts that working in the midst of the constant clash between the harsh outside reality of conflict and the unequal relationship between Israeli-Jews and Palestinians, on one hand, and the effort to conduct a dialogue that will increase equality, mutual understanding, and empathy, on the other hand, produces both difficult and exhilarating moments.

Facilitators' accounts bring invaluable insights "from the inside" on different psychosocial motivations leading to the choice to become facilitators, on the goals of the dialogue-encounter, on the political discussion dilemma, and on the impacts and limitations of dialogue work vis à vis the sociopolitical reality of the conflict.

In terms of making a difference, it is interesting to see that while the prominent psychosocial motivation that led our interviewees to become facilitators is their sense of responsibility for inducing social change, most of them see the effectiveness of their work, the difference that it makes, mainly in terms of personal change in the individual participants of the encounter and do not experience their work as bringing about more general, social change. This gap between the initial expectations from dialogue-encounters and facilitators' actual experience with their work can maybe serve as an indication coming from the "wisdom of the field" as to which psychological difference can dialogue actually make, and what are the limits of the effectiveness of reconciliation-aimed dialogues that are conducted in a situation of conflict. We see thus that although Avi's case, stated in the beginning of the chapter, of attitude change through encounters is not a single case, and there are probably many cases like it, still, the change remains on the personal level and is not generalized to the macro level of the whole society.

The findings of this study can contribute to a better understanding of the intricate psychosocial, cultural, and political issues in facilitated dialogues between groups in conflict and can suggest improved psychological strategies for the planning and implementation of dialogue interventions during ongoing conflict so as to maximize their potential impact. This study is envisioned as a first step toward an international comparative study of dialogue interventions in conflict-ridden areas.

Acknowledgment

The authors are grateful to the Truman Institute for the Advancement of Peace for the generous support of this study.

References

Bar, H., & Bargal, D. (1995). *Living with the conflict: Encounters between Jewish and Palestinian Israeli youth.* Jerusalem: The Jerusalem Institute for Israel Studies. (In Hebrew)

Bar-On, D. (1999). *The "others" within us: A socio-psychological perspective on changes in Israeli identity.* Jerusalem: Bialik Press. (In Hebrew)

Bar-On, D., & Kassem, F. (2004). Story telling as a way to work through intractable conflicts: The TRT German-Jewish experience and its relevance to the Palestinian-Israeli context. *Journal of Social Issues, 60,* 404–418.

Bar-Tal, D. (2000). From intractable conflict through conflict resolution to reconciliation: A psychological analysis. *Political Psychology, 21,* 351–365.

Bekerman, Z. (2000). Dialogic directions: Conflicts in Israeli/Palestinian education for peace. *Intercultural Education, 11,* 41–51.

Bekerman, Z. (2002). The discourse of nation and culture: Its impact on Palestinian-Jewish encounters in Israel. *International Journal of Intercultural Relations, 26,* 409–427.

Fisher, R. (1997). *Interactive conflict resolution.* Syracuse, NY: Syracuse University Press.

Freire, P. (1970). *Pedagogy of the oppressed.* New York: Herder & Herder.

Gergen, K., (1999, May 27–31). *Toward transformative dialogue.* Paper presented to the 49th Annual Conference of the International Communication Association, San Francisco, CA.

Halabi, R. (2000). Another Jewish-Arab encounter. In R. Halabi (Ed.), *Identities in dialogue: Arab-Jewish encounters in Whahat al-Salam/Neveh-Shalom* (pp. 9–15). Tel-Aviv: Hakibutz Hameuchad. (In Hebrew)

Kelman, H. (1998). Social-psychological contributions to peacemaking and peacebuilding in the Middle East. *Applied Psychology, 47,* 5–29.

Lewin, K. (1958). Group decision and social change. In E. Maccoby, T. Newcomb, & E. Hartley (Eds.), *Readings in social psychology* (pp. 197–211). New York: Holt.

Maoz, I. (2000). Power relations in inter-group encounters: A case study of Jewish-Arab encounters in Israel. *International Journal of Intercultural Relations, 24,* 259–277.

Ross, M. (2000). "Good-enough" isn't so bad: Thinking about success and failure in ethnic conflict management. *Journal of Peace Psychology, 6,* 27–47.

Salomon, G. (2002). The nature of peace education: Not all programs are created equal. In G. Salomon & B. Nevo (Eds.), *Peace education: The concept, principles and practices around the world* (pp. 3–14). Mahwah, NJ: Erlbaum.

Sonnenschein, N., Halabi, R., & Friedman, A. (1998). Legitimization of national identity and the change in power relationships in workshops dealing with the Israeli/Palestinian conflict. In E. Weiner (Ed.), *The handbook of interethnic coexistence* [An Abraham Fund Publication]. New York: Continuum, 1998.

CHAPTER 6

COMING TOGETHER: THEORY AND PRACTICE OF INTERGROUP ENCOUNTERS FOR PALESTINIANS, ARAB-ISRAELIS, AND JEWISH-ISRAELIS

Karen Doubilet

People-to-People Initiatives: Developing a Psychological Repertoire of Coexistence

The dream of peace was not realized upon the signing of the Oslo Accords, indicating that the Palestinian-Israeli conflict demands a solution that goes beyond the scope of diplomacy. Indeed, recent approaches to peace building emphasize that political agreement must be accompanied by a deep societal transformation, filtering down to the grassroots level. Such a transformation requires a fundamental shift in the personal attitudes of the people on both sides—toward the development of a new psychological repertoire that favors coexistence (e.g., Bar-Tal, 2004; Maoz, 2000). In fact, recent violence has sparked a renewed interest in people-to-people (P2P) initiatives (Hermann, 1999), which aim to reconcile the populations from the root. So while politicians are building a wall that separates the populations, the grassroots sector is attempting to build bridges.

P2P initiatives between Palestinians and Israelis—including dialogue groups, civil society programs, and intergroup encounters, which use various tools such as art and sports to bring the sides together—receive a large portion of the overall funding for coexistence programs in Israel (Maoz, 2004). P2P encounters are based on the idea that bringing people together can help to improve relations between the groups, promote positive attitude and behavior change toward "the other," diffuse negative stereotypes, and foster friendships between the sides. In light of the lack of contact that characterizes Palestinian-Israeli relations—in addition to those of Arabs and Jews within Israel—"intergroup encounters are one of the few remaining channels for relationship building" (Abu-Nimer, 2004, p. 405).

The Contact Hypothesis

The ethos of most intergroup encounter initiatives reflects the theoretical premise of the social contact hypothesis, outlined in Gordon Allport's celebrated book *The Nature of Prejudice.* It states that bringing hostile groups together, under specific conditions, can be an effective means of reducing prejudice and improving intergroup relations (Allport, 1954).

The conditions, which have since been elaborated and refined by numerous scholars (Amir, 1969; Cook, 1963, 1978; Pettigrew, 1998; and Sherif, 1966), include the following: (1) there must be equal status between groups, at least within the contact situation; (2) there must be institutional support (the presence of egalitarian social norms); (3) there must be "acquaintance/friendship potential," which means that contact must be "intimate" in nature and must be of sufficient frequency and duration for intergroup friendships to develop; and (4) contact must involve the mutual pursuit of a superordinate goal (a goal whose attainment requires the effort of both groups).

This concept was initially developed and applied in the 1950s in the United States in an attempt to ameliorate racial discrimination against the black minority. In addition to the purported harms of segregation, belief in the positive impact of contact was one of the chief arguments, culminating in the U.S. Supreme Court's decision to desegregate public schools in the seminal case *Brown v. the Board of Education Topeka,* 1954 (Kadushin & Livert, 2002, p. 120). Contact-based programs have since been implemented in other regions and have become one of the most prevalent models of coexistence education in intractable conflict settings, with reports estimating 275 coexistence programs in Israel alone (Abu-Nimer, 2004, p.406).

As Salomon (2002) and McCauley (2002) have emphasized, not all peace education programs are created equal. For instance, some programs involve weekly meetings over the period of a year, while others involve only a one-time intervention. Additionally, each program has its own raison d'être and modus operandi, with activities as diverse as interreligious dialogue, soccer, and drama utilized as vehicles for bringing the sides together. Similarly, there are programs that cater to every age group, although most initiatives target children and youth while they are still impressionable, and more susceptible to attitude change.

While significant funds are invested in P2P activities in the intractable conflict setting, research has shown that the impact of contact on participants' attitudes is not entirely clear. The intractable conflict setting presents several challenges in controlling some of the conditions for contact to have a positive effect, partially accounting for these elusive findings.

First, research in intractable conflict settings has demonstrated that power and status asymmetries are virtually impossible to neutralize within the encounter. Status differences between the two groups—the Jews (the occupiers) and the Palestinians (the occupied)—are inevitably contagious to the intergroup dynamic (Abu-Nimer, 2004; Maoz, 2000; Suleiman, 2004). For this reason, the protocol of most programs requires the encounter to be bilingual (Arabic and

Hebrew) with an equal number of Palestinian/Arab and Jewish facilitators. In spite of these efforts to balance the power, Abu-Nimer (2004) has noted:

> There is a clear asymmetric access to Arabic and Hebrew language in the encounter. Arab students often felt less comfortable than did their Jewish counterparts in expressing their views due to requirements or expectations to speak Hebrew during the encounter. (p. 408)

Suleiman (2004) and Maoz (2000) have warned that even if it were possible to neutralize asymmetries within the encounter, these equal status relations would merely reflect a microreality. An optimistic view is that this microcosm could eventually spill over to daily societal relations.

Second, lack of institutional support and social norms that favor equality present another major challenge to encounter programs in intractable conflict settings. For instance, segregation of Arab and Jewish schools in Israel may have a significant and detrimental impact, which is often overlooked, as it creates a context that contradicts the very premise of coexistence. While school segregation is a sad reflection of the reality that there are language differences and that Arabs and Jews generally live in separate enclaves, most people probably consider integration undesirable or even dangerous.

Segregation may have especially detrimental effects in intractable conflict settings. For instance, Johnston (1993) describes how segregation has undermined coexistence efforts in Northern Ireland:

> [as a result of segregation,] children have little opportunity to come into contact with those of another culture other than through myths, symbols and rituals, which perpetuate endemic fear and distrust, hostility and ultimately violent conflict. (p. 66)

Educational segregation denies youngsters the opportunity to get to know the other side, thereby reinforcing one-sided narratives of history, fear of "the other," and exacerbating prejudice. In this sense, "segregation has functioned as a passive incubator of prejudice and bigotry" (Johnston, 1993, p. 66).

Finally, the self-selection of participants presents another challenge to the intergroup encounter framework in the intractable conflict setting. Since participation in intergroup encounters is voluntary, these initiatives reach only those who are willing to meet with the other side. In the case of youth, parents or guardians must be willing to support their children's participation. Most programs include visits in each other's communities and villages, as well as co-ed overnight and weekend workshops, likely ruling out participants from religious and traditional backgrounds.

While Steinberg (2002) has stressed that contact programs can play a central role in bringing about bottom-up societal change, he cites the selection bias as a major limitation to these initiatives:

> [T]he limited grass-roots and people-to-people discussions often involved small groups of like-minded individuals discussing narrow issues . . . the evidence indicates

that the dialogue process was also limited by the self-selection of many of the participants, meaning that individuals or groups that were already more inclined by empathy
and understanding were more willing to participate in such dialogues. (pp. 7–8)

Similarly, the problem of selection bias has been partially implicated for the
lack of success of contact programs in Northern Ireland. Church, Visser, and
Johnson (2004) note that by virtue of self-selection, these initiatives exclude the
more extreme members of society, who are, perhaps, the people who could most
benefit from participation.

Finally, violence on the ground ultimately stymies any attempt to instill a
spirit of peace and cooperation. Nevertheless, organizations such as the Peres
Center for Peace continue their P2P efforts, even after setbacks such as Kas-
sam Rockets falling on a soccer field just prior to a tournament scheduled for
its Palestinian-Israeli "Twinned Peace Sport Schools" program. Even more
recently, a young Palestinian basketball enthusiast, participating in the program, was shot and injured during an Israeli raid on a Palestinian prison in
Jericho—but the boy continues to meet with his teammates from the twinned
Israeli community.

Encounter Models

The increasing popularity of contact programs has sparked interest and
created concern as to what makes an effective encounter. Accordingly, scholars
have recently turned their attention to mapping encounter models and the
psychosocial techniques that are used to improve intergroup relations. The
following section outlines the defining features of the various approaches and
techniques used to foster attitude and behavior change toward "the other."
Various encounter models are summarized in Table 6.1.

Intergroup Interaction versus Interpersonal Interaction

An important distinguishing feature between encounter models is whether
they advocate contact at the interpersonal level or at the intergroup level.
Interpersonal interaction refers to the extent that people relate to each other
as individuals (e.g., Fatma, Michal, David, Mohammad), while intergroup
interaction refers to the extent that participants relate to each other via group
membership (e.g., Arab-Israeli, Palestinian, Jewish-Israeli) (Tal-Or, Boninger,
& Gleicher, 2002). Both Maoz (2004) and Suleiman (2004) differentiate between
these types of interaction in their classifications of encounter models—with
interpersonal interaction characterizing their coexistence and psychological/
intergroup approaches respectively, and intergroup interaction characterizing
the confrontational and political/intergroup approaches.

Interpersonal interaction encourages participants to focus on each person as a
unique individual. The fact that Mohammad is funny and Fatma is a gifted artist,

Table 6.1 Summary Chart of Intergroup Encounter Models

The Coexistence Approach	The Confrontational Approach
• Interpersonal interaction • Emphasize similarities between groups • Work on a mutual goal (sometimes) • Foster tolerance (Maoz, 2004)	• Intergroup interaction • Confront group distinctions • Empower the Arab minority through direct confrontation with the Jews • Enhance awareness of power asymmetries • Reconstruct identities (Maoz, 2004)
Interpersonal/Psychological • Interpersonal interaction • Diffusion of category boundaries • Suppression of conflict and political discussions (Suleiman, 2004)	**Intergroup/Political** • Intergroup interaction • Increase awareness of power imbalance • Encourage discussion of political issues (Suleiman, 2004)
The Common Identity Approach • Recategorization into superordinate categories • Emphasis on group unity (Gaertner, Rust, Dividio, Bachman, & Anastasio, 1994)	**Distinct Identity Approach** (Hewstone & Brown, 1986) • Complimentary Role Technique • Focus on category boundaries and cooperation • Emphasis on cross-cutting categories (Doise, 1978) **Intragroup Approaches** • Single Identity Approach (Church, Visser, & Johnson, 2004) • Metacognition (Ben-Ari, 2004)

for example, constitute individual characteristics, which are irrelevant to their membership in the Palestinian group. This interpersonal orientation highlights the diversity of out-group members, thus weakening the power of the group stereotype.

The interpersonal approach assumes that new attitudes about out-group members will be generalized to the out-group at the category level. In the context of the intractable conflict setting, people's attitudes toward the out-group have been informed and influenced by deeply entrenched conflicting historical narratives and ongoing violent conflict. Therefore, if Fatma has animosity toward Jews and thinks of them as cold and greedy prior to the encounter, learning that Michal is a generous and caring person will not necessarily change her belief about all Jews. Indeed, studies have shown that positive experiences with individual out-group members are generalized only when that individual is seen as representing a "typical" category member (Wilder, 1984).

In contrast, intergroup models focus on confronting stereotypes in order to foster new attitudes that generalize to the group as a whole. Hewstone and Brown's (1986) Distinct Identity Model recommends giving members of the different groups separate but complementary roles, in order to maintain category distinctions in the context of mutual interdependence. The idea is that when contact is more cooperative and pleasant, new attitudes are more likely to be generalized to the entire out-group.

This model is reminiscent of Sherif's (1966) "superordinate goal" method, which was used to facilitate cooperation between competitive groups through mutual interdependence. For example, suppose that the groups were asked to plant a garden together. Michal, David, and Oren (Jews) may be given the task of digging, while Fatma, Mohammad, and Naser (Palestinians) are assigned to the task of planting the seeds. The groups' organization remains at the category level—the Jews as "diggers" and the Palestinians as "planters." However, the goal of planting a garden requires the cooperation of both groups. This focus on category levels is more likely to facilitate generalization of new attitudes to the group as a whole (Hewstone & Brown, 1986).

Emphasis of Similarities or Differences

Another distinguishing feature of encounter models is whether they aim to enhance similarities or differences between groups. The Coexistence Approach (Maoz, 2004), for example, endorses emphasizing similarities between the groups as a means of diffusing group stereotypes. Facilitators will attempt to highlight cultural and religious congruencies such as "We both like hummus" or the Muslim Arabs fast on Ramadan and the Jews fast on Yom Kippur. The Confrontational Approach (Maoz, 2004), on the other hand, advocates acknowledging differences between groups—such as differences in style of dress—rather than suppressing them. In a similar vein, the Psychological/Interpersonal Approach (Suleiman, 2004) advocates suppressing political discussions, thereby highlighting similarities on the interpersonal level; while the Political/Intergroup Approach (Suleiman, 2004) encourages political confrontation.

Recategorization: Common Group Identity Model (Superordinate Categories) versus the Cross-Categorization Model

In order to create the feeling of being a united group, the Common Group Identity Model suggests creating the perception of a superordinate category (a category that includes both groups) (Gaertner, Rust, Dividio, Bachman, & Anastasio, 1994). Intergroup sports teams, such as the Palestinian-Israeli soccer teams organized by the Peres Center for Peace, utilize this concept nicely. Using this technique, the "blue team" category, which includes both Palestinian and Jewish players, comes to constitute a superordinate category. When the superordinate category becomes salient, traditionally rival groups are more likely to perceive themselves as one unit.

However, research shows that newly established categories may be limited to the context in which they are established. In a famous experiment on black- and white-skinned miners, Minard (1952) found that, on the job, the miners perceived themselves as belonging to one group. The normally salient ethnic categories were replaced with one superordinate category ("miners") that included both groups. Outside of the mine, however, the men reverted back to the previously dominant "black" and "white" categories. In other words, once the soccer game is over, the blue team's dual identity becomes diluted and team members revert back into their separate Palestinian and Jewish categories.

However, the Distinct Identity Models that utilize the cross-categorization technique may provide a more stable solution. This technique makes in-group and out-group distinctions more complex by focusing on cross-cutting (or overlapping) categories that exist independently of one another. For example, one can be a Jew, a mother, a daughter, an architect, and an athlete at the same time. Doise (1978) first suggested that when categories cross-cut each other, they reduce the salience of the original category distinctions. Several studies have demonstrated that sharing at least one category dimension can reduce in-group bias (Deschamps & Doise, 1978).

Power Asymmetries and Politics—Confrontation versus Suppression

As discussed previously, neutralizing power and status asymmetries between groups is one of the most challenging conditions to meet in intractable conflict settings. The Coexistence (Maoz, 2004) and Interpersonal/Psychological (Suleiman, 2004) approaches attempt to rebalance the power by creating an atmosphere of equality within the encounter. These models generally discourage the discussion of political issues, fearing that conflictual discourse could result in polarizing the groups even further. However, as previously mentioned, critics have argued that this method creates an artificial microcosm of equality that does not represent reality.

The Confrontational (Maoz, 2004) and the Political/Intergroup (Suleiman, 2004) approaches attempt to confront asymmetries, increase awareness of power relationships, and reconstruct identities. In addition, these models encourage discussion of political issues. Rather than suppressing thorny issues, these approaches advocate putting the groups' real feelings on the table in order to achieve a sort of catharsis. In fact, the Confrontational and the Intergroup/Political approaches were actually developed by Arab facilitators in response to the imbalanced majority-minority dynamics of the workshops (Maoz, 2004; Suleiman, 2004).

Intragroup Approaches

As discussed previously, contact programs face special challenges in the intractable conflict setting. Inasmuch as the conditions for contact are almost impossible to meet in this context (Ben-Ari, 2004; Church et al., 2004), some critics argue that intergroup contact is altogether unrealistic. As a result of the recent violence, the military has restricted the mobility of Palestinians in the occupied territories, making it difficult to get the sides physically together. As a result, most encounter programs engage Israeli-Jews and Israeli-Arabs, rather than Palestinians, intensifying the self-selection bias on a nonvoluntary basis.

Accordingly, scholars have recently turned their attention to developing intra-group or unilateral models as alternatives to intergroup contact. In response to lack of success with intergroup contact programs between Catholics and Protes-tants, scholars in Northern Ireland have begun to endorse what they call "the Single Identity Approach" (Church et al., 2004). Similarly, Ben-Ari (2004), an Israeli scholar, has proposed the "Metacognitve Approach" as an alternative to contact. This approach aims to increase people's awareness of their cognitive processing so that they will exercise caution in forming social judgments.

It is important to note that intragroup techniques do not contradict intergroup models. In fact, scholars have suggested that they can complement intergroup methods by preparing participants for bilateral interventions (Ben-Ari, 2004; Church et al., 2004) and by promoting more sophisticated thinking about intergroup perceptions in general (Ben-Ari, 2004, p. 315). In light of the obstacles in the way of getting the sides together, intragroup models seem to offer a more realistic, although not ideal, alternative to contact.

References

Abu-Nimer, M. (2004). Education for coexistence and Arab-Jewish encounters in Israel: Potential and challenges. *Journal of Social Issues, 60*(2), 405–422.

Allport, G. W. (1954). *The nature of prejudice.* Reading, MA: Adison-Wesley.

Amir, Y. (1969). Contact hypothesis in ethnic relations. *Psychological Bulletin, 71*(5), 319–342.

Bar-Tal, D. (2004). Nature, rationale, and effectiveness of education for coexistence. *Journal of Social Issues, 60*(2), 253–271.

Ben-Ari, R. (2004). Coping with the Jewish-Arab conflict: A comparison among three models. *Journal of Social Issues, 60*(2), 307–322.

Church, C., Visser, A., & Johnson, L. S. (2004). A path to peace or persistence? The "Single Identity" Approach to conflict resolution in Northern Ireland. *Conflict Resolution Quarterly, 21*(3), 273–293.

Cook, S. W. (1963). Desegregation: A psychological analysis. In W. W. Charters, Jr. & N. L. Gage (Eds.), *Readings in the social psychology of education* (pp. 40–50). Boston: Allyn & Bacon.

Cook, S. W. (1978). Interpersonal and attitudinal outcomes in cooperating interracial groups. *Journal of Research and Development in Education, 12*(1), 97–113.

Deschamps, J. C., & Doise, W. (1978). Crossed-category memberships in intergroup relations. In H. Tajfel (Ed.), *Differentiation between social groups: Studies in the social psychology of intergroup relations* (pp. 141–158). London: Academic Press.

Doise, W. (1978). *Groups and individuals: Explanations in social psychology.* Cambridge, MA: Cambridge University Press.

Gaertner, S. L., Rust, M., Dividio, J. F., Bachman, B. A., & Anastasio, P. (1994). The contact hypothesis: The role of a common group identity on reducing intergroup bias. *Small Groups Research, 25*, 224–249.

Hermann, T. (1999). The sour taste of success: The Israeli peace movement, 1967–1998. In B. Gidron, S. N. Katz, & Y. Hasenfeld (Eds.), *Mobilizing for peace: Conflict resolution in Northern Ireland, Israel/Palestine, and Africa* (chap. 5). Oxford University Press.

Hewstone, M., & Brown, R. J. (1986). Contact is not enough: An intergroup perspective on the contact hypothesis. In M. Hewstone & R. J. Brown (Eds.), *Contact and conflict in intergroup encounters* (pp. 1–44). Oxford, England: Blackwell.

Johnston, J. (1993). Education for mutual understanding. In Y. Iram & Z. Gross (Eds.), *The humanities in education* (Vol. 1, pp. 65–76).

Kadushin, C., & Livert, D. (2002). Friendship, contact and peace education. In G. Salomon & B. Nevo (Eds.), *Peace education: The concepts, principles, and practices around the world* (pp. 116–126). Mahaw, NJ: Erlbaum.

Maoz, I. (2000). An experiment in peace: Reconciliation-aimed workshops of Jewish-Israeli and Palestinian youth. *Journal of Peace Research, 37*(6), 721–736.

Maoz, I. (2004). *Conceptual mapping and evaluation of peace education projects: The case of education for coexistence through inter-group encounters between Jews and Arabs in Israel.* The Hebrew University of Jerusalem. Retrieved November 2004, from http://construct.haifa.ac.il/~cerpe/papers/maoz.htm.

McCauley, C. (2002). Head first versus feet first in peace education. In G. Salomon & B. Nevo (Eds.), *Peace education: The concepts, principles, and practices around the world* (pp. 247–257). Mahaw, NJ: Erlbaum.

Minard, R. D. (1952). Race relationships in the Pocahontas Coal Field. *Journal of Social Issues, 8*, 29–44.

Pettigrew, T. (1998). Intergroup contact theory. *Annual Review of Psychology, 49*, 65–85.

Salomon, G. (2002). The nature of peace education: Not all programs are created equal. In G. Salomon & B. Nevo (Eds.), *Peace education: The concepts, principles, and practices around the world* (pp. 116–126). Mahaw, NJ: Erlbaum.

Sherif, M. (1966). *Group conflict and cooperation.* London: Routlege & Kegan Paul.

Steinberg, G. (2002). *Unripeness and conflict management: Re-examining the Oslo Process and its lessons* (Occasional Paper No. 4). Program on Conflict Management and Negotiation, Bar-Ilan University (2004 Course Reader), 81–111.

Suleiman, R. (2004). Planned encounters between Jewish and Palestinian Israelis: A social-psychological perspective. *Journal of Social Issues, 60*(2), 323–337.

Tal-Or, N., Boninger, D., & Gleicher, F. (2002). Understanding the conditions and processes necessary for intergroup contact to reduce prejudice. In G. Salomon & B. Nevo (Eds.), *Peace education: The concepts, principles, and practices around the world* (pp. 89–108). Mahaw, NJ: Erlbaum.

Wilder, D. A. (1984). Intergroup contact: The typical member and the exception to the rule. *Journal of Experimental Social Psychology, 20*, 177–194.

CHAPTER 7

RECREATING THE GOLDEN AGE: QUEST TO UNRAVEL THE GORDIAN KNOT

Abdul Basit

The quest for a peaceful resolution for the Arab-Israeli conflict has proven to be a Gordian knot. Despite significant attempts by many U.S. presidents to bring peace, we have witnessed only intermittent peace, followed by cycles of vengeance and outbursts of violence. Deep mistrust and prejudice between Arabs and Israelis have kept the flames of rage blazing. Though the Arab-Israeli conflict has a short history, going back only a few decades, it is responsible for the loss of tens of thousands of lives and massive destruction within the Holy Land.

Combating Myths

A number of misconceptions cloud the real issues at the heart of the Arab-Israeli conflict. It is, therefore, imperative to have a clear understanding of issues in their proper perspectives. The first is reflected in comments such as, "Oh. These Arabs and Jews have been fighting for centuries and it will go on like this. No one can stop them." The fact is that the enmity between Arabs and Jews is something new in the Middle East. The anti-Semitic movement originated and continued in Western countries for many centuries. The Nazi Holocaust happened in Europe, not in the Middle East.

Before the establishment of the Israeli state, Jews and Arabs had generally lived in peace in Middle East and other parts of the Muslim world. When the Arab empire ruled a large part of the world, stretching from the Asian steppe across the Mediterranean to Spain, Jews had complete freedom to worship. They lived under their own laws and enjoyed a large measure of self-government. During Moorish rule, for nearly 600 years in Spain, Jews not only held high positions but made valuable contributions in the fields of philosophy, science, and medicine. Most books dealing with the history of Jews regard the Moorish rule in Spain as the Golden period (Biale, 2002). As Moorish rule came to an end, both Jews and Muslims were expelled.

The second myth that must be dispelled is that the Arab-Israeli conflict is religious. In fact, Arab-Israeli conflict is essentially secular. Issues of territories and security were, and still are, the major areas of contention. Occasionally some high-profile religious extremists do make inflammatory statements to attract press and public attention, which convey the wrong impression that the conflict is religious in nature.

Though previous attempts to solve this thorny problem have failed, we must not be dejected. We must rise above all forms of obsolete ideas and old prejudices and try a fresh approach. We must not forget that nothing is constant in this world except change. Those who remain stuck in time and fail to make adjustment to changing circumstances become stagnant. Ibn Khaldun (1332–1406), known as the Father of Historiography predicted that civilizations will collapse if they cannot adapt their societies [their *asabiyya*] to altering world conditions (Glain, 2004).

Palestinians and Israelis must have an earnest desire to achieve a lasting peace that focuses not on the past, but on an optimistic future. Israelis and Arabs working together can make remarkable progress in many fields. The first goal is to convince the peoples of the region that change is a realistic possibility based on a shared history and complementary strengths.

Israel is a democratic and technologically advanced country with mature institutions for leveraging the brainpower and industriousness of its people. Arabs have wealth based on tremendous oil and gas resources, but lack the technical or operational know-how. If Israelis and Arabs make peace and start working together, perhaps a Golden Age can be recreated, in which Arabs and Jews living together in peace and harmony will astound the world with progress in nearly every field of human endeavor. It is not something unachievable. Even Golda Meir, addressing the United Nations, stated: "[T]he day must come when we shall live in amity and cooperation. Then will the entire Middle East become a region where the ten of millions of people will dwell in peace and then will its economic potentialities and rich cultural heritage achieve fulfillment" (Laqueur & Rubin, 1984, p. 167).

History of the Holy Land

Israel became a nation about 1300 B.C.E. and King Solomon built the Jewish Temple (*Beit HaMikdash*) in 950 B.C.E. This temple is mentioned in the Koran as the "Furthest Mosque whose precincts God has blessed" (17:1). Muslims all over the globe regard this temple as the third holiest site in Islam. In the Muslim world the temple is known as the Holy House (*bayt-al-Muqaddas*). The Prophet Muhammad initially designated Jerusalem as the first *Qiblah* (direction Muslims face during prayer).

In 587 B.C.E., King Nebuchadnezzar besieged Jerusalem, burned the city, and indiscriminately murdered inhabitants. The temple was destroyed; Jews were made prisoners and taken to Babylon. After 70 years of exile, during the reign of Cyrus the Great, Jews were allowed to return to Jerusalem and the temple was rebuilt in 515 B.C.E. Around 66 C.E., under the influence of some militant Jews, priests of the Holy Temple stopped offering daily sacrifices for the well-being of the Roman Emperor (Brandon, 1973). The religious argument of the militant Jews was sound according to Biblical teachings. Since only God should be worshipped, paying homage to the Roman Emperor was blasphemy. Romans had been watching these rebellious trends and finally decided to confront the enemy. First, Gestius Gallus tried to capture Jerusalem and when he was finally about to defeat the Jews, he suddenly ordered the operation to stop for no apparent reason. Why the Romans did this is still unknown. Jews were, however, excited and thought that it was a divine intervention to save Jerusalem.

After a few years, Roman General Titus started a full-scale war against the Jews with a firm determination to win. Jews fought fiercely, but despite their heroic efforts, the Roman army gave them a crushing defeat in 70 C.E. Since the battle was fierce and they lost many soldiers, the Romans were ruthless after victory. With vengeance they carried out a general massacre, causing great suffering and destruction. The temple was set ablaze, and Romans took the Great Menorah and the vessels to Rome. According to Josephus (a Jewish historian who was loyal to the Roman General and was present during this confrontation), Jewish losses were more than 1,100,000, and the number of Jewish prisoners was 97,000 (Brandon, 1973). Most historians, however, think that the figures given by Josephus were grossly exaggerated. The total destruction of Jerusalem in 70 C.E. marked the end of the Jewish state, leading to the exile of the Jews from Israel.

After more than 500 years, when Arabs conquered this region in 638 C.E., they were warmly received by the Jewish population. They ruled the region for more than 1,000 years, except when Crusaders controlled Jerusalem (1099 to 1187 C.E.). But in 1917 C.E., the Muslim rule of Palestine ended as British forces gained control of the region. However, the British rule did not last too long.

After two world wars, the British were crippled financially and politically. The dire consequences of World War II were especially gloomy. The realization deepened that, for maintaining a global presence, the financial cost would be debilitating. Also, in response to rampant anti-Semitism in late nineteenth-century Europe, Zionism started as a strong political movement that supported a Jewish homeland in the land of Israel, where the Jewish kingdom existed in history (Vital, 1975). The Zionist movement gained further momentum as the dimensions of the Holocaust became evident. "Jewish communities everywhere became increasingly anxious and united, and support for Zionist aspiration dramatically grew in strength" (Bickerton & Klausner, 2005). As the British realized the volatile situation in Palestine, it became clear that their days were numbered. They sought the help of the United Nations, and finally under the auspices of the United Nations, Israel was established as a nation-state on May 14, 1948.

The Current Feud

The Israelis sincerely believe that God gave them the Holy Land and they have undeniable right to return to the land where they lived 2,000 years ago. The Palestinian Arabs think that they have the legal right not to be displaced from their homeland where they have lived for more than 1,000 years. Many Palestinians believe that they have been forced to pay the price for the genocide of Jews in Europe, committed by Germans, not by Arabs.

Unfortunately, the Arabs and Israelis regarded the national goals of the other as incompatible with their own. The inevitable consequence of this diametrically opposed perspective was periodic skirmishes, renewed and continual clashes, small wars, and major wars. The tremendous hate and anger have been blazing like an inferno, very often resulting in merciless killings. Unfortunately, this kind of violence distorts vision, impedes understanding, and worst of all, blunts one's humanity. A brief history of events regarding Arab-Israeli conflict brings back the memories of wars, large and small, and merciless killings—thus reopening the psychological wounds. Here we want to mainly focus on building bridges, overcoming prejudices, and laying the foundation for a glorious future.

Sadly, the leaders on both sides (except Anwar Sadat of Egypt and Yitzhak Rabin of Israel) have consistently failed to rise to the occasion and show out-standing leadership and foresight. But did the leaders ever think what price their people paid for the land? It is the most precious price: blood of innocent men, women, and children. The inhabitants of the Holy Land have been living in constant terror and a siege mentality has developed on both sides. The truth is that there is no military solution to these problems. Military victories no matter how great will be fruitless. Therefore, an overriding interest in genuine peace is vital for both Palestinians and Israelis.

It is time to give a fresh start, broaden our horizon, look at the new dimensions, and become future-oriented rather than a prisoner of the past. President Anwar Sadat of Egypt said before the Israeli parliament: "How can we achieve durable peace based on justice? In my opinion, and I declare it to the whole world, from this forum, the answer is neither difficult nor is it impossible despite long years of feuds, blood, faction, strife, hatreds, and deep-rooted animosity" (Laqueur & Rubin, 1984, p. 595). The possibility of achievements and accomplishments is limitless, since the main ingredients needed for a great civilization are fortunately present.

One may ask why those who attain leadership positions fail to see this bright future. And why their policies have done so much damage to their nation and made the future of the nation bleak. It is my conviction that the leaders on both sides have fallen into a "deterministic trap." The Jews believe that God gave them the land so they have the absolute right to be there. Palestinians believe that they have been living there for more than 1,000 years and the state of Israel has no legal basis. Each side has a convincing argument and there is no doubt that, from spiritual and emotional viewpoints, the Holy Land is central for both Jews and Arabs. We can go on debating this ad infinitum, but it will be an exercise in futility.

Currently only one thing is absolute: Both Israelis and Palestinians are going to be there and share the same land. This truth must be faced directly by the Palestinians and Israelis, but not through dark glasses that distort the truth. Since this is an undeniable fact, the most important question is: What is the best way to live in peace and use combined strengths and assets to make the Middle East a major influence and respected throughout the world?

Right now this sounds strange and unbelievable. But this is within the grasp of both the parties. Edward Said rightly emphasized that we must establish a workable system of relationships to connect past, present, and future. His vision was that one day a process would develop to help connect Arabs with each other and with Jews, thus ending this terrible and costly struggle (Said, 1994). We must remember that just as there is no present that is entirely free of the past, there is no future that is entirely free of the present. It is incumbent upon the leaders to have a wide perspective that takes into account the present state of affairs. Only a realistic approach can pave the way for an optimistic future. How is this possible? Here are a few suggestions that may help achieve this goal.

- *Educational and Political Systems:* One of the primary means to promote peace between nations is to overcome biases and prejudices. And since this must start early, educational system both in Israeli and Palestinian schools must emphasize peace and eliminate all derogatory and hateful terms. If this is not done with sincerity and dedication, then all attempts to achieve peace are doomed to failure. If we continue planting the seeds of hatred and enmity, we get the fruits of death and destruction.

  Good political systems, especially a democratic system that allows freedom of speech and press and holds leaders accountable, usually lead to a progressive and modern society. Israel is a democratic country with an excellent educational system. It has produced great scientists, who have made valuable contributions in the fields of science, medicine, agriculture, military technology, and other high-tech industries. Unfortunately, Arab countries, despite enormous wealth, have failed to overcome handicaps and shortcomings and their conditions are gradually worsening (Glain, 2004). Due to exceedingly high rates of illiteracy, totalitarian regimes, tribal systems, official corruption, and ineptitude, Arab countries have stagnated. Science and technology remain virtually undeveloped, and the gap between the modern world and Arab countries has been widening. More ominously, so has the gap between the superrich well-connected Arabs and the poor masses. This leaves Arab youths feeling disillusioned, frustrated, and angry; and radical Muslims have rushed to capitalize on this reservoir. It is high time that Arab countries, instead of finding scapegoats, confronted those problems head-on. Undemocratic systems must be reformed and a representative government that is accountable to the people must be established. This will help bring a government that truly represents the people, and it will promote freedom of speech and the press. Then people and their representatives can decide how problems, no matter how intractable, should be resolved.

- *Fixation on Security:* Though total security cannot be achieved in an age of mobile, long-range armed forces, there are good reasons for Israel's fixation on security outside of terror attacks. One point that helps to understand the heightened fears of Israel is the lack of any normal relationship between Israel and Arab states. A nation that is not recognized by Arab and other Muslim states is bound to become suspicious and obsessed with the issue of survival. Since survival comes first, Israel's demand to establish normal relationship with Arab countries is fully justified. Establishing normal relationships, however, does not mean that Arab states have to fully agree with the Israeli policy. Egypt and Jordan, both Arab countries, have normal relationships with Israel, but they do not endorse all of its policies. This is one of the most crucial points that Arab and other Muslim states have consistently failed to recognize.

  It is said that to resolve differences and untie entangled problems is the sign of wisdom and prudence. But this cannot be achieved unless the competing groups are willing to communicate with each other. One must also emphasize that face-to-face negotiations greatly facilitate breaking the psychological barriers. A good sign looming on the horizon is that Pakistan is negotiating with Israel, perhaps wanting to establish a working relationship. Although the fanatics in Pakistan are furious about this move, President Musharraf will prevail.

- *Abject Poverty Breeds Hate and Violence:* The terrorists need to identify an enemy first. They can then brainwash the masses that all of their problems are due to their enemy. It is easy to find a scapegoat. History is full of examples where this strategy has been used with astonishing success. Communists exploited the poor and the deprived by blaming the capitalists for all their problems. Nazis convinced Germans that Jews were responsible for the economic and political plight of their country and thus justified the Holocaust. Impoverished Palestinians, living in a world that is completely indifferent to their fate, feel frustrated, angry, and hostile. Surrounded by a sea of trouble, they find the terrorist's message electrifying. Instead of accepting any responsibility for their plight, they have been able to find an easy target—Israel.

  Though Israel must bear some responsibility as its immediate neighbor, it is actually the responsibility of wealthy Arab states and G-8 nations to shoulder the economic burden of uplifting the daily living conditions of the Palestinians. The sad part of this story is that when aid was given to Palestinian leaders, widespread corruption ensued from top to bottom. Instead of improving the lot of the poor and needy, the leaders spent the money as they wished. But to help pave the way to peace, to drastically reduce Intifada (uprising), and to undermine the support for Hamas, Israel must also care for its poor neighbors. No matter how much Israelis are comfortable or uncomfortable with this approach, it is a wise investment in normalizing relationships.

- *An Iron-Fist Strategy Will Not Work:* Intifada and suicide bombings stem from emotional injuries and insults, and feelings of hopelessness and helplessness. In the beginning when Intifada started, the Palestinians were throwing stones and Israelis were trying to stop them with rubber bullets and at times real bullets. Perhaps we have forgotten the lessons that we learned from the Vietnam War. It is human nature that when a powerful enemy humiliates and imposes severe punishments, the hardships of struggle, bitterness, and suffering strengthen the will to resist. The enemies harden their attitude and make a steely resolve to fight to the finish no matter what. There has been a lack of understanding and empathy for the Palestinians in the state of Israel, who are their neighbors, and will remain their neighbors. Good neighborly relations with the Palestinians may result in promoting good relationships with Arab and Muslim countries of the world.

- *Israeli Settlements:* Israeli settlement in the occupied areas is a main stumbling block in any peace initiative. Whether it was done for pure security reasons, or it was an attempt to annex the areas, it definitely sent a strong signal to the Palestinians that their dream for a Palestinian state was just a glimmer on the horizon or a mirage. Most third parties, therefore, have been reluctant to condone this move on the part of Israel. It is also not workable if we examine the long-range strategy. If Israel intends to exist as a democracy, first, it cannot colonize the land of Palestinians. Israelis fully understand that the curse of dominating another people by force is the beginning of moral decline. Second, it cannot create a great Israel state where Palestinians are allowed to become citizens, because there are more Palestinians than Jews. Both options are untenable. Maybe the advice of President Jimmy Carter was prudent: "[T]rue peace must be based on normal relations among the parties to the peace. Peace means more than just an end to belligerency. Second there must be withdrawal by Israel from territories occupied in 1967 and agreement on secure and recognized borders for all parties in the context of normal and peaceful relations in accordance with U.N. Resolutions 242 and 338. . . . Some flexibility is always needed to insure successful negotiations and the resolution of conflicting views" (Laqueur & Rubin, 1984, pp. 608–609).

- *Issue of Palestinian Refugees:* One of the most emotionally charged issues is the return of Palestinian refugees who left their homeland in 1948 after the establishment of Israel. It is estimated that approximately 3 to 4 million Palestinian refugees are living in other Arab countries, and they would like to return. The Israeli argument is that since Palestinian refugees have been living in other Arab countries for many decades, they are better off staying there than returning to Palestine. And, the Palestinians argue that if Israel can bring Jews from Russia and other parts of the world to Israel, then those Arabs who lived in Palestine, their land for nearly 1,000 years, should be allowed to return. There have been serious discussions about this issue and various proposals have been made, including compensation (Kimmerling & Migdal, 2003). At one time, Israelis considered allowing 100,000 Palestinian refugees to return, but it did not work out.

  With the passage of time, memory fades, and the past gets lost or twisted in arguments of the present. As a result, attitudes about old issues change and hard realities dictate different priorities. If there is any final deal about the return of Palestinian refugees, which is most unlikely, it is estimated that it will cost nearly $40 billion, most of it for refugee assistance. The first step, I think, is to move toward confidence building, or as I would like to call it, trust building. Once confidence and trust have been established between Palestinian and Israelis, then attitudes about many difficult issues change—entrenched interests get out of the trenches and problems that appear tough become easy.

- *The Issue of Jerusalem:* The future of the old city of Jerusalem is most problematic. Israelis have strong emotional ties with Jerusalem, and the public opinion in Israel is unanimous on the retention of this city. It is hard to imagine that any party can dare to compromise on this issue. However, equally important and holy is the city of Jerusalem in Islam. As mentioned earlier, it was the first *Qiblah* (direction Muslims face during prayer). Muhammad with his companions offered prayer facing toward Jerusalem for almost 10 years. There are also holy shrines such as Dome of the Rock and Al-Aqsa mosque. It is also extraordinarily holy to the Christians. It is the place where Jesus was born, preached, and crucified. All the land surrounding Jerusalem is holy for all three monotheistic religions: Judaism, Christianity, and Islam.

From a purely political viewpoint, any action by Israel or Palestine to gain complete control of Jerusalem would be disastrous. There are four options: (1) Jerusalem becomes a part of Israel; (2) Jerusalem becomes a part of Palestine; (3) both Israel and Palestinians control Jerusalem in close cooperation; or (4) international trusteeship for the holy places of all the three religions in Palestine. It will be an uphill battle to wrestle with this issue, and no option will be easily acceptable to either party. When Jerusalem was under the control of Jordan, Jews were denied access to praying at the Wailing Wall, which was a most cruel thing to do. No matter which option is selected and agreed upon, one thing must be made abundantly clear: Muslims, Jews, and Christians alike should have complete freedom to worship and visit their holy places.

- *Fighting Terrorism:* Right or wrong, not only Arabs, but the entire Muslim world believes that unconditional and unwavering support by the United States for the state of Israel has been one of the major reasons why terrorists treat America as enemy number one. A more balanced and even-handed approach may have major impact on world terrorism (Rubenberg, 2003). Strange as it may sound, once the enmity between Arabs and Israel is changed into friendship, their coordinated effort could drastically reduce the driving force of world terrorism. The theory that terrorism is due to a clash of civilizations—between Islam and the West (Mannis, 2005)—is completely unsubstantiated (Huntington, 1996, 2004). Strictly speaking, Islam does not represent a civilization. It is a monotheistic religion, deeply rooted in Abrahamic faith, like Judaism and Christianity. And 1.2 billion Muslims in the world live in all of the five major continents, representing a mosaic of cultures. There are roughly 6 to 8 million Muslims living in the United States. Not only do they like America and its special emphasis on human rights and freedom of speech and the press, but they greatly appreciate the lack of discrimination in job opportunities. By establishing mosques and Islamic centers in various parts of the country, they have come to appreciate why secularism is necessary for a pluralistic society. The separation of church and state gives them and other religious groups the freedom to worship their religions the way they want. Some of the Muslims have made major contributions in the fields of science and medicine. They love the United States ardently and are more than happy to be American citizens. Arab-Israeli friendship and the active role of American Muslims can definitely bring enough pressure to make a serious dent in world terrorism and perhaps bring it to an end. We will not only save hundreds of billions of dollars, but we will have peace of mind, security, and economic prosperity.

Future of the Middle East

None of the suggestions outlined so far is easy to achieve. Undoubtably, we will encounter obstacles at every step. But these problems and issues have to be faced and dealt with in an amicable manner. When we deal with intractable problems, there are no simple solutions, only intelligent choices. When there is a sincere desire to achieve lasting peace and hope and expectancy for a better future, there is a basic shift in the negotiating paradigm—the unthinkable becomes thinkable, and the impossible seems possible.

It is my firm belief that in the future a Middle East region can emerge as a significant force in the world politic beyond its oil interests. And it is not a fantasy. Israel's democratic system has produced a modern society where citizens have equal rights and leaders are accountable. Israeli scholars have made significant contributions to science and technology, pioneering work in genetics, medicine, agriculture, optics, and engineering. Arabs are stagnant at present, but history shows that they are resilient and did rise to the occasion when their future was at stake, for example, during the Crusades and the reign of Genghis Khan. Furthermore, Muslim and Jewish scholars flourished in science, medicine, and technology during Moorish rule in Spain. As Professor Mannis (2005) stated: "Between 900 and 1300, while Northern Europe was plunged into dark ages, the medical sciences in the Mediterranean societies in which Islam was dominant experienced a period of renaissance which was to pervade medicine for the next hundred years." Ibn Sina (known as Avicenna in the West), the physician and philosopher, was one of the renowned figures of the Middle Ages. His book, *Canon of Medicine*, was used as the main textbook for teaching medicine in Europe into the seventeenth century (Glasse, 1989). The contributions of Arabs in other fields, such as ophthalmology, mathematics, and astronomy, were also significant. The great Arab philosopher Ibn Rushd (known as Averroes in the West) became famous in Europe and his books were translated into Latin. He was so highly celebrated in the West that a school arose in Europe, which was called "Latin Averroism" (Glasse, 1989). Libraries in Cordova were the envy of the West. So it would be a tragic mistake to underestimate the valuable contributions that Arabs can make to change the modern world.

As stated earlier, great civilizations thrive when certain ingredients are present in a peaceful atmosphere. Those essential elements, according to the experts (Coulburn, 1966; Gibbon, 1932; Kennedy, 1987; Mearsheimer, 2001; Spengler, 1962; Tainter, 1988; Toynbee, 1961), are (1) energy resources, (2) wealth, (3) manpower, (4) the will to strive for excellence, (5) freedom to exchange ideas and thoughts and develop new strategy, and (6) past history of overcoming insurmountable problems.

The Middle East is a vast region: Its wealth is abundant; its manpower is enormous. There is a past history of Jews and Arabs working together and making new discoveries, as evident in Spain. The democratic system of Israel may bring positive changes in the Arab worlds once they start working together, and the technological advancement of Israel will be a major asset to the whole region. This combination of wealth, manpower, and modern technology in a peaceful atmosphere will gradually lead the Middle East toward becoming a major player on the world stage. The region will not only be rich, but will be able to make steady progress in medicine, science, philosophy, and technology like Western countries. Maybe the descendents of Isaac and Ishmael, as God promised, will become great nations once again, and a Golden Age will reemerge.

References

Biale, D. (Ed.). (2002). *Cultures of the Jews*. New York: Random House.

Bickerton, I. J., & Klausner, C. L. (2005). *A concise history of Arab-Israeli conflict* (4th ed., p. 73). Upper Saddle River, NJ: Prentice-Hall.

Brandon, S.G.F. (1973). *Ancient empires: Milestones of history* (2nd ed.). New York: Newsweek Books.

Coulburn, R. (1966). Structure and process in the rise and fall of civilized society. *Comparative Studies in Society and History* (Vol. 8). London: Cambridge University Press.

Gibbon, E. (1932). *The decline and fall of the Roman Empire*. New York: Modern Library.

Glain, S. (2004). *Mullahs, merchants and militants: The economic collapse of the Arab world*. New York: St. Martin's Press.

Glasse, C. (1989). *The concise encyclopedia of Islam*. New York: HarperCollins.

Huntington, S. P. (1996). *The clash of civilization and the remaking of the world order*. New York: Simon & Schuster.

Huntington, S. P. (2004). *Who are we?: The challenges to America's national identity*. New York: Simon & Schuster.

Kennedy, P. (1987). *The rise and fall of the great powers*. New York: Random House.

Kimmerling, B., & Migdal, J. S. (2003). *The Palestinian people*. Cambridge, MA: Harvard University Press.

Laqueur, W., & Rubin, B. (Ed.). (1984). *The Israel-Arab reader* (4th ed.). New York: Facts on File.

Mannis, M. (2005). Al-Razi Memorial Lecture: The Islamic contributions to ophthalmology. [Summary.] *Journal of Islamic Medical Association, 36*(1), 12.

Mearsheimer, J. J. (2001). *The tragedy of great power politics*. New York: W. W. Norton.

Rubenberg, C. A. (2003). *The Palestinian: In search of a just peace*. Boulder, CO: Lynne Rienner.

Said, E. W. (1994). *The politics of dispossession*. New York: Vintage Books.

Spengler, O. (1962). *The decline of the west* (C. F. Atkinson, Trans.). New York: Modern Library.

Tainter, J. A. (1988). *The collapse of complex societies*. Cambridge: Cambridge University Press.

Toynbee, A. J. (1961). *A study of history*. New York: Oxford University Press.

Vital, D. (1975). *The origins of Zionism*. New York: Oxford University Press.

CHAPTER 8

DANCING TANGO DURING PEACEBUILDING: PALESTINIAN-ISRAELI PEOPLE-TO-PEOPLE PROGRAMS FOR CONFLICT RESOLUTION

Sari Hanafi

Introduction

For the past three decades, the discipline of international relations has distinguished between *conflict settlement* and *conflict resolution*. While the first approach prioritizes military and diplomatic intervention, the second approach consists of efforts to create "two-track diplomacy" between belligerent peoples, which means to facilitate negotiations between states on one level, and on the other level, to promote contact between the societal actors (e.g., the ethnic groups in conflict). In fact, the nature of protracted "ethnic" and colonial conflicts is society-wide and not, in essence, a matter between governments. Therefore, many people suggest in this context that the most appropriate "party" to deal with is the identity group, not the nation-state or even the "governing structure." Some researchers stress that the people of such societies need to be empowered before they can forgive, heal, and restabilize their lives (Montville, 1991).

While official government-to-government mediation does not address this issue, there is much that the approaches of nongovernmental organizations (NGOs) can offer. NGO initiatives fall under the category of "People-to-People Programs" and are applied in regions that have undergone national and ethnic conflicts. Such projects, as shown in Table 8.1, consist of cooperation in all domains: the private sector, culture and the arts, as well as dialogue and joint projects for civil society groups. In the Palestinian case, in the spirit of the peace process, and in line with the Israeli-Palestinian September 1995 Interim Agreement, many donors began to encourage and fund these programs. In fact, following the Oslo Agreement, mediation projects have developed in the Palestinian Territories targeted at the Palestinian-Israeli conflict to bring together national and international practitioners in training programs focused on conflict mediation skills. The Norwegian Applied Social Research Center (FAFO) implemented the first major people-to-people program.

People-to-people is not a specific program; rather the term refers to all projects related to the cooperation between Palestinian and Israeli groups. This includes cultural and educational activities such as summer camps, concerts, theatre, and the development of school curriculum on history, as well as environment projects and media. The variety of 158 joint projects funded by FAFO (Mu'allem, 1999) is shown in Table 8.1.

Regarding projects involving dialogue, there are dozens of projects encouraging Middle East dialogue implemented both in the region and abroad. Some of these projects were initiated prior to the Oslo Agreement, creating mainly face-to-face dialogue groups. The factors determining the success or the failure of these projects vary and include objective as well as subjective factors: language barrier, ubiquitous checkpoints, security fears of Israelis entering the occupied territories, and Palestinian concerns that they will be viewed as "collaborators".

The Palestinian National Authority and the Egyptian and Jordanian governments have generally been in favor of cooperation programs. Moreover, important forms of cooperation have been established between Israeli NGOs and Palestinian NGOs as well as some Palestinian ministries (such as the Ministry of Youth) before the arrival of Hamas. However, while the Palestinian NGOs have readily accepted this cooperation—as they live together with the Israelis—in general, almost all of the Arab institutions and NGOs still refuse to work in regional projects or bilateral projects.

Having said this, it is apparent that the presence of a third-party mediator often expedites cooperation projects. The EU-dubbed "Barcelona process," for example, was an occasion for many NGOs in the region to create networks for many sectors (human rights, environment, media, etc.) in which Israel was included. In the academic field, joint projects between universities and research centers in the Arab world and in Israel are quite prominent. In his inventory of

Table 8.1 Different Types of People-to-People Projects Funded by FAFO

Sector of projects	Number	Percentage
Different projects for adults (some are educational)	60	38
Cultural projects	21	13
Environment projects	16	10
Media projects	8	5
Twinning of school and education	13	8
Youth projects	40	25
Total	158	100

these projects, Scham (2000) counted 217 projects between Israel and some of the Arab countries: in the Palestinian Territories, 133 (62%); Egypt, 39 (18%); Jordan, 26 (12%); Morocco, 11 (5%); Tunisia, 6 (3%); and Other, 2 (1%). Some 195 projects among them cover many fields of research: social science, 49 projects (25%); medicine, 35 (18%); agriculture, 35 (18%); water, 30 (15%); environment, 11 (6%); education, 14 (7%); marine, 10 (5%); physics/technology, 6 (3%); and veterinary, 5 (3%).

Programs of cooperation increased in a significant manner because of the interest of the donor community to revive the contacts between Palestinians and Israelis, especially by the United States and the European Commission. However, the breath of people-to-people projects run jointly between two groups does not mean that such initiatives are uniformly admired; in fact, these types of projects remain problematic and have yet to be accepted by all civil society actors. Some evaluations of people-to-people projects identify negative aspects associated with the idea of the project and the manner in which it was implemented (Mu'allem, 1999; Scham, 2000). These type programs have become popular for the funding donors, but not always for the recipient society. In March 1999, an international conference organized by the Welfare Association Consortium (a coalition of three organizations to manage the World Bank fund directed to Palestinian NGOs) elicited strong criticism from the Palestinian scholarly and NGO communities on the topic of people-to-people projects. Projects are considered as neglecting the power structure between the Palestinians and Israelis in favor of the latter, and criticized on the basis that the Israelis are taking a lot of legitimacy from such projects. Some articles in local newspapers also reflected this heated debate against people-to-people projects. Building structures for peace seems, to many NGOs leaders, as neglecting the power structure between the belligerents.

For the donor community, this type of program is based on the idea that regardless of the achievements of the peace process, meetings between the two people are important and should be encouraged. If this idea is valid, then the manner in which it has been applied in practice has made the objective very misleading. The application of this program has two characteristics: the first one consists of gathering people who do not possess the sufficient requirements necessary to establish a basis for common ground. In this case the "meetings" between the Israeli and Palestinian partners become more of a juxtaposition of actors than a dialogue between them. The second characteristic is the total separation between political issues, on one hand, and academic, economic, and cultural issues, on the other hand.

This chapter examines issues related to the following two hypotheses: The first, concerning the conception of the approach, is that the structure of cooperation for both belligerent parties has a long-term impact on pushing the peace agenda. The second hypothesis, which concerns implementation, proposes that the context of peace making by political leadership has an impact on the success (or process) of the implementation of the people-to-people projects.

Conflict Resolution Methods

There have been few efforts to assess people-to-people programs in the region. One such effort done by Norwegian researcher Lena Endresen (2001) looks at people-to-people activities as part of the formal peace process and not outside of it, as the Oslo Interim Agreement (Annex VI and Article II) refers to the People-to-People Program. Endresen notes that the asymmetrical relationship between Palestinians and Israelis in the conflict has great influence on the implementation of these types of programs, and makes a close connection between making peace by the political leadership and building peace by people and the civil society. According to her, "five years later, the experience from the People-to-People Program suggest that this notion may be valid in cases where people build peace as a *supplement* to a peace that political leadership make" (2001, p. 26).

Palestinian researcher Nassif Mu'allem (1999), who has also conducted the only available Palestinian study on people-to-people projects, says they are more accurately called "persons-to-persons" projects. Significantly critical of this approach, Mu'allem concludes that normalization should proceed after the fulfillment of Palestinian national and legitimate rights and the establishment of an independent Palestinian state. After the launching of the second Intifada, voices emerged in the Palestinian newspapers that raised the question of whether Israeli peace organizations should prioritize working with their own public who refuse to acknowledge the rights of Palestinians as opposed to working with their Palestinian counterparts. For its part the PNGOs—the most important Palestinian NGOs network—called on its members not to proceed with joint projects with Israeli organizations, unless the latter "support the Palestinian right to freedom and statehood and a comprehensive, just and durable peace that meets Palestinian national rights" (Palestinian NGOs, 2000).

The Israeli-Palestinian Center for Research and Information (IPCRI) established an initiative to assess people-to-people programs in the Palestinian/ Israeli context, which showed mitigating effects of this program. The IPCRI research project included a workshop for those who have initiated, organized, and funded people-to-people activities, interviewed organizations and people involved in such programs (Baskin, 2001).

Outside of the region, some research has studied the experience of conflict resolution methods in conflict-ridden areas, such as Transcaucasia, Bosnia, Kosovo, where strife has been based on either an interstate or modern ethnic conflict. According to Baird, in the post–Cold War era, the main type of conflict results mainly from group psychology (1999). Hence, the methods of conflict resolution focus on the psychocultural aspect of the conflict (related to identity, "false consciousness," irrational myths, mistrust, and fear), at times neglecting the structural cause of the conflict related to colonization.

As an example of the focus on trust and mistrust, Hancock and Weiss (1999, p. 1) considered the "basic problem" of the Palestinian-Israeli conflict as one of trust: "Unlike the late premier Rabin, who grew to trust Arafat and was trusted in return, [former Israeli prime minister] Netanyahu has long had a personal dislike for the Palestinian leader. For his part, Arafat is suspicious of Netanyahu's real aims, with the Israeli leader being an unknown quantity even to most of his own people . . . It is our belief that current tensions between Israel and the Palestinian Authority are embodied, to a large extent, in the fractious relationship between Netanyahu and Arafat."

While it is true that psychocultural aspects can play a role in the process of the conflict, contributing to its escalation, duration, and intensity, this dimension cannot be considered the cause of the conflict. In this regard it may be that in the Palestinian case, people-to-people programs cannot tackle the psychocultural aspect of the conflict while disregarding the structural aspects of colonization. Otherwise, the logic of the conflict resolution effort is one that works to halt the violence while the conflict continues unabated. Certainly there are psychological roots underlying this conflict, especially insofar as the history of the conflict has been accompanied by a process of establishing, stabilizing, and defending coherent individual and collective identities. However, it is clear that the nature of the conflict has remained a territorial one based on colonial structures with bellicose forms of action occurring on a daily basis, such as ethnic cleansing (in Jerusalem), territorial expansionism (the settlements), and aggressive nationalism (the Jewish nature of the state of Israel).

Recently a project to evaluate the many initiatives on peace building was established under the rubric of the Reflection on Peace Project (RPP). During Phase I of its work (September 1999 through April 2001), RPP completed 26 field-based case studies that document the experiences of specific international, national, and local agencies working in postconflict settings, conflict-prone areas, and in areas of active warfare. In several consultations, practitioners reviewed and analyzed these cases. Through this process, a series of key issues emerged as critical across the many different types of conflict interventions. But the biggest concern was negative impacts that actually leave the situation worse than before the program started, rather than things that caused the program to fail or to be less effective than it could have been. The experiences from the case studies and workshops affirmed six categories of negative impacts: worsening divisions, increasing danger for participants, reinforcing structural or overt violence, diverting resources, increasing cynicism, and disempowering local people.

Beyond this general discussion two points deserve special attention: the role of the mediator and its neutrality, and the relationship of identity and "otherness" in people-to-people programs.

The Role of the Mediator and Neutrality

Some literature criticizes the neutrality of the mediator. Critics argue that powerful states have been criticized for not sufficiently using their political, economic, or military leverage in the form of carrots and sticks (rewards and sanctions), or that their behavior did go beyond mediation to arbitration (Miall et al., 1999 p. 12). In the conflict settlement process in the Middle East, the United States is not seen as neutral since it simultaneously provided arms and military funding to Israel, thereby contributing more to the militarization of the conflict. Contrary to the belief of many scholars, even Norway, a self-styled "neutral" small-state actor, was arguably not a truly effective peacemaker in its most famous mediation case, the Oslo Accords; while these accords claimed to recognize all of the parties and to pursue communicative action, in examining what happened, little was done to denounce the continuation of Israeli settlement policy during the implementing of these accords (Lieberfeld, 1999).

William Zartman, representative of traditional international mediation theory, went further in demystifying the mediation role. According to Zartman, neither in track one nor in track two are the motivations of the mediator or the facilitator peace-oriented. He portrays mediation as a geo-strategically manipulative activity, the aim of which is not long-term conflict resolution but a self-interested strategy of advancement by all individual parties in a conflict, including the mediator (2007, p. 45).

In moments of intense hostility between the belligerent parties, as with the current state of renewed conflict between Palestinians and Israelis, questions emerge about the efficacy of people-to-people programs. In general, the mediation of the third-party actor has been looked to as a technique that ensures the viability of this method of conflict resolution. On the basis of its neutrality, it is assumed that the mediator has the capacity to direct and advance the cooperation. However, it should be recognized that at times this neutrality could become a handicap (a burden) rather than serve as an asset in resolving the conflict, as Baird has described, in that mediators sometimes refuse to take a position, arguing that their "neutral" posturing is essential to their credibility in the long term (1999).

However, recently there have been new developments in this conflict resolution method based on the integrative approach or so-called Harvard Negotiation Method (Fisher, Ury, & Patton, 1991), which employs the value level of a conflict. The essence of this method revolves around a distinction between principles and positions, and between values and interests. Most mediators try to find compromises between the interests of each side without realizing the values that are determining these interests (Miall, 1992).

Relationship to Identity and "Otherness"

One of the major justifications for people-to-people projects is the importance of identity, not necessarily in the conflict itself but in the conduct of any conflicting relationship. However, identity is "more than a psychological sense of self . . . it is extended to encompass a sense of self in relationship to the world" (Northrup, 1989, p. 55). With this understanding, the relationship to "otherness" becomes a factor complicating the conflict. During the conflict, belligerents try to dehumanize and objectify "the other," projecting negative attributes onto "the other" and depersonalizing "the other" to support the separation needed to maintain one's own identity. Even if the rooted cause of a conflict is land, the lack of communication between the belligerents on both sides of the conflict reinforces the warped perceptions of what the other side stands for and what threat they really pose. Moreover, when it is a case of protracted conflict, the stereotypes and/or demonizing of the others can lead to a massive violation of human rights, particularly against the civilians.

Dialogue or Juxtapositions?

Following these characteristics of people-to-people programs, the dialogue between the two partners becomes a simple juxtaposition between people around a table where everyone tells small stories, making the dialogue a kind of narrative in the postmodern meaning: there are neither victims nor oppressors, or all are victims and oppressors. Moreover, there is no truth and all are relative. This is illustrated by a meeting that took place between Israeli and Palestinian teachers at the end of 1996. Without proper preparation, the participants exchanged stories, some about their life experience during the first exodus at 1948, while others talked about their suffering from problems related to the adaptation/assimilation in the Israeli society during the first years following their migration. While the meeting started warmly, it finished in violence between the two groups, with Palestinians feeling that no common ground had been reached with their counterparts. Another project consisted of bringing together Israelis and Palestinian journalists in Neve Shalom—a community of Israelis and Palestinians that is considered an oasis for peace. After a day of cultural activities and discussions about current news, the facilitators asked the group to write a common press communiqué about an event that happened that day. This communiqué stopped with the second sentence when some Israeli journalists announced that they do not recognize the West Bank and Gaza Strip as occupied land. The relative failure of both of these projects shows that there is the absence of a minimum basis for dialogue between the belligerents about the nature of their conflict.

Other projects also show mediocre results in the two societies and even in the belligerent groups. For example, Palestinian and Israeli cultural NGOs planned a project to hold two concerts in order to promote contact between the youth on each side. Two musicians trained together, and it was agreed that two performances should be held in East and West Jerusalem in July 1998. However, the Israeli public refused to go to East Jerusalem, and the Palestinians did the same concerning the performance in West Jerusalem. In the end, the two communities did not mix at all. In the final analysis, this project facilitated musicians and two composers meeting, but not the people.

In the same spirit, in the field of science, a project of cooperation was organized between two chemical laboratories in Al Quds and the Hebrew universities. Once the funds were obtained and divided between the two of them, the Israeli counterpart refused to meet with his Palestinian partner under the pretext of a lack of time. In fact, this easy availability of money encourages opportunism in both Palestinian and Israeli sides.

Separation between Politics and Other Spheres

The other logic behind the people-to-people program is the separation of the political sphere and the cultural and academic spheres, in the name of their respective autonomy. To illustrate this logic, I offer the example of a project of cooperation between Palestinian and Israeli civil societies, which reveals the dysfunctional nature of projects based on this separation logic. In the end of 1998, the Jerusalem Spinoza Institute called the Palestinian University of Al Quds (based in Jerusalem) to cooperate with it in order to organize an international conference in August 1999 entitled "Moral Philosophy in Education: The Challenge of Human Difference." Nothing could be more banal than such a project between two institutions on a subject such as education that touches directly the Palestinian and Israeli populations. However, between May and August 1999, a serious incident happened. The Ministry of Interior of Barak's government withdrew the identity document of Musa Budeiri, a director of the Center of International Relations in Al Quds University, a native and resident of East Jerusalem, whose family has lived there for hundreds of years under Ottoman, British, and Jordanian rule. He was given a tourist visa, valid for four weeks, and told that he would have to leave Jerusalem by August 22. Another problem emerged that the Israeli Ministry of National Education became a financial partner of the conference. In light of these two problems, Al Quds University hesitated between continuing the cooperation or stopping it altogether as a way of expressing solidarity with Professor Budeiri and protesting against the partnership with the Israeli Ministry.

The pros of keeping the collaboration going were supported by two arguments. First, the cooperation would persuade the Ministry of Education to recognize Al Quds University, taking into account that nonrecognition is purely political. The second argument is related to the first: it consists of trying to convince the Ministry of Interior not to expel the university administration, which is located in Jerusalem to the outside of this city (as announced once by an Israeli official). In fact, these two arguments show that the romantic view of cultural cooperation between two civil societies hides all the power imbalance between the two societies (between an occupied and occupying people). As the president of the Spinoza Institute argued: "We are here to put apart divergence and talk in science, philosophy and education, far from politics." Finally, the Al Quds University team decided to pursue the cooperation, hoping that the organizer would act in favor of Al Quds University's cause and Musa Budeiri's expulsion.

In the opening session, Sari Nusseibeh, the president of Al Quds University, contrary to his habit, gave a very moving speech exclusively about the case of Musa Budeiri and his family. To outline the roots of the Budeiri family in this city, he discussed a manuscript on Jerusalem history written by Musa's father, which has never been edited. Nusseibeh, the pioneer of dialogue between Israelis and Palestinians, finished his speech by saying that he is torn morally by these events, adding that the Israelis should not expect to conduct further dialogue with Palestinians as the latter are increasingly becoming tourists! Almost all of the participants were moved, but the organizers were not. The president of Jerusalem Spinoza Institute commented on Nusseibeh's speech saying that, "There is some military problems between Israelis and Palestinians which have not yet been resolved," while the rector of Hebrew University asked Nusseibeh where he could find the Budeiri manuscript as the Hebrew University would like to have it. Finally the organizers of the conference refused to send to the Minister of Interior a petition in favor of Budeiri and signed by the majority of the participants—arguing that there is separation between the academic and political spheres, and that as scholars they cannot take a position. However, the commission of recognition of universities, which is composed mainly of scholars, shows how the academic sphere is implicated in Israel's colonial project. According to the logic of the Israeli side, the application of this conception of "autonomy" of the academic sphere and the notion of "neutrality" of the people-to-people program is taken to mean abstaining from action or abstaining from taking a conscience position in favor of an interlocutor whose rights as citizen have been denied. In this case, the program "people-to-people" becomes a program of dominators-to-dominating or occupants-to-tourists. Following the same logic, one can talk about the non-recognition of the Palestinian side by the people-to-people approved projects that are signed only by Israeli and donor sides. The Israeli side is even afraid that clashes could ensue with the Palestinian side from the outset of the first sentence of the contract; for example, if the Palestinian NGO wants to designate the territories as Palestinian Territories, while Israel recognizes only the label Palestinian Authority.

To me, it is very clear that many projects in the people-to-people program do not pay any attention to the imbalance of power between the parties and sometimes even hide such discrepancies behind the equal number of participants, while the conception of the program is elaborated in the way that the colonial side decides the rules of the game. In the context of occupation, the line between the cultural sphere and the political is very blurry. In a recent article in the Israeli newspaper, *Ha'artz*, an author expressed his astonishment at the Arabic world's (and especially those with whom Israel has diplomatic relations) refusal to participate in the Jerusalem Film Festival, as this festival is a "pure cultural event." This astonishment would have diminished if the journalist had attended the Mayer reception in David Tower organized for the festival participants where this reception and dinner were dedicated exclusively to putting forth the idea of the unification of Jerusalem under Israeli control, with everything supporting this theme, from the first song inaugurating the reception to all the speeches, including that of then-Jerusalem Mayor Ehud Olmert, and finally to the prize given to the guest of honor, movie actor Kirk Douglas.

These observations of some people-to-people projects illustrate the problem of a program that functions independently or in isolation from the achievements of the peace process. Cooperation between the two civil societies cannot be undertaken in a manner so as to escape responsible action, and if need be, as in the Budeiri case, taking an active position supporting the occupied side. Failure to do so misrepresents reality and presents a false image of the conflict. While the Western and Israeli media focus their attention on this type of program, the number of settlers has increased three times since the launching of the peace process (from 160,000 to 480,000). This reminds one of the ART Franco-Germanic television channel's comments on Michel Khalief's film *Wedding in Galilee*. This channel presented the movie as an example of peaceful coexistence between Israelis and Arabs because the Israeli soldiers were invited to the Palestinian wedding, but the commentators neglected to note that the precondition imposed by the military forces in order for them to issue permission for the wedding—set during the period of curfew—was the very presence of the Israeli soldiers that these commentators were celebrating in their review.

The conclusion that I would like to draw here is not to undermine the reason d'être of people-to-people programs but to question the current form in which they are conducted—in a hasty manner and thwarting their own objectives. The way to resolve the conflict is not to ignore or hide it, but to present it openly in an honest manner in order to prevent it from accumulating and merging with other problems, creating irremediable rupture between the belligerents. Furthermore, the efficacy of the people-to-people approach is related not only to the approach itself, but to the degree of development of the ongoing peace process achievement. People-to-people meetings have no meaning if the first-track negotiation does not succeed to allow freedom of movement for Palestinians. Also, people-to-people programs will suffer if accompanied with the extensive settlement activities.

The idea of summer camps is a good example of effective people-to-people programs, as children are at an age in which they can change their attitudes. However, facilitators who have participated in such projects report that in some cases Palestinian children suffered trauma and alienation because of these camps. Playing for one day with Israeli kids in the playgrounds in Tel Aviv proved to be a source of great alienation and discomfort when these kids compared the comfortable situation of their counterparts (the Israeli children) in Tel Aviv with their own more dire circumstances in Dheisheh Refugee Camp.

While it is true that there are funds being funneled into people-to-people projects, some of these projects were a real success without funding. For example, I have followed intellectual dialogues between some Israeli historians and some Palestinian scholars debating issues concerning Palestinian and Israeli nationalism as well as Israeli colonial practices and been surprised that such meetings were so fruitful to the point that there were more discussions than dialogue, in the sense that the divergences between the Israelis themselves were wider than with the Palestinians and vice versa. These meetings were a laboratory for the emerging of new narratives.

References

Baird, A. (1999). An atmosphere of reconciliation: A theory of resolving ethnic conflicts based on the transcaucasian conflicts. *The Online Journal of Peace and Conflict Resolution*, *2*(4). Retrieved from http://www.trinstitute.org/ojpcr/2_4baird.htm.

Baskin, G. (2001). *Putting money into Israeli-Palestinian peace projects now? You must be crazy.* Israel/Palestine Center for Research and Information. Retrieved from http://www.ipcri.org/files/peace-now.html.

Endresen, L. (2001). *Contact and cooperation: The Israeli-Palestinian People-to-People Program.* Norway: Norwegian Applied Social Research Center (FAFO).

Fisher, R., Ury, W., & Patton, B. (1991). *Getting to yes: Negotiating agreement without giving in.* New York: Penguin.

Hancock, L. E., & Weiss, J. N. (1999). The conflict within: The interpersonal conflict between Netanyahu and Arafat. *The Online Journal of Peace and Conflict Resolution*, *2*(2). Retrieved from http://www.trinstitute.org/ojpcr/2_2hanwei.htm.

Lieberfeld D. (1999) Talking with the Enemy: Negotiation and Threat Perception in South Africa and Israel/Palestine. Westport, CT: Praeger Publishers.

Miall, H. (1992). *The peacemakers: Peaceful settlement of disputes since 1945.* New York: St. Martin's Press.

Miall, H., Ramsbotham, O., & Woodhouse, T. (1999) Contemporary conflicts resolution: the prevention, management and transformation of deadly conflicts. Polity Press.

Montville, J. (1991). The arrow and the olive branch: A case for track two diplomacy. In J. Volka & J. Montville (Eds.), *The psychodynamics of international relationships* (Vol. II, pp. 161–175). Lanham, MD: Lexington Books.

Mu'allem, N. (1999, November 27–28). *Palestinian Israeli civil society co-operative activities.* Paper presented during "Peace Building between Israelis and Palestinians" workshop, Helsinki, Finland.

Northrup, T. (1989). The dynamic of identity in personal conflict. In L. Kriesberg, T. Northrup, & S. Thorson (Eds.), *Intractable conflicts and their transformation* (pp. 55–82). Syracuse, NY: Syracuse University Press.

Palestinian NGOs. (2000). *Palestinian NGO Network conditions cooperation with Israeli organizations.* [Announcement by the General Assembly of PNGO]. Ramallah: Palestinian NGO Network.

Scham, P. (2000, September). Arab-Israeli research cooperation, 1995–1999. Middle East Review of International Affairs (*MERIA*) *Journal, 4*(3).

Zartman I. W. (2007) *Peacemaking and International Conflict: Methods and Techniques.* United States Institution of Peace.

CHAPTER 9

GREENPRINTS FOR PEACEBUILDING BETWEEN PALESTINIANS AND ISRAELIS

Yaron Prywes

The disciples of the wise increase peace in the world.

—*Talmud, Berkot (64a)*

The believers are but a single Brotherhood: so make peace and reconciliation between your two brothers.

—*Qur'an (49:10)*

Blessed are the peacemakers: for they shall be called the children of God.

—*Mathew (5:9)*

The Israeli-Palestinian conflict often takes center stage in world politics. This is remarkable attention given to less than 0.2% of the world's 6.6 billion people—approximately 10.5 million people total, including 5.4 million Israeli Jews and 5.1 million Palestinians in a landmass the size of New Jersey.[1] As a Jew born in Israel and raised in America, I have always found the topic highly relevant and interesting. But why do so many others? I believe this conflict permeates the world arena because many of the dichotomous tensions that exist between and within Palestinians and Israelis have widespread relevance: west vs. east, theocracy vs. democracy, rich vs. poor, religious vs. secular, modern vs. traditional, terrorism vs. militarism, security vs. freedom, nonnuclear vs. nuclear, and whites vs. people of color. Furthermore, events from the Israeli-Palestinian conflict ripple outward to the greater Middle East, Europe, Asia, Africa, the United States, and beyond, while conversely the conflict is deeply affected by global events. Productively addressing this conflict can have a global, positive impact. But peace builders work against time and history, since the longer these dichotomies are allowed to overpower shared goals, the more difficult it becomes to achieve peace. Efforts must be active, inspired, and thoughtful.

This chapter equips peace builders with numerous simple but powerful theories, which I collectively call "Greenprints." Functioning like blueprints for peace, they guide those who rightly resist oversimplification but naturally become overwhelmed with the complexity of this conflict. Greenprints, named after the color of the leaves of the proverbial olive branch—connoting peace—and the color of new growth and regeneration, provide peace builders with what political road maps have thus far failed to offer: fresh, useful, and creative ways of thinking. The greenprints can be utilized individually, but are most powerful when used together.

Greenprint #1: A Model of Nature and Nurture to Understand Peace Building

Kurt Lewin, a Jewish German-American researcher often credited as "the father of modern social psychology," explained that each person is shaped by an interaction between nature (inborn tendencies) and nurture (how life experiences mold individuals). Lewin (1933) captured this concept with his well-known equation, shown in Equation 9.1, which describes behavior (B) as a function of the person (P) and the environment (E).

$$B = f(P \times E) \qquad \text{Equation 9.1}$$

Lewin's formula can help individuals understand—and overcome—interpersonal conflict. For example, as a college student I took part in a Middle East Peace and Conflict training program, which enabled us to live with a Palestinian family in the West Bank, a Jordanian family in Amman, and an Israeli family in West Jerusalem. We also studied current political and social affairs and attended lectures by academics, political activists, and government officials. I'll never forget when my home-stay host Samer and I got into an argument about the accuracy of the Holocaust. What helped me stay engaged in dialogue with him despite experiencing strong negative feelings about his denial/minimization of what I perceived as historical truths was the realization that we are both products of our environments. Our positions and feelings relate to the groups with which we identify—me, a Jewish Israeli American and grandson of an Auschwitz survivor in contrast to him, a Lebanese Jordanian Muslim growing up in Israeli-occupied southern Lebanon; the history of conflict between our two peoples; and differences in our respective educational systems. Thus, Lewin's formula can help free people from "taking things personally" and provide a bit of necessary emotional distance from a potentially inflammatory and unproductive interaction.

Applying Lewin's formula to the Israeli-Palestinian conflict—as any other large-scale dispute—requires addressing all three of Lewin's variables: understanding each side's unique personal factor (P), the impact of each side's environment (E), and each side's peace-building behavior (B).

Greenprint #2: A Model of Identity to Understand the Person (P) in Peace Building

To further understand the person (P) in Lewin's formula, it is useful to consider another model that further elucidates identity—a crucial aspect in defining an individual and culture. Deconstructing the concept of identity can help participants in a conflict better understand why cross-cultural exchanges can be so profound and emotional. The Identity Iceberg, as shown in Figure 9.1, helps organize numerous elements comprising one's identity (Knefelkamp et al., 2005). Like an iceberg, many elements of one's identity are not readily perceived because they are hidden below the surface and can only be discovered through exploration.

For Israelis and Palestinians, primary elements comprising their identity include religious tradition, nationality (sometimes two), ethnicity, language, political affiliation, and gender. A comprehensive list is virtually unlimited, including varying levels of attachment to a neighborhood, profession, generation, military unit, sports team, group of friends, and university. Identities are also not

Figure 9.1 Identity Iceberg

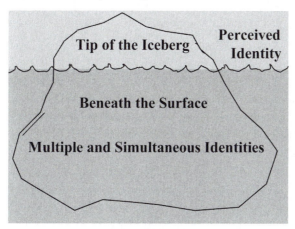

One's identity is like an iceberg. Only 10 to 15 percent is visible above the surface. The waterline correlates to the elements of an individual's identity that can be perceived, such as skin color or clothing.
Source: Knefelkamp et al., 2005.

static; they change according to the environment and also develop throughout a person's lifetime as one grows from child to adolescent, adult, and senior (Maalouf, 2000). For example, the meaning of being a woman is very different if living in the cosmopolitan city of Tel-Aviv or in the ultraorthodox community Mea Shearim.

The development of one's identity is thus a dynamic interplay between intrapsychic (how I see myself) and psychosocial forces (how others see me) (Knefelkamp, 2006a; Knefelkamp et al., 2005). Deeper clarity about who you are can be achieved through interaction with someone who is different in some fundamental way, or when someone sees you differently from how you see yourself. Successful Israeli-Palestinian peace-building programs help participants generate self-awareness about multiple and simultaneous similarities and differences, while maintaining a sense of unity within the group by identifying a shared goal or other common ground.

The lesson for all peace builders is that both *who* is present and *what* is being discussed will impact which identities come to the fore, and successful programs facilitate *how* participants manage those identities. The most effective programs acknowledge differences while maintaining a sense of unity, such as common characteristics or goals, and thus lay the groundwork for a new common identity to emerge, often around shared concepts of friendship, humanity, and peace.

Greenprint #3: A Model of Boundaries to Understand the Environment (*E*) in Peace Building

An exchange between a Palestinian and an Israeli is both an encounter between two individuals and an expression of intergroup relations (Alderfer, 1987). This means that the two individuals represent the groups with which they identify, and carry with them a perspective informed by that group and their environment. Thus, interactions between individuals from different groups are influenced by their respective group's experience with another group. Even if groups are not physically present, they are metaphorically "behind" individuals. This concept is visualized in Figure 9.2.

An important aspect to understanding the environment is defining its boundaries. The dashes defining the circles in Figure 9.2 show the boundaries connecting individuals with their two groups (Israeli and Palestinian), and a newer boundary holding the two interacting individuals together. The relative permeability of group boundaries—shown by the relative thickness or space between the lines in the figure—is another important facet of peacebuilding efforts as the boundaries represent the possibility for change and how groups regulate transactions with each other (Alderfer, 1987).

Boundaries play a major part in the Palestinian-Israeli conflict literally and figuratively, and physically as well as psychologically. Discussions about checkpoints, settlements, separation fences, terrorism, housing demolitions, models of

Figure 9.2 Peace Programs Seek to Strengthen the Boundary Holding Palestinian and Israeli Participants Together

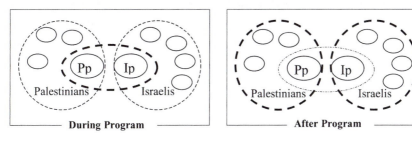

Key
Pp = Palestinian participant
Ip = Israeli participant

An exchange between a Palestinian and an Israeli is an interaction between individuals embedded within two groups. The thickness of the dashed lines represents the relative permeability of the boundaries, which may change as a result of program participation.

coexistence, Jewish democracy, solutions to Jerusalem, refugees, or UN resolutions are implicitly or explicitly a discussion about appropriate boundaries between or within groups. Power imbalances also impact these boundaries and their relative permeability.

Theoretically speaking, these "system boundaries" can be underbound (too loose), overbound (too rigid), or optimally bound (just right). Recent violence between Fatah and Hamas can be understood as a power struggle within Palestinians as to the proper boundary the group as a whole should have in relation to (economically and militarily superior) Israel. Generally, Fatah believes the optimal boundary with Israel should be more permeable than Hamas does, as indicated by Hamas' refusal to formally recognize Israel.

The goal of peace-building activities is to improve intergroup relations by addressing the psychological and physical boundaries separating two groups in conflict (Palestinians and Israelis, Fatah and Hamas) and to make overly rigid boundaries more permeable in appropriate ways. The "before" and "after" images in Figure 9.2 illustrate how boundary permeability may change during and after a peace-building intervention. Since thickness of the dashed lines represents stronger boundaries, the figure shows that even after participating in some well-intentioned peacebuilding program, some participants are unable to sustain connections.

The more group members feel mainly positive about their own group and mainly negative about other groups, the less permeable the group boundaries become. Impermeable boundaries can result in distorted cognitive formations about a group. Language—and the use of words and social categories—reflects the rigidity or permeability of boundaries since they condition members' perceptions of objective and subjective phenomena, and transmit theories and ideologies to explain members' experiences, affect issues, and influence their relations with other groups (Alderfer, 1987). For example, referring to Palestinians as "Arabs," consciously or not, can implicitly negate legitimacy of this group's claim over the land since it can be argued that if a Palestinian is only an Arab, then he or she has a "home" in any one of the 21 Arab countries in the world (thereby also serving to minimize injustice suffered by Palestinians). Similarly, referring to Israelis solely as Jews can imply a denial of the country's existence, and negate the legitimacy of whatever entity exists, Jewish biblical and historic ties to the land, and even UN Resolution 181, calling for the modern creation of the Jewish state.

Leaders play an important role—physically and psychologically—in boundary formation. For example, when Palestinian President Mahmoud Abbas and Israeli Prime Minister Ehud Olmert engaged in official bilateral discussions for the first time in December 2006, they greeted each other with an embrace and kiss on each cheek.[2] This singular public act carried many messages and layers of meaning. The leaders showed their constituency and the world that (1) they are willing to embrace a representative of "the other" despite deep animosity between the two peoples, (2) they did not hold each other personally responsible for the outbreak of the violent al-Aqsa (second) Intifada, and (3) they are trying to resolve their differences through peaceful dialogue. I also believe that their greeting was meant to (1) strengthen their own personal political standings (Olmert by demonstrating that Israel is trying to alleviate Palestinian suffering while maintaining its security, and Abbas by demonstrating that Palestinians are able partners for peace); and (2) strengthen Abbas's political standings given the rise to government power of the extremist group Hamas. Ironically, for Palestinians who already perceive Abbas as a sellout or as an Israeli collaborator who does not deliver results, the affectionate embrace may have further reinforced their view of his drifting too far from his group's boundaries. Effective leaders shape and improve their group's boundaries toward the enemy, while not letting their members feel alienated. This is admittedly a delicate balance to achieve.

Greenprint #4: A Developmental Model to Understand Peacebuilding Behavior (B)

The Developmental Model of Conflict Resolution posits that individuals hold different worldviews depending on their level of maturity (Danesh & Danesh, 2002, 2004).[3] These worldviews include a perspective on how the world is organized, principles that guide action, and a driving purpose. They also shape the conflicts people experience, their behavior in such situations, and their attempts at resolution. Table 9.1 shows various worldviews and their link to major stages of human development (childhood, adolescence, and adulthood), with resulting governing dynamics and strategies to resolve conflict.

Table 9.1 Developmental Model of Conflict Resolution

The corresponding elements of their worldview at each stage of development

Stage of Development	Childhood	Adolescence	Adulthood
Perspective	World Is Dangerous	World Is a Jungle	World Is One
Principles	Might Is Right	Survival of the Fittest	Truth and Justice
Purpose	Self/Group Preservation	To "Win"	Unity in Diversity

The corresponding mode and governing dynamic at each stage of development

Stage of Development	Childhood	Adolescence	Adulthood
Mode	A-Mode (Authoritarian)	P-Mode (Power)	C-Mode (Consultative)
Dynamic	Dominance & Submission	Competition	Divergence & Convergence

Source: Prywes adaptation of Danesh & Danesh (2002).

The model can be applied to individuals and groups (e.g., communities and nations), as well as to their conflict resolution processes (e.g., mediation, legal, political systems). As the figure shows, at the childhood level, the world is seen as a dangerous place, where "might equals right," and one's primary purpose is preservation. The governing dynamic at this stage—called "A-mode" where A = authoritarian—involves dominance and submission. This worldview and resulting behavior is appropriate when a child is very young, but as a child matures, this mode becomes oppressive and dysfunctional. This same dynamic appears on a societal level when a population's efforts to participate in an author-itarian government or express their dissenting opinions are suppressed. Like children under the thumb of a dominant parent, these societies may appear peace-ful on the surface since they are sacrificing their dissenting voice for security. Occasional outbursts—equivalent to childhood tantrums—inevitably occur, but are often dealt with swiftly and forcefully, restoring a state of strained calm. Such governments, operating on A-mode, are founded on a society's sense of insecurity, which can erupt into violence.

An adolescent worldview sees the world as a jungle, where "survival of the fittest" and "winning" are primary drivers. Resources are viewed as scarce, and thus one's gain is another's loss. Called "P-mode" (where P = power), this stage is also characterized by an internal struggle of identity formation and external competition for autonomy and independence. A large majority of individuals and societies in the world today operate primarily in this worldview, concerned about itself, and inviting competition and power struggles with others, fighting to have their point of view dominate, to be right, and to win at the expense of the other. While these are necessary phases of development, they have limits, are not always appropriate, and overreliance on them facilitates conflict and violence.

These stages can be seen to describe the governing dynamics and mindset of the Israeli-Palestinian conflict, characterized by insecurity, fear, and pain, the idea that "only the strong survive," and the need by both parties to assert their dominance and authority over the other in order to protect themselves. As a result of living and operating in a violent environment, people in this conflict are embedded in A and P modes of thinking and behavior. However, despite having adaptive origins, A and P modes now also have detrimental effects. Behavior driven by a need to protect oneself in the short term actually makes both Palestinians and Israelis *less* safe in the long run by continuing to nurture more violence, death, and destruction. Some people on both sides are beginning to realize—as Albert Einstein observed—that peace cannot be kept by force; it can only be achieved through understanding.

The third mode—"C-mode" or the consultative approach—represents the more mature phase regarding development and conflict resolution. In C-mode, an individual's and society's actions and fate are seen as fundamentally intertwined with the world around them. Truth and justice gain paramount importance. Resources are seen as potentially abundant for all if collaborative and creative efforts are deployed, consistent with the driving concept underlying this worldview: "unity in diversity." Unity—not to be confused with uniformity—is a conscious and purposeful convergence of multiple entities in a state of harmony, integration, and cooperation to create a new entity or entities. The new entity builds around a common goal and usually reflects more than the sum of its parts. For example, a two-state solution to the Palestinian-Israeli conflict would seek to create an independent Palestinian state, coupled with the emergence of dynamic, cooperative relationships between the two neighboring states to ensure mutual security and economic development.

C-mode moves away from an individualistic focus toward a focus on resolving conflict as a collective group enterprise. C-mode behavior is dynamic, actively seeking divergence of perspectives that lay a foundation upon which to build convergence. Thus, listening and consensus-building are essential skills in this mode.

Leveraging C-mode toward creating peace requires work in the form of a specific mindset and skill set. Table 9.2 details what I call the "consultative greenprint": a set of useful peace-building guidelines that help facilitate this C-mode state.[*] The consultative greenprint is a three-step peace-building and conflict-resolution process that involves (1) preparation, (2) exploration, and (3) integration. Each step has a number of guidelines that involve participants' head (intellect), heart (emotions), and hands (behaviors). It further represents a way to use conflict as an opportunity to grow and develop.

Table 9.2 A Consultative Greenprint: A Three-Step Peace Building and Conflict Resolution Model

(1) Preparation

Mental Preparation

- Get yourself into a learning orientation—mastering conflict is a lifelong process.
- Make a conscious choice to utilize Authoritarian, Power, or Consultative modes.

Emotional Preparation

- Acknowledge and work with emotions but make sure they don't derail the process.

(2) Exploration

Understanding

- Nurture mutual efforts to better understand the conflict and different interpretative positions.
- Develop increased self-awareness and knowledge of others.
- Seek to understand how your perspective relates to your own previous learning, background, and experiences.

Listening

- Agree to listen until you understand.
- Acknowledge that understanding does not imply agreement.
- Listen without preparing your response.
- Listen for the meaning and standpoint of others and the self.

Emotions

- Be free from the need to convince someone you are right.
- Stay in communication even when you are confused, angry, fearful, or unsure.
- Remember the impact of your communications on others is not always intended.

(3) Integration

Connect

- Acknowledge and build upon points of unity.
- See connections between various embedded systems.

Refine

- Develop the ability to critique in a mature manner.
- Search for the appropriate response.
- Seek understanding of multiple modes of inquiry and approaches to knowledge, and the ability to judge adequate and appropriate approaches from those that are not adequate or appropriate.

Build

- Take responsibility for your own perspectives, stances, and actions.
- Lead toward satisfying universal human needs of existence, belonging, and growth.
- Strive for sustainable solutions.

Conclusion: Ensuring Survival through a Declaration of Interdependence

As Austrian American physicist Fritjof Capra, a Buddhist Catholic, noted in his best-selling book *The Web of Life* (1997), the more we study the major problems of today's world, the more we come to realize that they cannot be understood in isolation. Consistent with this view, the many facets of the Palestinian-Israeli conflict are interconnected and interdependent, reflecting systemic problems. Divisive dualism and violence continue to dominate life in the region, with fears on both sides preventing those involved from recognizing that it is in everyone's best self-interest to move from childhood and adolescent approaches to conflict—defined in the A and P modes in the Developmental Model of Conflict Resolution—into more developed, adult approaches of the C-mode. Instead of competition begetting competition between the two cultures, cooperation would breed cooperation, and a high concern for self would enhance—not diminish—a high concern for "the other."

Reversing the trend of violence in the region requires systematically addressing underlying environmental issues (the E in Lewin's theory, including economic, educational, and societal problems) that create hatred and misunderstanding between and among Israelis and Palestinians; and being conscious of how groups and cultures inform perspectives and identities of individuals (the P in Lewin's theory). In addition, consultative behaviors and mindsets should be used (by individuals and leaders) to create optimal boundaries between groups that meet mutual needs for security, economic prosperity, and self-determination, and to facilitate cooperation to overcome extremism and to create sustainable security.

Effective political road maps for peace in the region will emerge if the greenprints described in this chapter are used to govern the process. These greenprints utilize individual and group dynamics models to understand—and resolve—the Israeli-Palestinian conflict. These solutions require a "declaration of interdependence"—a radical shift in perceptions, thinking, values, and behavior from a regressed, short-term, reactive, self-interest worldview toward one that is sustainable, enlightened, inspired, and built on mutual interest, cooperation, and unity.

Acknowledgment

I would like to acknowledge Dr. Judy Kuriansky for the opportunity to share my perspective on this critical topic, and colleagues and family who provided thoughtful feedback; in particular, Israeli conflict analyst Aelia Shusterman and editor Deb Aronson. Lastly, thank you, Dr. Knefelkamp, Dr. Alderfer, and Dr. Danesh—your work offers a fresh outlook on this often-depressing conflict.

References

Alderfer, C. P. (1972). *Existence, relatedness, and growth: Human needs in organizational settings*. New York: Free Press.

Alderfer, C. P. (1987). An intergroup perspective on group dynamics. In J. W. Lorsch (Ed.), *Handbook of organizational behavior* (pp. 190–222). Englewood Cliffs, NJ: Prentice-Hall.

Capra, F. (1997). *The web of life*. New York: Anchor Books.

Central Intelligence Agency. (2006, December 19). *The world fact book*. Retrieved December 27, 2006, from https://www.cia.gov/cia/publications/factbook/index.html.

Danesh, H. B., & Danesh, R. (2002). Has conflict resolution grown up? Towards a developmental model of decision making and conflict resolution. *International Journal of Peace Studies, 7*(1), 59–76.

Danesh, H. B., & Danesh, R. (2004). Conflict-free conflict resolution: Process and methodology. *Journal of Peace and Conflict Studies, 11*(2), 55–84.

Israeli Central Bureau of Statistics. (2006, December 28). *Population in Israel on eve of 2007*. Press Release. Retrieved December 27, 2006, from http://www1.cbs.gov.il/reader/cw_usr_view_Folder?ID=141.

Knefelkamp, L. (2006a, October 20). *Diversity within: The development of the multicultural self*. Plenary Speech at the Diversity and Learning Conference of the American Association of Colleges and Universities, Philadelphia, PA.

Knefelkamp, L. (2006b). Listening to understand. *Liberal Education, 92*(2), 34–35.

Knefelkamp, L., Graham, T., Ingram, L., Nielson, K., Prywes, Y., & Uyekobu, S. (2005, January 29). *Educational encounters at the intersection: Student intellectual, intercultural, and identity development*. Featured session at the Annual Conference of the American Association of Colleges and Universities, San Francisco, CA.

Lewin, K. (1933). Environmental forces in child behavior and development. In C. Murchinson (Ed.), *Handbook of child psychology* (2nd ed.), 590–625. Worcester, MA: Clark University Press.

Maalouf, A. (2000). *In the name of identity: Violence and the need to belong* (B. Bray, Trans.). New York: Penguin. (Original work published 1996)

Palestinian Central Bureau of Statistics. (2006, December 26). *Demographic and socioeconomic status of the Palestinian people at the end of 2006*. Press Conference. Retrieved December 27, 2006, from http://www.pcbs.gov.ps/.

Population Reference Bureau. (2006). *2006 world population data sheet*. Retrieved December 29, 2006, from http://www.prb.org.

PART II

GROWING, GRIEVING, AND TALKING TOGETHER

Either we are going to die together, or we are going to learn to live together. And if we are going to live together, we have to talk.

—*Eleanor Roosevelt, U.S. First Lady 1933–1945,*
first U.S. delegate to the United Nations

Never doubt that a small group of thoughtful, committed citizens can change the world. Indeed, it is the only thing that ever has.

—*Margaret Mead, American anthropologist*

A group of us sat in a New York apartment in 2004 as two young people told their story about pain and loss as a result of the Intifada, and how they transformed hate into compassion. Their stories are recounted in this part, along with other chapters describing innovative ways in which Israelis and Palestinians are communicating with each other and working together for mutual understanding and peace.

These techniques include engaging "the other" in dialogue—listening to each other's narratives to overcome stereotypes and see each other's humanity. Dialoguing is one of the recently popular means being used to achieve such mutual respect and rapport between people in conflict. This technique emerged out of the work of experts adapting the techniques of resolving conflict between blacks and whites as a result of the South African Truth and Reconciliation Commission, as well as the work of professionals facilitating reconciliation between Nazi perpetrators and Holocaust survivors though sharing narratives. A workshop approach—called "To Reflect and Trust"—has been applied to Israelis and Palestinians in conflict. The approach reflects a truly bilateral and international understanding, as it evolved from a collaboration of Israeli social psychologist

Dan Bar-On and Palestinian educator Sami Adwan, with psychiatrist Joseph Al-beck from the Harvard International Negotiation Initiative. In dialogue groups, participants hear the narrative (personal perspective and experience) of the "other side," and through that, become more aware and understanding of another truth besides their own. Distinct from debate, dialogue requires (1) letting others speak their truth, and (2) creating an atmosphere of respect and compassion, avoiding judgment. The ways in which dialogue works in exciting formats with Israelis and Palestinians are described in chapters in this part.

Another technique—also a favorite of mine—is called "nonviolent communication." It, too, is described in a chapter in this part. This interaction involves four simple steps which can be very effective when applied to diverse contexts of inter-personal relations. The four steps are (1) state the upsetting event, (2) describe your feelings, (3) identify your needs, and (4) and make a request. All healthy relationships also require what's called "compassionate listening"—paying keen attention to what "the other" is saying. Such interactions can help disputing parties achieve what I call the 3 As: acceptance, acknowledgment, and appreciation.

Another crucial element—I know as a clinical psychologist, relationship counselor and peace worker—that is essential for conflict transformation is feeling safe to speak your mind. A useful method that can accomplish this is called Open Space Technology. I saw first-hand an application of this to the Israeli-Palestinian conflict, in a training discussed in a chapter in this part. The experience engages others in a free exchange of ideas that lends to mutual support and creative problem-solving.

The phrase "Salaam Shalom" expresses the simularity of the two seemingly disparate cultures. The phrase implies that bridging the gap is possible. Efforts by interfaith groups—covered in this part—are proving that this is possible. As shown, too, in the work of unsung religious leaders all over the world profiled in *Peacemakers in Action* by the Tanenbaum Center for Interreligious Understanding, religiously motivated grassroots peacemakers have a vital role to play in resolving armed conflicts in Israel/Palestine and all over the world.

A cultural event that I attended at the Pakistani consulate in May 2006 was hosted by artist Mumtaz Hussain and dedicated to the Persian poet Rumi and the Turkish poet Igbal. The theme of the celebration sums up the spirit of chapters in this part: *"Each religion has a different path, but the destination is the same: peace and love."* That message is alive in the work of the Interfaith Encounter groups, described in a chapter in this part. In November 2006, as part of healing after the war along the Israeli-Lebanese border, one of these interfaith groups met with 30 middle school students. The students expressed their feelings and all came to one conclusion that reflects the spirit of all the efforts in this book: "We are different but equal."

CHAPTER 10

GRIEVING BUT GROWING: PALESTINIANS AND ISRAELIS IN THE PARENTS CIRCLE-FAMILIES FORUM

Boaz Kitain

So many of us on both sides of the conflict have lost loved ones. But we at the Parents Circle-Families Forum (PCFF) have resolved not to hold on to hate. In our organization—the Parents Circle-Families Forum—we grieve and grow together, as Israeli and Palestinian families committed to reconciliation. PCFF is an organization of more than 500 bereaved Israeli and Palestinian families who have all lost close relatives to the violence in the Middle East. The PCFF is one of a handful of truly joint programs still functioning despite the ravages of the ceaseless conflict. Our staff and management reflect our cooperative efforts. I am an Israeli and general manager of our Israeli group, who specializes in education and conflict resolution, and was the Headmaster of Neve Shalom/Wahat al-Salam Regional School, a unique mixed Arab and Jewish institution. I lost my son Tom in 1997 while he was on military duty. Aziz Abu Sarah is a Palestinian from East Jerusalem who was elected president of our Palestinian management. Below is his personal story about transformation, and also the story of a young Israeli woman who lost a loved one and who was also in our group. Both Aziz and Ya'ara have traveled to the United States to share their stories and talk about our organization.

A Conflict Close to Home: Two Stories

Aziz is now 27 years old. When he lost his brother as a result of the Israeli-Palestinian conflict, he was bitter and angry. But he did not let his resentment ruin his life. Here is his story in his own words.

Transforming Hate after Loss: Aziz' Story

A disaster can strike your nation, your state, or even the house of your next-door neighbor, but as long as it strikes someone else, it is still a distance away. Like many in Jerusalem, I grew up seeing many people die because of a "worthless conflict." I felt sad for them, but I continued to live my life just as before. My reaction was the same as others who see an accident on the side of the road, think "how sad," and drive on. However, my life changed forever the moment the disaster struck my house and my family, and the casualty was my brother.

In the spring of 1990, I shared a room with four of my brothers. One ordinary day I was woken at 5:00 A.M., as Israeli soldiers burst into my room. They asked us for our identity cards, and questioned the five of us. "Where were you yesterday? Did you throw stones?" They demanded the answers, and when they received none, they took my 18-year-old brother with them. My mother pleaded desperately with the soldiers, but in the end they took Tayseer with them. She would not hold him again until 11 months later, when he was released from prison.

Tayseer was kept without trial. He was interrogated and beaten for 15 days until he admitted that he had thrown stones at Israeli cars. During the 11 months he was imprisoned, we met him three times. Although we spoke with him through two fences, it was obvious that with each visit his health was deteriorating from the beatings. Finally, in the late days of March, he was released from prison. His condition was critical, and he was throwing up blood. We rushed him to the hospital.

Tayseer held on for about three weeks, before dying after surgery. I was 10 years old at that time, and Tayseer had been closest to me in age and closest to me as friend and brother. I could not accept his death. He had helped me with homework. He had accompanied me on my first day of school.

I became extremely bitter and angry. Even at 10, I understood that his death was not natural, and someone was responsible. I grew up with anger burning in my heart. I wanted justice. I wanted revenge.

In my high school years I started writing for a youth magazine. I was a consistent writer and wrote about two articles a week. I wrote with anger and bitterness, and used my pain to spread hatred against the other side. My success soon earned me the position of editor at the magazine. However, the more I wrote the more empty and angry I became. Eventually I grew tired of the anger, so I quit the magazine and tried to move out of the country.

I failed to get anywhere. After graduating from high school I found myself stuck in Jerusalem. I had refused to learn Hebrew growing up: it was the "enemy's" language. Now, to attend university or get a good job I would have to compromise. I started studying in a Hebrew Ulpan, an institute for Jewish newcomers to Israel. It was the hardest experience I had faced yet, but its results were the best I have encountered. It was the first time I had sat in a room of Jews who were not superior to me. It was the first time I had seen faces different from the soldiers at the checkpoints. Those soldiers had taken my brother; these students were the same as me. My understanding of the Jewish people started to collapse after just a few weeks of the Ulpan. I found myself confused, thinking, "How can they be normal human beings, just like me?" I was amazed that I could build friendships with these students and share their struggles. We went out for coffee together. We studied together. Sometimes we even found that we shared the same interests. For me, this was a turning point in my life.

I came to understand that unfortunate things happen in our lives which are out of our control. A 10-year-old could not control the soldiers who took his brother. But now as an adult, I could control my response to these hurts. They had acted unjustly and murdered Tayseer, but I had the choice, and I still have the choice, of whether to follow in the same direction.

Each day I live I refuse to become like those soldiers 15 years ago, and I choose to put aside the rage I worshiped as a teenager. I will always have this choice. It is a hard decision to abandon revenge, and an easy road to follow your feelings. Yet hatred begets hatred, and the same tools you use on others will be used on you. As a result, each day I must choose again to love and forgive those around me.

As humans, we try to rationalize our hatred. In our minds we demonize the enemy, and discredit their humanity. This is the lie that fires the conflict between Israel and Palestine.

Maybe I will never see the world restored to perfect humanity, but I still feel obligated to believe that the tools for peace are not tools of violence and hatred. More than this, I feel obligated to use my pain to spread peace, rather than using it to fuel a hatred that would have eventually consumed me. I believe we are all obligated to do our best to create peace, and not wait until it hits home. After all, there is no good war or bad peace.

Now I am 25 years old and co-host a radio show on Radio All for Peace (www.allforpeace.org), a unique Jerusalem-based radio station broadcasting in Hebrew, Arabic, and English, aimed at a wide audience amongst all people, and providing messages of peace, cooperation, mutual understanding, coexistence, and hope. My co-host, Sharon, also lost her brother and we both belong to the Parents Circle and speak for the forum, Israeli Palestinian Bereaved Families, where we work for appeasement in order to stop violence. Our show, "Changing Direction," highlights those who chose not to avenge or revenge, but to talk, accept, and work for a different future. The program is in the two languages—which requires the patience (to listen to the translation in the other language) but that mirrors the patience required for appeasement. As I say about this format, it bring "a new soul and a new message, even equality and almost revolutionary."

I am the head recruiter for a social organization that places young volunteers in housing for the elderly, orphanages, and schools that draws from groups of Christian youth and universities in Bethlehem, Abu-Dis, and Jerusalem, including the Hebrew University. I also travel to speak to schools and groups in different places. In 2005 I was a delegate on a tour of the Untied States, with Ya'ara Shapira, who had also lost her brother, speaking at gatherings sponsored by Meretz, an organization that fosters peace in the region and also a political party in Israel. We came to the United States to listen and to reach the hearts of people. Our message was: Instead of picking a side, be pro-solution.

We go to houses and talk to people about losing our loved ones and about mourning and not holding grudges. We go to schools and police groups and even to the West Bank. Sometimes I get frustrated that my own side is more hesitant to heal, but I am glad that the program is growing more on the Palestinian side.

We celebrate holy days together. I get invited to many people's homes. And I get many e-mails. One young man in Ramallah, Hassan, was in jail and when he got out, I took Jews to his home, so they could learn about each other and not harbor hatred. We are supposed to be enemies but we can relate to each other.

It is easier to shut down and let your emotions lead you. To turn is hard. Be aware there is another direction. My parents even joined the Parents Circle a year ago. My mother cried. For the first time, she knew that Israelis felt as she did. Now she regrets feeling good when Israelis hurt. My whole family has joined. We can make a difference. Break the circle that never ends, when you say, "He killed my brother. I will kill his brother." This is not the way. Tons of brothers have died and we have not achieved anything. I read something once that is inspiring, that said "Press for the end of the Madness." When you treat people as human beings, we will find solutions.

With all the hurt I have, I want to make it better.

Like Aziz, Ya'ara—a 21-year-old Israeli young woman—also lost her brother because of the conflict. In 2005, she traveled in the United States with Aziz to talk about her experience and her work with the Parents Circle-Families Forum (PCFF). This is her story in her own words.

A Lost Beloved Brother: Ya'ara's Story

My story begins 21 years ago. My name is Ya'ara. I am 21 years old and I am from Israel.

Since the moment I came to the world I had the best family in the world. They took care perfectly of every aspect of my life. They surrounded me with love and care, and nurtured all of my wishes and desires for the future. But those desires were a result of the education I received. Obviously my education came from schools and all kinds of after-school activities, but I had one major educator. One major mentor. That was my brother—Rotem, who was three years older than me. And at the age of three, I think he was expecting a young brother, not a sister. For sure he raised me as a boy—he taught me to love soccer—how to play it and love it, and the right team, and the same about basketball and all types of sports. I even behaved and acted like a boy, not a girl. But I acted like a special boy—as special as he was.

Rotem was my protector; In fourth grade when girls would get teased by boys, he decided to walk around the school and make sure that no girls got hit. And he was an unbelievable humanitarian, and life lover person. He adored any form of being on the planet and because of that he hated the way they treat each other. He conveyed those beliefs and feelings to me.

When Rotem was 18 years old he was supposed to go to the army like every other boy and girl in Israel. He wanted to go to a fighting unit. I couldn't understand it—how can that gentle soul hold a gun? How can he shoot at a person? I tried to ask him all these questions and more. I tried to tell him to go to a nonfighting unit (a sort of army units which you do all kinds of important works that do not include actual fighting). He refused. He said that he can't let other people do what he is supposed to do. He said he can't be against something he never really tried. He said he'd have to try. So he did. He joined a fighting unit—as a combat engineer, and was supposed to do four months of boot camp, as combat training. During those four months, he found that he could not shoot. He was a great solder in all other aspects, but he never shot his gun. He was supposed to practice a lot on his shooting, at ranges, but he couldn't form the act of using this vehicle—a gun. Luckily, he had amazing commanders who allowed him not to shoot and still finish his training. At the end of his training, he was supposed to transfer to a nonfighting position in that unit.

It was at the summer of 2000. I was between my 10th and 11th grade. I went with some friends of mine for a vacation in the Kineret. My second day there, on the beach, my best friend came calling me in a sort of hysteria. He said my mother is there. That it looks bad, like something is wrong. I started walking and inside I already knew what happened. I came standing in front of my shocked mother who just said the words, "Rotem is dead" and started weeping. That moment something inside of me died with him.

My brother had committed suicide. The only real time he ever shot was at himself. He left a note explaining everything—telling all the people how much he loved us all. How it had nothing to do with us, only with him—he did not belong here. He could not bear the pain of feeling all the sorrow of the world. He felt every pain of every person as if it was his own. As long as there is so much violence and mistreating in this world, he could not be a part of this kind of world. I found it ironic that he would forever stay a part of a system that is a symbol of everything that was hard for him on this planet. He was bound to stay a soldier forever.

In his letter he asked us to look at his paintings and poems. We knew he was a musician and artist. But when we started to look, we found things we never knew existed. All those things that had one cry, one request in them—stop this unhuman behavior. All the paintings, all the poems said, stop the violence, suffering and the wrongs, start acting in patience, with justice and compassion to one anther. These sayings got into my heart. I found a reason to live. I found I had a mission—a legacy—I had to do whatever I can, from that day on to see that these things will happen in the world. I thought to myself that I have to stop the next person from feeling this way. I felt I have to wake up everyday and see what I can do to make it somewhat better. Since that day I found many, many more reasons to choose life. I wasn't somewhat dead anymore.

One day, about a year and a half later, I found a way to pursue and make into action all the things my brother wrote and dreamt about. I met a group, called Parents Circle-Families Forum. Since then I have served as a counselor in the Parents Circle's Summer Camp for Israeli and Palestinian children and youth of bereaved families as part of my national service, and am involved in the daily work of the organization. In this group are people that felt the same way I did—they shared the same pain of losing the ones we love and the same notion that no one should be feeling this pain. They knew that there is nothing in the world worth having this pain. They do everything they can to spread acceptance and reconciliation between the two people here in this conflict we are in. Their so-called revenge is to be an example of tolerance toward the other side of the conflict.

The day I joined their battle I knew my brother was smiling down on me.

Healing from the Loss

Aziz and Ya'ara are two of the many young and adult members of the Parents Circle-Families Forum. They promote reconciliation as an alternative to fear, hatred, and revenge that plague their region, through various imaginative projects and programs that communicate, educate, and inspire more moderate approaches to peace building. Members of the Parents Circle-Families Forum have chosen to channel their grief into the pursuit of reconciliation and understanding. They demonstrate that even though they have paid the highest price in this conflict, they can acknowledge the other's pain and humanity rather than seek revenge for their losses.

Aziz and Ya'ara speak to individuals and organizations in their region and across the world. They held a tour in American campuses sponsored by UPZ. Other representatives of our group have spoken for the Committee on Mental Health for NGOs at the United Nations. They recounted the story of another member of PCFF, Robi Damelin. Robi lost her beloved son, David, on March 3, 2002. He was killed by a sniper while doing his reserve duties. David was doing his master's degree in the philosophy of education at Tel-Aviv University, was teaching potential social leaders, and was active in the peace movement.

The Parents Circle sees itself as a bridge between the Israeli and Palestinian civil societies and is accepted as such by the majorities of both sides. We believe a reconciliation process must be established by the people and for the people, apart from any political and national process, for without it any agreement will not be sustainable. Some people are afraid to get to know "the other" because if you know the person behind the stigma, you cannot hate them. They have the same blood color and listen to the same music. The long-term goal of the organization is reconciliation, to this end we draw on academic and grassroots experience from around the world, such as the work done in South Africa with the Truth and Reconciliation Commission. If the parents in our group can reconcile and forgive, then surely we can be an example to the rest of the world.

In both societies, bereaved families hold a unique authority and are highly respected, and therefore, sharing sessions in schools and organizations has special significance. Recently we managed to have a few of these sessions with Palestinian militants and with Israeli settlers. We are trying to reach out to extremists; it is harder than with the mainstream public, but possible.

A few members of our group, including Robi Damelin, an Israeli bereaved mother, and Ali Abu Awwad, a Palestinian bereaved brother and our Palestinian project manager, were profiled in the movie *Encounter Point* by Just Vision, about Israelis and Palestinians working together for peace.

Parents Circle Projects

Hello Shalom, Hello Salaam ("Hello Peace")

"Yes, there is someone to talk to" is the media slogan of our "Hello Peace" project—launched in October 2002 as an innovative free chat-line and phone system enabling individual Israelis and Palestinians to speak to each other directly through a technologically moderated toll-free system. "Hello Peace" proves that many Israelis and Palestinians are willing to engage with one another. With more than 900,000 phone calls made since the project's start, it has been an overwhelming success and is likely to have reached the broadest constituencies of Palestinians and Israelis ever engaged in a peace project during this conflict.

While not all calls are full of love and harmony, "Hello Peace" uncovers the lack of trust and empathy in an effort to encourage dialogue and humanize the conflict—in order to ultimately dispel the popular myth that "there is no partner for peace" and encourage deep social change in both societies. The project has received considerable media coverage in Israeli, Palestinian, and international media.

Lectures in High Schools

During the past few years, PCFF has developed an extensive educational program intended for high school students. Bereaved Forum members from both sides share their stories and conduct discussions in classes, aimed to root peace and reconciliation. Lectures allow teenagers to witness the possibility of choosing reconciliation over revenge, and get acquainted with the other side's fears and needs.

In just six months—from January until June—in 2005, our members conducted more than 650 lectures before some 20,000 youth and adults, Israelis and Palestinians, all over the country. That means they reached a significant percentage of all 16- to 18-year-old Israeli and Palestinian youth. Through these sessions, many of the student participants had the opportunity to meet a bereaved parent or family member from "the other side" for the first time. The vigorous debates during the lectures and students' written feedback attest that the lectures are a highly effective tool introducing the youth to tolerance and reconciliation as means to solving the conflict, and that our members are effective promoters of these views. By describing their own personal loss and their unwillingness to seek revenge, they inspire students to begin the long process of transforming their own legitimate feelings of suspicion, fear, and hatred toward the other side—stark realities of the Israeli-Palestinian conflict.

Youth Internet Project: Arabic-Hebrew Website

Our pilot Youth Internet Project is an ongoing activity as an adjunct to our encounter dialogue meetings between Palestinian and Israeli schools. This project runs a special blog software, allowing each participant to make personal postings on the site, write about themselves, their families, and hobbies, and share thoughts and photos.

The second stage of this Internet site starts a dialogue between participants, initially within a single nation, and then a binational dialogue. At the same time, the participants go through a series of single-nation seminars preparing them for a joint seminar.

Israeli-Palestinian Student Seminar

A three-day seminar for 41 selected high school students (20 Israelis and 21 Palestinians) took place in 2005. Out of the long list of schools who have hosted our dialogue meetings, we approached the Beit Safafa Palestinian High School and the Israeli Ankory High School in Ashdod. We had previously met all

11th- and 12th-grade students in both schools, and after our initial program, offered them a continual encounter activity with "the other side," facilitated by our PCFF members.

A teacher from Ankory High School in Ashdod, says about the program:

> Three days together—and many things changed: Many stigmas broken, many prejudices removed from both sides' minds, having been found baseless. We spent the time trying to get acquainted, to listen, and to try to understand each other. Accepting the other and understanding them are tasks not easily achieved. We managed to touch the most sensitive and highly charged issues of both sides and we are grateful for having gone through this because it was very beneficial.

Public and Media Campaigns

Our public awareness campaigns to promote the values of reconciliation, tolerance, and peace between Israelis and Palestinians appear on billboards, in newspapers, and on radio and television. One dramatic public display that drew considerable media attention was the Coffin Display in Tel-Aviv and at the United Nations in New York, and the Peace Tents held in Tel-Aviv and Gaza.

In another campaign that drew considerable media attention, Israeli PCFF members donated blood at a Palestinian hospital while Palestinian members did the same in an Israeli blood bank. An Israeli father who lost his daughter in a suicide bombing in Jerusalem said, "It is much easier to donate blood than to shed it in the ground for nothing."

Summer Camp for Israeli and Palestinian Children

The 2005 summer camp was almost cancelled because it was coincidentally scheduled for just the days of the Israeli disengagement from Gaza. Parents were worried and all but one of the permits came through only at the last minute. The 10- to 16-year-old Israeli and Palestinian youngsters of bereaved families spent four days together, rafting on the Jordan River, sailing in the Sea of Galilee, and visiting Haifa. The goal of the camps, started in 2003, is to create an environment for each child to begin to know "the other side," and to see themselves as an important part of the reconciliation process. The schedule promotes teamwork, creates shared experiences, and allows the youngsters to practice reconciliation, in hopes that over time they will see themselves as emissaries of reconciliation.

Yigal Elhanan, an 11-year-old Israeli camper, lost his sister in a suicide bombing: "It was annoying when people tried to console me, because I shut myself off." Yigal said: "I didn't want to listen to anyone, I was stuck in this frame of mind that they [the Palestinians] are all out to kill us . . . (now) I think that killing one another won't solve anything. Us kids, we'd bet ter start talking with one another before all the grownups die out there." Fellow camper, 13-year old Palestinian Urud Abu Awad, lost her uncle. "I lost my uncle, but Yigal lost his sister," she said. "He lost someone much closer to him. I can't even imagine that . . . such a person [a suicide bomber] should ask himself 'why do I do it?' Is losing someone dear a good enough reason? The Israelis are losing people dear to them too."

Promoting Reconciliation in Adult and Academic Communities

Our pilot project of Promoting Reconciliation in Adult Communities took place in several dozen communities in Palestine and Israel, supported by the Danish Foreign Ministry. We met a diversity of audiences. Our contact and involvement in the academic world has grown significantly as well, as we held dialogue-encounters at the Haifa, Tel Aviv, and Bar-Ilan Universities in Israel, and at the Palestinian Bethlehem and A-Najah Universities, as well as meetings with student associations in the southern West Bank. The academic staff in one Israeli university decided that they will include the meetings with our representatives as a regular part of their syllabus.

During 2005 we continued meetings with specific and unique audiences, and combining different interest groups. For example, in Israel, we convened with army officers and representatives from the military administration, senior citizens, school drop-out teenagers, various ethnic groups such as Ethiopian new immigrants, religious kibbutz members, and others. We also convened meetings with Palestinian government officials, the Shuhada El-Aksa militia group in Nablus, Deheishe refugee camp residents, women's organizations' representatives in Hevron, Palestinian rural communities (Dura, Idna, Sawia), and others.

The Voice of Peace: FM 107.2

The Families Forum produces an innovative bilingual radio program that is broadcast twice a week on the new "Voice of Peace." A one-hour show is co-hosted by a young Israeli woman named Sharon Mishiker with Aziz Abu Sara, a young Palestinian man, where they interview forum members, report about our events and activities, talk with students and participants in our workshops, and interview supporters and sponsors. Playing multicultural music adds joy to the program.

Delegations and Conferences

Since we believe that the public in both Israel and Palestine, with the aid of civil societies in the region and in the world, can produce substantial pressure on the leaderships in the region, the American and European leaderships, and the Arab states to reinvigorate the peace process, we lobby toward this goal. Our delegations meet with various religious and lay groups, institutions, personalities, government figures, and municipalities to spread our message and raise support for our work and vision.

Forum members have participated in conferences, seminars, and lectures in various places around the world: East and West Coast of the United States, Italy, Germany, France, and others. The growing number of invitations we receive is indicative of the interest and support that has been generated for the unique position and message of the forum within the Israeli-Palestinian conflict.

One of our member mothers sums it up well: "The path of reconciliation is better and shorter than the path of suffering and bloodshed."

Acknowledgment

"Ya'ara's story" by Jennifer Friedlin. *Marie Claire* magazine: March 2005. Reprinted with permission of *Marie Claire* magazine.

CHAPTER 11

COMPASSIONATE LISTENING WITH ISRAELIS AND PALESTINIANS

Leah Green

Sitting in a settlement in the West Bank, I am listening to an Israeli woman—the daughter of a Holocaust survivor. Her mother carried her across European borders in the dark of night to the "Promised Land" of her Jewish ancestors—the land of the prophets where she now lives. It's her misfortune that this land is situated in the disputed West Bank. A future peace agreement with the Palestinians or a unilateral withdrawal by her own government will likely prevent her from staying in her beloved community. I can feel her love for the land and it's heartbreaking.

Now I am listening to a Palestinian—a leader of Hamas—in Gaza. His rage is palpable, as he tells me about witnessing the murder of his father and other relatives as a young boy, and about how he was tortured by the Israelis as a young man. He still grieves from his arrest and imprisonment on the eve of the birth of his first child—a son he didn't hold for the first five years of life. I empathize with his feelings and think of times that I've imagined revenge for incidents trivial in comparison, and failed in forgiveness.

These stories are typical of ones I hear from Israelis and Palestinians on both sides of the conflict—experiences that led to my founding The Compassionate Listening Project. Our reconciliation efforts are based on the ideas of Gene Knudsen Hoffman, a Quaker peace maker who began introducing her ideas to the peace community 25 years ago (Hoffman & Green, 2001; Manousos, 2003). Hoffman's thinking was influenced by Thich Nhat Hanh, a Buddhist monk who challenges peacemakers to stay available to those on all sides of a conflict.

I've led Compassionate Listening training delegations for North Americans to Israel and Palestine since 1990. Carol Hwoschinsky joined me in 1996 in developing a training component for our delegations. Participants are trained to listen respectfully to people on all sides of the conflict, and to connect with the humanity of each person we encounter My goal in the Middle East is to build the international constituency for peace while offering a practical tool for conflict resolution on the ground.

The fundamental premise of Compassionate Listening is that every party to a conflict is suffering and that every act of violence comes from an unhealed wound. Our job as peacemakers is to hear the grievances of all parties and tell each side about the humanity and the suffering of the other. We listen with our "spiritual ear," to discern and acknowledge the partial truth in everyone—particularly those with whom we disagree. We put aside our own positions and help the speakers tell their story, stretching our capacity to be present to another's pain.

The first step in Compassionate Listening is to offer the gift of nonjudgmental listening to another person. We center ourselves, and bring an open mind and a loving heart (Hwoschinsky, 2001). We reflect back the facts, feelings, and values that we hear, always checking to see if we are hearing accurately; we do not interrupt, tell our own stories, or interpret what we've heard.

Compassionate Listening is not about agreement. We each have our own window on "the truth" and we validate people's rights to their unique perspectives. We do not argue, judge, or criticize. We do not offer advice or try to solve their problems. We ask open-ended questions that encourage the speaker to deepen in their story. We offer spaciousness, curiosity, and empathy.

We've learned that it is easy to listen to people with whom we agree—it's when we listen to those with whom we disagree, those we hold as "the other" that listening becomes a challenge. At times, we listeners get triggered from hearing something that we disagree with. In those moments, we practice techniques to manage our internal responses, and to bring ourselves back to connect with the humanity of the person we're listening to.

Granted we are not always successful in our own eyes. Sometimes a participant will succumb to their triggered state and make a challenging statement or a defensive remark. But Israelis and Palestinians alike appreciate our intention, which seems to be most important.

Listening with empathy and understanding to the heart of another human being builds trust quickly. Such listening is deeply healing for the one speaking and also for the listener.

Compassionate Listening is a powerful precursor to dialogue. When I have listened to someone, and he or she feels respected and understood, he or she often reciprocates with a desire to hear my viewpoint. Then, dialogue can begin. If dialogue is attempted too early, it can be unproductive, with each participant defending his or her own position and very little listening taking place. In Compassionate Listening, we learn to listen and speak from the heart. Both require practice.

When we sit with Israelis and Palestinians and hear their stories, regardless of where they fall on the political spectrum, it becomes possible to affirm their humanity at the deepest level. I have even found compassion for extremists on both sides of the conflict. This does not mean that I condone their actions, but when I hear their life circumstances, I can, at times, imagine myself making the same choices.

In the last decade, more than 450 American participants have listened to thousands of Israelis and Palestinians with the intention of discovering the human being behind the stereotype. Participants in Compassionate Listening training delegations come from all backgrounds and walks of life, and have a genuine interest in the experience, hopes, dreams, and suffering of Israelis and Palestinians from all sides. The delegations have resulted in an extensive network of informed leaders—including many religious leaders—across the United States, who stand for both peoples. They learn to put their preconceived opinions aside and listen to people they may previously have been too angry with or too afraid of. They learn to hold more of the complexities of the conflict. Many participants move into more of a leadership role in their communities upon their return. Their efforts within the United States are valuable, as this conflict continues to create harsh divisions among religious and political groups, on college campuses, and within the peace movement.

No one has declined a listening session with us. I contact people I read about or meet by chance who are doing courageous work. I contact others who have never had anything to do with reconciliation work, a friend's nephew, a colleague's neighbor ... It's not difficult to locate people in Israel and Palestine. From our work over the past 16 years, we have friends from all sectors of society and call on their help in setting up listening sessions and connecting us to new friends. We've sat with people in homes, offices, streets, refugee camps, the Israeli prime minister's office, the Palestinian president's office, and on military bases. We've listened to settlers, sheikhs, mayors, rabbis, students, Bedouin, peace activists, and extremists. I even brought an all-Jewish delegation to listen to Sheikh Ahmad Yassin, the spiritual founder of Hamas who was assassinated by the Israeli military in 2004. Listening to those we believe to be our enemies is not just a radical idea, but a pragmatic one. I truly believe that political solutions can come much more easily after the process that teaches us to see the humanity in others. How will political solutions come if people don't know each other, can't see the humanity of "the other," and can't discuss solutions together? Every voice is needed at the table, and listening is the first step in the relationship building process.

The trust that we've built with Israelis and Palestinians over the years has allowed us to bring them together for Compassionate Listening trainings. At times these trainings have been the first opportunity for each to meet the other on a human level.

"Hassan" participated in a Compassionate Listening training in 2002. At that time, he felt he had no future. He was three years out of high school, and very smart. He dreamed of using his skills for his people and wanted to become an attorney. But he was living under occupation, without any opportunity to study law or to find meaningful work. He suffered the tragedies of other young men in the area—checkpoints, inability to travel, friends and family killed in the war, imprisonment, and little hope of employment or the ability to marry. He began to fantasize about violence against Israelis. It's hard to imagine the degree of hopelessness he felt about his life and his future.

Through a colleague, he learned of our Compassionate Listening training in Bethlehem. The Bethlehem workshop created a safe and loving environment where Hassan's story was deeply heard. He learned communication and peace-building skills such as cultivating compassion for himself and those he considered his enemies, listening and speaking from the heart, and learning to find shared values underneath seemingly divergent positions. Hassan decided to enroll in our advanced training for Jews and Palestinians together. Unable to get a permit to come to Jerusalem for the training, he risked arrest and imprisonment as he snuck around the Israeli checkpoint to attend the training. Listening to the suffering of Israeli Jews for the first time and having his own suffering deeply heard and acknowledged by Israeli Jews for the first time, Hassan felt his humanity was restored. Through the structured exercises and small group work, Hassan was able to establish a profound sense of community and connection with people whom days before he had imagined were his enemies. For the first time in many years, he felt a sense of hope for himself and for the world. He began to get involved with positive initiatives, including a Palestinian peace center in East Jerusalem, where he is now employed. Two years later Hassan told me: "I was on a path to violence, but thanks to The Compassionate Listening Project I now have a pathway to peace, internally and externally."

Underlying the conflict, both Israelis and Palestinians are victims; both are suffering, both are wounded. While Israelis find it difficult to see Palestinians as victims, Palestinians find it hard to see Israelis' sense of vulnerability and fear. They see Israel as the fourth largest military power and experience the direct effects of Israel's military might. But if they had the opportunity to listen to Israelis as we have, they'd hear Israelis' tremendous sense of powerlessness and fear.

On their part, Israelis failed to see how patient Palestinians had been with the Oslo peace process that was supposed to lead to an easing of the occupation and statehood. After the Oslo handshake, the situation for Palestinians declined significantly. The second Palestinian Intifada (uprising) that began in 2000 was a revolt against the ongoing Israeli occupation. As Palestinians watch the continual confiscation of their lands to settlement expansion and the Wall, they are enraged and feel they have nothing more to lose. Suicide missions, while an expression of utter rage, hopelessness, and revenge, only serve to further alienate and retraumatize Israelis. Both are locked in the cycle of violence.

In all our years of listening to Israelis and Palestinians, we've learned that all are suffering, wounded, and want to live with security, justice, and peace. We've learned that people want to take risks for peace, and will take risks, if given an opportunity to really be heard.

References

Hoffman, G., & Green, L. (2001). *Compassionate listening: An exploratory sourcebook about conflict transformation*. Retrieved from www.newconversations.net.

Hwoschinsky, C. (2001). *Listening with the heart*. Indianola, WA: The Compassionate Listening Project.

Manousos, A. (2003). *Compassionate listening and other writings by Gene Knudsen Hoffman*. Torrence, CA: Friends Bulletin.

CHAPTER 12

Beacon for Peace in the Promised Land: Transforming Palestinian-Israeli Relationships with Nonviolent Communication

Hagit Lifshitz, Arnina Kashtan, and Miki Kashtan

Our cultural conditioning often leads us into the habitual game of responding to events and situations with judgments, blame, labeling, and demands. This familiar approach preserves and reinforces the experience of painful alienation among human beings, as it tends to create fear, guilt, and shame. Continuing to respond in these ways is unlikely to get us what we deeply want. We all pay a price in the long run when our needs are met at others' expense.

As an alternative, Nonviolent (Compassionate) Communication (NVC) helps us to act and encourage others to behave out of choice and caring, thus leading to give and receive from our hearts. Instead of focusing on thoughts, judgments, and opinions, we look for the core human feelings and needs that are alive in us and in others. NVC practice rests on the assumption that we all share the same feelings and needs: tenderness, closeness, understanding, safety, the desire to contribute, to matter to others, to be valued and loved. Arguments and fights arise mostly out of our different strategies to meet these needs.

This chapter gives an overview of the principles and steps in a unique communication skill that facilitates understanding, caring, and "heart-centered" interaction, and an example of how the skills in this technique are being applied with Palestinians and Israelis.

Marshall Rosenberg developed the practices of NVC in the 1960s in an attempt to support communities in creating peaceful desegregation. Soon the vast potential applications of this powerful technique led to a rapid spread across the globe.

Rosenberg has run workshops with people in the Middle East of various political persuasions (Palestinians and Israelis, secular and religious Jews, Israelis on the political left and right), and used NVC to help participants express feelings regarding the highly contested issues of the Occupied Territories.

In one interaction, a settler was willing to reexamine living in the West Bank if she could be truly listened to (Kashtan, 2002); in another, a Palestinian man at a mosque at Dheisheh Refugee Camp near Bethlehem went from calling Rosenberg names to inviting him home for a Ramadan dinner (Rosenberg, 2003).

Hundreds of thousands of people in dozens of countries and from all walks of life, including many professionals in the fields of mediation and conflict resolution, therapy and counseling, and group facilitation have been trained in NVC. Currently about 200 certified trainers offer NVC in 35 countries, with several in Israel and in the Palestinian territory.

The practice of applying Nonviolent Communication in the service of social activism is based on a combination of practical considerations and deep spiritual values. On the practical level, we listen with empathy to those with whose positions we disagree. This increases the chances that they will want to listen to us.

On the spiritual plane, listening with empathy to others is one way of putting into practice the fundamental values of compassion and nonviolence. Underlying the willingness to persist in identifying and attending to everyone's needs is a deep well of trust in the abundance of the universe and in the fundamentally benign nature of human needs. Thus, when we approach a conflict from the NVC perspective, we aim to connect with the underlying needs, and look together for ways to attend to them as equal to ours, and in harmony with all parties involved in the conflict.

The Nonviolent Communication dialogue entails four clearly defined steps. The first step requires transforming judgments into *Observation*. Expressions of what we see, or hear, or notice are separated from thoughts and evaluations. For example, one would say, "I see/hear/notice that . . . " instead of starting with what the other person did, which would likely stimulate defensiveness.

Steps 2 and 3 require expressing fully and accurately *Feelings* and *Needs* that are alive in relation to those observations. These two steps require our awareness and expression about the reasons for our feelings, which are our needs that are either met or unmet. When they are met, we might feel happy, satisfied, relaxed, or calm; and when they are unmet, we might feel frustrated, uneasy, in pain, or disappointed. Trainings use lists of possible feelings and needs to help participants identify them.

Step 4 of the NVC dialogue is making a *Request*. Here we offer to the other person our concrete "doable" suggestion as to the way she or he can contribute to our well-being and assist us in fulfilling our needs.

As the listener, we can open our heart with "empathic listening" to the other person. We listen carefully to the *Feelings* and the *Needs* of the person who talks, no matter how she or he expresses herself or himself, and reflect them back, in an attempt to check if we understand her or him fully and accurately. Such compassionate/empathic listening makes it possible to maintain our connection with the humanness of the other. This process often gives rise to surprising, creative results of mutual good will and generosity by all sides involved, even in previously insurmountable conflicts.

According to Rosenberg, use of language can reinforce "enemy images" of others. When we refer to corporate executives as "profiteers," our use of language implies greed; when we refer to lower-level managers as "bureaucrats," we imply uncaring; when we refer to people fighting for an opposing cause as "terrorists," we imply inhumanity. Learning to practice empathy requires being able to recognize in others' actions fears and longings similar to our own, regardless of their actions.

The use of NVC does not require that the persons with whom we are communicating be literate in NVC or even motivated to relate to us compassionately. If we stay with the principles of NVC, with the sole intention to give and receive compassionately, and do everything we can to let others know this is our only motive, they will join us in the process and eventually we will be able to respond compassionately to one another (Center for Nonviolent Communication, 2006). If we want to engage in social activism based on mutuality, trust, compassion, and nonviolence, we are likely to find that social change requires changing ourselves within while working on changing external structures. The experience of applying NVC in our daily life and in our social change work makes transformation possible.

Presenting the use of NVC in the context of the Palestinian-Israeli conflict is a unique opportunity to witness its healing power at its best, since this conflict is considered as perhaps one of the most difficult and complicated situations known. Some even consider it "impossible" to transform.

The following excerpt from a dialogue serves as a powerful example of just such transformation. It takes place during an NVC training for Israeli and Palestinian peace activists who are preparing a joint humanitarian project in a Palestinian village (referred to here as "Village B").

In this training, dramatic moments occurred when Israelis and Palestinians played their own or each other's role in an effort to transcend the pain preventing them from hearing each other with an open heart. A Palestinian man took the Israeli person's side and expressed his fears and worries as if he were Israeli. Similarly, Israelis took the Palestinian side. All were moved to express hidden fears, wishes, and hopes and be understood. This resulted in a sense of partnership, friendship, and closeness.

The facilitator is Hagit Lifshitz, the first author. Israeli participants are members of Middleway, a peace organization operating in Israel, and the Palestinians are residents of Palestinian Village B. Besides role-playing, other tools include verbal interactions to clarify needs and feelings, and to guide the participants through the steps of the NVC process.

The training focused on giving the participants an opportunity to experience the effect of healing energy present when compassionate listening and compassionate expressions are put into practice. It aimed at allowing the participants to recognize and feel the transformation, and at encouraging them to trust this process and make efforts to learn it and use it. It also aimed at showing them the concepts and the basic four steps of the process.

Phase 1: Exercising Expression of One's Feelings and Needs, Instead of Judgments, Accusations, and Demands

The facilitator first lets the participants[1] talk freely as they would normally, and then helps them reframe their expression to avoid judgmental expressions or arguments. She then guides them in realizing and transforming their speech into expressions of their feelings and needs.

WASEEM (A PALESTINIAN MAN) SAYS: Well, you Israelis come and go in our village and you say: "Oh, this is bad, this is woeful, this is unbelievable" about our poor condition and then you go back to your places and do nothing. Are we monkeys in the zoo? It may be better if you stay at your places and leave us alone!

FACILITATOR (GIVING INSTRUCTIONS TO WASEEM):   Say more of your feelings and more of your needs. What is important to you? What is painful underneath the anger?

WASEEM: I am very frustrated and disappointed with you Dorit, because I wish you used your power to stop the unjust occupation. I feel helpless and confused. I wish you realized what it means to be under occupation. I wish you knew how desperate I feel as I cannot take my child to the doctor, the soldiers refused to let my wife go through the fence when she urgently needed to go to the hospital, we have no work! I wish you could even imagine what it is like!

DORIT (AN ISRAELI WOMAN):   But what can we do? At least we try to do something for you! You—the Palestinians—want us to do the impossible! You don't understand that we cannot control the army and the government and change their policy toward you!

FACILITATOR TO DORIT: Speak about your feelings and your needs! Focus on your heart, not on your thoughts and judgments. Speak about what you appreciate and realize . . .

DORIT TO WASEEM: I hear your pain and despair. I hear a deep wish of yours that I and my friends will realize and imagine what many-sided suffering you go through every day. Is that it . . . ?

WASEEM: *Na'am* ("Yes," in Arabic). I wish you could be with us and witness our suffering.

DORIT: I feel so sad and helpless. I wish I knew what to do. I'd like to help and be there for you.

WASEEM: You hear me. I feel relieved and grateful.

DORIT: I am glad to hear this. I also wish to say something else to you. Would you be willing to hear this now?

WASEEM: Yes!

DORIT: I also need your acknowledgment and appreciation for what we *do* in this matter to better your situation in many ways. I wish we could work together to realize what we could do. I need your cooperation and help.

WASEEM: Oh, Yeah! I wish we spoke more in this way. I feel more hope and courage this way.

In this process, the participants have experienced and witnessed the effective power of staying connected with and expressing fully one's feelings and needs, as an alternative to accusations, demands, and analysis.

The facilitator now guides the participants to the next step of the process: the practice of compassionate listening to another person, however challenging it might be.

Phase 2: Exercising Empathic-Compassionate Listening to Another Person: Facilitator's Demonstration

In this second phase, the facilitator demonstrates empathic-compassionate listening. She listens to a participant who expresses his opinions, judgments, and expectations. She avoids any "answers," "arguments," "disagreements," or "agreements." Instead, she tries to focus, guess, realize, and reframe the participant's feelings and needs, willing to get his consent for her reframing. She keeps on doing that until the participant is ready for the next step.

YA'IR (AN ISRAELI MAN): (Upset and skeptical, he is reacting to the interaction between Dorit and Waseem earlier.) In real life, no one speaks like Dorit did to Waseem. It's artificial. They—the Palestinians—should have known that we, Israelis, have our own needs and feelings! Why should we be those who listen to them? This is impossible and unfair! It also makes them inferior to us!

FACILITATOR (FOCUSES ON HIS FEELINGS AND NEEDS): So, Ya'ir, is it your need to be heard, understood, and appreciated by your Palestinian partner, without judgments, analysis, arguments, answers? Do you wish to *get* this kind of listening from him in the same way you *give* it to him?

YA'IR: Exactly! I can speak this way, but it will not be true, and it's unfair, because the situation is more complicated than that.

FACILITATOR: So, you would like to speak all your truth, to share your deep feelings and needs and be assured that he is willing to do the same with you? You need the certainty that he is willing to explore with you your perspective empathically?

YA'IR: Yeah! I don't know if Waseem and other Palestinians are able and willing to give me that.

FACILITATOR: So, you need their confirmation that they want to do it and you need their support and cooperation for going deeper and talking about all the aspects of the situation from your perspective too?

YA'IR: Well, I realize that they have their own perspective, and I am willing to give them the same attention that I want them to give me. I believe this is important, if we are all brave enough and want to work together.

FACILITATOR: So, you have faith in such a dialogue and you wish your Palestinian colleagues would have faith in this too and would be willing to join you in this journey?

YA'IR: Yes. I wish they wanted to do this with me. I want to invite you, guys, to this kind of exploration as equals.

In this process the participants have witnessed a consistent focus on the speaker's feelings and needs, regardless of his way of speech. The facilitator kept guessing and suggesting to him the feelings, the needs, and the wishes he had and asked for his reaction and confirmation. This helped the speaker deepen his reflection on his own truth and express more accurately and widely what he had to express. This process also allowed the participants to understand more deeply and open up their own hearts to the speaker.

Now the facilitator guides the participants to the next step of their training, to practice compassionate listening as was demonstrated by the facilitator earlier.

Phase 3: Exercising Empathic-Compassionate Listening to Another Person: the Participants Practice

The facilitator now invites participants to practice compassionate listening. Ya'ir, who has just experienced *getting* compassionate listening, is now willing to *give* the same healing experience to his Palestinian friends. Then Abdullah, a Palestinian man, is encouraged to play the role of the Israeli woman and express what he realizes are her fears and needs, as if he were her.

It often happens that people's generosity and good will arise spontaneously after receiving such nonjudgmental deep listening. Their hearts open up and they are more capable of and willing to *give* from their hearts. This phenomenon encourages us to trust that the more we *offer* our compassionate understanding first to the other human being, the more likely it is that we will also *receive* it from that person's heart.

Moreover, as a result of this process during this training, Palestinian and Israeli participants felt inspired to take the role of the other, and express deep hidden feelings and needs that otherwise would not be expressed or mentioned. The general atmosphere was trust, support, love, and sharing. Eventually, this led them to a joyful and creative ability for cooperation and work together.

YA'IR: OK, I'll try to do what you [the facilitator] have just demonstrated with me.

YA'IR (LOOKS AT HIS LIST OF FEELINGS AND NEEDS AND SAYS TO WASEEM): Are you feeling unhappy, because you want me, us—Israelis—to understand your perspective better?

ABDULLAH (A PALESTINIAN MAN, PRETENDING HE IS DORIT AND SPEAKING AS IF HE WERE HER): I wish I could speak to you [the Palestinians] about our fears too. I wish you'd be willing to listen to us about the horrors we had in Europe from the Nazis!

ABDULLAH (SPEAKING AGAIN AS HIMSELF, A PALESTINIAN MAN): I hear your fears from us, as Israelis. I remember Israelis talk about the Arab expressions like "We'll throw them to the sea."

Silence in the room . . .

ABDULLAH: I feel shame. I realize now that we, Arabs, express our own fears and tension when we say things like that. I wish we knew how to express our needs and feelings in a different way.

Abdullah was able and willing at this point to do two different things: He could empathize with the Israeli fear and acknowledge it, by expressing it in a compassionate way, and he could also reflect on, realize, and express his own feelings of shame and fear and his motivation to explore this more. Yet, another Palestinian woman in the group, Ebtisaam, expressed herself in a different way.

EBTISAAM: You, Israelis, made us your victims. You suffered in Europe and you come and take our land here and make us your victims and you want us all the time to understand your suffering, as if this makes you right and just. We, Palestinians, had done nothing to you, Jewish people. Why should we suffer because you suffered? Go settle your conflicts with the European people, not with us!

As the general ambience is of mutual acceptance and open hearts, Ebtisaam's expression invites other people to reflect on and explore deeper their own experiences.

DORIT: I am feeling now grateful to Ebtisaam for raising this point. I can now connect with my fears and my experience of being the victim. I am feeling identified with Ebtisaam. I am feeling such a pain and sorrow now, and sadness . . .

Tears come down her cheeks. . . . Silence in the room.

DORIT: Oh, this is so Tragic. Could we Ever Stop this Cycle?

Silence . . .

RINA (ANOTHER ISRAELI WOMAN):   I want to share with you all something. I now realize that in order to be able to give this kind of listening to another person, I need a lot of compassionate listening to myself first. Before I can *give* it, I need to *get* it, express all my own fears and needs and emotions until the transformation unfolds.

EBTISAAM: I wish we had more of this kind of energy before we start our project together. Let's fulfill our need for support, encouragement, and preparation and enhance our cooperation energy in such a way.

These excerpts from the Nonviolent Communication training for Palestinians and Israelis show that the most important component of this four-step process is the intention and the willingness to stay focused on feelings and needs, and on offering compassion as a way of transforming the situation into mutual giving and receiving from our hearts. This shows that it requires at least one person who is willing to stay with the sole intention to give and receive compassionately, and do everything she or he can to let others know this is her or his only motive. The others will join in the process and eventually everyone will be able to respond compassionately to one another. This "compassion in action" allows spontaneous and creative ways of reciprocal support and cooperation.

Note

1. Names are changed to protect participants' confidentiality.

References

Center for Nonviolent Communication. (2006). Retrieved May 11, 2006, from www. cnvc.org.

Kashtan, M. (2002, September–October). No enemies, no demands. *Tikkun, 17*(5), 73–74.

Rosenberg, M. (2003). *Nonviolent communication: A language of life* (2nd ed.). Encinitas, CA: Puddle Dancer Press.

CHAPTER 13

FOOD FOR THOUGHTS OF PEACE: JEWS AND PALESTINIANS SHARING DIALOGUE AND DINNER

Judy Kuriansky, Lionel Traubman, and Elizabeth Traubman

At any family meal, consider this food for thought: Put peace on the table. It's a principle behind the Living Room Dialogues, run by California couple Lionel and Elizabeth (Len and Libby) Traubman, to bring Palestinians and Jews together to share a good meal and their stories—for mutual understanding.

Says Len, dialogue co-founder and retired pediatric dentist, "Whenever we sit down together to break bread and to strive to meet the conditions for a good relationship, it is a sacred and blessed place." His wife, Libby, a retired clinical social worker, adds, "When we feed our stomachs together, we feed our souls."

That's exactly what happened one December holiday, when Len and Libby hosted eight Palestinians and eight Jews at their home to share holiday memories, music, candle-lighting—and of course, a celebratory dinner. The group included Holocaust survivors, Palestinian refugees, and Arab and Jewish college students.

"Picture Muslims, Christians, and Jews, Palestinians, Israelis, Jordanians, and Americans, all in a living room listening to each other, sharing hurts and hopes, and blessing one another," says Len. "It was the perfect reflection of the holiday spirit, and of our motto of 'neighbors forever' and 'for all peoples, equally'."

Of course, it all began and ended with a full table—with fruits, pita, hummus, fool mudammas, and lokum, a Middle Eastern candy also known as Turkish delight.

Four of the Arab students—Lama, Reem, Sara, and Mais, three from East Jerusalem and one from Jordan—were studying in America but unable to go home for Christmas or Ramadan. Having met two of them at a Family Peacemakers Camp, Len and Libby opened their home to the young women to create the feeling of family for the holiday.

The next morning, long-time dialogue partners and close friends Nahida and Adham Salem hosted the Holy Land visitors for breakfast. The Salems now live in Ramallah but come back to America to spend time with their children over the holiday. They met Libby 13 years ago when she came into their deli.

"Libby asked for some Middle Eastern food for a fundraiser and we agreed," Nahida explained. "It took Libby a year to convince me to be part of the dialogue group. Finally, I figured I can't lose anything by getting to know the 'enemy,' so I agreed. Then I showed up at one of their dinners with four of my Palestinian friends, and was Libby surprised!" Later Nahida convinced Jewish couples to join in.

For the morning gathering, Nahida prepared a feast of Middle Eastern foods: baklava, hummus, falafel, homemade bread, zatar, homemade cream cheese, and fava beans. She told Libby how to make the fava bean favorite dish: boil the beans with chopped garlic and parsley, add a little lemon juice. Top with olive oil and serve with pita bread.

Palestinians and Jews have a deep connection in their love of delicious food, Len explains, making meals an important part of the Living Room Dialogue— what the 30 Arabs and Jews have named their evenings of quality listening to personal narratives with a full range of emotions in the safety of each other's homes. Sharing life experiences, feelings, and culture inevitably leads to feeling shared humanity and equality. Each evening begins with food, ends with food, and contains finger-food throughout the meeting.

"Palestinians and Jews are both good cooks," says Libby. "You can say that the conflict is really between the kitchens—to see who can put out the best spread, be the most generous and creative." "The proof is in the pictures taken when the group first started and then twelve years later," says Len. "You can see how many of us have grown—in size as well as spiritually and emotionally."

The dialogue groups started in July 1992, when Len and Libby brought together a small group of American Jews, Palestinians, and supportive others in their living room in San Mateo, California. They had just helped Israeli and Palestinian citizen leaders meet in the California redwoods to forge the historic 1991 document, "Framework for a Public Peace Process," preceding the Oslo Accords. By 2004, with six local dialogues established, they initiated the First Midwest Palestinian-Jewish Dialogue Weekend held in Duluth, Minnesota, and the next year, the second gathering was in Louisville, Kentucky.

The idea for the groups dates back to the 1980s when Len and Libby helped launch the successful Beyond War movement in response to the global threat of nuclear war. From many initiatives with Soviet officials and citizens—and Len teaching himself Russian—the couple realized the secret to working toward peace: nothing could replace face-to-face relationships with the "enemy."

Later, in the early 1990s, they initiated successful black-white "meal-sharing" events in their hometown of San Mateo. Their meal-sharing was based on a model in South Africa, when the Koinonia Southern Africa movement brought together courageous black and white citizens in "meal groups" to counter apartheid. The women and men met together in public despite social taboos and physical risk to their lives, and explored ways to break down stereotypes and build bridges of understanding.

The experiences began to reverse fear, mistrust, and ignorance of one another and helped change the fabric of national relations in South Africa. The model proved successful when applied in other parts of the world for groups with ethnic, social, and political differences.

In Len and Libby's gatherings, African American and Caucasian couples met in a meal-sharing group once a month for a year in each other's homes—providing a private, nonthreatening environment allowing them to relax and open up to new ideas and insights. They recounted highlights of their life journeys— childhood, significant events, setbacks and successes, disappointments and joys. Then others around the table asked questions, starting lively and even challenging exchanges and communication.

"Lifelong stereotypes melt away," says Len.

The successes yielded insights on how to apply that model to the Middle East situation. Hundreds of examples of relationship-building successes are on the website (http://traubman.igc.org/global.htm).

Participants—Palestinians and Jews—alternate taking up to 30 minutes to tell highlights of their life stories, including their birthplace, family, childhood and adult experiences, highs and lows, successes and failures, beliefs and values, obstacles and disappointments, meaningful events, goals and dreams. They also share personal stories, revealing lives and experiences never heard before by "the other side," even though they are often painful or shocking to hear. The others listen without judgment, asking questions at the end, to clarify but not confront. In this way, "adversaries" get to know one another on a personal level, build trust, and overcome stereotypes and assumptions learned in their separated and distanced communities.

"We remind people that the idea is to build trust, understanding, and relation-ship, not to object, deny, or judge," says Len. "An enemy is one whose story we have not heard" is the repeated motto of the dialogue movement.

At the first dialogue meeting, participants often say, "I don't have a story," "My story isn't important," or "You wouldn't be interested in my story." By the second or third gathering, group members get better at sharing their story and realize that their story matters.

In the beginning, too, some participants might be overly cordial or overly assertive about their views, without listening carefully to each other. They are reminded that casual conversation, dogmatism, and win-lose debate differs from "sustained dialogue" that involves compassionate listening, respect for authentic personal narratives, and motivation to learn. In later meetings, they listen in-tently and realize how their lives have been similar, and yet quite different, lead-ing to greater understanding.

It is often difficult to get both Palestinians and Jews to join the meetings or to speak freely, as both can be afraid to trust others, especially to new acquaintances, about their feelings and opinions.

"This cannot be just a hobby or quick fix, but requires dedication," explains Len. "Change takes time and continuing a relationship."

To teach people about the groups, Len and Libby send free-of-charge printed guidelines, videos, and success stories (Traubman & Traubman, 1997a, 1997b). They also travel the country teaching others how to organize the meetings. Requests come from their worldwide e-mail circle of more than 2,500 deeply interested citizens and institutions. Good dialogue, they teach, is an exchange of ideas and experiences, suspending judgment, to truly listen and staying in the process even when your closely held beliefs are challenged or threatened.

"When divergent views converge," says Len, "you discover a new social intelligence."

The Living Room Dialogues are thriving—the San Mateo group of 30 Jews and 30 Palestinians has met more than 170 times—with six groups in the San Francisco Bay Area and more than 50 others across the United States from Rhode Island to Hawaii, in homes and on high school and college campuses.

Dialogues are also thriving on the East Coast, in the New York area—in Brooklyn, Manhattan, and Westchester—and have been held on college campuses like NYU, Fordham, and Queens College. Marcia Kannry founded the Dialogue Project (www.thedialogueproject.org) in 2001 and has more than 20 years' experience in multicultural and interfaith organizations. A Jewish American who lived in Israel, Marcia says the groups flourished after 9/11 when Muslims and others felt the need to reach out to their neighbors. The stated mission of the Dialogue Project is to break through walls of silence among people of diverse faiths and ethnicities—Palestinians, Israelis, Jews, Muslims, Christians, and "interested others." Father Khader El Yateem, the Palestinian Christian minister of the Salaam Arabic Church in Bay Ridge, Brooklyn, is a dialogue participant, board member, and hosts dialogues in his church. Once bitter toward Israelis when he was imprisoned for six months, he remembers a soldier who retrieved his Bible and looked after him; he now explores forgiveness and acceptance with members of his dialogue circle—including an Israeli Rabbinical student, Jewish activists, Palestinian Americans, and others—and is teaching his six children not to hate Jews.

Marcia points out that, for many of the participants, dialogue is their first encounter with people whom they have viewed only as "the other," in a safe environment where they can speak their "truth." Conversations occur under the guidance of a trained facilitator, with agreed-upon guidelines: confidentiality, speaking from personal experience, no interruptions, and listening actively (taking in the words and intent of the speaker rather than listening in order to construct a response).

At a recent community meeting with a panel discussion about dialogue, the audience was asked to separate into pairs, and to take turns telling each other their story, with one person talking while the other just listens. Then they repeat back to each other what they thought they heard, to validate each other's story. This is the listening process that is fundamental to the dialogue.

At a dialogue I attended, one Israeli woman told her story about her fiancé being killed many years earlier. Her Palestinian partner had a difficult time reporting back what she had told her, explaining that she was so impacted and upset by the story about the murder. This reaction sparked valuable sharing and opened the way for mutual understanding.

Marcia told me of many powerful dialogue interactions. A second-generation Palestinian Muslim American, who celebrates her culture through dance, dress, and worship, discovered a place where she can speak with Jews on an equal footing about her family's history and land in Palestine. An international student was able to acknowledge her fears living in the world as a Jew and Israeli. A former soldier in the Israeli army whose brother is a "settler" was able to explore his concerns about security as he listened to a young Palestinian American woman dressed in a hijab tell him about the effects of the Wall on her family.

"In dialogue," Marcia says, "we do not shy away from difficult topics. In fact our circles begin with an exploration of 'hot' words, words that carry a strong emotional content, like 'jihad,' 'Zionism,' 'the Wall,' and 'terrorist.'" This exploration allows participants from the outset to experience the dialogue circles as a place where their deepest concerns can be stated and, importantly, can be heard. "Participants feel empowered when they are able to articulate their stories and perspectives," says Paula Pace, chair of the board of the Dialogue Project and lead facilitator. "From that place of strength, they are then better able to hear and feel compassion for the experience of 'the other.' Trust can develop when people recognize honesty, even when they might not agree with what is being said."

"Dialoguers have begun to challenge their own assumptions and to hear the heart as well as the words of 'the other,'" says Marcia. "We have found that participants are able to reach across the political divide—even as it increases—to experience each other's humanity."

The understanding of dialogue groups is that (1) all stories are valid and valued; (2) an enemy is one whose story has not been told; (3) Jews and Palestinians share values and a common future; (4) both have a right to equal dignity, peace, and security; (5) relationship building—and not blame, hatred, and violence—leads to peace; (6) citizens must be included in any peace agreements; and (7) the UN, the United States, and other nations, as well as all Jews, Palestinians, and supportive others, should all assist in any peace process that engages ordinary citizens in compassionate and constructive dialogue.

Besides listening, "meal-sharing" continues to be a prominent part of Len and Libby's Living Room Dialogues—revealing, metaphorically, a hunger to learn.

"The way to a person's heart is through the stomach," says Libby, explaining their belief that this is especially true to bring peace between Israelis and Palestinians since food is such an important part of both cultures.

"In the beginning, this is about heart connections," adds Len. "Sitting the family down at a meal is the place where we come together, so why not to bring the two 'families' of the cultures together?"

A few years ago, a large number of families did come together—420 Jewish and Palestinian Americans and others—for an historic relationship-building dinner-dialogue in San Francisco, called "Building a Common Future."

"We enter into these new relationships at the 'human' level, rather than at the point of political differences," says Len. Palestinians and Jews in the group have met with congresspeople and state department officials, teleconferenced with the U.S. ambassador to Israel, hosted a Palestinian foreign minister in a Jewish home and an Israeli minister of justice in a Palestinian home for food and heart-to-heart dialogue.

Still, their bedrock principle is reflected in a statement by former U.S. Assistant Secretary of State and negotiator of the Camp David Accords, Harold Saunders: "There are some things only governments can do such as negotiating binding agreements. But there are some things that only citizens outside government can do, such as changing human relationships." As anthropologist Margaret Meade said, "Never doubt that a small group of thoughtful, committed citizens can change the world. Indeed, it is the only thing that ever has."

The puns about peace and food are endless. As one participant said, "If the negotiation table doesn't work, the meal table can." Judy Bart Kancigor, creator of CookingJewish.com (www.cookingjewish.com) says, "If Israelis and Palestinians would meet in the kitchen, it would save a lot of bloodshed."

The food of both cultures is similarly Middle Eastern. Both share hummus, falafel, and tabouli, although Nahida Salem says the Palestinian versions are spicier than the Jewish ones. Jewish recipes include more Western and Eastern European dishes, consistent with the background of the emigrants. These include potatoes, beets for borscht, raisins in rugula cookies, and of course, ingredients for the famous chicken soup. Common in Arabic food are dried beans and mint, the spice za'atar, flat leaf parsley, orange flower flavoring, salted chick peas, and of course, garlic and onions. According to scholars, the Prophet Mohammed's favorite foods included yoghurt with butter or nuts, cucumbers with dates, pomegranates, grapes, and figs.

Important sharing and discovery, says Libby, often comes around the meal preparation and clean up, besides the actual dining. Recognizing the power of food for peace, Len and Libby and their local dialogue partners put together a book of recipes from participants from both cultures, some of which have been passed from generation to generation. The collection, *Palestinian and Jewish Recipes for Peace* (Traubman & Botto, 2004), includes sample meals, complete with appetizers, soups, salads, entrées, side dishes, breads, and desserts. Each section starts with messages of peace with word play, such as, "For the garden of your daily living, plant four rows of squash: Squash stereotypes, squash indifference, squash blame, and squash violence."

Eric Gattmann contributed his mother Bertha's recipe for marble cake, and Hilda Gattmann shared her grandmother's chocolate almond cake.

"Our best recipes are not for 'fast foods,'" says Len. "When you take a lot of time to prepare, it gives you hours to talk together in the kitchen and then around the table." For that reason, not all the recipes in the book are for food—some "recipes" describe how to have a better dialogue or how to listen without judgment—skills crucial in resolving and preventing conflict. There are photographs, and stories behind some dishes about what they mean to a person or family, reminding them of a special ceremony, event, or relationship.

Nazih Malak, a Palestinian Muslim, shared that his favorite holiday while growing up was Eid Al Fitr—the breaking of the fast after the month of not eating from sunrise to sunset during Ramadan (commemorating the revelation of the Koran to the Prophet Mohammed). To break the fast, family and friends feast on favorite foods such as tabouli, baklava, and stuffed grape leaves (that can take two weeks to hand roll). Nazih recalls how the children complained of hunger and prayed to get sick to have an excuse to stop fasting.

Nermeh Nazzal recalled that one year after she was married, her husband Jiries challenged her to prepare New Year's dinner for his whole family, without any help from his mother. Nermeh made all the favorite Arabic appetizers—hummas, kibeh, sfiha (like pizza), and falafel—and proved she could do it.

The favorite holiday for Maida Kasle, a Jew with Russian roots, was Passover, when all the cousins came and gathered around the piano and sang. Raeda Ashkar's favorite holiday is New Year's Day in Nazareth, when family and friends have a huge party and lunch on kebeh and stuffed cabbage rolls, symbolic of rolling into the New Year.

"So many people get to appreciate each other and their culture, and see how different but how similar they are in their celebrations and their identity," says Libby. They also pass on their recipes to generations and across cultures.

Henriette Zarour from Beit Jala passed on to her two daughters her mother's recipe for special Easter cookies—called Mamoul—shaped like the crown of thorns or like the sponge used to wipe the lips of Jesus as he carried his cross.

Nijmeh Hadeed, a businesswoman from Ramallah, recalls Christmas back home as a special time with gifts and good food. Her favorite dish at holiday time is Mahshi.

Recipes

Mahshi (Rice and Lamb Stuffing)

1 cup uncooked rice
2 cups uncooked ground lamb
Salt, pepper, and allspice (to taste)
Butter (to taste)

Mix 1 cup of uncooked rice, 2 cups of uncooked ground lamb, salt, pepper, allspice, and a little butter. Remove the meat of four to six small white zucchini or baby eggplants. Stuff them with the prepared meat/rice filling. You can also use the filling in rolled grape leaves. Cover the stuffed vegetables with tomato sauce. Place in a small pot, cover, and bring to a boil for about 5 minutes and then simmer for another 40 minutes to an hour. The stuffing mix is delicious when used in small white zucchinis, baby eggplants or rolled into grape leaves. The number will depend on the size of the vegetable used, but smaller is better. Serves 4 to 6.

Tabouleh

¼ cup cracked wheat
2 large bunches of parsley
4 tomatoes
2 cucumbers
1 bunch mint
2 lemons
1 cup of extra virgin olive oil
Salt to taste

Fill bottom of bowl with the wheat. Soak with cold water until soft, then drain. Chop parsley and mint fine. Chop tomatoes and cucumbers into chunks. Mix together. Mix juice of 2 lemons and olive oil in the salad. Add salt if needed.

Chicken Jerusalem

40 oz. chicken breasts, cut into serving pieces
½ cup flour
2 tsp. vegetable oil
½ lb. mushrooms, cut into pieces
6 oz. marinated artichoke hearts
2 cups tomatoes, chopped
2 cloves garlic, minced
½ tsp. oregano
Freshly ground black pepper
½ cup sherry

Heat oil in frying pan. Dredge chicken pieces in flour and brown in the oil. Place the chicken in a casserole with the mushrooms and artichoke hearts. Stir garlic and spices with tomatoes and pour over chicken. Bake at 350 degrees Fahrenheit for 1 to 1½ hours or until tender, adding sherry during the last few minutes of cooking time.

Potato Kugel

3 eggs
3 cups potatoes, grated and rained
⅓ cup potato flour
½ tsp. baking powder
1½ tsp. salt
1 onion, grated
4 tsp. melted butter or fat

Beat eggs until thick. Stir in remaining ingredients. Turn mixture into a greased baking dish and bake at 350 degrees Fahrenheit for one hour, until browned. Serve hot.

Dining Prayer

An opening prayer before the meal is very important. Len and Libby use this one:

> We are troubled and sad that governments continue to lack the will to enact a just peace.
> We also believe that politicians ultimately follow the people.
> Governments alone cannot move beyond war without us.
> Thus, we will continue our efforts in the "public peace process" that increases face-to-face relationships and changes the hearts and minds of more and more citizens.
> Therefore, we gather together this evening. . . . To reaffirm:
> We are neighbors forever and interdependent.
> We want the best for each other and will
> resolve all conflicts without violence,
> beginning with listening.
> Working together, we will
> build our common future
> for the good of both peoples, equally.

A Season of Light and Hope

Hope prevails, as it did around the table at Len and Libby's "Season of Light" holiday dinner. Mais, a college freshman from East Jerusalem, had always doubted that there were people on the other side who were serious about change, but the evening gave her hope. Reem also found hope: "I have been given such a privilege to experience this evening's kind of hope. Of course, it will take more than my one candle light, but many lights to finally touch enough others."

Sara, a Jordanian student, wants that message of hope to go back home. "Back home they are still very inhibited from doing this. . . . People from this room need to take this back home." Lama is optimistic, "I know that one by one, citizens—people like me—will make a difference . . . to a new individual, society, and nation." She is already making a difference, as a staff member of the organization Building Bridges for Peace.

After a breakfast feast at the Salems' house, Len and Libby took the four young women to the Golden Gate Bridge—symbolic of their own bridge for peace.

Acknowledgment

An original version of this article first appeared in *The New York Daily News*, December 25, 2005.

References

Traubman, L., & Botto, F. (2004). *Palestinian and Jewish Recipes for Peace*. San Mateo, CA: Jewish Palestinian Living Room Dialogue Group. [101 pp]. Available from http://traubman.igc.org/recipes.htm or e-mail: LTraubman@igc.org.

Traubman, L., & Traubman, E. (1997a). *Reconciliation Resource*. San Mateo, CA: Jewish Palestinian Living Room Dialogue Group. [8 pp].

Traubman, L., & Traubman, E. (1997b). *Building Relationships: Basis for Change*. San Mateo, CA: Jewish Palestinian Living Room Dialogue Group. [25 pp].

CHAPTER 14

BEGINNING THE DIALOGUE
IN FAITH

Reverend Cheryl M. Walker

Recently, I had the honor of opening a public dialogue hosted by the Dialogue Project, a group dedicated to employing dialogue as a technique for reconciliation in the Israeli-Palestinian conflict. Not knowing much about the group I went to its website (www.thedialogueproject.org) to find out more about the people involved in the project and what they hope to accomplish. After reading about their goals, I was quite pleased that my church was asked to host this dialogue, and would be used to facilitate the process—something that in our world of rhetoric and dogma is sadly lacking on all sides of the political fences.

One of the things I saw on the website was a brief description of the differences between dialogue and debate. Where dialogue seeks to inquire and learn, debate seeks to sell and persuade. Where dialogue seeks to unfold shared meanings, debate seeks to gain agreement on one meaning. The list continues but I would add one other difference between debate and dialogue. Dialogue begins in faith, debate begins in ideas.

In debate there is the idea, and the idea is what matters. The goals of debate are to sell the idea, defend the idea, and eventually gain agreement on the one idea. But with dialogue, the starting point, I believe, is faith. The theologian Carter Heyward defines faith as a "process of leaping into the abyss not on the basis of any certainty about *where* we shall land, but rather on the belief that we *shall* land." We enter into dialogue in this way. We do not know how we will be transformed, but only that we will be transformed. And we have faith that the transformation will bring us closer to our ideal selves and the world closer to that all-too-elusive dream of one beloved community where the inherent worth and dignity of all people is affirmed and respected.

Of course, by definition dialogue means that we are engaging with someone else. And so we begin the process of dialogue with faith in the innate goodness of people. We have faith that "the other" seeks the same goal of transformation that we are seeking and that they are doing so with good will in their hearts, just as we do so with good will in our hearts. If we did not have that faith, we would not begin the dialogue process. What would be the point? So we begin our dialogue with faith in ourselves and faith in others. We take the leap into the abyss, holding each other's hand.

The road won't be easy—there will be times when you think it will "never end."

When that happens, have faith; believe we can change the world.

Yet we can get "stuck" sometimes, in faith, we get stuck in the words. We need not call the holy by the same name to have faith in that mysterious presence that binds us all one to another in spirit. We may not use the same words to describe the beauty of the world and life in this world, yet we can reach out and see the holy and the divine in each of us. And we need not worship alike to know that the power of love shall always triumph over the power of hate. We may not express our *religions* in the same way, but as we engage in the process of true dialogue, we need to express our *faith* in one way—the way of respect and peace.

Things can be difficult and we may very well come to doubt both our commitment and the commitment of others to the process of change. It is at this time that we need to hold on tighter to our faith in the goodness that resides in all humanity. When it seems that change will never happen, hold on tighter still to the faith that transformation happens and that if we try, we can build a land of peace and justice for all people. We begin in dialogue, and we begin in faith.

Reference

ThinkExist.com Quotations. "Carter Heyward quotes." *ThinkExist.com Quotations Online.* Retrieved April 1, 2007, from http://einstein/quotes.carter_heyward.

CHAPTER 15

BELIEVE IT CAN HAPPEN: THE INTERFAITH ENCOUNTER APPROACH TO THE ISRAELI–PALESTINIAN CONFLICT

Yehuda Stolov

To understand my work in interfaith encounter with Israelis and Palestinians, I have to take you back to when I moved to Jerusalem after my graduation from high school in order to study in a Yeshiva (a Jewish religious academy). This Yeshiva was established about 50 years before, by Rabbi Abraham Yitzhak Hakohen Kook, who was a remarkable deep thinker and a man of farsighted vision. I studied there for six years, then completed my army service, and studied at Hebrew University in Jerusalem, where I earned advanced degrees in physics and Jewish thought.

These studies created two major understandings that shape who I am and inspire my life and work. First, I learned that all views contain heavenly sparks and have their role in the divine process of bringing humanity and the world back to God. This led me to the second realization, that interfaith dialogue and conversations about faith with Christians, Muslims, Jews, and others—if conducted in the right way—can be a powerful force in building bridges between the different communities of the Holy Land and Middle East, and help solve the current conflict.

When I look at the Palestinian/Arab-Israeli conflict, I see a political conflict fueled by prejudices, fears, lack of trust, and hatred toward "the other." One experience makes it possible to overcome these negative attitudes: When we engage in deep and positive interaction with each other about faith, we overcome prejudices and fears and replace them with mutual understanding, respect, trust, and friendship.

Our "interfaith encounter" approach to resolving the conflict is broader than traditional interfaith dialogue, because the primary goal is no longer just learning about the religion of the other person, but instead, encouraging exchange between participants; thus, the emphasis on "encounter"—not meaning to struggle, but in the humanistic sense of the word, meaning to come together in understanding. Consistent with this, the main process for the interfaith encounter approach is no longer learned lectures, but small dialogue/encounter groups. As the number of groups grew and our activities grew, four years ago we formed the Interfaith Encounter Association (www.interfaith-encounter.org).

The work at the Interfaith Encounter Association (IEA) has been life-changing for me: I have let go of my prejudices about Christians and Muslims and instead have constantly growing respect for these religions and their followers.

The Uniqueness of the Interfaith Encounter Approach

Three characteristics designate the unique contribution of the Interfaith Encounter Association approach in the effort for construction of peace and reconciliation. The first is that, contrary to the common view that religion is the problem, the IEA believes that an efficient way to bring people together is through interfaith understanding and that the best way to gain such understanding is deep and positive dialogue through interactive encounter. People who study together and exchange feelings and views about their personal understanding of their religion overcome prejudices and fears, develop trust and friendship, and learn to accept each other and thus come closer to harmony. In this way, religion is a bridge—rather than a breach—between people. As most people of the Middle East—whether Arabs and Israelis; or Jews, Muslims, Christians, and Druze; or religious and nonreligious—are closely linked with their religious identity, this process is a major key for the peace process.

The second unique characteristic is that the IEA works for peace in a highly nonpolitical way. We do not have an official stand, nor agreement among members about the exact nature of an Israeli-Palestinian agreement, the solution for Israeli-Lebanese relations, or any other political issue. Political views of participants are private and have no significance in interfaith encounter programs and activities. This attitude allows people from all parts of the political spectrum—including those considered "radicals," "extremists," or "fanatics"—to actively participate and contribute to the advancement of the peace process. Everyone is included—even those who may not be considered candidates for dialogue by other approaches.

Finally, IEA is based on involvement at the grassroots level, and civic participation. The masses engage in the process, and very little effort is invested in political, or even religious, leaderships. When citizens form a civil society movement for social change and when this movement is wide enough, leaders will follow.

The power of the Interfaith Encounter approach is self-evident to anyone who has experienced it, but it has also been supported by scientific research. A study in cooperation with the Project for Arab-Jewish Dialogue—under the auspices of the Program in Conflict Resolution in the Political Studies Department at Bar Ilan University under the coordination of Dr. Ben Mollov—examined changes in the attitude toward "the other" of participants in interfaith retreats compared to a control group who did not participate. The findings showed that the more the people defined themselves as "religious," the more negative were their initial attitudes toward "the other"; but these people made a dramatic shift to a more positive attitude during the interfaith retreat.

How Does the IEA Actually Work?

Our work is based on several principles: to respect and accept "the other"; that religion is our point of connection; that we believe in one God; that hatred doesn't suit us; that with love we will conquer negative feelings of people; and that with tolerance, listening, and feeling "the other," we can gain love.

Programs include meetings, study sessions, weekend retreats, and longer conferences, as well as study visits and special projects to target special needs.

Personal Transformation Stories

The transformational quality of a good interfaith encounter is evident to anyone who takes part in an IEA activity. Personal testimonies prove this.

Leah writes: "I came to Israel 9 years ago—a very right-wing thinker. I had thought that by coming here, I was fulfilling a religious and Zionist dream. What about the Arabs? Maybe if we're lucky they'll all leave. That's how I thought at first. And I wasn't the only one. . . . I read about IEA in *The Jerusalem Post*, which got the better of my curiosity. Who were these brave people who decided to go against the grain and meet each other? I was shocked to see Palestinians and Israelis sit down together and dialogue—in the middle of the Intifada—to find commonalities in their respective religions in order to respect and understand one another. I e-mailed the organization and promptly got an invite to the next weekend retreat which was happening in two weeks in Jerusalem. . . . I had never spoken to any Palestinian before, other than waiters at restaurants and I was shaking. It was so frightening for me to meet people who were my sworn enemy. The Palestinians said they came to the weekend because they didn't believe that Israelis wanted peace and dialogue and had to see for themselves. I was quite surprised to hear that.

"Through dialogues such as the ones that IEA has at both its weekend retreats and monthly meetings in various cities, I've seen how the ignorance we have had about the other, turns into respect and understanding. In the time since I've joined IEA, I have hosted people at my home for Jewish celebrations for them to learn about our customs and in turn, they have invited me to their homes for Christian and Muslim celebrations. This can only have a positive effect on our families, our neighbors, our neighborhoods and God willing, even further than that."

After a young-adults Israeli-Palestinian retreat, Aiman from Nablus said, "It was the first time for me to watch a Jewish prayer and I felt the urge to dance and clap hands. It is the first time and I feel I connect to it and love it from the inside."

Ali, also Palestinian, said, "For me to see the Jewish young adults ponder and argue how to conduct the prayer, made me feel connected to them as it reminds me of myself and my friends trying to find our ways in the older religious paths."

Eliran, who is Israeli, said, "The retreat changed many things for me as in the first time I can connect on a personal basis with Palestinian friends and find with them a common language—the language of the heart. For me, to see them discussing to the point and with open hearts and knowing that it took them ten hours to pass the hour and a half way, going through troubles and risks, shows how much we are together."

Amir, another Israeli, realized, "Young people have strength and commitment to peaceful ways and nonviolence, and it was so wonderful to meet the other side and know that this is exactly what they want."

Aida, a Palestinian-Israeli, summarized others' experiences, stating, "I believe in the power of every person to change the reality. Each of us, no matter what is his or her place in the society, has that responsibility. It is a personal decision to be a source of light, love, and giving. It is a personal decision to work toward inner and real peace—first for me and then for others—redeeming my soul and my spirit through the decision to be on the side of God, the side of love. So many young people today are so busy in survival they forget how much they are contributing to the continuation of the sad situation by not participating in the life of the society. Especially in our region it is an existential must—we all are part of the doing and its consequences."

The Circles

Interfaith encounter programs are organized, conceptually and practically, in four geographical circles.

First Circle: In Israel

The first circle is the citizens of Israel. For most Jewish-Israelis, both religious and secular, "Israeli" equals "Jewish." While most know that there is a nonnegligible non-Jewish minority of Arabs in Israel and can even quote their numbers, their immediate association to the concept "Israeli" does not include non-Jews. Or even if Israeli non-Jews are recognized, they are referred to as one monolithic unit, without real knowledge of the differences among them in religion, attitude, way of life, level of education, or personal differences. This ignorance results in lack of sensitivity, prejudice, and even discrimination on the part of Jews, and in anger and frustration on the part of Arabs. Tackling this challenge through interactive dialogue brings acceptance of the other, positive interchange, and even social justice.

In order to achieve the larger goals of peace and reconciliation, Jews must understand and accept the fact that they live in the Middle East and have to face its inhabitants and interact positively with them, and Arabs must understand and accept the fact that the Jews of Israel are not European colonists but an integral part of the future of the Middle East. This first step toward the harmonious integration of the Jewish minority of Israeli society into the Arab majority of the Middle East is most likely the harmonious integration of the Arab minority within the Jewish majority inside Israel—since inside Israel is the only place where massive interaction between the two societies takes place. Because the people live in such close proximity within this circle, it is possible to work on harmonious intercommunal relations in neighboring towns, villages, and neighborhoods.

The IEA accomplishes this by forming ongoing interfaith encounter groups that bring together citizens from neighboring communities who otherwise have hardly any interaction. Each group is led by an interfaith coordinating team that reflects the diversity of religious contexts in the area—with one member for each religious context. Each group is a semiautonomous unit, with full freedom and responsibility to organize the ongoing encounters and their content. These groups gradually develop a strong sense of a joint community and actually build a minicommunity in which the relations are harmonious without suppression of differences. In this way, the groups serve as a model for larger communities, demonstrating and providing a seed for what's possible in relations that can expand to include more parts of society.

This first circle includes a constantly growing individual membership of 6,000 Jews, Muslims, Christians, Druze, and Baha'i affiliates, and cooperation with other organizations and institutions.

Second Circle: The Israeli-Palestinian Circle

The second circle includes all people of the Holy Land, namely Israelis and Palestinians, as these two peoples are destined to live together in the same small piece of land. Therefore, the second step toward harmony in the Middle East is building harmony between these two communities that have suffered so much from one another and yet are so close to one another; have so many fears and prejudices to overcome and yet have so much mutual curiosity and shared interests. Interfaith dialogue plays a major role in developing conversation between the two communities, in exposing the real similarities and differences, and in learning to live together peacefully and harmoniously.

This second circle includes close cooperation with seven Palestinian organizations from across the Palestinian National Authority areas that share IEA's vision. Retreats and conferences take place, along with special women's and young adults' conferences; programs of joint study of language, religion, and culture; and exchanges of family visits.

Even during the peak years of the Intifada, starting in the second half of 2002, IEA managed to maintain regular retreats with three Palestinian partners. With the hope for the improvement of the situation, hope grows to include more partners in active programs and to form ongoing Israeli-Palestinian groups similar to those among Israeli citizens.

Third Circle: The Middle East Circle

The third circle is the inclusive Middle Eastern one. It includes participation of IEA in the establishment of the Middle East Abrahamic Forum (MEAF) together with Palestinian, Egyptian, Jordanian, Iranian, and Turkish organizations, as well as individuals from Qatar, Kuwait, Lebanon, Morocco, and Tunisia, enlarging the number of organizations involved, and participants in the annual conference and variety of activities.

Three points that were formulated by an Egyptian colleague as the guiding principle of the Middle East Abrahamic Forum summarize the approach of all IEA programs and activity circles:

- People participate in the dialogue as people of faith, expressing their religious views and not as representatives of national entities or political viewpoints; therefore, every issue discussed, theoretical or practical, is addressed from its religious perspective.
- Dialogue involves two or more points of view and requires that the participants listen to the other as well as expressing their own views.
- Every religious viewpoint can be expressed but attention is given to the way of expression; as you do not want to be embarrassed or offended, do not embarrass or offend the other.

Fourth Circle: Everyone Who Really Cares Can Join the Global Circle

The key for the success of such a grassroots strategy as reflected in the interactive Interfaith Encounter approach is mobilizing large popular participation. Conflict can only be resolved when a large social-change movement is created where a substantial part of each society has experienced the encounter and acceptance of the other. To accomplish this requires cooperation of many activists and development of diverse projects suited for people of various backgrounds, ages, and genders.

One does not have to live in the Middle East to actively participate in the interfaith encounters. It is wrong to think that when a dispute arises between two sides, it is their sole business and the rest of the world can remain neutral. Even if one is not directly affected, remaining indifferent—or even worse, taking a side—fuels the clash. In the context of the conflict in the Holy Land, this effect is apparent, as clashes between Israelis and Palestinians often induce tensions between Jews and Muslims, and sometimes even between Christians and Muslims, in many other parts of the world. From my physics background, I relate this to Newton's third law that when A influences B, B also influences A. In the case of the Holy Land, growing realization of this fact is leading to increasing development of the fourth geographical circle of IEA's activity: the global circle.

To achieve the global circle, people outside the region can participate in interfaith encounter work, toward harmonious coexistence in the Holy Land and in the Middle East. There are several ways they can do this. This includes reading and sharing stories from IEA programs that are e-mailed to more than 20,000 subscribers and posted with photos on the website. The stories record positive developments in the intercommunal relations in the Holy Land and the Middle East that are rarely reported in the mainstream media. Another way is by forming a Friends of Interfaith Encounter group such that conducting parallel dialogues gives moral support to the well-being of people in the Holy Land and their efforts at harmonious intercommunal relations, and, at the same time, actively builds well-being and harmonious intercommunal relations in the friends' own location in the world. Another way is to enlarge the network by spreading the word about interfaith encounter to Israeli contacts, Palestinian contacts, Middle Eastern contacts, and others around the world.

Success

After IEA's Jerusalem celebration of the International Day of Peace, Noa, a Jewish-Israeli, effectively captured the feelings of both Israelis and Palestinians when she wrote: "The most important effect this meeting had on me was to see many more people I didn't know before who are involved in interfaith activity. Many times as I walk the streets of Jerusalem, I think that this city can be a wonderful spiritual oasis—a place for celebrating the difference of culture, language, and belief. Last night the yard of Bet Tabor Jerusalem seemed to me beautifully rich with the diversity of humankind. The potential of this city was visual and clear."

Ongoing Work

In November 2006, an Interfaith Encounter group met for several workshops facilitated by a psychologist in order to help members cope with stress caused by the war along the Israeli-Lebanon border. When two women died of katyusha rockets, the female population was terribly traumatized. During the war, the women in the group had volunteered at the community center, especially helping to escort children to activities where the rockets would not reach. The meetings continue to reinforce the impact and importance of our work.

CHAPTER 16

Dialogue in the Midst of an Ongoing Conflict: A Group Process of Israeli Jewish and Palestinian Students

Shoshana Steinberg and Dan Bar-On

Introduction

Intergroup encounters have been widely used since the early 1980s as a means of promoting coexistence between the Jewish majority and the Palestinian minority, which makes up one-fifth of the population in Israel. In the context of the wider Arab-Israeli conflict and the Palestinians' living in the Occupied Territories struggle for the creation of an independent state, the relations between the Palestinian Israeli citizens and the Jewish Israelis are very complex. The two groups live in separate neighborhoods and do not meet on a daily basis.

The Palestinians demand equal rights and recognition as a national minority. For the most part, the minority group perceives the Jews as those involved in sustaining a situation that denies their legitimacy as citizens of Israel and negates their historical and lawful rights to a national home. At the same time, many Jewish Israelis see their expressions of solidarity with other Palestinians as a threat to the country's security. The initiated encounters offer an opportunity to discuss issues related to the relations between the two groups, which may result in better understanding of each other.

Many studies have aimed to assess the effectiveness of intergroup encounters. Assessment of the results has been hampered due to a lack of instruments that can be used to follow group processes (Bar & Bargal, 1995). Most of the studies concentrate on evaluating the final product and less on group processes. Therefore, their contribution to knowledge about in-group and intergroup communication is limited.

In recent years, qualitative research methods have been used, contributing to directing attention to processes that take place during the encounters. Studies point out power struggles (Maoz, 2000) that run parallel to the developmental processes that groups undergo.

In the present study, development is defined as a change in the quality of the discourse, which is assumed to be a sign of a shift in the way individuals perceive themselves, "the other," and their relationship. The quality of the discourse is defined by using a typology consisting of seven categories that constitute one axis. At one extreme is "ethnocentric talk": each side concentrates on itself, the discourse is characterized by stereotypic views of the other, the participants do not listen to each other. The opposite extreme is defined as "dialogic moment," which is characterized by mutuality, equality, and listening. This is a moment of cognitive and emotional understanding. The theoretical framework for construction of this typology is the dialogic perspective on communication (Bakhtin, 1981; Buber 1965). According to this perspective, the "objective truth" is less important. Meaning making is related to the construction of one's collective identity. It emerges from the encounter between self and other and the self is conceived as a process that continually develops in and through the relationships with others through dialogical interaction.

Not every conversation is a dialogue that leads to self-understanding and to understanding of the other. Dialogue, according to Buber (1965), is more than an exchange of information. It is a process and quality of communication in which the participants meet. Dialogue exists in moments since the conditions needed appear rarely and for short periods of time.

Developing the Typology for Categorizing Discourse

A review of the research literature that deals with group encounters shows that most existing studies use questionnaires before and after the course of encounters. We found no tool for classifying different levels of dialogue. The construction of the typology was based on the analysis, using Rosenthal's (1993) hermeneutic case reconstruction method, of fully transcribed group session recordings of workshops. The workshops took place at Ben-Gurion University as a year-long undergraduate course on intergroup processes in the Jewish-Arab conflict.

The groups consisted of eight Jewish and eight Palestinian Israelis who met weekly for three hours. The co-facilitators were two professional group leaders (Jewish and Palestinian) from the School of Peace at Neve Shalom who used the collective approach that encourages interaction in terms of national (as opposed to personal) identity. (This school is located within Neve Shalom, the only cooperative Jewish-Arab village in Israel, staffed equally and run jointly by Israeli Jews and Palestinians, that conducts workshops, interventions, and professional trainings.) The purpose of the encounters was to discuss the conflict, to express feelings, to learn about the differences and the similarities between the cultures, and to reexamine the way the participants define themselves in connection with the "relevant other."

Analysis of the discussions led to the emergence of seven categories that differentiate kinds of discourse. We will describe the categories and the differences between them.

Typology for Identifying Categories of Discourse

1. *"Ethnocentric talk":* The participants use argumentation, do not share their feelings. Each party seems to be talking to itself, not to the other. The two groups conduct two monologues, which do not meet.
2. *"Attack":* The participants accuse each other, use labels such as "racists," "terrorists." As opposed to the first category, here one side actively relates to the other, but the talking is ethnocentric.
3. *"Opening a window":* One side expresses feelings and tries to share their experience with the other, but the other side does not want, or is not capable of, understanding reality from the other's perspective. The term given to this category is based on the concept of the "double wall" that was used by Bar-On (1999). At times, one side opens a window in his or her wall, but is confronted by the other's wall.
4. *"Recognition of differences":* The sides discover that their perceptions of the other may be wrong. Furthermore, they recognize the differences between them, and how much they do not understand each other. This recognition is a turning point of abandoning the illusion of understanding the other, which is based on stereotypic perceptions. It enables a switch to a conversation based on recognition of the distance between the participants as separate and unique entities. The participants become conscious of the fact that the only way to reach understanding is by listening and making an effort to see reality from the other's perspective.
5. *"Intellectual discussion":* The participants use argumentation, do not tell personal stories, and do not express feelings. However, they listen to each other, and react to the other's arguments. The conversation may lead to cognitive understanding of the other.
6. *"Inclusion of differences":* A discussion between equals, characterized by sharing feelings with the others, differentiation among individuals, listening, reacting in a nonjudgmental way, and trying to understand the other's point of view.
7. *"Dialogic moment":* A kind of empathy to the other that seems to exemplify concepts such as a moment of cognitive and affective understanding, of "real meeting" as defined by Buber (1965), of participating in the other's experience without losing the "self."

The following examples illustrate the various categories. (PM = Palestinian Male, PF = Palestinian Female, JM = Jewish Male, JF = Jewish Female)

"Ethnocentric Talk"

The discussion takes place during the first meeting. The Palestinians talk about their feeling of not being a part of the Israeli society.

AHMAD (PM):   I will never feel that I am an Israeli.
RON (JM):   I don't have a problem with this. I'm asking you why you feel uncomfortable. You say that you don't have entertainment activities. It's

	your own doing. It's because you don't organize yourselves properly.
ANWAR (PM):	What can I study except for social science . . . if I study engineering . . . I'll be working as a school-teacher . . . everyone ends up teaching . . .
RON:	I studied economics, engineering, and business administration and I taught at school. There are many people who have a problem finding a job.

By saying that he will never feel that he is an Israeli, Ahmad wants to stress his national identity, which is a very important element in the conflict between the two groups. The Palestinians want to be accepted and included as citizens of a separate collective identity without assimilating into the Jewish majority. It seems that Ron intends to convey "openness" by stating that Ahmad's identity is of no importance. His statement conveys the message that he disregards Ahmad's expectation for recognition. Ron repeats the question asked earlier: Why don't the Palestinians feel good in Israel and answers it without waiting for a reply.

Anwar talks about discrimination. Ron ignores the asymmetrical power relations, and the minority group's dependence on the good will of the majority. This conversation does not seem to lead to better understanding of the other. Each of the sides seems to be self-centered. Each has his agenda. Each has a self-image that he wants to convey. The Palestinians talk about national identity, discrimination, and alienation. Ron tries to preserve his positive self-perception as being benevolent by ignoring the other side's messages.

"Attack"

The discussion takes place after an incident in Hebron. An Israeli soldier started to shoot at civilians. Only by chance, no one was injured. The shooting stopped when he was overpowered by another Israeli soldier. The media reported that the shooting soldier is mentally unstable. Omar, a Palestinian participant, brings up the incident. He looks and sounds angry.

OMAR:	They all come out crazy. Ami Popper[1] too, they are all crazy! . . . They show in the newspaper, on TV, and say that he is insane . . . they are the chosen and the perfect people and they don't have people who are not OK, and the one who kills is crazy . . . This is not the way you solve a problem.
HANNA (JF):	We truly agree . . .
OMAR:	They never admit . . . It annoys me. Now they will say that he is temporarily insane.
AYA (JF):	There is such a thing . . . If you ask me, every act of killing is some kind of temporary insanity.
FATMA (PF):	They try to save him, this is called saving . . .
OMAR:	You justify him, you save your self-image.

The Palestinians attack and members of the other group respond by intellec-
tualization. Omar accuses the other group of making up excuses in order to
protect the soldier who, he believes, is sane and knew what he was doing. The
Jewish participants try to defend themselves. Hanna speaks for the group and
says that they all agree with Omar. It is not clear whether she really agrees with
him. It may be that by agreeing she hopes to change the subject of the discussion.
Another Jewish participant, Aya, tries to defend her group's good name by offering an explanation for the shooting. It seems that Omar chooses to express his
anger and frustration by attacking the other group and by defining it. In comparison to ethnocentric talk, here even by attacking it, this way of communicating can be seen as an attempt to reach out to the other group.

"Opening a Window"

During the fourth meeting, Ahmad tries to explain the Palestinians' bond to
the land.

AHMAD:	My parents used to live in a village that was five kilometers away from the village where we live now. We were moved out of there [in 1948], and until now we do not feel that we belong in our village. We live in the same area, but do not have a feeling of belonging. Almost every weekend we climb a hill and look at the place where our village was. My mother, my father and my uncles start crying, and I myself, although I was born here, feel that I belong there together with all of them. I identify with them. [Ahmad looks sad, speaks softly.] Why is there a kibbutz over there? Why?
ANAT (JF):	If you don't feel that you belong here, why don't you go live in the territories? My parents came from somewhere else. . . . I do not feel a connection to the land from where they came.
MIRI (JF):	I feel that I belong to Israel but not to Beer Sheva.

Ahmad tries to convey the feeling of uprootedness that his parents feel although they live very close to the place where they were born. Living for a long
time in the new village does not make it "home" for them. Ahmad speaks with
pain. His words and body language convey his strong identification with his family. It is obvious that Ahmad feels that his parents were treated unjustly. His
message is: Nothing can compensate for being moved away from one's own home
and land. Ahmad shares his feelings of sadness, mourning, and frustration, but it
seems that the Jewish participants do not get the message or defend themselves
from its deeper meaning.

"Recognition of Differences"

The Arab group visited Bir-Zeit University. They state that they felt at home
there, as opposed to the feeling of not belonging at the university where they
study. The Jewish students ask why they do not enroll there, and ask them if they

intend to go to live in the Palestinian State when it will be established. The Palestinians are surprised to hear this question. They reply: Absolutely not!

AVNER: You are saying something, which is very strange to hear. You say that if the Palestinian state will be established you are not going to live there.

NASSER: You want to get rid of us! Why should we go?

AVNER: The question is how can you come . . . as a person who does not intend to move to the Palestinian state, and say that you have demands? [Turns to the Jewish students.] I want to understand their point of view, how do they demand an independent state, in which they do not intend to live . . . you are not going to live there?

NASSER: I cannot live there.

AVNER: Why?

NASSER: Because there is a people and land . . . Most of the Palestinians, when a state will be established, will feel that they belong there. Here they do not feel the cultural and social life . . . they will not leave their land and go with their people . . . do you understand? . . .

AVNER: So here we have the information that the establishment of a Palestinian state, even if its capital will be Jerusalem, will not resolve the Arab-Israeli conflict . . . you are fighting for a state in which you do not intend to live . . . I can say that I identify with the struggle for the establishment of a Palestinian state, but today I was absolutely surprised that the conflict will not be resolved the day the Palestinian state will be established.

NASSER: So the solution is to throw us out . . .

AVNER: It is not true! *You want to be a minority. That's what you want!* If I did not have a country I would have gone anywhere in order to live in my country without any connection to land . . .

During this discussion, the participants speak to each other on a personal level. They use "I," "you," and the other's first name, and there are descriptions, stories, and expressions of feelings, listening, and attempts to understand the other. But the two groups do not share a common rationale, which, according to Habermas (1984), can be used for arriving at an understanding and agreement. Avner, who is a son of immigrants who left the countries of their birth in order to live in a Jewish state, thinks that the most rational solution to the Palestinians' feeling of not belonging is to move to the Palestinian state. Their connection to the land seems absurd to him, and he cannot understand it. Avner tries to convince the Palestinian Israelis that their attitude is not rational, but does not succeed. The discussion uncovers deep differences in values and perspectives (between statehood and land), a gap that seems impossible to bridge. Avner expresses his frustration by almost shouting: "You want to be a minority! That's what you want!" Both sides repeat the same argumentations, until they become aware of the basic differences in perspectives and the futility of their efforts to convince the other. The Jewish participants realize that their former perceptions of the other were mistaken.

"Intellectual Discussion"

The topic of the discussion concerns religious extremism on both sides.

NASSER: These people [the Hamas] use religion. They say that this is Jihad [a holy war].

AVNER: We also have Goldstein[2] and Popper. They do not represent religion. Their religion is not my religion. It is like the religion of the Hamas members. I hope it's not the religion of other people who believe in the Koran.

NASSER: The same religion belongs to all people, but some use it . . .

AVNER: The same thing happens on our side . . .

The participants of both sides use argumentation and present their positions and evaluations of the situation. They listen, react to one another, and do not try to compare who is right and who is a victim. Here the use of "we" and "our side" does not mean "as opposed to you." The two groups find something in common. The conversation leads to cognitive understanding and agreement.

"Inclusion of Differences"

Toward the end of the year, a Palestinian participant, Fatma, shares a personal experience with the group.

FATMA: I will tell you what happened to me about a month ago. I called the Egyptian consulate. I wanted to register for a master's degree program in clinical psychology. They asked some questions about grades, language, and at the end he asked me: "Where do you live?" In the Galilee. Then he understood. He asked what is written in my ID. I said to him: "Israeli." He said: "Go away, you are Israeli, there is no room for you here." [Fatma is crying.]

ORIT (JF):   So what you are saying is that it does not matter. You say that if people will say I'm Israeli, the other side won't accept it . . . the Palestinian side will also not accept it. Are you afraid of assimilation?

FATMA: I'm afraid of being left with nothing.

ORIT: What do you mean? Without any identity?

FATMA: Yes, with no identity at all.

Fatma expresses emotions. Orit asks questions in order to better understand Fatma. They talk as person to person, not as representatives of groups. Orit's reaction shows that she understands Fatma's feelings of humiliation and rejection, and is capable of responding to these feelings, but still keeps some distance from them.

"Dialogic Moment"

The topic is the Kfar Kassem[3] massacre. The Palestinians compare it to the Holocaust. The Jewish participants strongly object to this comparison. They claim that the Holocaust is a historical event, which cannot be compared to any other event in the history of humanity.

Amina, a Palestinian participant, tells a story she heard from her grandfather and from her father about an event that happened in 1952. When her father was 13 years old their tribe was driven to the Jordanian border awaiting impending expulsion. Her father described how he feared for his father's life until they were allowed to return to their village, after the intervention of a high-ranking Israeli officer, whom he remembers as being tall and strong, and suddenly appearing in a white jeep. Amina's description of the events as seen through the eyes of a terrified boy conveys the cruelty of the situation. The personal story evokes an emotional response from a Jewish female participant, Orit.

ORIT: I want to talk about something that happened to me during the last hour. When I hear about the Holocaust, I see all these children in the black-and-white movies and all the atrocities. It's very hard for me to compare it to any other historical event. It seems so unusual and different. I had great difficulty listening to you. But I think that Amina helped me very much. The story that she told about her father, I suddenly realized . . . The Holocaust is very emotional for us. It is a personal event . . . a very emotional one. Suddenly your story sounds so horrible, that I understand why Kfar Kassem is so . . . I see the connection. I see your pain even greater than my pain. I do not have a relative who went through such a terrible experience.

Orit identifies with the feelings of fear, helplessness, and pain conveyed by Amina. The personal story evokes empathy. Through this story Orit realizes what the historical memories of both Palestinians and Jews have in common: the feeling of suffering inflicted by others. Orit's response reminds us of the way Buber (1965) referred to dialogue and dialogical moments—it is a moment of cognitive and affective understanding. It seems that Orit succeeds "to step into the Palestinians' shoes" and see reality from their perspective.

Discussion

The goal of encounters between groups in conflict is to achieve change and to make progress in intergroup relations. Until now, no instrument has yet been developed that can enable observers and researchers to follow the group process and identify development of intergroup communication. The tool introduced here allows the examination of nuances during the group discourse. It is assumed that changes in the way the parties speak to one another reflect changes in their perceptions. The types of discourse described in the typology reflect different ways of viewing the self, the other, and the relationship. The categories can theoretically be located on a scale progressing from simplistic to more complex perceptions.

"Ethnocentric talk" reflects a monolithic view of self and other (Bar-On, 1999). The conflict is perceived as a zero-sum game (Bar-Tal, 1995). Thinking in terms of black and white is, according to Bar-Tal, an outcome of protracted conflicts. Groups involved in long-lasting and violent conflicts develop psychological conditions that help them cope with the continuous threat and violence. These conditions include a positive view of one's own collective while the other is seen as the mirror image. Each of the groups sees itself as right, moral, and peace seeking while the other is seen as the opposite: the immoral aggressor who is not ready to compromise. Each side perceives itself as the victim. The groups tend to avoid each other.

During the encounter "ethnocentric talk" can be seen as a way of avoiding the other. While being in the same room, each group seems to be self-absorbed. There is no turning to the other as a separate and unique entity. Each party assumes that it knows who the other is (Gurevitch, 1988). This assumption of "knowing," based on stereotypic definitions, contributes to conducting two monologues that do not meet.

"Attack," like the former category, reflects a monolithic perception of self and other. By attacking, one tries to convey the message that he or she is the one who is right, the victim, while the other is wrong and guilty, but as opposed to ethnocentric talk, there is an attempt to reach out to the other.

"Opening a window" is an attempt to invite the other into one's world by sharing feelings with him or her, that may be seen as a sign of recognition of the other and of caring about the relationship. Sharing of feelings may lead, according to Gurevitch (1988), to dialogue and to mutual understanding. However, the attempt to achieve dialogue fails when the other side does not trust the opponent's intentions. When one suspects that he or she is being manipulated or is afraid of the consequences of accepting the other's emotions, one responds by ignoring the other's expression of feelings. Geldman (2000) states another reason for not responding to the other's feelings: in conflict situations, closeness and understanding of the other are perceived as signaling moral justification of the other side's position and one's own wrongdoing.

The category "recognition of differences" can be seen as a turning point in one's perception of self and other. It means recognition of the other's "otherness" and realizing that reality can be seen differently from another perspective. Gurevitch (1988) sees recognition of the distance between the self and the other, and the ability "to not understand," as a necessary step toward dialogue that may lead to understanding.

"Intellectual discussion" is characterized by listening and relating to the other's arguments. Listening is seen as a sign of recognition and respect (Buber, 1965). It helps gain new information and may lead to agreement between the opposing sides.

"Inclusion of differences" is a kind of dialogue where each side contributes to mutual understanding by sharing personal stories and experiences, expressing feelings, asking questions in order to get information (as opposed to rhetorical questions), a process of gradually getting closer to understanding how reality is seen from the other's perspective (Broome, 1993). However, as we saw in the example—a certain distance from the emotions of the other is maintained.

A "dialogic moment" is a moment of cognitive and affective understanding, of real meeting one another. It is the result of an egalitarian "I-You" relationship (Buber, 1965), and of the belief that there is no "objective truth," which leads to a joint effort to create shared worlds of meaning.

Our research brings up two theoretical questions. First, whether in encounters between groups in conflict, the developmental process is linear or chaotic. Does the group discourse develop in stages—from the first to the seventh category as could be inferred from the contact theory (Allport, 1954) and human relations approaches (Johnson & Johnson, 1997), or, are the changes chaotic as one could infer from the point of view of the conflict group model (Sonnenschein, Halabi, & Friedman, 1998): that the group process is an interaction between the pressure of the conflict reality outside the group and the internal group process? Therefore, one cannot expect a linear process to take place, based only on the internal group process.

Our analysis shows that chaotic changes occurred (Steinberg, 2004). The process was characterized by ups and downs, progress and setbacks. The quality of discourse was affected by the power relations that exist between Jews and Palestinians in Israeli society outside, political and social events, the facilitators' interventions in the group, and the achievements in dialogue that the group made as the year progressed. The factors that we identified as barriers to dialogue were opposing narratives about history and the origins of the conflict, collective identity based on victimhood, and the political situation. The factors contributing to understanding between the groups were symmetrical power relations, recognition of the other's "otherness," sharing feelings and listening. We found that, after dialogic moments, a regression to ethnocentric talk occurred. This appears to be a means of getting ready to confront the harsh reality on the outside. However, regression is partial and temporary.

In parallel there is another theoretical question of what is the goal of the group process: the Buberian approach that emphasizes the affective understanding between groups and individuals (in the form of the dialogical moments in the present analysis), or a more minimalistic approach that would value reaching intellectual understanding (category five in the analysis) as a desired goal in such intractable conflictual situations, like the Israeli-Palestinian situation. The authors of this chapter differ in their opinions about this question. Bar-On believes that by emotional identification with the other group, participants might find themselves becoming an isolated sect, apart from their external social context as long as the conflict is still going on outside the group. Therefore he does not expect it to last more than these few moments at a time. Bar-On sees cognitive mutual understanding as less problematic. He asserts that people can meet the harsh reality while keeping within themselves the discrepancy between the agreement inside the group and the disagreement outside. Steinberg believes that lack of empathy is a barrier to understanding. She sees personal stories and expressions of feelings that evoke empathy as a means leading to understanding the other. She does not see dialogic moments as the desired goal to be reached, as the encounters are not isolated from the ongoing conflict in outside reality. However, she thinks that one has to experience those short moments of real meeting and of perceiving "the other" as an equal human being in order to be ready to see the other's perspective, which is necessary for reaching an agreement.

The tool presented here offers theoretical and practical implications. On the theoretical level, the instrument can contribute to an understanding of the process that occurs in encounters between groups in conflict. On the practical level, professionals who organize group encounters can use the tool in order to plan their encounters effectively. Group facilitators can use it to analyze the discourse together with group members, thereby gaining insight into the quality of discourse and changes that may or may not be occurring. It can serve to prepare group facilitators to expect regression after progress and understand its causes.

Acknowledgments

The present analysis was supported by a research grant of the Abraham Fund and a grant of the Herzog Center for Diplomacy and the Middle East at Ben-Gurion University of the Negev. The authors thank Professor Shifra Sagy of the Department of Education at Ben-Gurion University, one of the seminar teachers; Rabah Halabi and Michal Zak from the School of Peace at Neve Shalom who facilitated the encounters; and students who took part in the discussions.

References

Allport, G. W. (1954). *The nature of prejudice.* Reading, MA: Addison-Wesley.

Bakhtin, M. M. (1981). *The dialogic imagination: Four essays* (M. Holoquist, Ed.). Austin: University of Texas Press.

Bar, H., & Bargal, D. (1995). *Living with conflict.* Jerusalem: Jerusalem Institute for Israel Studies. (In Hebrew)

Bar-On, D. (1999). *The indescribable and the undiscussable: Reconstructing human discourse after trauma.* Budapest: European University Press.

Bar-Tal, D. (1995). *Barriers on the way to peace.* Jerusalem: The Institute for the Study of Nurturing in Education. (In Hebrew)

Broome, J. B. (1993). Managing differences in conflict resolution. In J. D. Dennis & M. Hugo (Eds.), *Conflict resolution theory and practice* (pp. 97–107). Manchester, UK: Manchester University Press.

Buber, M. (1965). *Between man and man* (R. G. Smith, Trans.). New York: Macmillan.

Geldman, M. (2000). More thoughts about empathy. *Alpaim, 19,* 63–77. (In Hebrew)

Gurevitch, Z. D. (1988). The other side of dialogue: On making the other strange and the experience of otherness. *American Journal of Sociology, 93*(5), 1179–1199.

Habermas, J. (1984). *A theory of communicative action: Vol. 1. Reason and the rationalization of society.* Boston: Beacon Press.

Johnson, D. W., & Johnson, F. (1997). *Joining together.* Englewood Cliffs, NJ: Prentice-Hall.

Maoz, I. (2000). Power relations in intergroup encounters. *International Journal of Intercultural Relations, 24*(4), 259–277.

Rosenthal, G. (1993). Reconstruction of life stories. In *The narrative study of lives. 1*(1), 59–91.

Sonnenschein, N., Halabi, R., & Friedman, A. (1998). Israeli-Palestinian workshops. In G. Weiner (Ed.), *The handbook of coexistence* (pp. 600–614). New York: Continuum.

Steinberg, S. (2004). Discourse categories in encounters between Palestinians and Israelis. *International Journal of Politics, Culture and Society, 17*(3), 471–489.

CHAPTER 17

OPENING A LITTLE SPACE—AND
A LITTLE BREATHING ROOM—
FOR PEACE

Lisa Heft, Carol Daniel Kasbari, Avner Haramati, Tova Averbuch, and Harrison Owen

In June 2002 a group of Palestinians and Israelis gathered in Rome to meet in Open Space—to imagine a day beyond the current conflict that has been the source of such pain and grief. The meeting was sponsored by the Italian Ministry of Foreign Affairs, Education for Life (an international nonprofit foundation promoting dialogue with and between Palestinian and Israeli civil society), and the Roman arts center Centro Dionysia. The meeting was facilitated by Harrison Owen with his colleagues, Avner Haramati and Samar Daoud, assisting.

Dialogue is as much about listening—truly listening to another's experience—as it is about talking. It is not always about reaching agreement or finding solutions—sometimes it is about opening a little space between people so they can hear each other across their differences and honor those differences. Open Space Technology (Heft, 2002, 2003; Owen, 1997, 2002, 2004) is a method for convening people originated by Owen and used around the world, often when the stakes are high, the issues so complex that it is hard to see a way through them, and the time for solutions was yesterday. Participants host conversations on topics for which they have true passion and interest. There are no facilitators for those small group discussions—everyone shares responsibility for his or her own engagement. The guidelines for these discussions include: Whoever comes is the right person; whatever happens is the only thing that could have—even a seeming tangent in a conversation could yield a jewel of discovery; whenever it starts is the right time; and when it's over, it's over—if your discussion ends early, join another conversation in progress. If your discussion runs overtime, follow it and see what you discover. And if you are in a conversation where you are neither learning nor contributing, respect the group and yourself by leaving to join another conversation—or take a walk and return refreshed and ready to reengage. Your best work is needed. In taking good care of yourself, you also give your best to the group for the task at hand. Finally, be prepared to be surprised—if you hold too tightly to your own agenda, you may miss an amazing discovery that can emerge from passionate people speaking—and listening—together (Heft, 2002; Owen, 1997).

Open Space (OS) has been used to share best practices, rebuild communities after war, increase efficiency and revenue, design land use, create new products, discuss ethnicity and culture, develop strategic plans, and bring perceived adversaries together. It has been used by rabbis and imams sharing thoughts about peace, Haitians building literacy programs, South Africans working together after apartheid, students, parents, managers, activists, engineers, and architects.

For the Rome meeting, there were many challenging premeetings to bring together diverse people from "left and right"—not just the usual peacemakers—to build partnerships and co-ownership. This contributed greatly to the depth of conversation at the meeting. This pre-work—on the nature and complexity of the invitation to participate, and on the delicacy of selecting diverse participants while navigating heightened emotions and assumptions—was difficult and exhausting but essential to the success of the event. It involved the combined work and dedication of sponsers, steering committees and supporters on all sides negotiating, mediating and using all their best resources and connections.

> Maybe we would find a way. That way would not be easy, having many dark and fearful places. But we could not avoid the dark, or we would never see the light. And so we started. (Owen, 2002)

Owen invited the participants to announce discussion topics they would like to host—whatever had heart and meaning for them. Conversations began in groups of 2 or 20 as they talked, struggled, shared their grief, rage, and experiences. As the day continued, people moved from issue to issue in a room full of circle conversations.

> Sitting in that space, I felt an incredible flow of passion, desire, hope, exasperation and fear—it was all coming out. But as we came to the end of the day, there was a peace which did not exclude conflict but somehow transcended it. We gathered in the circle and shared as Palestinians and Israelis passed an olive branch each to the other. (Owen, 2002)

The next day the discussions continued.

> It was deep and it went deeper. The waves of pain and fear rolled on. There was nothing to do but simply be there with it all. After all, this was why we came together. And yet through it all I knew that the hope had been real, the space had been open, we had seen some light. We could carry both the light and the darkness and continue the journey—our choice. At the end of the final day, the olive branch was passed again. The last to speak was the head of the Islamic community in Rome, who said, "The Koran teaches us that to kill one person is to kill us all. And to save one person is to save the world. We must take whatever steps we can." (Owen, 2002)

After the meeting, participants reflected upon their experience (Kasbari, Haramati, & Averbuch, 2004). These included statements like:

We witnessed how people from the two sides of the conflict connected in a fantastic way and discovered their humanity. What made the meeting successful is that the human dimension, and not the system or state, was in the center of it. This meeting was a sweet moment in the middle of anger.

This meeting was an overwhelming experience at every possible level. While eating, drinking, or discussing issues, we felt we had a strong sense of mission. We wanted to break taboos. We had passed all the rituals of name-calling and finger pointing.

This was an inspiring, empowering, and exciting experience that I wish I could have more often. There was once a time when I felt that I wanted to kill someone because of what he had to say—but here I was smiling instead.

It brought about a feeling of emancipation—gave hope to people by listening to their stories and narratives. Storytelling, as a basic element of survival, humanizes people.

OS allowed us to show everything without tricks. It showed the real nature of people and provided an enabling system for communicating. Although this was at times difficult, no one walked out, neither physically nor psychologically.

Open Space enabled people to talk without inhibitions. It created a situation where we could not hold back things. Most amazing was how it makes us flow.

OS worked fantastically when we were dealing with the most upsetting and complicated issues like security. Although the discussions were hard it really worked despite the ongoing blood circle. I can't see how it will solve the conflict. Maybe it doesn't work in this sense. But it will bring the respect to each other and reduce the fear and the distrust that the conflict brings.

I also realized that if I invest more in myself, structure my priorities as a citizen, communicate better with others about my hopes, inspirations, and fears, and open up, without lying, about my feelings, I'll gain people's trust. This is what I did in Rome. I was taking off my skin and saw others do the same. This is something I didn't think was possible before the meeting.

Israeli and Palestinian participants also shared what they learned about themselves and each other.

During the meeting, I got to know Israelis personally. This was better than reading about them or learning about them from their news. I learned about them from their personality. We became individuals, humans.

I learned that we have to move from sympathy (which is based on my worldview, my ego) to empathy (which is released from my ego, an understanding that demands stepping out of myself and entering the existential experience of the other) for the Palestinians. To experience their experience.

If we want to make peace we need to build trust and in trust building two things are critically important: empathy and introspection. Empathy so we could understand the other in his own way and introspection so we could take responsibility for past mistakes and wrong perceptions.

Israelis and Palestinians making peace is like a couple in a process of divorce: they make the decision, as adults, that they don't want to live together any more, yet they have to make up their minds whether to develop a new independent narrative and go each to their own new life or continue to attack and bury one another. Our role now is to take responsibility for the well-being of our mutual children.

The meeting gave me an alternative way to look at things related to our life, conflict, and people. It forced me to put myself in their shoes and see things in a way I never saw before, even when I lived with them daily.

We didn't reach agreements but all the social barriers fell down. Open Space enabled people to meet in a very open and flowing way, to physically touch one another, to do something naturally together.

Change takes practice. People muddle through. Mistakes are made, lessons are learned, we listen, we stop listening, and then we try again. Conversation by conversation, if we keep opening the space for true listening and dialogue, a sometimes imperceptible change . . . happens. And person by person, moment by moment, breath by breath . . . the threads of peace and understanding can be found and slowly woven together. And when in doubt, the only thing to do is to open a little more space . . . and keep the conversation going . . .

References

Heft, L. (2002). *Opening space for collaboration and communication.* Retrieved January 28, 2007, from http://www.openingspace.net.

Heft, L. (2003, July). *The open space idea book.* Berkeley, CA: Author.

Kasbari, C. D., Haramati, A., & Averbuch, T. (2004, January). The practice of peace in practice: The Israeli Palestinian example—Qualitative research on the Israeli Palestinian Open Space Gathering, June 6–9, 2002, Rome, Italy. [Unpublished report.] Jerusalem and Holon, Israel.

Owen, H. (1997). *Open space technology: A user's guide* (2nd ed.). San Francisco: Berrett-Koehler.

Owen, H. (2002). *Opening space for peace.* Retrieved January 28, 2007, from http://www.openspaceworld.com/opening_space_for_peace.htm.

Owen, H. (2004). *The Practice of Peace.* Circle Pines, MN: Human Systems Dynamic Institute Press.

PART III

THE ARTS AND HEROES IN BUILDING PEACE

Distance is created by fear and lack of knowledge. When you see how similar we are, the fear disappears.

—*Ayala, a teen in the photography arts program for youth sponsored by Givat Haviva Jewish Arab Center for Peace*

We laugh at the same things. We have to work together, we can't do it alone.

—*Ortal, teen in Givat Haviva sailing program*

Service to humanity should be a team sport.

—*Ed Artis, humanitarian featured in the documentary "Call to Action"*

In creating together, people open their hearts, drop their defenses, and discover deep appreciation and connection. That's a solid psychological phenomenon, and a fact: that creative efforts and cultural exchanges are a useful and effective common meeting ground for peace, providing activities that explore one's self and bridge gaps between others. Creative projects are springing up both in the Holy Land and other countries to bring Arabs and Jews, Palestinians and Israelis, and people from other religions and countries together in activities for peace—cooking, camping, climbing mountains, and even cross-country trekking. Such activities, presented in the chapters in this Part, are aimed at breaking down physical and psychological barriers as a metaphor for making deep connections.

Sports like soccer and karate are also increasingly playing an important part in providing a fertile field for peace. An excellent historical example of this is the "ping-pong diplomacy" of the 1950s, when previously closed China extended a groundbreaking hand in peace and invited the U.S. ping-pong team to compete—proving that if people can relate, so can countries. By singing, sailing and staging dramas, young people are making their voice heard in support of peace. They are even learning how to solve the region's environmental challenges, in programs like that of the Arava Institute. Camps provide another ideal opportunity for young people to bond in friendship, in a fun and relaxed environment, especially when their home countries are in conflict. Many of such opportunities abound, from the well-known Seeds of Peace to other retreats which allow a safe haven for learning about each other, bonding with respect and understanding and empowering people to carry the lessons of peace back to their family and communities. In the following chapters, analyses of the outcome of several of these experiences reveals valuable insights into how they work, why they don't, and what can be done.

Some programs covered in the following chapters have made headlines—deservedly so—for their ambitious and effective efforts in bringing together Arabs and Jews, Israelis and Palestinians. Others have not hit the news, but are profoundly significant nonetheless. These fit what New School for Social Research sociology professor Jeffrey C. Goldfarb calls the "politics of small things." In his book *The Politics of Small Things: The Power of the Powerless in Dark Times* (University of Chicago Press, 2006), Goldfarb points out that change is accomplished by "working together beyond the confines of political divisions on a regular everyday basis." The everyday efforts presented in this part highlight the power of replacing bullets and bombs with creative efforts that bring friendship and cooperation necessary for peaceful coexistence.

CHAPTER 18

YOUNG LEADERS ON THE FRONT LINES FOR PALESTINIAN-ISRAELI PEACE

Rachel Brandenburg

While I note with frustration that there is no telling when a negotiated political settlement might be achieved between Israelis and Palestinians, certain initiatives between citizens give me hope. These initiatives are unique not only in their approach to conflict resolution, but also in that they are coordinated primarily by students, for students. These initiatives facilitate important cross-cultural sensitivities and sensibilities that will undoubtedly make a difference when the students involved today become the leaders of tomorrow.

Each generation raised to hate without knowledge of or exposure to the other postpones the potential for future peace and reconciliation. Challenges to exchanges and engagement between young people exist—through travel restrictions between Israel and the Palestinian territories and through geographic distance between individuals in the region and in the United States. Despite challenges, a handful of Israeli, Palestinian, Israeli-Arab, and American young people are developing conflict resolution skill-building programs, coexistence-building exercises, Arab-Jewish dialogue, and other creative programs to further Israeli-Palestinian youth's understanding and reconciliation on a communal level in the region, and to bridge the gap between communities in the Middle East and in the West. This chapter reviews some of these programs.

The New Initiative for Middle East Peace (NIMEP), Tufts University

Shortly after the start of the second Intifada in September 2000, a small group of Jewish American, Israeli, Arab, and Palestinian students at Tufts University convened to begin a weekly on-campus Jewish-Arab dialogue. Recognizing stark differences in their perceptions and opinions of the Arab-Israeli conflict, yet interested in understanding these differences, they met for two hours each week, to converse, debate, argue, and share personal stories related to the Middle East. Through laughter and tears, relationships developed and students who started off as strangers became close friends. As students graduated and the participants in this dialogue group changed, the nature of the conversations evolved as appropriate.

After participating in the dialogue group together for over a semester, a handful of students—American Jewish, Israeli, Lebanese Palestinian, Iranian, Saudi, Jordanian, and myself (an American Jew)—having developed an understanding about each other's positions on the Israeli-Palestinian conflict and other regional confrontations, felt compelled to do something beyond sitting around and talking about the problems in the Middle East.

We conceived the New Initiative for Middle East Peace (NIMEP) in 2003 as a forum for students interested in the Middle East to engage in productive dialogue, academic research, and hands-on exploration of the region. It was to be a student think-tank, and a means to engage the on-campus and broader local communities in productive discussion and consideration of a future resolution to the Israeli-Palestinian conflict. We dreamed that one day we would travel to the region together to discover the situation on the ground, and engage local academics, students, and politicians in dialogue about prospects for the future. Within only three years, and with tireless efforts of a number of driven and dedicated students, the guidance of professors and others who believed in our capacity to succeed, and the constant support from the Institute for Global Leadership at Tufts, our hopes for NIMEP have been achieved, and our dreams have been realized—far beyond what we would have then imagined (http://www. tuftsgloballeadership.org/NIMEP/index.html).

In February 2003, we had the fortunate opportunity to consult the president of Al-Quds University and former Palestinian Authority official Sari Nusseibeh, and the former head of the Israeli Shin Bet (Israeli national intelligence services) Ami Ayalon, regarding our plans. They had come to Tufts to present their own coexistence-building initiative—the People's Voice Campaign—and graciously gave us a morning of their time. Ten months later, 12 Tufts students—Jewish, Christian, Muslim, American, Israeli, and Palestinian—were en route to Israel and the West Bank for NIMEP's very first fact-finding mission. There we met with Israeli and Palestinian academics, students, journalists, politicians, activists, and others, in Haifa, Jerusalem, Tel Aviv, Ariel, Ramallah, Hebron, Bethlehem, and Dheisheh Refugee Camp. Upon return to Tufts, NIMEP leaders Matt Edmundson and Matan Chorev created a documentary chronicling the trip and what we had learned, which has since been screened to more than 1,000 people.

The documentary featured the perspectives of individuals with whom we spoke, on issues such as the separation barrier, security concerns, and a future settlement on territory, as well as reflections from students in our delegation. One Muslim student who had never previously visited Israel said, "I went into the trip thinking I was going to get some clarity on the situation, but only realized how much more complicated it is after being there and seeing it. I always talk about how when I get older I want to devote my life to human rights and conflict resolution, but it's very difficult to see how far there is to go, especially in this region." Another student commented on the uniqueness of the Old City of Jerusalem, "The aura inside the walls of the Old City was truly unique and holy but was not exempt from the harshness of the political reality. Even the most sacrosanct places in the world were being corrupted by the hand of human irresponsibility."

Another student, reacting to an afternoon spent with students and faculty at Bir Zeit University in Ramallah, said, "The students are Bir Zeit are much like ourselves in many ways, but the atmosphere in which they live is a completely different reality from anything we know. Whereas students at Tufts, for example, involve themselves in student groups such as Tufts Democrats or Republicans, their equivalent political action groups include Hamas, Fatah, and Islamic Jihad. What we consider cultural groups here are only beginning to appear on their campus. Because life for them is so directly impacted by politics, the political sentiment on the Bir Zeit campus is considered a representative microcosm of political sentiment in the city of Ramallah. This is completely different from politics on college campuses in the U.S."

The trip enabled students and faculty to better understand their own, each other's, and their Israeli and Palestinian counterparts' respective religions, cultures, politics, and societies in a way that could never have been achieved without the person-to-person interaction.

NIMEP has continued to conduct on-campus programming and individual research, and attract additional student involvement. After the successful trip to Israel and the West Bank, two Iranian Tufts students worked tirelessly to coordinate a trip for undergraduate and graduate students from Tufts and the Fletcher School to travel to Iran. With an invitation from the School for International Relations in Tehran, five Tufts undergraduates and five Fletcher graduate students engaged in a two-week dialogue on the future of U.S.-Iran relations with a cross-section of Iranian individuals, including students, academics, a journalist, an artist, athletes, religious clerics, representatives of the Armenian and Jewish communities, and others. As the first American student delegation formally invited to the country since the Iranian revolution in 1979, we traveled to Esfahan, Shiraz, the holy city of Qom, and went hiking through the Kooh Mountains.

A student delegation to Egypt followed, in coordination with a delegation from Northeastern University. In the winter of 2005, a NIMEP trip to Turkey brought together Turkish, American, and Israeli students to explore national, ethnic, and religious identity in Turkey. Students visited the major cities of Istanbul and Ankara, and smaller towns and villages in the southeast and eastern coast of the country.

To chronicle our trips to Israel and the West Bank, Egypt, Iran, and independent student research trips, we created the first annual NIMEP research journal in 2004. Entitled *NIMEP Insights*, the journal included student and faculty research, reflections and photographs related to the Israeli-Palestinian conflict and broader Middle East. The first issue included my article on Israeli-Palestinian coexistence-building initiatives; an analysis of the portrayal of Jewish and Arab Israelis in Israeli and Palestinian television; and a discussion of the role of feminist nonviolence and peace movements in Palestinian society during the first Intifada; and other topics such as Iran and U.S. foreign policy in Iraq. *NIMEP Insights* was entirely student-produced and has now seen two successful issues.

Student involvement in NIMEP has grown from five students to more than 40, and the group has become a familiar face both on the Tufts campus and in communities NIMEP students have visited and engaged. According to co-founder Matan Chorev, "NIMEP has shown its ability to sustain itself beyond the original cadre of founders. The numerous programs and projects it has spawned have taken on lives of their own. Partnerships with local NGOs, professors, and a vast student network continue to grow deeper and the tent is becoming ever larger. The future of NIMEP on Tufts campus is secure."[1]

Middle East Education through Technology (MEET)

Israeli and Palestinian high school students rarely have the opportunity to interact with one another face-to-face, especially after the outbreak of the second Intifada. But three Israeli students changed that. Israeli students Anat Binur, Assaf Harlap, and Yaron Binur were studying abroad at the Massachusetts Institute of Technology (MIT) in Boston, Massachusetts, when they got the idea for a program using technology and business to educate Palestinian and Israeli youngsters about interpersonal and professional skills, while learning to work together. In its nonprofit educational program, called Middle East Education through Technology (MEET), students from the United States travel to Israel to train the Israeli and Palestinian students.

"We decided that since the three of us were studying abroad and gaining tools from top universities—in computers, education, and management—that we would create a program that would make a difference back home where we live," says Anat about the program she and her friends established in 2004.[2]

MIT students, chosen for their dedication, enthusiasm, and leadership potential, spend up to three summers in Israel teaching the high school students computer skills. Professors develop the curriculum, and direct the summer training.

"We believe that if you take Palestinian and Israeli youth who are 15 years old and bring them together and create this common language of business and technology while they study together with others they would otherwise never be exposed to, and empower them together," Anat says, "then 20, 30 years from now, these are the leaders of the future." The students discover similar interests, abilities, and goals.

Holding the program in the Middle East allows the teens to develop relationships within the reality of their daily lives. For example, an Israeli student, Shiri, volunteered to help a Palestnian student after the latter missed classes because of getting stuck at a checkpoint. As one male Palestinian MEET student says, "I never thought I would get to be close with Israeli kids. Now when you see us working together, it is hard to know who is an Israeli and who is an Arab." An Israeli student says similarly, "I never thought I would befriend an Arab. . . . I was a settler and now it's all completely different. I have understood that we are both human beings. We simply have different opinions and we both want different things, but we are doing it the wrong way."[3]

Says Abeer Hazboun, MEET's director, "After four years of many hardships during the second Intifada, most people in the Middle East had already lost their faith in any solution . . . however . . . it was amazing to see MEET's students—15-year-old teenagers—working together on a common passion which was the computer. And during breaks, you would see them playing around and shouting each other's names in different languages, Abdullah, Yohanan, Intisar, Miri . . . "

The MIT students also get valuable experience. One American student said, "Working at MEET has been an opportunity to see past the 'events' level and look to the individuals. I've been pleasantly surprised by how quickly political and cultural differences fall away when our students are focused on the common goal of mastering difficult computer science curriculum."[4]

The first summer's five-week curriculum typically includes Java programming, problem solving, and teamwork and leadership skills. The importance of national and cultural diversity in teamwork is emphasized in team-based assignments. During the year, they meet every month to advance their projects and continue to develop team skills. The next summer they can return to learn entrepreneurship, and business and project management skills. During the year, they can apply their new skills with real-life clients in business or university settings. In the third summer, they can be teaching assistants or do an internship in a regional high-tech company. The first graduates of all three years of the program finished in 2006. Says Anat, "A student who graduates MEET is part of a family—a family of support that includes the academic world and the business world."[5]

The MEET program (http://www.m-e-e-t.org/news.html) is respected in the business community and recently received a generous gift from a wealthy Palestinian businessman (that allowed them to acquire a permanent office and computer lab space) and a donation of 15 computers from Sun Microsystems Israel.[6] Daimler-Chrysler has actively advocated for Israeli business investment in the program. Besides support from MIT professors and students, Hebrew University of Jerusalem allows MEET to use university space and resources. The program has been featured on television and in print media in Israel and the United States, including Israeli Channel 10 News, Radio Shams, and *Ma'ariv* newspaper, and *The Washington Times*.[7]

Ahmed, a Palestinian MEET student, says, "MEET affects not only the participants but also their friends and families. We can use the tools and experience we gained in MEET to create a new joint community."

Students in the MEET program gain practical professional skills but also confidence in themselves, and in future reconciliation between Israelis and Palestinians. Young people who had never met "the other" or ever imagined a Palestinian or Israeli as a peer now call each other friends and recognize the humanity across all sides of the conflict. They become a part of a growing personal and professional network aimed at productive engagement of peoples, businesses, and communities across the divide.

Soliya

The Internet is being harnessed as a learning tool for Palestinian, Arab, and American youth in another program, called Soliya, founded in 2002. Co-founders Lucas Welch and Liza Chambers wanted to enable students from colleges in the United States and Arab world to communicate directly from their homes or classrooms, in real-time, about global issues and cultural differences (www.soliya. net). Unlike the aforementioned initiatives, Soliya does not bring together Israeli Jews and Palestinians; however, the Israeli-Palestinian conflict is a matter of concern for the American, Arab, and Palestinian students involved and a topic frequently addressed nonetheless. Participants in Soliya's Connect Program "meet" face-to-face online for two hours once a week in groups of eight, including four American university students and four university students from the Arab world, facilitated by two trained facilitators. Each group has its own Web page and online resources to use throughout the semester. Students also follow a curriculum outside the dialogue time.

The name *Soliya*—*Sol* meaning "sun" in Latin and *Iya* meaning "beam of light" in Arabic—appropriately reflects the organizational goal: "to shed light on the relationship between the US and the Arab and Muslim world in a way that promotes understanding, respect, and joint action."[8]

Liza spent many years working in conflict zones around the world, including the Balkans, Middle East, and South Africa, doing transformative dialogue work and facilitation training. Lucas came to Jerusalem as an ABC news producer. After teaching media at Bir Zeit University and completing research on Internet communities at Harvard University, he saw that new Internet technologies could be used to stimulate the dialogue experience at extremely low cost and thus reach a broader cross-section of society. "By integrating media into the dialogue program," says Liza, "I saw that you could give participants the tools they need to bring what they learned to a broader audience."[9]

Soliya's Connect Program helps students develop friendly relationships while learning new Internet technologies and media skills to express their ideas and opinions effectively to a wider audience. It also helps them recognize and confront media bias. Students participate in a joint final project for the semester program. Past projects have included newspaper articles that are submitted to Common Ground News Service, a newswire organized by Search for Common Ground to serve regional and U.S. national publications. Other students have produced documentaries, with raw footage from television outlets such as the British BBC, Reuters news service, and Al-Jazeera. Policy memos that students produced are submitted to another initiative of Search for Common Ground, developing strategies for U.S. engagement with the Muslim world.

"For me, the weekly dialogues were amazing," says an American Soliya participant from the University of Iowa. "Sitting down to talk to such a diverse group of students offered the opportunity to dig into a number of issues, which ranged from personal affairs to large-scale political maneuvers. I began to foster a more complex perspective about Middle Eastern students and our interactions."

An evaluation of the program after the spring 2005 semester showed that 83 percent of the participants reported being motivated to learn more about the relationship between the United States and the Arab and Muslim world. Nearly three-quarters of the Arab participants and 83 percent of the American participants predicted that they would now play a larger role than they expected, informing their peers about U.S.-Arab relations, and had the skills to make a positive contribution to world affairs. Forty-three percent of Arab students and 70 percent of American students felt that the program contributed to their ability to understand and recognize bias in the media. Four out of ten students signed up for facilitator training, joint video projects, and Cooperative Action projects. The number of students who have elected to participate in similar continued engagement activities has been consistent across all past semesters.

A male student from Virginia Commonwealth University said, "This was the most rewarding class I have taken so far in college. I was able to gain a wealth of knowledge and meet people from across the world. I think these are the steps we need to take in order to make a difference in today's world community." A female Kuwaiti student from the University of Kuwait said, "The program introduced me to a new concept that is you don't need to travel to interact with people who have different ideas about a subject. It provided an environment where you wanted to discuss what you felt."

About two-thirds of participants felt that the program helped them develop skills that would assist them in resolving everyday conflicts. As a female Egyptian participant said, "I got to learn how to become a good listener, I learned that I can accept other views or try to convey mine in a decent way without having to challenge the other view. I gained more knowledge about many political issues that I hadn't been concerned with before, I learned about many different cultures and learned to accept our differences. I really learned a lot."

Since 2003, the number of student participants continues to rise and expand to universities including Al-Akhawayn University in Morocco; American University in Beirut, Cairo, and Kuwait; Birzeit University and Al Quds University in the Palestinian Territories; Dar Al-Hekma College in Saudi Arabia; South Valley University in Egypt; and campuses in the United States, including the University of North Carolina, University of Iowa, Tufts University, Harvard University, Carnegie Mellon and Bryn Mawr Colleges.

In 2004, Soliya was named among the "World's Best Emerging Social-Entrepreneurs" by global social venture fund Echoing Green, and has recently received grants from the United States Institute for Peace (USIP), the Norwegian government, and Kingdom Holdings.

The program's success is summed up by the reactions of a female Lebanese participant, who said, "Soliya encouraged and inspired me to take a more proactive role in my community by providing me with the tools for discussion, expression, and engagement."

Other Youth Programs

Building Bridges for Peace—the flagship program of a Denver- and Jerusalem-based conflict-resolution organization called Seeking Common Ground—brings together an ethnically and religiously diverse group of young women ages 16 to19 from Israel, the Palestinian Territories, and the United States for an intensive summer program in Jerusalem. The teens work together to develop leadership skills and effective communication techniques, and engage in activities that promote the status and empowerment of women. The students can continue activities from their home communities throughout the year.

Windows is a Hebrew-Arabic magazine that conveys the messages of young Israelis and Palestinians across the divide, through writing, art, and photographs. Founded in 1991, its form and content have evolved with the political situation. A Windows Palestinian-Israeli Friendship Center was opened in Tel Aviv in February 1999, and Windows' activities expanded to include lectures, movies, and encounter programs.

OneVoice is a grassroots organization that engages youth along with older age groups to network with ordinary Israelis and Palestinians as well as experts, dignitaries, celebrities, and spiritual leaders to educate people about themselves and "the other," and about nonviolent means for resolving conflict. Its Proclamation of Principles for Reconciliation, distributed among Israeli and Palestinian societies, raises awareness and deliberation over key issues aimed at a political settlement. OneVoice Youth leaders have represented the initiative worldwide, traveling across the United States to speak to American university campuses. In April 2006, a OneVoice youth leader was elected to the Israeli Knesset.

AID (Americans for Informed Democracy) is an organization that helps college students develop campus activities and community "town hall meetings on issues related to democracy"; but its "Hope not Hate" initiative also facilitates dialogue between Arabs and Americans aimed at mutual understanding. The editor of this volume, Dr. Judy Kuriansky, facilitated a workshop for this purpose at its annual meeting in 2005.

Young writer, storyteller, and conflict-resolution practitioner Carol Grosman is working with photographer Lloyd Wolf since 2002 on a book, performance, exhibit, and dialogue workshop—called Jerusalem Stories—to present the stories of Jerusalem residents from diverse backgrounds (tour guides, artists, housewives,

victims of violence, cab drivers, shopkeepers, students, religious and secular people, older people and youth) to resolve hostility by highlighting common feelings
and experiences of those who live in the extraordinary city of Jerusalem.

Conclusion

Despite the tension and strife surrounding the Israeli-Palestinian conflict,
some young people are learning about each other as human beings and friends,
rather than as offenders and enemies. Educational and cultural exchange between young people living in historically conflicted regions is an important step
toward resolution and reconciliation.

As a young person myself, these programs offer me hope. I am reminded of a
song I first heard and called my favorite at age 10, although the lyrics have taken
on new meaning for me over time and as I learned more about the Israeli-
Palestinian conflict. Written almost three decades ago (on the eve of the 1977
peace negotiations between Egyptian President Anwar Sadat and Israeli Prime
Minister Menachem Begin), *Yihiye Tov* ("There Will Be Goodness"), by Israeli
singer David Broza and poet Yonatan Gefen, describes a reality—war—and an
attitude—cautious optimism—that have remained relevant in the context of the
Israeli-Palestinian conflict:

> There will be goodness, yes, there will be goodness. . . . The children wear wings and
> fly off to the army, and after two years they return without anymore answers /
> People live with anxiety, looking for reasons to breathe / But between the hatred
> and the murder, they still talk about peace.

The work of NIMEP, MEET, Soliya, and other initiatives helps me continue
to believe that one day yet, "there will be goodness, yes, there will be goodness."

Notes

1. M. Chorev, personal communication, March 20, 2006.
2. A. Binur, personal communication, March 27, 2006.
3. Israel Channel 10 News, July 28, 2004. Retrieved March 15, 2006, from http://www.m-e-e-t.org/impact.html.
4. E. A. Sylweser, Computers build Middle East ties, *The Washington Times*, July 26, 2005. Retrieved on March 15, 2006, from http://washtimes.com/upi/20050720–022727–1863r.htm.
5. Israel Channel 10 News. Retrieved on March 15, 2006.
6. MEET Newsletter, Winter 2006. Retrieved on March 15, 2006, from http://www.m-e-e-t.org/news/winter06/index.html.
7. E. A. Sylweser, Computers build Middle East ties, *The Washington Times*, July 26, 2005. Retrieved on March 15, 2006, from http://washtimes.com/upi/20050720–022727–1863r.htm.
8. L. Chambers, personal communication, March 29, 2006.
9. L. Chambers, personal communication, May 17, 2006.

CHAPTER 19

JUST VISION: IN SEARCH OF ISRAELI AND PALESTINIAN MORNING-AFTER LEADERSHIP

Ronit Avni

An orthodox Jewish supporter of the illegal extremist group Kach is now one of the most renowned Israeli feminist peace builders. A Palestinian imprisoned for a decade as his friends built a bomb to detonate against Israelis now works to bring Palestinian and Israeli youth together. A former West Bank settler who supported the ultra-ethnonationalist Israeli Moledet party now stands with the women of Machsomwatch to monitor soldier conduct at checkpoints. A wounded Palestinian spends four years in prison. He then forms an organization to promote nonviolence among Palestinian society and also works alongside Israeli bereaved parents.

These are some of the amazing people we encounter as we research and document Palestinian and Israeli civilians who are what I refer to in half-jest as "morning-after" leaders—people who have gotten past romantic hopes for peace but who nevertheless step forward to serve their communities in times of painful sobriety, when pessimism, hopelessness, and fear characterize daily life.

Giving voice to these individuals is one of the aims of Just Vision—to widen their influence by connecting them to one another, to journalists, policymakers, and supportive communities.

I became involved in this work in the late 1990s as a volunteer for two human rights organizations in Israel, at the height of the Oslo peace process. At the

---

This text is based on an acceptance speech delivered at Auburn Seminary's Lives of Commitment Award Ceremony on June 9, 2005, and an article from Ronit Avni's essay, "Inverting the Shame-Based Human Rights Documentation Model in the Context of the Palestinian-Israeli Conflict," in *American Anthropologist*, March 2006.

time, the Israeli economy surged, new diplomatic relations formed, and a general sense of optimism pervaded the mainstream Israeli public.

Yet in the West Bank, Gaza, and East Jerusalem, Palestinians had already lost hope. The excitement they felt at the beginning of the Oslo process several years before was supplanted by disillusionment and distrust as their economy shrank, settlements grew, and local corruption festered.

The gulf between these two worlds was palpable and painful for those of us at the grassroots level who interacted with, and cared about, both societies. When the Oslo talks collapsed and violence resumed, any lingering thoughts of peace seemed to vanish. This is when "morning-after" leaders began to emerge.

Since then, in the face of devastating violence and pain following the collapse of Oslo, thousands of ordinary people stepped forward to end the bloodshed, to preserve human rights, and to promote reconciliation among Israelis and Palestinians. These sobered civilians refuse to abandon their fellow citizens to an endless cycle of violence. Regardless of any personal feelings of hurt, blame, or betrayal, these civic leaders recognize their own power to ameliorate the situation, and act. Their dedication to their communities drives them to operate outside the mainstream consensus, even at personal, political, or professional risk to themselves and to their families. Their work is more important now than ever.

At the height of violence in 2003, I launched Just Vision in order to find, reach out to, and publicize the work of Israeli and Palestinian peace builders. Sadly, amid profuse television broadcasts and newspaper reports of violence and violations, the media often ignores and thus marginalizes those people who embody the values of tolerance, equality, respect, nonviolence, and due process. Since they receive limited attention or mainstream backing, the staff of Just Vision works to highlight what they are doing to improve the situation, and encourage Israeli, Palestinian, and North American audiences to learn from such courageous individuals and to support their efforts.

Just Vision's core staff of Palestinian, Israeli, North and South American women has met with hundreds of bereaved parents, religious leaders, artists, educators, urban planners, Holocaust survivors, farmers, and economists from every geographical location, sector, and religious denomination who have been crossing checkpoints and boundaries to build a different future. These Israelis and Palestinians are by no means unanimous in their analyses of the root causes of the conflict, or its ideal resolution. Yet the differences between them may prove both informative and constructive.

Just Vision is interviewing 180 of these civic leaders in Arabic, Hebrew, and English, and teaming up with teachers to create curricula about their activities for use in classrooms, with a focus on how each of us can be agents of change.

There is Dr. Sami Adwan and Dr. Bar-On, two courageous educators who piloted an initiative to have Palestinian and Israeli teachers co-draft history textbooks that feature the two, often dissonant, narratives without glossing over complexities.

There is Orly Noy, who immigrated to Israel from Iran and is now the Hebrew language host and producer at All for Peace, the first radio station to broadcast in Arabic and Hebrew, staffed by a team of Palestinians and Israelis.

There is Khulood Badawi, a Palestinian citizen of Israel who is active on a leadership level with many joint Jewish-Palestinian organizations, including the Association for Civil Rights in Israel (ACRI), Ta'ayush, and the Women's Coalition. Khulood seeks to raise awareness about Palestinian realities on both sides of the Green Line through demonstrations, meetings, and public relations campaigns.

Interviews with these and other individuals are online at www.justvision.org with channels for getting involved so that audiences worldwide can support these inspiring people. In the interviews, we explore: Who are these peace builders? What are they doing? Why? At what cost? What lessons have they learned along the way that could prove beneficial to others seeking to follow their lead? How is it that many survived losing their children, their homes, their liberty, and their sense of security and now pursue a nonvengeful path? The Parents Circle: Bereaved Families Forum, for instance, consists of more than 500 Palestinian and Israeli families that have lost next of kin to the conflict. Its members are doing everything in their power to preserve lives on both sides.

We are also examining and publishing the history of this conflict in an exciting new way: Rather than presenting the bifurcated, contested narrative about the history of this issue, which juxtaposes a singular Palestinian perspective with an Israeli one, we are asking all 180 interviewees to name up to ten historical events, and up to four personal events that have shaped their understanding of the conflict and inspired them to take action. We are aggregating the responses so that audiences can see the points of agreement and divergence among those Palestinians and Israelis most committed to resolving the conflict through nonviolent means.

Of all these 180 interviews, we chose a few particularly riveting stories that we have turned into a feature-length documentary film, called *Encounter Point*. It features the stories of a former Israeli settler, a Palestinian ex-prisoner, a bereaved Israeli mother, and a wounded Palestinian bereaved brother who cross paths in one of the most explosive regions in the world. Over the course of the film, they must confront hatred in their communities and fear within themselves.

As one of the lead characters, Shlomo Zagman, jests: "People on the Left and the Right see it all clearly. They have slogans, which they write on stickers and place on cars. But if, like me, your position is a full page, how can you make it a sticker? Who will read it?"

The film premiered in the spring of 2006 at the Tribeca Film Festival, and won the San Francisco International Film Festival Audience Award. *Encounter Point* was screened before the United Nations, and in more than 50 cities worldwide, including and festivals from Jerusalem to Dubai. *Encounter Point* is co-directed by Julia Bacha, the co-writer and editor of the documentary film *Control*

Room, about the U.S. military and Al Jazeera coverage of the U.S. invasion of Iraq.

As we produce the online interviews and distribute the film, we are engaging with media makers, to ask that they pay more attention to the very people who are preaching tolerance, democracy, and nonviolence. These trailblazers are helping to curb and heal the pain that we have all caused. They are compromising, organizing, and making amends.

For instance, Itamar Shapira is a member of Combatants for Peace, a joint organization of Palestinians and Israelis who formerly took part in the armed conflict and are now leveraging their status as former fighters to call for reconciliation.

Ibraham Issa was once firebombed for launching the Hope Flowers school, which teaches democracy and tolerance. It was the first Palestinian school to teach its students Hebrew in a future-driven effort to foster understanding.

Through the sustained political and civic engagement of these courageous individuals—with help from the international community—I believe that these efforts will ultimately lead to systemic and constructive transformations in the direction of a peaceful, rights-respecting, equitable, and dignified future. The question is: How long will it take, and how many among us will join them?

CHAPTER 20

COMING SOON TO A THEATER NEAR YOU: THE ISRAELI-PALESTINIAN CONFLICT AT THE MOVIES

Meir Fenigstein
As told to Rachel Summer Claire Friedman

> Then Moshe says to me, You know what Hanna? The only thing it is sure in Israel, it is the Intifada and the war.
>
> —*Hanna, Free Zone*

Yes, we have continued conflict in Israel. And sometimes it seems as if it's never going to end. However, one thing that I am sure about Israel is that there is one kind of shooting that should be encouraged as much as possible among Israelis and Palestinians: shooting movies! I'm convinced it's one way to cope with all the suffering that continues to occur.

For 21 years, as the founder of the Israel Film Festival and the IsraFest Foundation, I have witnessed Israeli cinema evolve and mature into a sophisticated medium of creative expression with the ability to entertain audiences around the world, to show people that Israeli life is more rich and complex than the news flash of dead bodies after a suicide bomb attack, and to offer powerful new perspectives on the past, present, and future—hopefully one with less pain.

Many of the films we have shown are about life in Israel during wars and the Intifada, and relations between Israelis and Palestinians. I want to give people a view of the people who are living the war. Since films reach wide public audiences, they're a way to bring the situation among Israelis and Palestinians to public knowledge and reflection.

One of the best examples of how you can't escape the impact of the conflict on everyday life is a film that opened the 2002 film festival—*Trumpet in the Wadi*. Based on a very popular novel by Sami Michael, the movie is set in a working-class Arab-Jewish neighborhood in Haifa. Alex, a short, chunky, and quirky

Russian Jew moves into the same apartment building as Huda, an Israeli-Palestinian woman with whom he quickly becomes smitten. We start out laughing and optimistic about love surviving through a difficult time of Arab-Israeli discord, but Alex goes off to do his compulsory military service, and we end up crying and hating how the conflict tears people's lives apart.

Another good example is a film about the city of Ramleh where Israelis and Arabs live side by side and might care about each other if not for the political conflict.

Psychological Insight into the Culture and the People

Research proves the importance of movies in people's psyche, and the role films can play in helping people to talk about issues they would not ordinarily be exposed to. Watching movies and talking about them has been shown to be useful in therapy (Wedding, Boyd, & Niemiec, 2005). In the "talkback" technique, audiences process what they see by having a professional psychologist moderate discussions with the audience after a performance (Kuriansky, Walsh, & Laszczak, 2004). Many times after our films, we have such discussions with the filmmakers and other experts to give people an opportunity to discuss their reactions and feelings.

People can understand what is going on in Israel through documentaries, such as the story behind Rabin's assassination, or through docudramas, such as the conflicts that young soldiers feel between the positives of learning discipline and the negatives of having to fight.

Life in Israel is consumed with the "situation" (of the Intifada), but life does go on—people face everyday troubles, such as a daughter's suicide over incest as in *Out of Sight*, the film that opened the 2006 film festival.

In the Beginning

The theme of the pain of people is always in the back of my mind since my parents were both Holocaust survivors. Even though I try not to always think about it, you can't have parents who are Holocaust survivors and not think about how Jews were treated. I was born in 1950, two years after the state of Israel was formed.

I developed a strong interest in music as early as the first grade, when I played the drums at my school's morning assembly. My father bought me my first full drum set when I turned 15, and three years later when I went into the army like every sabra, I joined the Entertainment Division and five of us started performing for soldiers all over the country. I first really understood the importance of entertainment during rocky times of war when we performed for Israeli soldiers for six months during the Yom Kippur War and saw how we brought some relief into those soldiers' lives when they were so miserable in that horrible war.

Our rock band, Kaveret, became the leading rock band of the decade, like the Beatles (humbly) of Israel. When we disbanded in 1976, I went into acting and then to study music in Boston. By coincidence, someone asked me to bring a few movies from Israel back to Boston. When I went to a distributor in Israel to ask for the movies, he asked me, "Why just bring back two films. Take six and make a film festival." I said, "Hey, that's not a bad idea . . . " So, I went back to Boston and put together the first Israeli Film Festival, showing six films over four days—that's how it all began.

Dealing with Conflict

I then expanded to show 10 Israeli films in New York. My three goals were to do something with a vision, to be connected to the arts, and to connect people to Israel. That first year in New York was very difficult, but I believed in my vision and dream to bring the Israeli film industry to America.

The festival is not political but we have shown controversial films; during 1994–1998 we showed more of them because it was during the Oslo Accords and people were optimistic about peace, so people accepted them more. Things are different now. The situation is so inflammatory, that it's more difficult to show controversial films. But I still believe that watching a film about the situation can make it easier to handle it and to talk about the issues because it gives you a little distance, making it safer to talk.

Such films are even more important now because Israel is in the news, especially with the new Palestinian political party in power and everyone watching to see what happens, and wanting to get a sense of what is really going on regarding the political, cultural, educational, and social sides of Israel instead of just seeing what is shown on the news—that people criticize is so biased.

Movies don't have to have a social message, but some that I pick do. I'd like to think that some help Middle-Eastern-Western relations. In 1998 we showed a film called *Circus Palestina*, based on a true story about an Eastern European circus on tour in the West Bank that discovers that the lion has gone missing, and people who join the search make unlikely alliances.

Beyond Conflict

The fact that the festival continued despite the terror of the Intifada—and even 9/11 in New York—proves the importance of the creative arts in the midst of political conflict. When noted psychologist Dr. Judy Kuriansky was the master of ceremonies of the festival in 2002, she pointed out how when people are suffering, escape into films is a healthy release. At that event, Bette Midler serenaded HBO Chairman Michael Fuchs (who was honored) with her song "The Wind beneath My Wings"—symbolic of how important support is in times of terror. We also honored Eli Weisel—a teenage Holocaust survivor and symbol of how to survive terrorism.

Crossing Borders

> Mona's wedding day was the saddest day of her life. She knew that once she crosses
> the border she will never be able to come back to her family in the Golan Heights.
>
> —*The Syrian Bride*, 2004

In the last few years, we have been showing more films by Arab-Israelis. Last year, a big hit at the festival was *The Syrian Bride*, a film that won more awards internationally than any previous Israeli film. The movie is a collaboration between director Eran Riklis, an Israeli Jew, and Palestinian-Israeli screenwriter Suha Arraf; most of the cast is Palestinian-Israeli; and the script is a staggering multilingual combination of Arabic, English, Hebrew, Russian, and French. Mona, a Druze woman living in the Israeli-occupied Golan Heights, is about to be married to a Syrian television star from across the border. But because of the restrictions at the border, she has never been able to meet her groom, the wedding has to be held at the border, and once she crosses, she will not be able to return to see her family. Things don't go exactly as planned, and in the end, we get a powerful message about how politics can ruin people's basic innocent needs and desires. Importantly, the film doesn't blame one side or the other, but rather the bureaucracy perpetuated by both sides. And it leaves people questioning borders and boundaries, whether political, cultural, or personal.

The Jewish-Israeli and Palestinian-Israeli collaboration on the film is itself a type of "border crossing"—of a new type of cinema that is helping show that borders shouldn't matter. Another example is *Free Zone*, by renowned Israeli director Amos Gitai. A relationship develops among three women—Rebecca, an American played by the famous actress Natalie Portman; Hanna, an Israeli played by Hana Laszlo who won Best Actress at the Cannes Film Festival for this role; and Leila, a Palestinian played by Hiam Abbass—during a car ride across the Israeli-Jordanian border into an area in eastern Jordan set up as an economic free zone.

As Israeli filmmakers have more co-productions with Palestinians, we're going to see a new genre of films dealing at these levels that will be very interesting and a bridge to bring so-called enemies together.

Looking to the Future

We've shown more than 500 movies to more than half a million people in power cities in America (like New York and Los Angeles) with the largest Jewish and Israeli communities, not just in small screenings in a temple but on the big screen at a public movie theater. It's a big production for such a small country.

Some exciting things are happening in the Israeli film industry today. The Israeli government now distributes $15 million to support films; in 2004, one million people went to go see Israeli films in Israel compared to just 36,000 five years before; larger budgets and better technology have improved acting and the quality of the films that now get international attention and awards. This all spells potential for spreading understanding through the films, for making the possibility of peace and human relationships more of a sure thing than the persistent war.

Sometimes I get discouraged, but my mission is so strong that I keep on. Movies can't necessarily change decisions of leaders, but they can definitely help give another point of view. America has certainly changed a lot of the culture of other countries through its movies. But it takes time—maybe not this year but it's going to happen.

The film festival has been happening for more than 20 years—the largest international showcase for Israel with more than 500 movies shown to half a million people. So many changes have happened in Israel over that time, and in relationships among Israelis and Palestinians, yet filmmakers in both populations continue to work. At some points because of the conflict, Israeli and Palestinian filmmakers have been afraid to work together—but now we are seeing some hope for collaboration. That is a contribution of film to peace.

References

Kuriansky, J., Laszczak, M and Walsh, N. (2004, July). *The talkback technique: A useful psychological tool in audience processing.* Paper presented at the 112th annual convention of the American Psychological Association. Honolulu, HI.

Wedding, D., Boyd, M. A., & Niemiec, R. (2005). *Movies and mental illness: Using films to understand psychopathology.* Seattle: Hogrefe & Huber.

CHAPTER 21

SALAAM SHALOM: SINGING FOR PEACE BETWEEN PALESTINIANS AND ISRAELIS

Kjell Skyllstad

On the occasion of former Israeli Prime Minister Shemon Peres's 80th birthday in 2003, former U.S. President Bill Clinton took the stage with Israeli-born teenage singing sensation Liel Colette, together with 40 Palestinian and 40 Israeli children to sing John Lennon's song "Imagine." The words were evocative of peace efforts in the region, with lyrics like "a brotherhood of man," "nothing to kill or die for," and the chorus "I hope someday you will join us and the world will be as one."

The concert was a demonstration of the power of music for peace. This chapter explores that power, and its application to promote positive Israeli-Palestinian relations. As a music educator and researcher, involved for many years in international collaboration for peace, I am convinced that music can be a tool for integration, inclusion, group cohesion, collective cooperation, repairing social relationships, and facilitating dialogue between groups in conflict. This has all been demonstrated in unique artistic projects bringing together Palestinian and Israelis, as described herein.

The magic of music for conflict transformation is brought out in works such as *The Magic Flute* by noted composer Wolfgang Amadeus Mozart, where the main protagonists are faced with sensory stimuli that open up for new insight, and help break away from old conventions and prejudice.

The famed psychologist Abraham Maslow in *Toward a Psychology of Being* explains how strong sensory impressions or *peak experiences* facilitate a sensation of expanded time and place, leading to a positive change in self-appraisal and world outlook, and to the establishment of new relationship to others (Maslow, 1968, p. 101).

A central figure in music therapy, Kenneth Bruscia ascribes this experience to music therapy, saying: "Therapy should facilitate peak experiences, those sublime moments wherein one is able to transcend and integrate splits within the person, within the world. Since the arts facilitate the occurrences of peak experiences, aesthetic endeavors are seen to be a central aspect of life and therefore of therapy" (Bruscia, 1987, p. 33).

Neurophysiologists explain how such sensory stimuli remove emotional blockages through simultaneous neural breakthroughs, leading to permanent encoding in the synaptic structures.

One of my research studies, "The Resonant Community," showed that intercultural music making breaks down prejudice in children, leading to reduced ethnic conflicts in school (mobbing and harassment) while strengthening individual identity and self-esteem among minority children (Skyllstad, 2003, pp. 376–385). This project report had a significant influence on music education policies and practices in many countries during the following years, including Israel, where curricular reforms aimed at moving Israeli music education in an intercultural direction were put in place. As a follow-up, Dr. Edwin Seroussi, now professor in the Department of Musicology at the Hebrew University, and director of the Jewish Music Research Center in Jerusalem, reported hiring 40 new instructors to teach Arabic music traditions at his former workplace, the Bar-Ilan University of Tel Aviv.

One of the most respected figures in the movement for cultural dialogue between Palestinians and Israelis was Inbal Perelson, born in Kibbutz Amir and working within the Alternatice Information Center (AIC), a joint Israeli-Palestinian peace center. Shortly after being appointed editor of the AIC Hebrew journal in 1999, she was killed together with two of her colleagues in a flash flood that surged through the canyon near the Dead Sea—just a few months before she had published an in-depth study of the place of music in mediation and conflict transformation.

In this study she reports how right in the heyday of the Intifada, Israeli singers joined Israeli, Palestinian, and Arabic artists in performing peace songs, often combining Hebrew and Arabic texts. This was seen as a protest against official cultural policy that would enforce cultural separation. The popular Israeli singer Alon Olearchik at an annual children's' song festival in 1986 performed the song "Shalom Salaam" together with the Arab singer Anal Murkus. The words were:

> Believe there is reason enough
> In the world
> To make peace now between people
> It's time to make peace
> Not tomorrow, but today
> Shalom Salaam
> Shalom Salaam.[1]

Another song—"Moshe and Mussa" was written as part of an Israeli-Arab kindergarten project in Jaffa. Two children, Moshe (a Jew) and Mussa (an Arab), tell of their friendship:

Moshe and Mussa two friends
Moshe and Mussa go to kindergarten
Sometimes silent, sometimes crying
Sometimes laughing, sometimes singing
By the port of the city of Jaffa
Everyone will sing this song
Shalom aleihem, Aleykum Salaam
There's nothing like a twosome to tour the world.

Another song for peace by Israeli songwriter Uzi Khitman goes:

Here we are, you and me
And me and you
With two voices
And one song.
(Perelson, 1998, pp. 113–128)[2]

Friendship and collaboration is exactly the idea that made the following event such a remarkable demonstration of the power of song. During an Intifada demonstration, the well-known Israeli singer Amnon Abutbul was hit in the head by a rock hurled by a Palestinian demonstrator. Rather than thinking of revenge, Abutbul began to ponder in what ways he could contribute to bringing peace. After being released from the army, he found out that near his kibbutz there lived a Palestinian poet from Nazareth, Fatchi Kasem. He contacted him to tell his story and share his thoughts. Together in a few days they wrote a peace song in Arabic, called "Zaman el Salaam," expressing the longing of both peoples for peace:

Like an ocean—Peace, my love, has a wide embracing soul
There are times of ebb and flow in days of struggle and sorrow
Between storms and thunder feelings burst out my love:
Time for Peace—Inshallah
There is a time from far away I long like a lone star in the sky
There are times of ebb and flow in days of struggle and sorrow
One of the lightning the rainbow glows and I will know the time has come
Time for Peace—Inshallah.

But still the song had no music. Then out in the Negev desert, Amnon heard a violin sobbing. It sounded very Arabic. It was the violin of the master violinist Yair Dalal, who honors both Arabic and Jewish traditions (but sadly, was poorly treated by bigots on both sides when he toured Europe with a Palestinian ensemble from Bethlehem). Born an Iraqi Jew, Yair had for years actively supported and promoted Arabic music traditions in Israel and initiated interethnic cultural encounters in the Middle East as well as in other regions around the world.

This was the music that Amnon wanted for their peace song. Two days before the signing of the Cairo agreement, the song was released on a CD. Did it influence the negotiations? Could song be an instrument of peace? The artists had no way of finding out at that time.

But they got a new chance. For the celebration of the anniversary of the Oslo Accords in 1994, famous Finnish singer Arja Sajonmaa was looking for music and heard about the song and Yair. She wanted a choir to come to Oslo to reach the emotions through poetry and song. Yair was already well known in Norway. We had exchanged ideas on initiating multicultural music projects, as a way to prevent racial conflicts in school and society at large, so he was quick to respond. By the time of the Oslo Accords, I had just finished the three-year research project, The Resonant Community, in 18 Oslo schools that demonstrated the effectiveness of intercultural music making in resolving ethnic conflicts. With this success in mind, the arena was clear for another daring venture.

And so it happened that 50 Palestinian, 50 Israeli, and 100 Norwegian children were involved in a unique musical exchange project for peace. Unable because of the political situation to come together, children from the Palestinian territories and from Israel met at separate localities for rehearsals.

Then, on September 13, 1994, after long, unresolved negotiations in Paris and a whole night of fruitless talks in Oslo, PLO Chairman Yassir Arafat and Israeli Foreign Minister Shemon Peres showed up, exhausted and disappointed from the lagging negotiations. Before an audience of 8,000 people, the children performed the peace song, in three parts and three languages, accompanied by the Oslo Philharmonic Orchestra conducted by Zubin Mehta, and the Israeli-Palestinian orchestra with its leader Yair performing on his *oud* (the guitar-like queen of Arabian instruments).

In the intermission the two leaders sat down together, this time agreeing upon a new document, asserting their commitment to peace and resolving to move on with the Oslo Accords. Before a stunned audience, the Norwegian Foreign Minister, Björn Sverre Godal, announced that a peace document had just been signed.

How could this happen? What potential for emotional and conceptual impact lies in music performed by a multicultural ensemble? What did the event signify for the participating musicians, the children, the live audience, the politicians, and the large international television audience who watched the live performance?

For Norwegian educators and for Yair, who had recently witnessed the success of the first intercultural music project in Oslo, which I referred to, it was a confirmation of our conviction that music has transformative powers.

How did this transformation come about? First of all, the peace song "Zaman el Salaam" reflected a real-life experience, human suffering brought about by war and ethnic conflict, where the wounded singer seeks out his enemy to make a plea for peace. Then there was the marriage of words to music, music born out of the experience of multiethnic music making, of Yair's Israeli-Palestinian orchestra performing across borders—the fruit of a long interaction. Added to all this was the effort of the rehearsals, when both groups practiced songs from both the

Palestinian and Israeli musical heritage. And finally there was the social ritual of the final performance, serving as an initiation of the children into peacemaking. And there was the support by key devoted artists, an internationally famous conductor, a world-class orchestra, politicians from both sides, and a huge public audience identifying with the children, accepting and endorsing their message.

The beauty of the children's singing and their call for peace lives on, surviving even in the face of seemingly insurmountable political hurdles and setbacks. It even echoed and survived that fateful night on the Tel Aviv square when Ytzak Rabin was killed by a shot fired through the peace song in his breast pocket. And the words of "Zaman el Salaam" will continue to echo in "times of ebb and flow, in days of struggle and sorrow." Because someday "out of the lightning the rainbow glows and I will know the time has come. Time for Peace—Inshallah."

Notes

1. Excerpts from *Power Relations in the Israeli Popular Music System* by Inbal Perelson. Popular Music, Vol. 17, No. 1 (Jan. 1998), pp. 113–128. Reprinted with permission of Cambridge University Press.

2. Excerpts from *Power Relations in the Israeli Popular Music System* by Inbal Perelson. Popular Music, Vol. 17, No. 1 (Jan. 1998), pp. 113–128. Reprinted with permission of Cambridge University Press.

References

Bruscia, K. E. (1987). *Improvisational models of music therapy.* Springfield, IL: Charles O. Thomas Publishing Co.

Maslow, A. H. (1968). *Toward a psychology of being.* New York: Van Nostrand.

Perelson, I. (1998). Power relations in the Israeli popular music system. In N. Dibben & K. Negus, Eds. *Popular Music 1998* (Vol. 17, no. 1), 113–128. New York: Cambridge University Press.

Skyllstad, K. (2003). Creating a culture of peace: The performing arts in interethnic negotiations. In F. E. Jandt (Ed.), *Intercultural communication: A global reader.* 376–383. Thousand Oaks, CA: Sage Publications.

Chapter 22

Kites Fly for Peace: Staging Palestinian-Israeli Peace

Neil Ryan Walsh, Judy Kuriansky, and Lorenzo Toppano

On a roof in the Old City,
laundry hanging in the late afternoon sunlight:
the white sheet of a woman who is my enemy,
the towel of a man who is my enemy, to wipe off the sweat of his brow.
In the sky of the Old City a kite.
At the other end of the string, a child I can't see because of the wall . . .

—*"Jerusalem," by Israeli poet Yehuda Amichai (1988)*[1]

Introduction

On May 20, 2005, more than 45,000 kites soared in the air throughout Israel and thousands more were raised around the world, in a show of solidarity for peace in the Israel/Palestinian Territories. Mothers, fathers, children, Palestinians, Israelis, and others participated in the event, called "10,000 Kites." The organizers included the Los Angeles–based organization by the same name, the Association for Arts in the Community and Cross-Cultural Dialog founded by Israeli artist Adi Yekutieli with Palestinian artist George Nustas, and the Liberty Hill Foundation, which supports grassroots organizations. All these groups support peace through artistic projects (www.10000kites.org/mission).

Why kites? 10,000 Kites Executive Director Yael Samuel says kites are particularly appropriate because they can be seen by people on the other side of the "security fence" that separates Israel from the West Bank. "Kites are a way for ordinary people on both sides of the fence to show that they want peace and who want their neighbors on the other side to know it," he says (Samuel, 2005).

The First Kite Flyer

The spirit of that day—when 10,000 kites flew in the air and symbolically transcended borders—inspired Lorenzo Toppano to write a musical, *The First Kite Flyer*. A phrase in the Koran that emphasized the unity of Judaism, Christianity, and Islam provided further inspiration:

> In the name of God, the Compassionate, the Merciful Say ye: "We believe in God, and the revelation given to us, and to Abraham, Ismá'íl, Isaac, Jacob, and the Tribes, and that given to Moses and Jesus, and that given to all prophets from their Lord: We make no difference between one and another of them: And we bow to God." (Koran; *Sura 1 Sura 2: 136*)

The story centers around a boy who flies his kite over the borders that define his homeland. Though set at the time of Israel declaring statehood, it is not about the struggle to build a Jewish state, nor about the Arab diaspora living in Palestine, but about the human element of the situation: the people, relationships, and human spirit transcending a seemingly impossible situation.

Many people are surprised to hear that anyone could write a musical about one of the most archetypically intractable conflicts in the world. A well-known producer from Chicago snipped to Toppano, "Why don't you just do a musical on open heart surgery?" While it may seem that the serious theme of the Israeli-Palestinian conflict would be inappropriate in this particular theatrical genre, the production teams' intention is to bring light onto the dark subject of the Israeli-Palestinian conflict—as a way to contribute to peace.

The First Kite Flyer is really a love story, says Toppano, with the issues of the region as a backdrop. The relatively peaceful coexistence between Jews and Arabs at the time of the British occupation is exemplified in two supporting characters who rely on each other: Moishe, a Jewish farmer, and Abdullah Al Gazhi, who sells Moishe's melons and grain in his small store. The shop owner's son, Shadi, returns from school in England with his Jewish friend Ben, who falls in love with Shadi's sister Layli. But happy times are disrupted when a British land surveyor announces that the town will be divided in two by a fence. The fence separates Moishe's and Abdullah's homes, and also Ben from his friend Shadi and the love of his life, Layli. As the fence closes in on the stage, the Arabs and Jews on both sides are caught in chaos, hurrying to new homes. Ben and Layli, now separated from each other like Romeo and Juliet, must profess their love through the fence.

The musical is a good example of how the Israeli-Palestinian conflict is an inspiration for artistic productions, and how the real situation is serving as a means to tell dramatic stories of human relationships.

How His Bride Came to Abraham

The Romeo-and-Juliet theme used in *The First Kite Flyer* is also dramatically portrayed in the play *How His Bride Came to Abraham*. Abe, an Israeli soldier on patrol wounded by a roadside bomb, is discovered—and nursed—by a Sabra, a young keffiyeh-clad Lebanese woman. Their cultures clash, but after an evening of intense talk and mutual understanding that leads to surprise intimacy, Sabra wakes and dons an explosive belt. The pair is discovered and shots are heard. The 23rd Psalm ("The Lord is my shepherd") is then heard in Hebrew, Arabic, and English.

Veteran playwright Karen Sunde wrote the play in 1994 after traveling to the Middle East to research a United Nations commission for a play about peace-keeping missions for the U.N.'s 45th anniversary. When a producer suggested she write about the Israeli-Palestinian issue, she first thought, "That's impossible," but became captivated with capturing the relationship between enemies discovering humanity and even intimacy. The play has since been performed off-Broadway and at a high school, underwritten by the International Catholic Organizations Information Center. Its message, Sunde feels, is even more relevant today. "It takes place in a no man's land but where anything is possible," she explains (2006).

Sunde's message is: "Anyone should come out of the play desiring the happiness of his enemy's child." Her hope is that the play stimulates the desire for peace and reconciliation. While Sunde wrote her play at a time of more peaceful relations between Israelis and Palestinians, it seems even more relevant in these days when the conflict, as well as individuals' efforts for peace, are intensified.

In an expression of the meaning of the play, the female lead actress—Maya Serhan, a Palestinian—wrote to Sunde in 2003. "I had not yet come across a Palestinian/Israeli play or film that brings together all the feelings of pain, love, hate, anger, horror or fear in the hearts of a Palestinian refugee or an Israeli soldier," she said. "It is not a political argument or a play that casts blame on the other side. It's a love story. It's two people who grew up learning to hate the other . . . eventually finding the lover and warmth in the other." The male lead, an Israeli ex-combat soldier, Amir Babyoff, told Sunde that performing in the play helped him deal with feelings he had been unable to articulate and that her writing this play was a *mitzvah* (good deed). "We have the opportunity as artists, actors, and creators to step forward without taking sides and create that hope through a wonderful story," he said. "We must push forward while a glimpse of [that hope] is in the air."

Their comments show how even the actor—as well as the audience—can be challenged and transformed by a production dealing with this topic.

Theatre as a Source of Change in Individuals and Communities

Theatre has long served as an escape from the everyday world, as well as a ritual setting that provides an holistic environment, allowing experience through the senses instead of just the intellect (Hesley & Hesley, 1998; Johnson, 1987). But theatrical productions have also been used for broader social purposes: as a tool to present complicated ethical dilemmas to audiences, to question mores of a society, and to convey ideas about social change. This is evident in productions like Aristophanes's *The Frogs* about righting the wrongs of a dysfunctional society, Verdi's operas extolling justice and democracy in the French-occupied Italy of his day, Kurt Weil and Bertolt Brecht's anti-Fascist theatre in Germany during the 1920s and 1930s, and American activist theatre like the modern-day AIDS-themed plays of Larry Kramer. Community-based grassroots arts groups in countries plagued with conflict or under dictatorial regimes can be seen as building blocks for constructing a "civil society," native forms of democracy, or strategies for conflict resolution (Goldfarb, 2006).

The Stage for Peace in the Arab-Israeli Conflict

An increasing number of plays have characters who are either Palestinian or Israeli and are purposefully meant to cast a light on the defining issues of the region. Palestinian playwright Betty Shamieh's noted play, *Roar*, presents the experience of a Palestinian family living in a Midwest city of America (Detroit) which has a large Arab community. Israeli playwright Misha Schulman's play *Fist* deals with the turmoil within a conservative Israeli family when one son reveals that he refuses to continue serving in the military because of injustices of the occupation of Palestine.

Also of note, an increasing number of productions—as is the case of the love stories in plays by Sunde and Toppano—have characters from both sides, demonstrating the relationship between individuals from both cultures immersed in the conflict. Some artistic groups even gear their productions specifically toward promoting dialogue, peace, and mutual understanding between groups in conflict, like the Israelis and Palestinians. Many of these are listed by the Jewish Theatre in the section of its website called "The Arab-Israeli Melting Pot" (www.jewish-theatre.com/visitor/article_list.aspx?articleGroupID=86). For example, the Arab-Hebrew Theatre of Jaffa promotes multicultural and peaceful coexistence between Israelis and Arabs by hosting an Israeli and an Arab theatre company that puts on shows together. The group holds festivals that show Arab and Israel plays back to back with mixed audiences, works closely with women's groups, and conducts seminars for the community of Jaffa by celebrating both Arab and Jewish culture (The Arab Hebrew Theatre of Jaffa, 2003).

In one production—a ballet adaptation of *Romeo and Juliet*, with Romeo as an Israeli Jew and Juliet as a Palestinian—the director purposefully intended to show audiences his feelings about the conflict: that love and humanism can overcome hatred. This version of the Shakespearean story, however, has a happy ending in that the lovers regain consciousness. In doing so, the ending reflects the director's wish for the conflict to be solved. The ballet was performed to full houses in Budapest in 2006.

Productions centering on the conflict are crossing borders. Palestinian actor/playwright Saleem's play, *Salam, Shalom . . . A Tale of Passion* is the story of two men—an Israeli and a Palestinian—studying in California and living in the same dorm. The autobiographical story—written in 1995 after Saleem broke up with his Israeli boyfriend—has been shown throughout the United States, as well as in Australia and New Zealand. Even playwrights of other nationalities are focusing on these issues. British playwright Robin Soans spent a few weeks in Israel and was inspired to write a play, *The Arab Israeli Cookbook*, about different aspects of the conflict from the point of view of ordinary people. To ensure authenticity, he consulted 80 people in the region of all religions and ethnicity. Eight actors play 39 characters who are Israeli, Palestinian Muslims, and Christians. The play centers around food because, as Soans describes, "Both Jews and Arabs are passionate about food. . . . They have that in common. I thought if I started out talking to them about their love of cooking, I could find out about the daily lives, without getting right away into their hostilities and grievances" (Yugend, 2005). Like the Australian Toppano, the British Soans was an outsider to the Middle East but was inspired by the humanity of Israelis and Palestinians and decided to do his part for peace in writing his play.

Even musical productions embody the spirit of Israeli-Palestinian cooperation. The West-Eastern Divan Orchestra is a classical music project founded in the 1990s by the late well-known Palestinian author and academic Edward Said and the Israeli conductor Daniel Barenboim. This group brings together young (aged 14 to 25) musicians from Israel and throughout the Arab world to create music during summer workshops, which culminate in professional performances around the world (Cera, 2006). Barenboim says, "The destinies of the two peoples are inextricably linked and, therefore, we have to make tremendous steps to achieve things that are good for the Israelis and good for the Palestinians, too. But oh, there is such ignorance" (Moir, 2006).

Theatre as Healing

Peace Child Israel is a project in which Jewish and Arab teens create their own versions of plays that dramatize the issues they face in relationships with each other. In one play, *Alice in the Holy Land*, the characters see all points of view (Doubilet, 2007). In another, *The Other Side*, the teen actors realize that they are not "Arab" and "Jew" but more "brother" and "sister." The project, founded in 1988 by actress Yael Drouyanoff and funded by the Abraham Fund and the New Israel Fund, performed the plays during a 2006 tour of America.

Theatre in the service of peace education and the promotion of tolerance for Israeli and Palestinian youth from kindergarten to high school is also evident in the performances of *Viewpoints*—a joint Israeli-Palestinian performance initiated and coordinated by the Peres Center for Peace (the Peres Center, with the Adam Institute for Peace, has extended this approach, using the medium of film in its cinema workshops). A website, further supported by the European Union, gives students an opportunity to comment on the activities after the performance.

The "Talkback" Technique and Enhancing the Power of Theatre as a Medium of Social Change

Special appearances by the actors and directors after a performance have become increasingly popular, offering an added experience to the audience as well as promotion for the production. When a play presents complicated social themes or psychological issues, such panel discussions are increasingly including psychological experts to help the audience process the experience. In the "talkback" technique developed by Kuriansky, audiences are given a short questionnaire relevant to the topic of the play before (and sometimes after) the performance. The pre-performance responses are calculated during the performance and the results shared with the audience as a trigger for discussion (Kuriansky, Walsh, & Laszczak, 2005; Walsh, Kuriansky, & Laszczak, 2005). These talkbacks have been done after plays addressing relationships as well as social issues, like AIDS. Talkback sessions after a play about the Israeli-Palestinian conflict can help the audience process complicated emotional responses and challenging issues in peace building. This can be particularly useful, since attaining peace in the Middle East conflict can be an abstract ideal that can leave most people feeling overwhelmed, confused, or ineffective. Therefore, a focused discussion can even help individuals conceive realistic strategies to contribute to people's understanding and reconciliation of vast differences.

This format has been done in some cases. For example, the theatre series of the 2006 Culture Project/Impact Festival—an annual arts festival focused on human rights, social justice, and political action—featured several plays dealing with the Israeli-Palestinian issue, with stimulating audience discussions afterward. In *Six Actors in Search of a Plot*—co-written by Palestinian Muslim playwright Muhammed Ahmad Zaher and American Jewish director/choreographer Billy Yalowitz—three Palestinian and three Jewish Israeli actors try desperately to find a neutral story they can agree to tell, but each attempt gets mired by political views of the Palestinian-Israeli conflict. A subplot of two females enacting birth rituals as in-utero twins with a rare life-threatening blood syndrome serves as a metaphor for the birth of two states: Israel and Palestine. On the night Kuriansky saw the play, the audience was eager to know how the actors really felt. Yalowitz described how the Palestinians and Jews argued about nearly every line during the first rehearsals. The play had been produced by Temple University and Peace Child Israel in their style of spontaneously created dramas with the intention for the audience to get actively engaged in the same struggle as the actors over how to share different narratives.

Some productions which directly address the conflict would greatly benefit from a talkback. Such was the case when Kuriansky and Walsh went to see the play, *Desert Sunrise*. The play stimulated many intellectual and emotional reactions. Judging from the hours-long conversation that two authors of this chapter had with the playwright after seeing the play, the audience members, would have also benefited greatly from processing afterwards.

In the play, an Israeli soldier, lost in the Palestinian desert between Hebron and Jerusalem, meets a Palestinian cave dweller who has stolen away from his home to meet his soon-to-be-bride. In the hot desert sun, they initially clash and threaten to kill one another, but eventually bond. The fiancée suddenly arrives—and dons an explosive belt. Other soldiers then arrive and the situation turns tragic.

The play's one-month runs were extended three times off-Broadway at the Theatre for the New City. Twenty-eight-year-old Jewish director and playwright Mischa Schulman, who was born in Jerusalem, intended the work to present a balanced perspective and a sympathetic picture of both sides, and so was somewhat surprised when he encountered some criticism. As he recounted, "About 20 percent of Palestinians were upset, mostly because one of the characters is a suicide bomber, and about 20 percent of Israelis feel the soldier is not presented more sympathetically" (Schulman, 2006).

The intertwined relationship between the Israeli man and the Palestinian man is powerfully exemplified by a game they play to pass the time in the desert sun. One starts the story of his dream, and the other adds to the storyline, and then they take turns embellishing the story. In doing so, their initial fighting transforms into laughter. Building a dream together is a metaphor for establishing a dream between their people and divergent cultures. This technique is similar to an exercise Kuriansky uses in couples therapy—"shared storytelling"—whereby partners build a common story or fantasy by taking turns contributing sentences (Kuriansky, 2003). This story stem or shared storytelling exercise is used to develop better communication and connection for healthy interpersonal relationships. As suggested in this play, the technique can serve as a model for broader application in larger cultural groups, as with Israelis and Palestinians.

Recommendations

Professionally facilitated talkbacks after a play dealing with the theme of conflict like that between Israelis and Palestinians, and with peaceful resolution, can be organized into special events, where audiences are prepared for such an intense experience. Exercises to facilitate dialogue can include a story stem game such as used in the play *Desert Sunrise*. Audience members can even be paired according to their differing opinions about issues presented in the play. Because the conflict is potentially such a heated issue, audience members should be carefully prepared and even briefed on "rules" like respecting personal boundaries and avoiding judgments. Talkbacks can also provide the production team with valuable audience feedback; for example, Palestinian playwright Saleem never published his play, but constantly evolved the story based on audience reactions.

Conclusion

Theatre productions are a valuable medium to address challenging social issues, but can also be an opportunity to start a dialogue about relevant issues presented in plays with themes of contemporary conflict. Artistic organizations are increasingly using theatre to address issues raised by the Israeli-Palestinian conflict, focusing on human relationships between the people rather than on political positions. Audience processing of difficult material can be achieved through the technique of "talkbacks"—discussion forums after the performance that encourage dialogue, moderated by a professional with a mental health or mediation background. Theatre presents a valuable art form for audiences of all ages that can entertain but also facilitate dialogue aimed at deeper understanding of seemingly intractable conflicts like that in the Middle East.

Note

1. From "Jersusalem" a poem by Israeli poet Yehuda Amichai (1988). The Selected Poetry of Yehuda Amichai, Newly Revised and Expanded edition: 1996. The University of California Press, Book Division. Reprinted with permission.

References

Amichai, Y. (1988). *Poems of Jerusalem.* New York: Harper & Row.

The Arab-Hebrew Theatre of Jaffa. (2003). *About the theatre.* Retrieved May 5, 2006, from http://www.arab-hebrew-theatre.org.il/eng/about/about.htm.

Cera, Stephen. (2006, April 17). The night they played Ramallah. *Maclean's,* p. 67.

Goldfarb, J. (2006). *The politics of small things: The power of the powerless in dark times.* Chicago: University of Chicago Press.

Hesley, J. W., & Hesley, J. (1998). *Rent two films and let's talk in the morning: Using popular movies in psychotherapy.* New York: John Wiley & Sons.

Johnson, R. A. (1987). *Ecstasy: Understanding the psychology of joy.* New York: Harper & Row.

Kuriansky, J. (2003). *The complete idiot's guide to dating.* Indianapolis: Alpha Books.

Kuriansky, J., Walsh, N., & Laszczak, M. (2005, November 25). *Using the "talkback" technique to facilitate discussion after a creative media event and to survey audience members' opinions on psychosocial issues.* Poster session presented at the New School for Social Research, Department of Psychology, New York.

Moir, J. (2006, April 6). The maestro and his demons: On the eve of delivering his first Reith Lecture, in an exclusive interview, Daniel Barenboim tells Jan Moir how music makes sense of the world. *The Daily Telegraph* [London], p. 27.

Samuel, Y. (2005). *10,000 kites: Frequently asked questions.* Retrieved May 5, 2006, from www.10000kites.org/faq.htm.

Samuel, Y. (2005, June 6). Personal communication.

Schulman, M. (2006, May 13). Personal communication.

Sunde, K. (2006, June 13). Personal communication.

10,000 kites. (2006). *Mission and vision.* Retrieved May 5, 2006, from http://www.10000 kites.org/mission.htm.

Walsh, N., Kuriansky, J., & Laszczak, M. (2005, November 4). *The "talkback" technique: A useful and innovative psychological tool in audience processing of psychosocial issues in mixed media events.* Paper presented at the Greater New York Conference on Behavioral Research, John Jay College of the City University of New York, New York.

Yugend, T. (2005). *Cooking up a meaningful plot in LA* [Original source: *The Jewish Journal*]. Retrieved May 5, 2006, from http://www.jewish-theatre.com/visitor/article_display.aspx?articleID=1397.

Chapter 23

Alice in the Holy Land: Dramatic Discoveries of Arab and Jewish Youth in Peace Child Israel

Karen Doubilet

Due to fiscal cut-backs, the Israeli Ministry of Education is forced to integrate an Arab high school and a Jewish high school. Following decades of war, mistrust and segregation, these students will have to meet face-to-face, sit next to each other in class and in the lunchroom, and play together on the same soccer team in gym class. The kids are stunned, parents are infuriated, everyone is fearful—and amidst the charged atmosphere, a fight breaks out.

Nevertheless, the schools are integrated, and the Arab and Jewish students are forced to grapple with some serious themes—identity, prejudice, and fear. As time passes, the students learn to get along—there is even a forbidden romance, and when a Jewish boy serenades his Arab classmate, love transcends difference. One day in gym class, the teacher points out that the students have split themselves up into mixed teams on their own accord—signaling a significant step forward, and a symbol of emotional barriers that the students have overcome.

However, the strength of this bridge is tested several years later when Danny—now an Israeli soldier—and his friend Mohammad come face to face at a checkpoint.

—*From the play Roadblock, created and performed by Arab and Jewish students from Qualansua and Emek Hefer, 2005*

Intergroup encounter programs have become an increasingly popular framework for bringing together Arabs, Palestinians, and Jews in Israel and the Palestinian Authority (PA). The image of such programs certainly has great appeal: a group of diverse youth playing together, holding hands, exchanging phone numbers, sharing a plate of hummus—all implying hope for peace. This picture becomes even more powerful when viewed contextually—in the face of daily violence and suffering, deeply ingrained ethnocentric attitudes, competing narratives of history and victimhood, and collective memories of trauma and persecution. In fact, bringing the sides together at all—let alone getting them to hold hands—constitutes a great challenge and is an admirable achievement.

The alluring picture described sparked my desire to examine intergroup encounter programs for my doctoral research in conflict management. In this chapter, I reflect on my work assessing the impact of participation in a program called "Peace Child Israel" (PCI) on participants' attitudes and behaviors toward "the other." Founded in 1988 by David Gordon and late Israeli actress Yael Drouyannoff, PCI is a grassroots, nongovernmental organization that hosts an encounter program for Arab and Jewish youth. The program utilizes theater as a vehicle to promote coexistence, educate for democratic values, and encourage understanding and mutual respect.

The program—which has grown and blossomed under the direction of the dedicated and passionate Melisse Lewine-Boskovich—matches groups of Arab and Jewish teenagers from neighboring schools and community centers all across Israel. The youth from the twinned communities embark on a year-long creative journey, meeting on a weekly basis (alternating between the Arab and Jewish community)—and for occasional weekend workshops. The meetings are bilingual, and each group of 20 to 30 youth is led by two professional facilitators— one Arab and one Jewish—with backgrounds in education, theater, social work, group facilitation, or other relevant fields.

The impressive curriculum addresses issues such as identity, stereotypes, fear, as well as cultural similarities and differences. A variety of theatrical techniques, such as role-playing, reverse role-playing, collage, improvisation, and movement teach compassionate listening, critical thinking, and nonviolent communication. The intergroup process ultimately culminates in an original drama, reflecting the group's experiences and dialogue over the previous year. The emotionally engaging plays are performed in Arabic and Hebrew for family, friends, and public schools across the country. Some participants stay on for a second year of the program called "Du Drama," which seeks to cultivate these youngsters into leaders.

As a teenager, I was involved in educational theater in Canada; I knew what an intense experience the process of creating a play with a "message" could be, and this is partly what drew me to examine an encounter program that utilizes drama as a tool for social change. The experience of observing this process in an intractable conflict setting—such as in the Israeli-Palestinian context that I am connected to historically and emotionally—has been incredibly powerful. In fact, as an "objective observer," I often have to restrain my overwhelming urge to jump in and participate at the meetings, especially when they get heated and emotional. As a student of the Palestinian and Israeli conflict, I understood the protracted nature of Arab-Palestinian-Jewish relations on an intellectual level prior to my work with Peace Child; however, this experience awakened my interest in the deep emotional component of intergroup relations and conflict.

Research has shown that children in this region begin to develop negative attitudes about "the other" side in early childhood (Bar-Tal & Teichman, 2005).

These attitudes are not only transmitted by their parents, but are also embedded in cultural norms and social institutions. Through the socialization process, children are tacitly and actively taught to fear and revile "the other." With the exception of a small number of mixed communities, Arabs and Jews generally live in separate enclaves and attend segregated schools, polarizing the groups even further and reinforcing hostility. As such, encounter programs constitute one of the few opportunities for youths to meet and interact with one another in a protected environment.

In 2005, one of PCI's groups created a play whose plot provides an appropriate metaphor for what I have observed unfold in the encounter process. The play relays the story of two nations that are separated by an enormous wall. Each nation is told that the people on the other side of the wall are monsters. One day, a young girl ventures into the forbidden, and climbs over the wall to the other side only to discover that there are no monsters at all; the story of the monsters was in fact a myth, falsely perpetuated by her parents and society, whom she now resents intensely for lying to her all those years.

Currently, the average Jewish Israeli is probably uncomfortable, at best, with the idea of entering an Arab village, let alone the Occupied Territories. For most Arabs and Palestinians, the thought of getting lost in a Jewish town is probably similarly threatening. These are some of the themes that arise in the encounter process. Whether stopping for a bite to eat in "the other's" territory constitutes a truly justifiable, or simply invisible, boundary, the perception that grave danger lurks on the other side of the wall indeed exists. Peace Child participants have the opportunity to cross that boundary in a protected environment, to get to know each other, visit in each other's villages and communities, and many times become friends—dissipating the fear and apprehension. The wall that was conquered in the play reflects the wall between the Arab and Jewish participants that I observed come down in the encounter process—as the encounter unfolds, the monster becomes humanized.

How the Drama Works

Twenty-five students gather in a classroom—some enter with trepidation and discomfort, and others with a real desire to get to know "the other." Everyone is aware of who they are sitting beside. Some make a very conscious decision to sit next to a counterpart from "the other side," knowing that it socially desirable to sit in a mixed arrangement.

The youth are divided into small groups (Jews with Jews, and Arabs with Arabs), and are instructed to prepare a skit about "getting lost in the counterpart's community." The Jews are angered by the Arabs' skit in which they get lost in a Tel Aviv market, and are accused of being terrorists. The Arabs are similarly perturbed by the Jews' skit, which conveys their fear of being lynched in an Arab village, where there are plenty of camels. This exercise is followed by a charged discussion—some wish to go home, others suddenly have stomachaches.

In the end, most of the students do not abandon the process—the experience deepens their relationship, they develop an understanding of "the other side's" narrative, and many times they even become friends.

As Israeli Stav Davidman, class of 2006, said, "Although it seems to me that I haven't made much of a difference, I know I've changed quite a lot of things, because now there are at least 40 Arabs who know that there are good Jews too, and there are about 30 Jews who know that there are good Arabs too." Omaima Khalifa, an Arab youngster from Sheikh Dinun in the class of 2002, learned that "change is always possible," and Muhammad Tribieh from Sakhnin, who was in 10th grade when he came to the camp, made friends. "I made a Jewish friend called David," he said. "And he taught me a lot about Jewish culture, how people spend their time, how *they live*." Tenth-grader Inbal Shaked from Yuvalim in Misgav was doubtful about becoming friends at first, but said, "In the end we all laughed at the same things, ate together, worked together as partners. And you learn so much from just listening to a wider point of view than what you hear in the news."

Parents are also positively affected. Muhammed's father, Wadji Abud Tribeih, said, "I didn't tell Muhammad to join, he wanted to. But I think it's right that we ask how we can help each other, and such programs in which you sit together, provide an opportunity to slowly, slowly, raise our consciousness" (Gelfond, 2002).

This scenario of friendship and trust is idyllic, and constitutes a microreality. The sociopsychological dimension of Arab-Jewish hostility goes much deeper than the ethnocentric attitudes present in most societies. There is, in fact, real—and not just imagined—danger; suicide bombings, military operations, house demolitions, and checkpoints are a daily reality. This reality creates a major challenge for encounter programs and often leaves those involved feeling frustrated. Just when a group is finally making progress, participants' cell phones start ringing; mothers call frantically in response to breaking news—another bomber has detonated. The youth, who were just dancing and singing about coexistence together on stage, may soon have to face each other in a different context—Danny as an Israeli soldier and Muhammad as a desperate Palestinian trying to get his dying father across a checkpoint to an Israeli hospital.

This dilemma leads to the million-dollar question: What is the impact of encounter programs? Will Danny relate to Muhammad and other Arabs differently had he not participated in such a program as Peace Child? And will Muhammad relate differently to Jews after participating in the encounter? Additionally, can the microcosm of peace and coexistence that exists in the encounter spill over to the macro level?

At this point, we do not know to what degree the outcomes of encounter programs carry over to society at large. The fact remains, however, that even in this hotbed of intractable ethnopolitical conflict, Arab/Palestinian and Jewish children are holding hands, singing songs of peace. In this sense, I view the encounter as providing a vision and hope for coexistence. Peace Child Israel is part of a movement of peace builders who, in spite of the odds, remain devoted to building a bridge between these divided populations. Even if the bridge is shaky, the effort is one step toward peace. As German educator Hermann Rohrs has said, "seen against the progress of human history . . . making society a more humane place is a task which can by its very nature only be accomplished in tiny stages" (1993, p. 39).

One class at Peace Child did a play called *Alice in the Holy Land*—a take-off on the popular tale of *Alice in Wonderland*. As one student described her experience—and the impact of the Peace Child program: "Alice wandered around the Holy Land talking to everyone and listening to every point of view. She was objective and saw all sides. Alice was taking the path we all need to take."

References

Bar-Tal, D. & Teichman, Y. (2005). *Stereotypes and prejudice in conflict: Representations of Arabs in Israeli Jewish society.* Cambridge: Cambridge University Press.

Gelfond, L. (2002, August 9). Alice in the Holy Land: Jewish and Arab teenagers are creating their own version of wonderland through Peace Child. *The Jerusalem Post,* p. 20.

Rohrs, H. (1993). The pedagogy of peace: A fundamental science of practical relevance for the humanization of life. In Y. Iram & Z. Gross (Eds), *The humanities in education* (Vol. 1, pp. 39–44).

CHAPTER 24

COPING WITH CRISIS:
SEEDS OF PEACE AND THE INTIFADA

Edie Maddy-Weitzman

At the outbreak of the second Intifada,[1] the following comments by Palestinian and Israeli teens were posted on an Internet listserv for participants in Seeds of Peace, a peace education program bringing together youth from conflict regions. Tanya,[2] an Israeli, asked, "How can I go to a peace camp while there is a war going on inside my country? How can I fool myself with the thought that everything is okay while there are people that are shooting at babies?"

Mona, a Palestinian from Ramallah, argued that Palestinians shouldn't meet with Israelis while their tanks were parked by her house and Palestinians were being killed by Israelis. She posted, "You want us to talk about peace, about co-existence (all those dreams). Why not talk about fear about the tanks, about death and human body parts all over my universe?"

Hela, an Israeli, responded to Mona with reasons why it was all the more important to attend a peace education program during this time of conflict, saying:

> I don't think you should look at it as playing while your people are suffering but as talking while our people are fighting. . . . Building peace at a time of war may be hard and it may be washed away and we'll need to start from the beginning. But you can't wait for a time of peace to start building peace.

Clearly these teens were questioning the value of continuing to bring Palestinians and Israelis together in light of the new reality posed by renewed violence.

Their interchange reflects the challenges confronting peace education programs attempting to operate in the shadow of violence and during the breakdown of governments' peacemaking initiatives. Recently, researchers and practitioners of intergroup encounters taking place in the context of the Israeli-Palestinian conflict have debated the advisability, feasibility, and purpose of conducting peace education in such a situation (Adwan & Bar-On, 2004; Bar-Tal, 2004; Baskin & Al-Qaq, 2004; Halabi & Sonnenschein, 2004; Maoz, 2004b; Salomon, 2004). This chapter examines this debate and addresses the following questions: Should these programs be held at such times, and if so, what should they look like? What objectives can they hope to achieve, and what challenges do they confront? Indeed, can peace education be at all effective in the context of an intractable conflict such as the one between Israelis and Palestinians?

For the past five years, I have been examining the Seeds of Peace program as it continued to operate during the Intifada. Using a qualitative research paradigm, multiple data collection procedures were employed, including interviews of participants and staff members, observations of Seeds of Peace activities, and daily postings by the participants on an Internet listserv. I looked at the challenges confronted by program organizers and participants during a time of heightened strife as well as the strategies used in seeking to overcome those obstacles.

The Seeds of Peace Program

Participants in the Seeds of Peace program—"Seeds," as they call themselves—attend three-week sessions at the Seeds of Peace International Camp in Maine, established in 1993 by the late John Wallach. The mission of Seeds of Peace is expressed in its motto "empowering the children of war to break the cycle of violence" and in the following statement: Seeds of Peace "is enabling people blinded by hatred to see the human face of their enemies. It is equipping the next generation with the tools to end the violence and become the leaders of tomorrow" (Seeds of Peace, 2005).

Participants, aged 13 to 15, are nominated by their schools, must be able to converse in English, and pass a rigorous selection process held by their governments. The teens come from a variety of backgrounds; in many cases their families have experienced suffering either directly or indirectly as a result of the Israeli-Palestinian conflict. Some are grandchildren of refugees or of Holocaust survivors, or have had relatives killed in one of the several wars between their peoples. Each government's delegation of campers is accompanied by adult chaperones who are educators or community leaders.

None of the teenagers had met youth from the other side prior to the camp experience. Many arrive with deep-rooted negative images of one another. Israeli campers tend to perceive the Palestinians as violent (as one Israeli said, "I didn't think they would all be terrorists, but I would generalize sometimes"), inferior ("I didn't see them as equal people"), and dehumanized ("I just didn't think of how they live, and where they live and who they are").

Palestinian campers' main associations of Israelis, prior to the camp experience, are as violent soldiers and settlers, occupiers, violators of their human rights, and people who aren't human. As one Palestinian said, "I thought of Israelis as being a different nation, aliens from another planet. They only have guns in their hands. They don't have people ten years old or thirteen years old."

At the camp Israelis and Palestinians eat, sleep, and live together, engaging in numerous joint activities, including sports, art, and drama. The hallmark of the program consists of daily dialogue sessions, led by professional facilitators, in which the teens present their respective peoples' views on the Arab-Israeli conflict, air grievances, discuss their histories, and share stories of their lives. After returning home, participants can continue their involvement in Seeds of Peace through the follow-up program operated out of the Jerusalem Center for Coexistence, located in an area bordering Arab and Jewish neighborhoods.

Seeds during the Intifada

It is important to understand the hostile landscape in which the Seeds of Peace program has been operating during the past five years. Israeli and Palestinian societies have been significantly affected by the ongoing violence, leading to despair and increased mutual demonization (Bassiouni, 2003). In both communities, it is considered disloyal or unpatriotic to have contact with the other side at such a time. For Israeli Seeds, speaking out for the need to dialogue with Palestinians or expressing empathy for their suffering could result in being ostracized. For the Palestinian Seeds, the situation is even more complicated and dangerous; meeting with the people with whom its community is fighting risks being labeled as "normalization" and, even worse, collaboration.

Many Seeds underwent a deep crisis following the beginning of the Intifada and the death of a Seed, Asil Asleh, who was killed by Israeli police at a demonstration of Arab Israelis. Overnight their reality had been radically altered; suddenly, they found themselves catapulted into the middle of a nightmare. Palestinian Seeds had to cope with the fact that the Israeli soldiers shooting at Palestinians were fellow citizens of their Israeli friends. Israeli Seeds had to contend with the fact that Palestinians undertaking violent actions against Israeli soldiers and civilians were compatriots of their Palestinian friends. Furthermore, in some cases, Israeli Seeds were serving in the Israel Defense Forces (IDF), stationed in the West Bank and Gaza just as some Palestinian Seeds were throwing rocks at Israeli soldiers.

SeedsNet: Communication via Cyberspace

The Seeds of Peace organization was confronted with the challenge of how to sustain its follow-up program with Palestinian and Israeli Seeds during the Intifada, due to the inability of many of the Palestinians to access the Seeds of Peace Center in Jerusalem because of restrictions placed on them by Israel, and the Palestinian belief that face-to-face meetings were inappropriate under existing circumstances. One central means of communication between the participants took place via cyberspace through SeedsNet, an online secure Internet listserv providing Seeds of Peace graduates with a daily forum in which they could maintain dialogue across borders. SeedsNet—sent to more than 2,000 participants daily—became a "virtual coexistence" where Seeds could hold discussions, debates, and arguments, as well as ask questions and share information.

During times of heightened strife, SeedsNet provided participants a safe, alternative outlet for receiving information about what was happening on the other side, news that might not otherwise be heard. Palestinians and Israelis wrote about how the conflict and violence affected their lives, painting a concrete, vivid, and personalized picture of the suffering and hardships they were enduring. Palestinians wrote about how the occupation impacted them on a daily basis, including restrictions and humiliation they experienced at checkpoints and destruction to their homes and cities by the Israeli army. Israelis wrote about suicide bombings that had killed friends or acquaintances, or their own close calls on the scene of a bombing. Their stories humanized the daily headlines, giving names and personal information about the people suffering and killed, as well as showing the effects these deaths had on their loved ones. For example, Tanya, an Israeli, wrote about her reaction to the killing of two Israelis while eating in a restaurant in Tulkarem. She received a response from Sami, a Palestinian who lives in Tulkarem, saying, "I just want you to know that neither I nor all the other people that I've been asking lately, support the killing of the two men that just simply came here to eat hummus."

Many participants attributed great significance to the fact that SeedsNet is a closed and secure listserv, enabling them to feel safe about the opinions they express, without worrying about repercussions of their statements in their communities. SeedsNet further served as a support network and therapeutic outlet, where Seeds could maintain relationships and express doubts, anger, frustration, and despair. One Israeli described how whenever he felt angry about regional events taking place, he would post a message to SeedsNet in order to "feel much calmer and I can have people respond to it and hear what other people have to say about it. It's kind of like an Advil." A Palestinian noted that writing to SeedsNet serves as a release for many of the Palestinian Seeds, "the tanks are next to their houses, or a bomb just happened next to their houses, so for them to tell it to the other side and get feedback. . . . It helps in controlling their anger and frustration."

SeedsNet also helped the teens maintain optimism and hope regarding the future. One Israeli stated, "It means that there's still hope if people are still talking to each other on SeedsNet. I don't think there are many groups that keep on doing it, Palestinians and Israelis, talking to each other on a daily basis." A Palestinian said that following a terrifying incident in which her sister was almost injured by Israeli soldiers, which she described on SeedsNet, "My in-box was filled with e-mail from people who had read about it on SeedsNet. And honestly it did help me a lot and uplifted my spirit."

To be sure, not all of the postings enhanced positive communication. Some writers' jokes were misunderstood. At times some Seeds verbally attacked others, using threatening and offensive language. In one case, a Palestinian posted a message that the time had come for Israeli children to die as opposed to Palestinians, and that a certain Israeli Seed had better leave his settlement soon, "before we kick you out of there." At such times, Seeds of Peace staff members intervened on SeedsNet, reminding the participants of their goals and how they were more likely to be achieved through respectful communication. A SeedsNet Monitoring Committee of volunteers was established, which formulated a list of rules and guidelines for the writers, advising respect and tolerance, banning cursing and violent threats, and recommending that the smile symbol (:-) be used to indicate a joke, to prevent misinterpretations.

Of course, not all participants, especially the Palestinians, have regular access to the Internet but the opportunity for online communication during a time of conflict can be very effective, particularly when the participants are unable or unwilling to engage in face-to-face contact.

The Induction of Israeli Seeds into the IDF

One of the thorniest issues facing the program and participants, called the "IDF dilemma," emanated from the fact that Israelis enter the military at age 18 and could be ordered to serve in the West Bank and Gaza. Since the outbreak of the Intifada, many more Palestinian Seeds than previously have experienced direct contact with Israeli soldiers on a regular basis at checkpoint crossings and via incursions by the IDF into Palestinian areas. The idea that Israeli Seeds would become soldiers fighting against Palestinians was often incomprehensible and overwhelming for both sides.

In Israeli society, serving one's country is the expected norm and typically looked upon with pride, but the act of having befriended Palestinian teenagers posed a major quandary for many Israeli Seeds, whereby, as one Seed said, this selfless act and duty of serving one's country "is the same act that kills my partner." Several Israelis reflected upon the great confusion, anxieties, and contradictions they experience upon receiving their induction notices. The message learned from Seeds of Peace about the other side being human is perceived by some Israelis to be incongruous with army service. As an Israeli Seed stated:

> If you're in combat, you have to believe that you're fighting the enemy. And if Seeds of Peace succeeded, and the enemy has a face then you're just killing people. And no one wants to kill anyone, especially when they're 18, 19, or 20.

Some of the Israeli Seeds saw some potential benefits to serving in the army while preserving the values they learned from Seeds of Peace, reasoning that it would be better for Palestinians if people like them were at the checkpoints. As one Israeli asked, "Who would you want sitting at a check point or serving the country—a Seed who has been opened and enriched with others' opinions and knows of different options, or a crazed, narrow minded person?"

Some Israeli Seeds tried to resolve the IDF dilemma by serving in noncombat units such as public relations, media, and intelligence, or even (as some female Seeds did) declaring themselves to be conscientious objectors. Several veteran Israeli Seeds took the initiative of organizing seminars for younger Israeli Seeds who were approaching the age of military service, to review a variety of perspectives on this subject.

Many of the Palestinians had great difficulty reconciling the fact that their Israeli Seed friends are, or will be, serving in the same army as soldiers who have been causing death and suffering to their people. A Palestinian addressed Israelis on SeedsNet, describing how she and her family were suddenly awakened in the middle of the night by soldiers banging on her door and pointing a gun at her family:

> I have Israeli friends, I go to Seeds of Peace, I believe that we can live together, we work to try and get a solution among us "we Seeds." But if one of you guys is a soldier, even one of my best Israeli friends, don't ever expect from me to see you in the way that I used to. When you're wearing this suit, when you are holding your gun, when you kill my friends, my people, and maybe one of my family members, and even me, I don't still see you as a Seed.

Some Palestinian Seeds expressed envy toward the Israeli Seeds who had a means to express their patriotism and fight for their country that Seeds of Peace appeared to deem legitimate, whereas they perceived that engaging in their own armed struggle would be viewed negatively by the organization. Several Palestinian Seeds insisted that Israeli Seeds not participate in the army, and attempted to pressure the Seeds of Peace organization to take a position against Israeli Seeds serving in the army.

Government Sponsorship

Another challenge to the program emanated from government sponsorship and involvement. On the positive side, official support contributed greatly toward the legitimacy of the program, a factor that alleviated parental anxieties about sending their children to a camp where they would interact with the "enemy." Moreover, being selected to attend the camp by the government was considered prestigious and an honor. Authority support was particularly important for the Palestinians who could be accused of engaging in normalization activities with Israelis, a widely held taboo, and marginalized from their society.

But government involvement also compromises certain aspects of the program. Through contact with the other side, participants may question some of their government's policies and positions, resulting in tensions within the respective delegations. This was evident when several of the female Israeli Seeds declared themselves to be conscientious objectors—prompting the Israeli Ministry of Education (for whom refusal of military service was unacceptable) to complain to the Seeds of Peace organization.

By providing a transformational experience in which participants come to humanize the adversary and focus on issues pertaining to justice and human rights, peace education may encourage participants to question the status quo and seek to alter the system, whereas governments tend to promote the status quo. Organizations conducting interventions between groups involved in intractable conflicts must consider the impact of receiving governmental support, especially if this restricts the freedom and independence of the participants and/or the program.

Recently, with the establishment of a Hamas-led government in the PA, the situation has become even more complex. Hamas opposes sending Palestinians to the Seeds of Peace camp. Consequently, the 2006 campers were chosen from Palestinian private schools with the support of PA President Abbas, thus bypassing the new Hamas government.

Increased Asymmetrical Power Relations

The extreme asymmetry in power relations between Israelis and Palestinians during the Intifada on the macro level also impacted the program. As noted by James Bennett (2004), a basic source of asymmetry between Israelis and Palestinians stems from the fact that "one side has a state; the other does not." Within the external context of the relationship between Israelis and Palestinians, Israelis are the stronger party, holding the reins of power and control, and having economic, political, and military superiority (Maoz, 2004a; Salomon, 2002; Suleiman, 2004). Furthermore, Adwan and Bar-On (2004, p. 517) point out that during the current Intifada, although both parties have suffered from the bleak realities of the conflict, Palestinians have significant less control over their lives due to the occupation and living under the rule of the Israeli army, resulting in "restricted freedom of movement, curfews, border checkpoints, and great fear of shootings, killings, and house demolitions."

This increased asymmetry made it extremely difficult for some Palestinians to justify their continued participation in Seeds of Peace. One challenge that emerged at the beginning of the Intifada resulted from the organization's politically neutral stance. Some Palestinian Seeds could not understand or accept this position, especially when they experienced military incursions. They were greatly disappointed with the lack of political action taken by the organization on their behalf and the absence of organized demonstrations and condemnations of the Israeli government's actions. Indeed, some Palestinians interpreted the lack of political action to indicate that the organization was supporting the asymmetric status quo. In 2005, a Palestinian wrote, "To Seeds of Peace: you want to make a change? Bring all your Seeds and come and demonstrate against the racism that's happening, the checkpoints, and the wall."

Moreover, many Palestinians could not legitimize participation in joint activities with Israelis, dictated by Israeli-imposed restrictions. Many of the face-to-face activities were held in Jerusalem or in locations controlled by Israel. In order to attend them, Palestinians from the West Bank and Gaza had to first obtain permission from the Israeli authorities and pass through checkpoints. One Palestinian said she could not possibly participate in a Seeds of Peace seminar on human rights held at the Jerusalem Center, when in order to reach Jerusalem she first had to cope with checkpoints, a violation of her human rights. Another Palestinian criticized Seeds of Peace for holding activities in areas controlled by Israel, stating that the process of needing permission to travel took away from the dignity of Palestinians and served only to promote Israeli needs. He wrote:

> The fact is when we give Israelis the satisfaction of meeting with Palestinians we are only saying that, "It's okay. Don't feel that guilty about what is going on. Look, I've come all the way, crossed checkpoints, all to see you and make peace with you." Surely that must make an Israeli feel better and make him think, "Hmmm, maybe it isn't that bad"—when it really is.

Failure to attend to issues of asymmetry within the program negatively impacts the participants, undermines the program, perpetuates the external status quo of inequality (Abu-Nimer, 1999), and "reinforce(s) existing negative attitudes and relations in which one group is dominant or regards itself as superior to the other" (Maoz, 2004a, p. 446). Seeds of Peace employed several approaches in order to address this problem of asymmetry, including the use of a mixed model, increased reliance on uninational programming, and focus on leadership training in one's own community.

Use of a Mixed Model

Within the field of peace education, debate exists as to whether such programs should highlight individual or group identities. To what extent should the national identities of Palestinians and Israelis be emphasized? This issue has been at the heart of much of the recent research on intergroup encounters taking place between Arabs and Jews in Israel, and between Palestinians and Israelis (see Abu-Nimer, 1999, 2004; Halabi & Sonnenschein, 2004; Maoz, 2000, 2004a; Suleiman, 2004).

One approach used by many programs is that of the coexistence model or decategorized approach, based on Allport's contact hypothesis (1954). Such programs emphasize individual identities and highlight similarities, cooperation, and intimacy between individual members of the conflicting groups. In this model, group membership is minimized and controversial political issues are avoided (Suleiman, 2004). A major criticism of this model is that interpersonal interactions are emphasized to the detriment of addressing the actual conflict between the groups (Abu-Nimer, 1999, 2004; Halabi & Sonnenschein, 2004; Maoz, 2000; Suleiman, 2004).

As a result of this dissatisfaction, a second model was developed, referred to as a categorized (Horenczyk & Bekerman, 2002) or confrontational (Maoz, 2004a) approach. In this model, participants are related to as representatives of their groups rather than as individuals. Center stage is given to intergroup processes, core conflict issues, national identities, and power relations, as opposed to interpersonal relations.

However, shortcomings of this method have been identified, including that it can inadvertently strengthen the in-group–out-group schema and lead to greater anxiety (Horenczyk & Bekerman, 2002); that participants' identities may be circumscribed as they are pigeonholed into the fixed category of Arab or Jew Abu-Nimer, 2004); and that the absence of personal relations may impede lasting effects beyond the meeting room (Bar-On, 2002).

A new approach, referred to as a mixed model, has recently been employed in intergroup encounters (Maoz, 2004a). This approach includes both categorization and decategorization techniques, addressing interpersonal and political-intergroup dynamics. At certain points in the encounter, expression is allowed for discovering similarities and relating as individuals, whereas at other times, interaction is based on collective identities with emphasis given to conflict issues and power relations (Maoz, 2004a).

The Seeds of Peace program employs a mixed model approach, focusing on both individual and group identities, on coexistence and confrontation. Opportunities are created for the participants to interact and get to know each other both as individuals and as members of groups in conflict. For example, at camp participants can interact with each other on a personal level during mealtimes, sports, and other activities, discovering common interests and forming cross-group friendships, and as members of groups in conflict during the daily dialogue sessions in which issues pertaining to the conflict and the external asymmetry are addressed.

Several researchers have noted that a significant objective of peace education programs consists of learning about the collective narrative of the adversarial group, its history, suffering, and aspirations (Abu-Nimer, 2004; Adwan & Bar-On, 2004; Salomon, 2004). The Seeds of Peace program is designed to provide access to the other side's narrative through daily facilitated dialogue meetings. Many participants noted that they learned important aspects of the other side's collective narrative that helped them understand the behaviors and actions of the other side. Moreover, they indicated that they had learned to apply critical thinking skills, question their sources of information, and seek additional perspectives. Israelis mentioned learning about the *Nakba* ("catastrophe"), referring to the massive displacement of Palestinians in 1948, turning many of them into refugees, and Palestinians mentioned learning about the Holocaust and its significance for the Jews. It should be noted that understanding the narrative of the other side does not necessarily imply agreement with these positions. As one Israeli stated, "I might not agree with him, but I can understand why he thinks this and that."

This mixed model can lead to powerful outcomes. One Palestinian stated that before she met the Israelis, she believed they knew they had stolen the land, lied about it, and knew they lied about it. However, after befriending Israelis and listening to their narrative, she discovered that their attachment to the land is genuine; she now seeks a compromise so that both sides can live together. An Israeli said that by listening to a Palestinian friend talk about life in Hebron, and seeing photos of soldiers patrolling around this Palestinian's home, he came to truly understand life under occupation.

Considering which model is best, it is noted that many Palestinians indicated that having opportunities to address conflict issues was critical. In this way, they could speak about attaining their rights and a just solution to the conflict, perceiving that they were doing something worthwhile for their people. In contrast, many Israelis seemed to find the opportunity to get to know the other side on an individual basis and to form cross-group friendships a significant experience. This suggests that Israelis may have preferred a decategorized approach while Palestinians may have preferred a categorized approach. For Palestinians, interacting at the intergroup level may be an attempt to acquire a sense of equality and power within the encounter setting. However, it should be noted that many of the participants interviewed for this study indicated that the combination of both a coexistence and confrontational approach was meaningful. Maoz (2004a), in an evaluation of 47 intergroup encounters between Jews and Arabs in Israel, found that only 21 percent used a mixed approach. Based on the findings of this study, more programs, particularly those targeting teenagers, should consider adopting this model.

Uninational Programming

Another strategy that Seeds of Peace employed during the Intifada was an increased reliance on uninational programming (although special face-to-face events were also held) and projects in which participants could "make a difference" in their communities despite the ongoing conflict. Such activities greatly appealed to Palestinian Seeds since attention was shifted away from interactions and relationships with Israelis to an internal focus on improving Palestinian society, making it more acceptable for them to participate. For example, at a seminar entitled "Walking the Walk, not Just Talking the Talk: Community Activism in the Shadow of Conflict" held in Jericho, 55 Palestinian Seeds volunteered at a refugee camp where they conducted activities with the refugee children and painted the gymnasium. Discussions were also held, centering on ways that Palestinian Seeds could contribute to their home communities, even during a time of conflict. One Palestinian said, "If there's a curfew and you have children in your neighborhood not going to school, you can help them with their studies." Another Palestinian said that these seminars motivated her to volunteer in her community and overcome feelings of hopelessness and despair. An important aspect of these activities is that they are considered to be legitimate and positive in the eyes of the Palestinian people, thus alleviating concerns about engaging in a peace education program that also includes Israelis. Furthermore, these activities fostered leadership skills and helped build self-esteem, empowering the participants.

Attempts were made to adapt activities appropriate to the real-life context of increased strife, asymmetry, and to the needs of the participants. To that end, Seeds of Peace solicited graduates' feedback. For example, some Palestinian grads wanted to see more focus on uninational activities with Seeds of Peace Centers in their home communities so that they wouldn't have to contend with obtaining permission from the Israeli authorities in order to attend events at the Jerusalem Center. As a result, Seeds of Peace opened an office in Ramallah and hired Palestinian staff to conduct programs locally.

Programming for the Alumni Seeds

A major shortcoming of many peace education programs is the short-term nature of their interventions. Few peace education programs operate with the same participants for more than one year (Abu-Nimer, 2004; Nevo & Brem, 2002). In contrast, the Seeds of Peace program conducts long-term follow-up programming for participants, geared to their developmental needs. For example, some programs include academic components, focusing on timely themes, such as the role of the media during conflict; and the teaching of professional skills, such as conflict mediation. Furthermore, Seeds of Peace empowers alumni by involving them in the planning and implementation of activities, thus giving participants a sense of ownership for the programs. The organization also hires alumni as counselors and facilitators at the camp and at regional centers.

At a leadership summit in the summer of 2005 held at the camp in Maine, 120 alumni Seeds, now in their 20s, continued intergroup dialogues and participated in workshops on business, politics, media, and conflict resolution. This summit offered them opportunities to develop professional skills, receive career advice from experts, learn how to assume leadership roles in their fields of interest, and develop collaborative projects. Some participants had been unable, or had refused, to meet with members of the other side earlier in the Intifada, like Mona, who four years earlier had said she wouldn't meet with Israelis while tanks were parked outside of her home in Ramallah.

Today some of the graduates are pursuing professions that target youth and education. A Palestinian Seed said she wants to become a history teacher, teaching in a way that children "are not given a message to hate or be prejudiced or feel superior. I would also like to let them know that yes, you have been taught history that way but someone else in a different part of the world has studied the same incident in a different way." An Israeli said he intends to focus on peace education for young children and encourage them to learn Arabic, "I think in the books, don't leave out anything, tell everything and give all the facts. Get the kids educated towards peace and hope that Palestinians will do the same. And learn Arabic so you can talk to the Arab people in Arabic." Others are studying media and communications, hoping to influence how the conflict is reported in their communities. Still others are studying law, political science, and international relations, with plans to impact their society's legal and political systems.

Conclusion

The renewal of Israeli-Palestinian violence in autumn 2000 posed a fundamental challenge to the viability of Seeds of Peace. Although dialogue did continue, there remained a number of acute problems. These include the induction of Israeli Seeds into the IDF, government sponsorship, and increased asymmetrical power relations between Israelis and Palestinians on the macro level. While some obstacles persisted, several strategies helped the organization "survive" the Intifada, including the use of online communication, employing a mixed model, an increase in uninational programming, the creation of special alumni programming, and empowerment of the Seeds in designing and implementing programs.

There is no doubt that operating peace education programs during the Intifada posed many challenges. However, the results of this study of Seeds of Peace indicate the merits of conducting peace education programs in a time of heightened conflict. As noted by other researchers, these include achieving the following objectives: preserving ties between the two sides by creating "islands of sanity" (Adwan & Bar-On, 2004, p. 514); preventing further dehumanization (Maoz, 2004b); heightening participants' awareness of the reality in which they are living (Halabi & Sonnenschein, 2004, p. 374); and cementing the infrastructure for expansion when top-down peacebuilding initiatives resume (Baskin & Al-Qaq, 2004; Maoz, 2004b). Perhaps Ziad, a Palestinian Seed from 1993, best expresses why it is critical for peace education programs such as Seeds of Peace to continue to function during a time of acute violence:

> Today we have people on both sides who are opposed to the peace process and the idea of peace. . . . the voices of extremism became stronger . . . That's why I believe Seeds of Peace should survive because I think that Seeds of Peace is the enemy of the extremists. . . . Peace is established between enemies not friends. I think Seeds of Peace plays the most important role when the gaps between the people are very great, when there's hatred and misunderstandings. . . . It's important that the Seeds of Peace program goes on.

Notes

1. The violent Palestinian-Israeli confrontation that began in autumn 2000.
2. Pseudonyms for the Seeds of Peace participants are used, with the exception of Asil Asleh.

References

Abu-Nimer, M. (1999). *Dialogue, conflict resolution, and change: Arab-Jewish encounters in Israel.* Albany: State University of New York Press.
Abu-Nimer, M. (2004). Education for coexistence and Arab-Jewish encounters in Israel: Potential and challenges. *Journal of Social Issues, 60,* 405–422.

Adwan, S., & Bar-On, D. (2004). Shared history project: A PRIME example of peace-building under fire. *International Journal of Politics, Culture, and Society, 17*(3), 513–521.

Allport, G. W. (1954). *The nature of prejudice.* Reading, MA: Addison-Wesley.

Bar-On, D. (2002). Conciliation through storytelling: Beyond victimhood. In G. Salomon & B. Nevo (Eds.), *Peace education: The concept, principles, and practices around the world* (pp. 109–117). Mahwah, NJ: Erlbaum.

Bar-Tal, D. (2004). Nature, rationale, and effectiveness of education for coexistence. *Journal of Social Issues, 60,* 253–271.

Baskin, G., & Al-Qaq, Z. (2004). Yes PM: Years of experience in strategies for peace making. *International Journal of Politics, Culture, and Society, 17*(3), 543–562.

Bassiouni, M. C. (2003, November 13). Laudable in rekindling hope. *Bitter Lemons, 17*(1). Retrieved November 15, 2003, from http://www.bitterlemonsinternational.org/previous.php?opt=1&id=17#67.

Bennett, J. (2004, August, 15). Sharon's wars. *The New York Times,* p. 31.

Halabi, R., & Sonnenschein, N. (2004). The Jewish-Palestinian encounter in a time of crisis. *Journal of Social Issues, 60*(2), 373–387.

Horenczyk, G., & Bekerman, Z. (2002, April). *Perceptions of group identities in Arab Jewish short-term encounters.* Paper presented at the Interactive Conflict Resolution Conference, Jerusalem.

Maoz, I. (2000). Power relations in intergroup encounters: A case study of Jewish-Arab encounters in Israel. *International Journal of Intercultural Relations, 24*(4), 259–277.

Maoz, I. (2004a). Coexistence is in the eye of the beholder: Evaluating intergroup encounter interventions between Jews and Arabs in Israel. *Journal of Social Issues, 60,* 437–452.

Maoz, I. (2004b). Peace building in violent conflict: Israeli-Palestinian post-Oslo people-to-people activities. *International Journal of Politics, Culture and Society, 17*(3), 563–574.

Nevo, B., & Brem, I. (2002). Peace education programs and the evaluation of their effectiveness. In G. Salomon & B. Nevo (Eds.), *Peace education: The concept, principles, and practices around the world* (pp. 271–282). Mahwah, NJ: Erlbaum.

Salomon, G. (2002). The nature of peace education: Not all programs are created equal. In G. Salomon & B. Nevo (Eds.), *Peace education: The concept, principles, and practices around the world* (pp. 3–14). Mahwah, NJ: Erlbaum.

Salomon, G. (2004). A narrative-based view of coexistence education. *Journal of Social Issues, 60,* 273–287.

Seeds of Peace. (2005). *Homepage.* Retrieved December 15, 2005, from http://www.seedsofpeace.org/site/PageServer.

Suleiman, R. (2004). Planned encounters between Jewish and Palestinian Israelis: A social-psychological perspective. *Journal of Social Issues, 60,* 323–337.

CHAPTER 25

SAMEN IN ZEE: ISRAELIS AND PALESTINIANS IN THE SAME BOAT CAMP

Sophie Schaarschmidt

Samen in Zee means "all the in same boat." It was chosen as the guiding principle for a unique initiative of four students from the Netherlands who brought together Belgian, Dutch, German, Israeli, and Palestinian youth. This initiative was carried with the thought that respect and understanding of divergent groups can only be achieved by getting to know one another—on equal terms—as individuals and cultural beings. The meetings were organized as a sailing camp, where participants were figuratively—and literally—in the same boat together.

The week's program consisted of learning modules of nonviolent communication and conflict resolution, and a mediation training—as the main constituent of the program—in addition to country presentations and sharing personal conflict experiences; as well as leisure and cultural events such as sailing lessons, a multicultural evening, and a trip to Amsterdam with a canal tour, dinner at a pancake bakery, and visits to three religious houses (a mosque, a synagogue, and a church) and the Dutch Amnesty International Office. The latter involved a courtroom activity creating opposing views of the universality of human rights.

Two Samen in Zee sailing camps took place: in August 2004, and a year later, in August 2005. The camps were held in the small village of Uitwellingerga in the north of Holland at a small private sailing farm, chosen for its peacefulness and surrounding landscape, privacy, and access to sailing lessons. The setting, field visits, program flexibility, and open-mindedness and cohesion of the group contributed to the uniqueness of the experience.

The group in the first camp consisted of the youth, youth leaders, workshop facilitators, sailing instructors, and organizing team. For the second camp, the organizing team consisted mainly of youth who had participated in the first camp and were committed to reprise the project. Major factors remained consistent, including the setting, workshop leaders (myself and British nonviolence trainer Marcus Armstrong), youth leaders who recruited the participants, sailing instructors, objectives and substance of the program, and countries of origin of the participants (Belgium, Netherlands, Israel, and the Palestinian Occupied Territory of the West Bank), but there were some changes in the youth organizations involved and some slight modifications in the program.[1]

The third camp—which was again planned by former volunteer participants of the second camp—took place in 2006 and it was also greatly successful. The youth of the third camp are now organizing a follow-up camp with the same participants to build on their experiences (www.yep2007.eu). They have received funding approval from the European Union. They plan to meet for the purpose of developing joint projects and to learn about becoming agents of social change and peace in the Middle East. This is a wonderful result of the third camp. However, voices have been raised that another "Samen in Zee" sailing camp should be organized for the following year since the youth feel that these camps have contributed a lot, not only to their own lives, but also to their communities.

This chapter addresses various important issues concerning the process and outcome of these camp experiences:

1. What were the motivations and the objectives of the camps?
2. What happened during the camps, particularly with respect to reconciliation efforts between Israeli and Palestinian youth?
3. Were the camps successful?

While the framework of this chapter is too limited to discuss in great detail the theories and success of conflict resolution trainings or to develop a new framework to evaluate such projects, some points and observations will be raised that are of interest to those working in the field of conflict resolution and peacebuilding.

Background

The project idea developed from a discussion about intercultural training and the Israeli-Palestinian conflict between the author and a fellow student, Menno Ettema, both enrolled in master's courses in the psychology of culture and religion at the University of Nijmegen in the Netherlands, and volunteers in the Euro-Med Youth program of the European Commission dealing with intercultural training, international voluntary service, and conflict resolution. Both had participated in a Euro-Med Youth camp in Israel called "Beyond the Borders," which brought together Dutch, French, Israeli, Palestinian, and Turkish youth in a kibbutz in Israel. This camp failed to decrease existing stereotypes between Israeli and Palestinian participants, apparently due to the aggression and emotionality evident in the group discussions and on the visits and tours, despite the opposite objective of the camp. Returning from this camp fairly shocked from this interaction, the author and her companion developed their initiative and presented it at a workshop at a Euro-Med Youth seminar in Haifa in December 2003, with participants from mixed professional and cultural backgrounds (Cyprus, Greece, Israel, Italy, Malta, Portugal, Spain, and Turkey). The positive reception inspired them to develop contacts and submit a proposal in February 2004. In addition to that, the author had a more personal motivation, being a German woman educated about the dreadful history of World War II and the treatment of the Jews in the *shoah*. Worried about the lack of justice, equality, and peace in the Holy Land and in the world, she believed that with this project, she could make a small contribution toward understanding and respect—something that is missing in any conflict in the world. Admittedly, this thinking might seem naïve and romantic. Indeed, the experience of the two youth camps resulted in a more critical reflection on the initiative and its objectives.

The First Camp

The first camp started off with a workshop including icebreakers and name-games, participants giving introductions and personal statements about hopes and fears regarding the coming week, followed by the first sailing lesson. One exercise, for example, was a sentence completion whereby participants put an ending to the phrase, "The sun shines on everyone who . . ." The afternoon workshop involved exercises to describe "cultural codes" and "cultural diversity," as well as a group meeting in nationality-mixed groups to reflect about the experiences, and an evening where participants engaged in "country presentations."

The idea of the country presentations was to give the other participants facts about each participating country (its population, size, main income, etc.). In the planning sessions, the Israeli and Palestinian youth leaders had demanded to avoid political discussions about the Israeli-Palestinian conflict, and to restrict the week's program to general education on nonviolent communication and conflict resolution. However, we were conscious of the fact that a presentation of "the Palestinian land" might never be apolitical since it by nature reports loss of land incurred by the state of Israel. Interestingly—to the apparent surprise of the youth leaders whose objective had been to avoid a discussion about the Israeli-Palestinian conflict—the Palestinians' country presentation could best be summarized as a powerful demonstration of their deprivation and inequality, whereas the Israelis' country presentation started very cautiously about geography and climate (i.e., nonpolitical issues) but was completely taken over by a Palestinian-Israeli who raised political issues. Some Palestinians were clearly very eager to express their feelings and explain their situation. This evening evoked a lot of emotions and frustrations among the Israeli, Palestinian, and Palestinian-Israeli group members. The Israeli group felt betrayed since their nation was portrayed as "evil" by the two Palestinian groups, and were eager to defend their position and claim legitimacy and understanding for their situation.

In reaction to this, and to prevent dissention, we felt the workshop program for the week needed some adjustment by holding workshops about "nonviolent communication" and "conflict resolution"—originally planned for the end of the week—earlier in the program, and abandoning the originally planned workshops on "identity" and "intercultural communication." Two workshops on nonviolent communication (NVC) were scheduled for the following two days in order to bring those principles into use in the mediation workshop where political issues would be brought back into the discussion. Principles of transactional analysis were taught by role-playing an agreement between a mother and her child. It was hoped that learning skills of nonviolent communication and compassionate listening would help participants conduct a mock authentic mediation session discussing and negotiating issues in the Israeli-Palestinian conflict on a rational, intergroup level rather than riddled with emotional and personal issues. The last thematic workshop, scheduled one day before departure, focused on the future: how to bring social change in a nonviolent way into practice. The question was asked, "What could be the role of youth in accomplishing social change in their environment?"

This approach seemed to work for most participants, evidenced by the decreased distress and animosity in the Israeli, Palestinian, and Palestinian-Israeli participants. The workshops contained theoretical and psychological input about processes in conflict resolution and ways of nonviolent communication that were put into practice using role-play, group and individual exercises, and moments of reflection. The work was on two levels: personal, in being encouraged to be himself or herself in the first place; and second, cultural, in being encouraged to be Israeli, Palestinian, Palestinian-Israeli, Dutch, German, or Belgian. Examples used in the workshops derived from various (mainly interpersonal) conflicts between partners in a relationship (e.g., colleagues at work, minorities and majorities in a society) with the aim of creating an understanding of conflict dynamics. Participants were allowed to discuss their personal conflict-related incidents, but boundaries were set to keep discussions on the political level well defined and limited. Political discussions were initiated mainly by the Palestinians and Palestinian-Israelis, with the result that the Israeli participants sought to redefine the discussion to stick to the personal level. Occasionally personal issues became so intertwined with national issues that participants were confused, at the expense of the possibility for any meaningful dialogue—at such times the organizers intervened to stop the discussions.

In general, the youth were all very eager to learn about the NVC model and different approaches to conflict resolution. They liked the activities and expressed the significance and value of this information for their personal lives. The group atmosphere during the workshops, sailing, and free time was relaxed and joyful; the group mixed well and seemed to enjoy being together, interacting as human beings rather than as representatives of cultural agendas. The other "foreign groups"—Dutch, Belgian, and Germans—clearly played an important role, in the way that these youth treated the Israeli and Palestinian participants on equal terms, and stimulated discussions with individuals from both groups during free time. The European youth wanted to know more inside information about the conflict and hear the personal stories that the other participants could tell about how the conflict was affecting their lives. This created authenticity, in that true stories were shared and true feelings expressed in an atmosphere of "communal" caring. The interaction of the participants during the sailing lessons and the evening activities was not to be underestimated as a valuable source of relaxation and camaraderie between the participants.

The mediation session presented tense moments, as the participants were aware that the group would now switch to discuss political issues, thereby testing whether the participants had learned to develop relationships that would resist heated argument, or whether the discussion would again divide the participants into rival camps. The mediation consisted of two parts: (1) uninterrupted speech time for each group, and (2) the mediation between the two groups itself. Although we were aware of the fact that the Palestinians and the Palestinian-Israelis faced different problems with the Israelis, it was decided during discussion with the youth leaders of all three groups that the two Palestinian groups should form one group for the mediation whereas all three groups would get the opportunity to speak during the uninterrupted speech time. The mediating group consisted of three spokespeople per group. In the Palestinian group there were two Palestinians and one Palestinian-Israeli. The Dutch, Belgian, and German groups appointed one person each to become a mediator. Altogether there were three mediators and three spokespeople per group participating in the round table discussion of the mediation.

During the uninterrupted speech time each group presented the story of its people based on hard facts that were illustrated by personal examples, which were presented in a very emotional way. The tone was not aggressive and none of the groups blamed another group for being responsible for the situation.

When, after a small break, the spokespeople took their seats in "camps" opposite each other at the mediation table, the atmosphere was so tense that one could hear people breathe. The youths who were acting as spokespeople kept calm but were obviously very nervous, and felt a burden to speak on behalf of their groups and negotiate existential questions (i.e., basic and significant to issues of existence, such as the life of an Israeli Palestinian citizen in the Holy Land). The Israeli delegation was especially distressed, having to face two different sources of contention: from Palestinians and from Palestinian-Israelis. Moreover, they seemed to feel inferior by the presence of these two Palestinian groups that were ready to negotiate their rights and needs—a situation that seemed to be the reverse of reality where Israelis would be perceived as the superior party in a negotiation.

However, the parties managed to establish a dialogue with each other, using the methods they had learned in the NVC workshops: listening to each other and presenting their demands and needs in the least violent way possible. This opened new opportunities for more intense communication, and created an atmosphere of mutuality with two equal partners negotiating a common future. It was clearly observable (by how they talked about the issues) that the youths were aware of the fact that their futures were entangled with each other and that they could only solve the conflict together, when both sides accepted to move toward each other. The moment the Israeli group reduced their control over the Palestinian group and accepted their autonomy and legitimacy (listening carefully without posing opposing opinions), a dialogue of equality evolved, which led the participants to search for solutions from which both parties could benefit. Although it was impossible to come up with solutions in such a limited time, the youths felt they had undergone a valuable experience with each other that laid a basis for their relation with each other during the rest of the week.

Challenges of Preparing the Camps

Preparing the approach, method, and content of the camps had not been an easy task. First of all, none of the organizers had prior experience in setting up such activities. Second, although our studies provided us with basic scientific models of intergroup relations, and conflict and cross-cultural identity issues, we had not learned to put this knowledge into practice. Third, we had to fulfill the guidelines of the YOUTH program of the European Commission, which was funding the project, and we had to negotiate our ideas with the youth leaders of the four partner organizations involved in the project. An additional difficulty was that we could not benefit from the experience of other organizations that had been organizing a project like ours since we did not know of projects of this kind in Europe, Israel, Palestine, or elsewhere. With all this in mind, we knew this project would be experimental. We spent many hours discussing the approach, goals, and usefulness of our project, and were well aware that the overall goals might never be reached—to achieve "peace" itself. Short of that, we resolved that projects like ours could usefully raise awareness among participants and encourage them to build bridges instead of walls—to engage in dialogue with each other in order to understand each party of the conflict better and accept each others' reality.

This experience could also be valuable to the European partner groups, despite their peripheral position regarding the Israeli-Palestinian conflict, which could play a valuable role as observers and mediators, and could get a better picture of the different realities for Israelis and Palestinians and the value of stimulating dialogue between them. This appeared to be exactly the role they chose during the camp. Their presence helped to legitimize both identities and give them equal prominence. At the same time, the nature of the NVC workshops provided a good framework for learning about conflict resolution and nonviolent communication in general that applied to the European participants as well. As a result, those workshops were reported to be useful by the majority of the participants, regardless of their country of origin.

The Second Camp

The second camp was built on the framework of the first camp, including the relaxation activities, but with some changes in the program; for example, addressing the issue of the national identity of the participants early in the first evening—during the country presentations—in order to stimulate a necessary group-defining debate between the participants right from the start. Since group-identity could be emotionally unsettling for the participants, we encouraged them to approach political issues from a personal background; for example, in verbalizing statements in this way: "The Israeli-Palestinian conflict impacts *me*, as an Israeli/as a Palestinian [in Israel], in such a way . . . " This process follows the principles of nonviolent communication and thus these workshops were scheduled early in the week, to prepare participants for the negotiation of political issues during the mediation session.

The second camp was hampered by the four-day delayed arrival of the Palestinian group because of visa procedures; only the Palestinian youth leader had been granted a visa in time to arrive at the start. This forced us to reschedule the program once again; continuing the NVC workshops at the beginning of the week, but postponing the mediation session until the arrival of the rest of the Palestinian group. The country presentations were kept on the first evening, with the Palestinian presentation done by their youth leader. As expected, an emotional discussion evolved from the subject matter of that presentation; however, the group atmosphere stabilized during the following days. The group awaited the arrival of the Palestinian group with great excitement, preparing a special welcome on the main plaza in Amsterdam.

The two-day visit to Amsterdam served as an effective get-acquainted opportunity, providing an amiable atmosphere on return to the farm for continuation of the workshop program—introduction to mediation and the mediation session. Despite that the Palestinians missed the NVC workshops, the mediation session went well; however, the mediators had to interfere more often—compared to the first year's camp—to clarify the ground rules (e.g., of being open, no verbal or physical aggression, no blaming or judging).

In addition, while the participants made serious efforts to establish a dialogue, the dialogue between the Israeli and Palestinian spokespeople of the second camp was less deep and more confrontational with less mutual listening (requiring more intervention by the mediators) compared with the year before. As with the year before, the time was too short for the development of any solutions. Yet, the participants expressed relief and increased awareness about the issues from this experience.

The task of the mediation session was to come to a written agreement reflecting some common view—not as a political paper but to raise awareness about what the other side experiences (e.g., that an Israeli youngster sees what occupation means to a Palestinian) and rethink their opinion. The spokespeople in the first camp agreed that the occupation has to end because it stands in the way of peace. In the second camp, the Israeli spokespeople slightly changed their view of suicide bombers (not the action but why they do it, as a desperate way to get attention for the situation). One Palestinian girl said during the mediation: "If there were no suicide bombers, there would not be a Palestinian issue anymore";

this made a deep impression on everyone, as they realized that for the Palestinians, this would have meant death for their nation.

Evaluation

After the week, the organizing team met to evaluate and share impressions and observations of the camp. Discussions covered broad issues and critical evaluations, including that activities should be imbedded into a conceptual framework. The short-term success of the camps was evident from the reports of the participants, and from their ratings on an evaluation form. In a round-table discussion of the participants at the end of the camp, and in a questionnaire that was used in the second camp to evaluate the project, the youth were overly positive about their experience. Suggestions were made for some little things to be improved, mainly about practicalities like providing more comfortable beds and serving dinner earlier and including more international food like rice and pizza. Yet the approach, method, and workshop content was neither criticized nor challenged by the youth or youth leaders.

After the communication sessions, participants noted that the experience was "powerful," "enriching," and "moving," and that they "learned a lot," and "got to know different opinions." Others noted that they felt "unfinished," "tired," "self-conscious," and "needed more training and practice." Overall, the participants liked the camp very much. In two particularly moving comments, a Palestinian girl said this was the most moving experience of her life, and an Arab-Israeli said, "You give me the hope back."

However, the long-term success was less obvious. The youth had created an Internet forum as a means to keep in touch with each other, and thought about various ideas for further action and awareness-raising in their own communities (e.g., to raise white balloons in the cities where the participants lived). However, few proposed ideas were implemented, and after half a year, most of the youth lost contact with each other. Discussions on the Internet forum became more and more apolitical with time, and led to sharing personal stories, jokes, or songs. Although a few enthusiastic youth took responsibility to plan another camp, the organizers felt that the efforts to create ongoing relationships had failed. The question arose whether the camps really contributed to a more differentiated understanding about the existing realities in the Israeli-Palestinian conflict. For that reason, one of the organizers posted the following questions on the Internet forum:

> However, I was thinking about the camp and about you, and about the situation in your countries, especially the situation in Israel and Palestine. I was thinking about what the contribution of the camp was for you. Did it really help you to find hope for the future? Did it help you to be able to look at the "other side" less biased or did you decide for yourself that THIS Israeli named . . . , and THIS Palestinian named . . . is okay and a good person, but the groups (THE Israelis or THE Palestinians) are not? Did it help you to become aware of the power relations in your conflict with one

party clearly holding the power over the other . . . ? Did you become aware about the fact that this conflict which might have developed from a fight about land and resources in the first place became a conflict about national identities? And what are you doing now with this awareness? What does this mean to you as being a member of your national group, either the Israelis, Palestinians or as a Palestinian in Israel? . . . If a sailing camp only resulted in having nice friends somehow, or knowing that we can eat hummus together as human beings, what implications does this have for the conflict? I can imagine that the Palestinians and Palestinian-Israelis liked the camp in its nature but might question the usefulness of it. Nothing has changed in their bitter realities, so where do we go from here? And for the Israelis, how helpful is it to have met a Palestinian who behaved like a human being whereas in the media Palestinians are all terrorists?

The struggle of the organizing team to evaluate the success of the camps underlines the need for a conceptual framework in which group encounter approaches are discussed and reviewed.

Conceptual Framework

Existing Models

The search for a conceptual framework for the group encounter approaches was challenging. Although many such encounters have been happening (with various conflict groups throughout the world), it was difficult to find documentations of evaluations used by these approaches. The following is an overview of some classifications of group encounters in the psychological literature, and their differences.

A useful classification of such camps (group encounters) is provided by Katz and Kahanov (1990) with the following two social psychological theories forming its basis:

1. The first theory—*Realistic Conflict Theory* (Sherif, Harvey, White, Hood, & Sherif, 1961)—proposes that a real conflict develops from a lack or shortage of resources or significance of land for two or more conflicting parties, leading to stereotyping, prejudice, and hatred toward the other(s). When two or more conflicting parties interact with each other, it is hypothesized that competition increases these perceptions whereas cooperation and the just distribution of resources between them.

2. The second theory—*Social Identity Theory* (Tajfel & Turner, 1986)—proposes that personal identity is defined by belonging to one or more groups that we give significance to, and conflict derives from differences between two or more of these different significant identities. Personal values and self-esteem are gained from "positive distinctiveness"—the attempt to distinguish oneself as having positive qualities separate from others. This distinction leads to "in-group favoritism"—the valorization of the own (salient) group identity at the expense of an "out-group" identity perceived as inferior, and less positive. Stereotyping, according to this theory, becomes a "human condition" whereby people will always be

prejudiced against one another and favor their own group above another, especially in a conflict situation with the other group.

For their classification, Katz and Kahanov (1990) arrive at the following three
"types" of group encounters: (1) workshops in the spirit of "human relations"
tradition; (2) workshops emphasizing "cross-cultural" learning; and (3) workshops based on the "conflict resolution" approach.

The human relations approach focuses on—as its name suggests—relations
between individuals in conflicting groups. Many such approaches focus on a superordinate identity—an identity everyone could identify with, for example,
being European, Muslim, or a human being. Negotiation becomes less salient in
such an approach because commonalities are emphasized that do not have to be
negotiated.

The cross-cultural approach focuses on raising awareness about cultural differences believed to account for tension and conflict between cultural groups. If
those cultural groups meet on equal terms, negotiation is not necessary, since it
is believed that understanding the differences would lead people to accept them.
This can be challenged, given what might happen if cultural differences are perceived as threatening to one's own culture.

The conflict resolution approach focuses on negotiating the needs and goals of
the conflicting groups with efforts to bridge existing differences and reach a
compromise. Group members are seen as representatives of their respective
groups and negotiation happens on the intergroup level; individual differences
are unimportant for the negotiation. Understanding is considered of little help in
the negotiation, since it concerns goals and needs that the parties want to see
achieved or satisfied.

Workshops in the tradition of human relations usually focus on dialogue on
the individual level, whereas workshops emphasizing cross-cultural learning
and workshops based on the conflict resolution approach focus normally on dialogue on the intergroup level. Whereas the first two types of the previously
noted classification are based on (different) conclusions drawn from the Social
Identity Theory—(1) in order not to prejudice, we have to create a common
identity; and (2) in order not to prejudice, we have to raise awareness about cultural differences—the last type is based on the Realistic Conflict Theory that a
fair negotiation will satisfy our needs and therefore we will experience less intergroup problems, which will lead to less prejudices.

On a more basic level, Katz and Kahanov's (1990) typology reveals a difference
between the types outlined with regard to their primary goal, which is *understanding* versus *negotiation*. Models directed to understanding are based on the
assumption that enhanced understanding of one another's situation and perspective encourages mutual dialogue that will eventually help to settle a conflict.
Models directed to negotiation are based on the assumption that a conflict would
be settled by having adversaries negotiating their needs in a dialogue on the
political level. Two of the three types described by Katz and Kahanov (1990)

would, according to this division, be categorized as "understanding models" (workshops in the spirit of human relations tradition and those emphasizing cross-cultural learning), whereas workshops based on the conflict resolution approach would be categorized as "negotiation model."

A different typology was proposed by Ben-Ari and Amir (1988) who classified group encounters according to their intention: (1) to reduce fear of each other and create familiarity by getting in contact with the rival group (contact model); (2) to get to know and understand the rival group by learning about the culture and specific problems the group is facing (information model); (3) to understand one's own (individual) stereotyping and the psychosocial dynamics of the conflict (psychodynamic model). All models are aimed at *understanding* in one way or another, by either becoming familiar with each other on the interpersonal, intercultural, or intrapersonal level.

Our Unique Model

Our camp experience leads us to add the two dimensions—understanding and negotiation—to the three existing types. This is based on the hope that (1) enhanced understanding of each other's situation, perspective, and needs encourages mutual dialogue, and that (2) this dialogue will open up the opportunity for the conflicting parties to negotiate their needs on a more political or intergroup level.

Our camp encounter is therefore a combination of the different approaches. The NVC workshops are clearly interpersonal and intrapersonal, demanding individual reflection and awareness of psychological dynamics that play a (key) role in conflict situations. Our workshops gave a lot of attention to feelings in a conflict that are obviously nonnegotiable. In contrast, the mediation session is based on negotiation on an intercultural level, moving inter- or intrapersonal issues to the background. The NVC workshops, visits to religious houses, country presentations, and the intercultural evening aimed at providing information and therefore creating *understanding* of each other's (ethnic, religious, or personal) background. In contrast, the mediation session aimed at *negotiating* needs between the conflicting parties, regardless of the understanding that the participants developed.

However, it was predicted that mutual dialogue (as defined in the mediation model as a dialogue in which both parties would be open, concentrating on solutions and agreements, and listen to each other carefully without blaming or judging or using verbal or physical aggression) would evolve more easily if the participants could do both—that is, define the existing realities not only in terms of needs and goals of the respective groups, but also in terms of different realities of the groups.

Our observation was that the Israeli and the two Palestinian groups came to the camp with different needs: whereas the Israeli group had the need to get to know the "enemy" in order to reduce their fear, the Palestinian groups had the need to get recognition for their suffering and discrimination and to get legitimization for their threatened national Palestinian identity (as being equal to any other national identity in the world) and raise awareness about this in the whole group. Therefore, the Israeli group was more comfortable with the approach of the "understanding model" used in the NVC workshops, because it served their need to be treated as individuals and not to be called "a people." In sharp contrast, the Palestinian groups were more comfortable with the approach of the "negotiation model" used in the mediation session, which served their need to talk about the conflict as a real and bloody battle for the right of existence fought between the two peoples. This vast difference has implications for follow-up projects. The logic of the "understanding model" would suggest that the youth would benefit from a well-built follow-up program that kept them actively involved with each other to deepen the friendships that would develop during the camp. The logic of the "negotiation model," however, would suggest the opposite: those participants should come to the camp well-prepared with strengthened (national) identities that allow them to negotiate their needs and goals (self-) confidently.

In conclusion, the youth might benefit from both approaches despite the fact that it is difficult to conclude whether our camp encounter integrated both successfully, or could satisfy the needs sufficiently in the future (e.g., the Israeli need to reduce their fear by "meeting the enemy" and the Palestinian need to get recognition of their suffering and be accepted by the "other side" with regard to the "national identity"). We are in the process of improving our model through thoughtful reflection and evaluation of our experience. Yet, our model holds hope for raising awareness about the Israeli-Palestinian conflict—on the political, interpersonal, and intrapersonal levels—for Europeans, Israelis, Palestinians, and the public elsewhere in the world.

References

Ben-Ari, R., & Amir, Y. (1988). Intergroup confrontations in Israel: Assessment and paths of change (in Hebrew). *Psychology, 1*, 49–57, as cited in Halabi (2004).

Halabi, R. (2004). *Israeli and Palestinian identities in dialogue: The School for Peace approach.* New Brunswick, NJ: Rutgers University Press.

Katz, Y., & Kahanov, M. (1990). A review of dilemmas in facilitating encounter groups between Jews and Arabs in Israel (in Hebrew). *Megamot, 33*(1), 29–47, as cited in Halabi (2004).

Sherif, M., Harvey, O. J., White, B. J., Hood, W. R., & Sherif, C. W. (1961). *Intergroup conflict and cooperation: The Robber's Cave Experiment.* Norman: University of Oklahoma Press.

Tajfel, H., & Turner, J. C. (1986). The ocial identity theory of intergroup behaviour. In S. Worchel & W. G. Austen (Eds.), *Psychology of intergroup relations.* 7–24. Chicago: Nelson-Hall.

CHAPTER 26

CHILDREN MARCH FOR PEACE

Richard C. Goodwin

It was a hot morning in Caesarea, at 8 A.M. on September 21, 2005 when 1,500 Arab and Israeli kids between the ages of 9 and 12 gathered to clean the debris off the beach to prepare for their three-kilometer march on the beach strip to Kisr Al-Zarqa.

Their T-shirts and hats with Arabic and Hebrew lettering read "Children's March for Peace." It is my vision that kids should make their voices known in the peace process, and most important, that Israeli and Palestinian children can—and should—show solidarity on their efforts for peace.

Children are all too often left out of the peace equation, yet they suffer anguish and fear every night when they go to sleep—worrying not only about themselves, but about their parent's safety in these times of terror. Kids want a better future, and because they will live longer than we adults, we need to create peace so they can enjoy the fruits of a better life.

Some organizations now attempt to get youth involved. The word *youth* usually refers to teens. Certainly teens can verbalize opinions and take action better than younger ones—but it is my firm belief that younger children, even preadolescents, need to not only be protected from terrorism but also should be proactive in the pursuit of peace.

At the same time as the march on the beach strip to Kisr Al-Zarqa, a second march started from the Lubieh forest near Golani junction, with another 1,500 Arab and Jewish children. Marching on the beach and in the forest made a purposeful statement about not only cleaning up the environment but also about making peace on all terrains.

The kids—all of whom were enthusiastic to participate—came from Arab and Israeli schools in the area. In fact, so many children wanted to take part that we had to cut off the number at a certain point. Of course, we also provided security, though there were no incidents.

The date—September 21—was purposefully picked to celebrate International Day of Peace as declared by the Untied Nations.

The activities lasted until noon, with a final ceremony attended by many mayors, local council leaders, and public figures. Each participating school received a gift package, including sports equipment, and each child was given a book about dolphins (symbols of peace) and 10 copies of a letter urging their families and friends to work to deepen the dialogue, pluralism, peace, and care for human rights issues.

The event cost $40,000, and was worth every shekel.

How did I get it going? I threw a cocktail party for the more than 50 organizations participating in my Middle East Dialogue Network. At the event, I described the project and 35 of the 50 organizations agreed to pitch in. The deputy director of Givat Haviva, Mohammad Darawshe, chaired the preparation committee and did a brilliant job.

With this big success under our belts, we were able to do four more in the next two years, with a total of over 10,000 children participating. The children ended the summer march of 2007 on the steps of the parliament and gave members of parliament a plan they had prepared for peace and for a better future. These events have shown everyone that young kids can have a tremendous influence for peace in Israeli society.

The Children's March for Peace is one of my pet projects that are part of the organization I founded, the Middle East Peace Dialogue Network. The word *dialogue* is key. It is my belief that the only way that true peace can be accomplished is when former enemies develop a meaningful dialogue.

Trust is key in any relationship. From a psychological perspective, centuries of mistrust—between the three great religions, Muslim, Christian, and Jewish—have been impeding peace in the Middle East. The problems faced by the people today are further compounded by politicians who have, from time to time, an agenda that is not always in the best interest of peace. I want leaders—and the people—to see from the success of the children's marches that, "If the people will lead, the leaders will follow."

I am convinced that coexistence is possible. The proof, for me, lies in the success of the peacemaking community of Neve Shalom/Wahat al-Salam. This community is made up of 50 percent Israeli Jews and 50 percent Israeli-Palestinians of which one-third are Christian and two-thirds are Muslim).

It is the goal of the Middle East Peace Dialogue Network (MEPDN) to support groups, institutes, organizations, centers, and individuals throughout the region that encourage communication and dialogue between the many and varied nationalities, cultures, religions, and political philosophies, and that also encourage leadership among youth for the general advancement of peace and democracy in Israel, the Palestinian Authority, and the greater Middle East.

Dialogue can take place in many ways, such as through economic development, the arts, workshops, and lectures.

We have many activities. These include compiling a database listing organizations, groups, institutes, and centers (locally and internationally) interested in the promotion of peace and democracy in the Middle East. We keep records of educational and cultural events and host guest speakers, workshops, conferences, and special programs related to resolution of the Middle Eastern conflict. We also send press releases about ongoing activities; expand mailing lists to use for information and fundraising; distribute a newsletter with commentary, news, solicitation of contributions, and a calendar of upcoming events; maintain a website with links to other sites and resources; develop, fund, and promote educational programs on Middle East topics for children, teens, and adults which include guest lectures, dialogue groups, cultural gatherings, and camps/retreats.

Money is an important part of keeping peace programs going—so many peace initiatives get benched because of lack of funds. Our financial support comes from private individuals, corporate donations, charitable foundations, and religious organizations. It is part of my philosophy that "money is a loan from God and if you use it to help others, she will see that you get more." I continually find that the more I give, the more I seem to get back.

Young kids deserve our support, and they deserve peace. The marches prove that they are willing to extend efforts themselves to reach that goal.

CHAPTER 27

COOKING, CLIMBING, CAMPING, AND OTHER CREATIVE COOPERATIONS BETWEEN PALESTINIANS AND JEWS: SUCCESSES AND CHALLENGES

Judy Kuriansky[1] and Tali Elisha

> I need you in order to be me . . . We can only be free together . . . We can only be safe together.
>
> —*Archbishop Desmond Tutu, Noble Peace Prize Laureate, describing the spirit of Ubuntu at the 2006 Clinton Global Initiative meeting*

In spring 2006, two Israelis and one Palestinian found their lives dependent on each other when they made the climb up Mt. Everest—one of the most difficult and challenging mountains in the world. They had all trained vigorously for several years before making the trip with a multicultural team that included Christians, Buddhists, a Hindu, and an atheist. The lone Palestinian, Ali Bushnaq, a 43-year-old father of three born in Nablus, said some friends would not talk to him because he agreed to climb with Israelis, but he decided to go anyway.

The trip was the brainchild of American climber Lance Trumbull, founder of the Everest Peace Project (www.EverestPeaceProject.org). His goal: to build peace between people who come from divergent cultures by intentionally making them rely on each other in extreme surroundings and circumstances.

"Our Everest Climb for Peace provided the world with inspirational stories, pictures and video that portrayed courage, friendship, and teamwork," Trumbull said (2006).

Sadly, Bushnaq collapsed and didn't make it to the summit; pneumonia made him too dizzy and weak to continue. Upon hearing the news, 39-year-old Israeli climbing instructor Micha Yaniv cried. Bushnaq was also brought to tears when his other new Israeli friend, David "Dudu" Yifrah, radioed Ali, waiting at advance base camp, saying, "I have a special surprise for you. I have a flag with sewn-together Palestinian-Israeli flags with me and I'm going to unfold it here at the summit, and I'm dedicating this climb to you in the name of peace." An emotional Ali proclaimed, "You are now my brother."

This remarkable expedition is one example of the innovative ways Jewish Israelis and Palestinians are coming together in the shadow of conflict and terrorism. The experience is grounded in the well-known "contact hypothesis" in social psychology (Allport, 1954), which posited that working together toward a common goal is one of four key conditions for a positive outcome of intergroup relations (other conditions are equal group status within the situation, cooperation, and support). The well-known Robber's Cave summer camp study further showed that solving a common problem and working together toward a common goal resulted in positive attitudes toward previously conflicting groups (Sherif, 1966; Tal-Or, Boninger, & Gleicher, 2002).[2] This chapter presents many impressive and varied efforts—supporting these principles—in bridging the divide between Palestinians and Israelis, and signaling healing and hope. It also explores the challenges and limitations of such endeavors, especially given the contemporary political climate.

Of course, it would be naïve to think that these projects are sufficient to bring about a solution to such an entrenched and complicated conflict. Gone are the more hopeful times just after the Oslo Accords, when joint projects flourished. The present socioeconomic situation is dire, the cultural divide wide, and politics more volatile and violent. Grassroots organizations struggle to maintain educational collaborations, training programs, dialogue groups, and cooperative projects of all kinds but sadly many have been sabotaged by lack of funds, political strife, fear, and even travel restrictions. For example, four Palestinian yachtsmen from the Gaza Strip couldn't participate in a "Sail for Peace" in 2005, crossing the Mediterranean from Tel Aviv through the Suez Canal, because of delays in getting travel permits.

Physical, logistical, and real barriers (checkpoints, the separation wall, visas, real and threatened violence) all limit collaborative efforts. So do psychological blocks (blame, distrust, discouragement and even ingrained attitudes and deep-seated hatred). Grassroots cooperation is further affected by the larger context of the socio-economic-political and cultural environment. Civil war between Hamas and Fatah has made civil partnerships even more precarious. With an unstable situation, project coordinators cannot be assured that their plans will go smoothly.

Yet committed individuals—private citizens (health professionals, philanthropists, human rights activists, and others)—persist in their commitment to partnership and peace. They are shining beacons of hope in a dark situation. As citizen ambassadors of peace, they are examples of how people in conflict zones can appreciate, respect, and trust each other. Their efforts are referred to as *people-to-people*—or more academically, *bottom-up* or *track-two*—diplomacy, signifying unofficial actions by citizens, conflict resolution specialists, businesses, or non-governmental organizations on the ground, as opposed to *top-down* or *track-one* diplomacy conducted between heads of state, ministries, or other officials. My favorite example of track-two citizen diplomacy is the so-called ping-pong diplomacy that was pivotal in opening up relations between China and the United States, when Americans were invited to a ping-pong competition by the Chinese during Nixon's presidency.

From ping-pong years ago to the modern-day mountain-climbing expedition, sports proves to be a fertile field for forming friendships and cooperation in spite of cultural conflict. PeacePlayers International brings Jewish and Palestinian boys and girls aged 10 to 16 together to participate in basketball and life-skills activities, to learn leadership skills, and to live together as friends. The soccer field provides the grounds to kick off cooperation in many programs, especially for kids, offered by organizations like the Peres Center for Peace (www.peres-center.org) and Givat Haviva Jewish-Arab Centre for Peace (www.givathaviva.org.il). The world's most popular game also became a vehicle for peace on a professional level when in 2005, for the first time, Israeli Arab players teamed with Jewish sportsmen to play in international matches. The Jewish-Arab club, which also has a 50–50 management team of Jews and Arabs, got to the finals in their first season playing in an international tournament. But according to the club's president, Alon Liel—a former foreign ministry director-general and former Israeli ambassador to Turkey—the team's greatest success was not on the field, but off.

"We are not engaging in sport only," Liel said. "The United Club is an important test case in Arab-Jewish co-existence" (Ben-tal, 2005). A soccer fan, Liel got his inspiration for the power of sport to bring cultures together when, as a special envoy to South Africa in 1986–1988, he noted how the South African Football Association helped black South Africans get ahead, thereby ameliorating the impact of apartheid. The present team is supported by the European Union, Swiss, Americans, Dutch, Turks, and of course, the British, who are major soccer enthusiasts.

The spirit of trading the battlefield for the sports arena was spawned at Delphi in ancient Greece. Centuries later in 2004, Delphi was the site of another such sporting effort, called Budo for Peace, where *Budo* is Japanese for "the way of stopping conflict." Six Palestinian and six Israeli young students of marital arts, along with youngsters from other areas of conflict such as Kosovo and Cyprus, traveled to Greece for a weekend pilot program, which was the brainchild of an Israeli sixth-degree Black Belt, Australian and Israeli-emigre Danny Hakim. Bowing to each other in the matches is a way for youngsters to learn mutual respect.

Taking advantage of the popularity of the upcoming Olympics, a "Peace through Sport" campaign was launched in Amman, Jordan, to use sport as a means to instill dialogue, tolerance and peace among young people living in conflict regions. Plans included a camp in Jordan in September 2007 to bring young people together with Olympic athletes from countries in conflict.

But the picture is not always rosy and one cannot be Pollyanna and think that playing together can wipe out ingrained cultural divides—or mores. In a film called "*Shadye*," screened at the Human Rights Watch 2006 International Film Festival, a 17-year-old Muslim girl from a small Arab village in northern Israel becomes a world karate champion. But at a match in South Africa, when the

Israeli team coach asked the Palestinian team coach to train their teams together, the latter declines, saying, "That would give the impression that we are living in peace . . . [when we are not]." By at the end of the film, Shadya marries and is forbidden by her husband to pursue her sport.

Peace is not only being played out on the sports field, but also on the kitchen table. At dialogue groups organized by a dedicated California couple, Arabs and Jews also prepare and share meals from their respective cultures (Kuriansky, Traubman, & Traubman, 2007). Similarly, considering their cuisine as a contribution to the peace process, a group of two dozen Arab and Jewish cooks formed a group called Chefs for Peace. "Cooking together, we create, we become our true selves, we open our imagination," they say. "People discover and experience a universal and heartfelt connection."

Israeli master chef Sasi Habeh and Palestinian maitre d' and sous-chef Jamil Amleh were a good example of partners cooking for peace, even though their Mile End Jerusalem Steak House in Montreal is now out of business (for reasons beyond their control). Of course any business can go belly-up, but the story of their collaboration is inspiring. The men's friendship dates back to when Habeh was a soldier and helped Amleh pass at a checkpoint. Though both devout in their respective Jewish and Muslim religions, they each made concessions for the sake of their restaurant: Amleh agreed that alcohol could be served—not acceptable to Muslims; and Habeh conceded that the restaurant could stay open on Friday nights and Saturday despite the "no-work" mandate of the Jewish Sabbath. The food, music, and murals were from both cultures. "My friends thought I was crazy, getting involved with an Israeli," said Amleh. "But we wanted to show everyone that our two peoples can live together and work together." Said Habeh, "There are always extremists. But I'd like to think Jamil and I represent the majority opinion when it comes to wanting to put down arms and coexist. Jamil and I are more than friends. We are brothers" (Brownstein, 2005).

From a psychological perspective, feeling the spirit of brotherhood reinforces a sense of self and belonging, fulfilling normal needs for affiliation. Social identity theory emphasizes in-group association (Tajfel & Truner, 1986). But affiliation with the so-called out-group—and extending brotherhood to the other—also affords psychological gains, including self-esteem, pride, and a sense of goodness.

Given the limitations of meeting in the region and the dangers of cooperation, Palestinians and Jewish Israelis are often forced to meet on more neutral foreign soil—hosted in countries like Norway, Italy, Germany, Cyprus, and Turkey—in meetings organized by third parties. For example, the 2006 International Conference on Education for Peace and Democracy organized by the Israel/Palestine Center for Research and Information (IPCRI) was held in Antalya, Turkey. And, Japanese youth invited Israeli and Palestinian students to Japan to learn how to communicate with one another at a Japan-Israel-Palestine Student Conference over a period of five years (www.jipsc.org). Says Ayumi Yamamada, head of the JIPSC research section, "We call it 'Mutual Understanding' because young Palestinians and Israelis like to come to Japan to see how a country gave up fighting, and also in Japan we want to learn more about the troubles of young Palestinians and Israelis." Korean students—who had been sent by their provincial government as "peace messengers" to hold peace talks at Bethlehem University in the Palestinian territory and at Hebrew University in Israel—invited 10 Palestinian students and 10 Israeli students to South Korea to participate in a peace camp program—called "KOPAIS (Korean, Palestine, Israel) Friends: Making Peace Together." At the camp—held August 25–September 6, 2005—the students dialogued, played soccer, and visited temples. Finally, together they drew up a "Peace Declaration" to pursue peaceful coexistence.

Of course, collaborations between Arabs and Jews outside the region are easier than for those in the conflict zone. For example, in 2006, two San Diego residents, Palestinian Nader Elbanna and Israeli-born Miko Peled, raised $84,000 to send more than 1,000 wheelchairs to the Holy Land. The two men gathered contributions from organizations like the Rotary Club, and also from bags of coins collected by kids who participated in walk-a-thons. Half the wheelchairs were destined to go to Palestinians and half to Israelis, and almost all are for children, many of whom are victims of violence. Sixty-year-old father-of-six, Elbanna, who owns a medical supplies business, met 44-year-old father-of-three martial arts teacher, Peled, at a Jewish-Palestinian Dialogue meeting.

Educators can be important partners in peace, as evidenced powerfully in the team of Palestinian professor Sami Adwan and Jewish social psychologist Dan Bar-On, who have developed a unique educational program and booklets for Palestinian and Israeli youth to learn their own narrative and understand the narrative of the other (Adwan & Bar-On, 2007). In another educational effort, Palestinian Ghassan Abdullah and Orthodox Jew Adina Shapiro, founders of the Middle East Children's Association, organized a meeting of hundreds of teachers to share curriculum (Centerpoint Now, 2005). And IPCRI's education conference brought together 270 Israelis, Palestinians, and international participants from all over the world (Spain, South Africa, Austria, Iran, Bosnia, the United States, and others)—including peace and conflict resolution facilitators, human rights activists, educators, practitioners, researchers, and community organizers—to meet, share their work, and build relationships. Lack of sustainability has challenged people-to-people initiatives, but the valuable email exchange of information and resources set up by the IPCRI organizers is flourishing on the computer network.

Yet, even these important educational efforts are not without problems. For example, local government officials have not yet embraced the curricula devised by the Adwan–Bar-On team. Lacking local support, projects have to seek outside international support: for example, Adwan and Bar-On have brought their educational program to schools in Virginia and are appealing to U.S. Congresspeople. Other problems the team faced: some local teachers dropped out of the project. One Palestinian quit after being humiliated at a checkpoint. "It can be frustrating," Adwan told an audience gathered for his lecture as part of the week-long 6th Annual Global Understanding Convention—"Global Solutions: Sharing Resources, Shaping Peace"—at Monmouth University. "But we continue anyway."

Camping grounds have long been a common ground for bonding, and at least a dozen such projects abound based on the principle of creating retreats for youth from diverse backgrounds. These include the well-known Seeds of Peace, as well as others whose names perfectly describe their intent: Building Bridges for Peace, Kids4Peace, and Peace It Together. The name of one yearly gathering, "On the Way to Sulha," evokes an indigenous Middle Eastern way of reconciliation where the word "Sulha" in Arab culture describes the ritual which marks the end of the conflict (Ben Itzhak, 2006). All offer Jewish and Arab adolescents a reprieve from violence and conflict in their communities by taking them to a safe environment to foster understanding and trust, form friendships, and learn leadership and communication skills. The programs are designed to include dialogue (about pain and hope), workshops to learn about each other's culture, interfaith prayers or rituals, and fun (sports, games, music, dance, performances and parties). I've experienced the value of such camping, over four days at the annual Oseh Shalom~Sanea al-Salam Family Peacemakers Camp, dialoguing by day and singing songs in English, Arabic, and Hebrew over campfires by night. At a closing ceremony centered around a paper dove flying on a flagpole, a Palestinian summed up the experience to a Jew, "Meeting you has made me put aside the war that just happened, to see the beauty of the people and how we all care about the same thing—a happy life for our families, and living together in peace. We can do it, one at a time" (Kuriansky, 2006, p. 261).

Residential summer camping projects for youth are continually being developed, since such programs are a safe place for participants to express themselves, learn, and have fun—all to facilitate bonding not possible in their home communities. One such project—PeaceInsight—is bringing together a group of 16 Israeli and Palestinian teenagers who may never have met anyone from "the other" community, to a campsite in England. "It is said that the single flying movement of the butterfly may provoke a tornado on the other side of the world," say the organizers. "We hope that bringing together young Israelis and Palestinians may contribute to creating consciousness and a storm of love that touches and involves all humanity."

The challenge is to bring home what is learned. Research shows the difficulty of this, in a similar way that people with addictions often relapse once they return to their environment where cues restimulate unwanted behavior patterns. Youth who formed strong friendships with the so-called "other" find themselves, once home, prey to prejudices of their local network. To counteract this, participants are encouraged to keep in touch through meetings, text messaging, e-mail, and even telephone conferencing. But old attitudes interfere with friendly exchanges. And even though participants are encouraged to spread their lessons to friends, families, and communities, they often encounter resistance.

Technology is increasingly being harnessed for international connections in these grassroots peace efforts. A favorite example of mine is MEET (Middle East Education through Technology), where students from the Massachusetts Institute of Technology engage businesses like Sun Microsystems and Daimler-Chrysler to work with academia to educate Palestinian and Israeli youngsters. The companies donate computers, and American graduate school professors and students provide teaching expertise. Through learning computer skills, the youngsters also develop skills for peace building and forging partnerships between companies and communities to build a better future. The program is a model for other countries, as evidenced by the interest of attendees at a workshop I organized at the 2006 United Nations' NGO conference where a MEET student presented about the program. Particularly rewarding was the fact that audience members from diverse cultures wanted to know how to apply the model in their country.

The power of computers as a tool for peace in the Middle East is also evident in a new computer game called "Peacemaker." The software allows the player to pretend to be the Israeli prime minister or the Palestinian president, and to make diplomatic, economic and security decisions. Windows pop up to present scenes— like a suicide bombing or an air strike—to which the player must respond. Players learn that choices lead to consequences. For example, as Palestinian president, the player may order an end to martyrdom, but risk losing the next local election. If as the Israeli leader, the player orders an air strike after a Palestinian suicide bombing, the result may be escalated Palestinian violence in retaliation but not responding can lead to local criticism and also being voted out of office. The goal of the game is to make compromises and reach peace agreements.

Young people represent the hope for the future—but also for the present. This is evident in many programs involving youth (Steinberg & Bar-On, 2007; Doubilet, 2007; Goodwin, 2007). Among unique programs involving young people is the activity—"A Message of Peace"—which is part of the program of "Journeys for Peace." In a moving exercise, Israeli and Palestinian children from 10 to 12 years old pick either a "condition for peace" or a "consequence of war." The youngsters then formulate questions related to their personal choice and pose them to leaders from a variety of disciplines—like former UN Secretary General Kofi Annan, U.S. President Clinton, and the Dalai Lama—and then form a united "Message of Peace" that puts together their two realities from the Israeli and Palestinian perspective into a united "hope for peace." The boys and girls then share their message with other children inside their classrooms, and outside the school in their family and communities. "As time goes on, the kids develop a strong sense of self-esteem that allows them to respect and love each other, instead of hate and not caring for the others," says a director of the program, Sergio Kopeliovich. "The real 'Journey for Peace,' he says, "begins in each one of us, in every boy and girl. Kids are not just the future, kids are the present, which is why 'Journeys' is the conscience that motivates them to be early 'awakened peace speakers' who could change the near future, and the present days in the region."

Women are also partnering for peace. On International Women's Day, celebrated around the world on March 8, about 20 Israeli and Palestinian women met in Jerusalem to network with each other and with American women in Washington, D.C., through video-teleconference. The networking was organized by Peace X Peace—an American group that connects women around the globe in groups (called Circles) and also through the Internet, teleconferencing and even using Skype (a software allowing free calls over the Internet), to share their stories on topics from relationships to health, money, politics, and parenting. A technique they promote—consistent with the trend in positive psychology today—is "appreciative inquiry," or affirming strengths and assets. The women from both cultures exchanged phone numbers and promised to meet again. One woman from East Jerusalem and an Israeli woman promised to exchange Arabic and Hebrew lessons. In another effort by women, the United Nations Fund for Women (UNIFEM) brought together Palestinian and Israeli and international women leaders and activists to establish an International Women's Commission to guarantee women's participation in the peace process in the region.

"Women don't have a vested interest in maintaining military power and hegemony . . . and they don't need guns for their egos," says female Palestinian peace activist Maha Abu-dayyeh-Shamas in *Can You Hear Me? Israeli and Palestinian Women Fight for Peace*—a 51-minute film produced by New York–based filmmaker Lilly Rivlin, focusing on the role of women in peacemaking (www.lillyrivlin.com). Another main figure in Rivlin's film, orthodox Jewish peace activist and mother, Leah Shakdiel, agrees that women have a different—and even superior—approach to the conflict. "When violence breaks out, men's approach is to turn away from each other and stop talking," she says, while women, on the other hand, understand that the opposite is necessary: to keep talking in order to stop the violence. Sadly, the two women's encounter descends into debate and bitterness. But the film shows that progress is made. The women continue to participate in a Coalition of Women for Peace. Also, Maha and another Israeli peace activist had made a major accomplishment: appearing before the UN Security Council to insist that UN Resolution 1325—calling for inclusion of women in all official peace negotiations—be applied to Israeli and Palestinian women.

Some experts believe that women are more supportive of reconciliation than men. Melodye Friedman is the founding director of Seeking Common Ground, a Denver-based female-centered conflict resolution program for teen girls. "Just as race, religion, political ideology and other identities influence co-existence, so does gender," says the psychologist. "Women possess qualities inherently embodying a more collaborative approach to strengthen intergroup relations and tend to approach conflict resolution from a place of gender inclusion, collaboration, consensus and empathy ('I feel your pain')." This leads to more inclusive leadership which builds peaceful relations and creates more inclusive communities, she explains. Since 1994, about 700 young women have attended the two-week intensive summer experience and follow-up in their home communities in the United States, Israel and Palestine.

Peace activist Saida Nusseibeh is also a proponent of the gender perspective. A pioneer of Jewish-Arab peacebuilding—Nusseibeh was a co-founder of one of the earliest dialogue programs, the Jewish Arab Dialogue and Education in Europe (JADE) started in the early 1970s. She is now active in the United Religious Initiative–Middle East North Africa region, and is planning a project targeted for mothers and daughters. Talking with me during a visit to the Citadel in Amman, Jordan, the city where she now lives, she told me, "I believe that mothers and daughters together are a powerful force for peace."

Even strong bonding established in intensive experiences can splinter under stress. This happened on a joint expedition with Palestinians and Israelis. Their first adventure went smoothly—a month-long expedition in 2004 from Chile to a mountain in Antarctica, which they named "The Mountain of Israeli-Palestinian Friendship." But a year later, the next trip—the 2006 Journey Across the Desert, meant to cross the Sahara from Jerusalem to Tripoli—was fraught with friction and problems. A Palestinian, Sheik Taha (second in command at the Al Aqsa Mosque), was denounced by several Palestinian newspapers for his efforts for peace. Fearing his standing in the community would be jeopardized, he dropped out. In another snafu, Israeli team members were not allowed to enter Libya, causing dissension in the group and leading another member (an Afghani refugee) to depart. Another impediment to entry—when Israel would not issue visas a second time to the Arab team members (a Palestinian and an Iraqi)—caused more tension.

In contrast to these tensions, some extraordinary friendships were formed. For example, a 40-year-old Israeli man whose mother was killed in a suicide bombing and a 24-year-old Palestinian woman whose cousin died in her arms after being shot by an Israeli soldier, spent nights teaching each other Arabic and Hebrew. The spirit of comraderie was evidenced further at the end of the trip, when the whole team planted an olive tree together at the foot of Mt. Sinai, a holy place claimed by all three faiths (Jewish, Muslim, and Christian). The tree would mark the end of their journey, and the beginning of a friendship that would change their lives (http://breaking-the-ice.de).

Artistic endeavors also provide common ground. An exhibition in March 2006, called "Fasatin-Smalot"—meaning dresses in Arabic and Hebrew—showed dresses from both cultures that reflect issues of identity. Another version of an art exhibit meant to inspire peace is a recent project of the Parents Circle-Families Forum. Ceramic bowls made by more than 100 Palestinian and Israeli artists all on the same theme of "Offering Reconciliation" symbolize how a common vision can bridge differences between interpretations and peoples. Art also serves as the vehicle for peace for an Arab former police officer who fulfilled his dream when he established an art gallery 10 years ago in his hometown of Umm al-Fahm, an Arab town in Israel. The gallery made international news in 1999 when Yoko Ono had an exhibition in the Arab town—to purposefully show equality since she had exhibited her work in the Israeli Museum in Jerusalem.

Mixing cultural traditions in art for Israeli-Palestinian peace was also evident in a project initiated by the Israeli and Palestinian Forum. Artist Adi Yakutieli decorated Chinese lanterns with two figures under the motto "It won't stop until we talk" printed in Arabic and Hebrew. On an evening to commemorate International Peace Day in 2006, the lanterns—commonly used in Buddhist ceremonies for peace and central to the fifth anniversary of the 9/11 World Trade Center Memorial Annual Floating Lantern Ceremony organized by the New York Buddhist Church at which my world music band (www.towersoflightsong.com) performed—were carried into a big hall in a city between Bethlehem and Jerusalem by adults and children. A moment of silence was observed for victims of the conflict on both sides.

Filmmaking is also being used to promote cross-cultural understanding. The documentary *Encounter Point*—being shown around the world—follows the stories of a Palestinian ex-prisoner, an Israeli settler, and a breaved Israeli mother and a breaved Palestinian's brother. On a smaller scale, the Creative Arts Network in Canada brings Israeli, Palestinian, and Canadian teens together in a camp atmosphere in Canada to produce short documentaries, animations, or dramas. The youngsters are free to explore any topic as long as the theme relates to conflict resolution. One film showed teenagers describing what peace sounds and tastes like. In another students film with a Romeo and Juliet theme, a Palestinian male and his Israeli girlfriend are painfully separated by a checkpoint.

Another impressive visual arts effort is Givat Haviva's "Through Our Eyes" photography project where Jewish and Arab teens "look" at each other and get to know each other from new angles through the images they take. They visit each other's homes and take pictures of unfamiliar surroundings to learn about each other's lifestyles. Through the experience, the youngsters develop bonds of friendship. Other projects at their Center for Peace (www.givathaviva.org) include "Children Teaching Children," All for Peace Radio, workshops, courses for women to strengthen common bonds, and a joint Israeli, Palestinian, and Jordanian newspaper—called *Crossing Borders*—edited by young people, with 30,000 copies going to 500 schools in the three countries.

Individuals and groups are increasingly documenting their experience. Len and Libby Traubman's DVD, *Dialogue at Washington High*, shows tenth grade high school students engaging in a new quality of listening. The Traubman's DVD, *Peacemakers: Palestinians and Jews Together at Camp*, traces the experiences of Muslim, Jewish, and Christian families from all over the world sharing community at summer camp (http://traubman.igc/vidcamp.htm). In another film project, director Debra Sugarman filmed five Israeli and Palestinian teenage girls in an RV on a road trip across America on the premise of hoping to meet George W. Bush (www.dearmrpresidentthe movie.com). Along the way, they find pain and sorrow but also friendship and forgiveness. Turning also to film, David Michaelis and Jamal Dajani—a Jew and a Palestinian who met while working at a San Francisco television station—made a travelogue of their experiences on the Jewish and Arab side of Jerusalem. Among the people they documented in their film, called *Occupied Minds: A Palestinian-Israeli Journey beyond Hope and Despair*, are a father whose daughter was killed in a suicide bombing, a Palestinian militant, and peace activists.

Some programs target a particular activity to dispel mistrust and foster cooperation, while others offer a panoply of services. For example, the Peres Center for Peace supports programs for Jews and Arabs in almost every conceivable arena—from education to health, sports, and agriculture, including joint botanical experiments. Recent projects include a forum of more than 100 Israeli and Palestinian peace and dialogue groups which met in Jordan; a "Peace Match" soccer game featuring the Real Madrid team against the Peres Centers' Palestinian and Israeli professional players, held in Israel for the first time; and a conference in Israel on chronic disorders in children attended by over 70 Palestinian doctors.

In contrast to such diversified programs, one targeted group—called Combat-ants for Peace—was formed by former soldiers from both sides joining together for peace. About 90 former soldiers first met in secret—to avoid expected disap-proval from their governments—but since March 2005 have been meeting openly to dialogue, promote peace, and publicly spread their message against violence.

Conflict is a deadly serious matter, but as a psychologist, I know that laughter eases anxiety. One young man—dubbed the "laughter ambassador"—conducted a laugher workshop at a Jewish-Arabic conference for artists at the YMCA in Jeru-salem. Realizing the power of laugher as a therapeutic tool to stop the cycle of feeling sadness, hate, and victimization, Alex is now doing laughter workshops—and plans laughter clubs—for Israelis, Jordanians, Turks, and others. Another example of laugher as an antidote to hate is "StandUp for Peace," a comedy act formed by a fellow Friar (a membership entertainment club in New York and Los Angeles, to which I also belong) and Brooklyn-born Jew, Scott Blakeman, who teamed with New Jersey–bred Palestinian-Sicilian Dean Obeidallah. The two met at benefit shows for Seeds of Peace, an organization that sponsors camps for Arab and Jewish teens to live and learn about each other. Performing since 2002 for audiences of Arabs and Jews at colleges, comedy clubs, and community centers, Blakeman (2006) says, "Just by standing on stage together, and bringing Arabs and Jews together in the audience, we're making more progress than they are right now in the Middle East. When peace talks resume, we want to be the opening act."

These projects, varied in nature, all provide proof of the possibility—supported by time-honored social psychological theory—that people divided by differences can work together and form bonds of friendship and cooperation that can lead to peaceful relations. Common ground has already been found for Palestinians and Israelis in many sports and related artistic endeavors as described above. New grassroots ventures are continually being formed, and opportunities seem end-less, given the creativity and devotion displayed by the two peoples. This pro-vides great hope for people-to-people peace in the future. Yet, such projects have to reach a critical mass in order to make a difference in the general society and impact policy; large enough numbers of people are not yet actively involved de-spite groups like One Voice and Peace Now, who do active recruitment. And to be effective on a large scale, such projects have to involve multistakeholders, includ-ing faction leaders, politicians and governments. Impressive as they are, these projects still do not represent the majority of people involved in the ongoing conflict, and can sometimes be seen as preaching to the already-converted—those who want to cooperate and make peace—leaving out mass numbers of others, including those in power and those with extreme or dissenting views.

"You have to go out of your cozy environment and even face fears of disturb-ing the peace, in order to get to peace," said educator Sami Adwan at the Peace-building and Trauma Recovery: Integrated Strategies in Post-War Reconstruction conference at the University of Denver (Adwan, 2007). "You have to work within your community, but also go outside the community, and bring in other groups. You also have to go where the people are, like in the schools."

As a good model of this, the associate vice president for academic initiatives and professor of political science at Monmouth University, Saliba Sarsar, arranged for Sami Adwan and Dan Bar-On to come to his campus as Fulbright scholars-in-residence in Spring, 2007. Adwan and Bar-On's educational efforts are described earlier in the chapter. During the semester at Monmouth, they met with local authorities, taught a course titled "Education: Multiculturalism, Conflict and Peacebuilding," and were featured on a panel discussion (Adwan & Bar-On, 2007). "Having such eminent scholars here on our campus is critical for our student body to meet real people doing exemplary grassroots projects to bring about peace in seemingly intractable situations," says Sarsar (2007). The author of *Principles and Pragmatism: Key Documents from the American Task force on Palestine,* Sarsar himself is involved in dialogue activities between Arab Americans and Jewish Americans—for which he received the 2001 Humanitarian Award from the National Conference of Community and Justice. Finding like-minded people willing to promote your work is crucial.

Efforts such as these require emotional strength. "It takes energy to maintain professional and personal relationships, given all the roadblocks," says Adwan. He outlines two choices: (1) take it easy and just stop, or (2) continue working on peacebuilding projects despite the open conflict. The latter, which he calls "peace-building under fire"—also the proposed title of his book—is his choice. An important lesson that he and Bar-On—his co-director of the Peace Research Institute in the Middle East (PRIME)—learned is that compromise is key (as in any healthy relationship). The two scholars discovered this while taking a year and a half to produce their pamphlet about narratives. Ultimately, they realized that it was impossible to write one narrative or even a bridging narrative—instead both sides had to write their own collective narrative. They also left a space in the middle of the pages for students to write their own personal narrative. Compromise was also key in designing the cover. Since the Palestinian flag uses the color green and the Israeli flag uses the color blue, the PRIME coordinators mixed the colors to create a new one. And, since Palestinian teens objected to the image of the Israeli flag—which reminded them of the military occupation—the scholars settled on two male figures in respective cultural dress, cultivating trees.

Another key psychological requirement for partnerships is trust. But trust has been lacking between Palestinians and Israelis, blocking efforts at working together or sticking it out through problems when they arise between partners. Psychologists like Gary Reiss are helping Israelis and Palestinians rebuild trust in workshops directly addressing such feelings. His seminar "Sitting in the Fire: Training in Conflict Resolution in the Midst of War Zones" gives participants skills to express opinions and feelings in a non-threatening way. The techniques are part of "World Work," a process-oriented psychology technique (Reiss, 2006).

Executive Vice President of Search for Common Ground Susan Collin Marks is convinced that "love" is the fundamental ingredient to the effective peacemaking process. "In the face of the fear that pervades our world and our lives, the only way through it is love," Marks told a workshop group held at the Marble Collegiate Church in New York (2007). "We can use other words, like the 'legitimacy of the other,' but really I think the word 'love' is the most powerful word . . . love evokes the most powerful energy in the world." As the senior associate of the international conflict resolution program at Columbia University, the former 1945 Jennings Randolph Peace Fellow at the United States Institute for Peace, and also a native South African, Marks knows of what she speaks. She served as a peacemaker and peacebuilder under the auspices of the National Peace Accord during South Africa's transition from apartheid to democracy—a process chronicled in her book, *Watching the Wind: Conflict Resolution during South Africa's Transition to Democracy*. The workshop, which I attended, was meant to build awareness about the methodology of conflict transformation by exploring participant's relationship with conflict. In one exercise, participants took a position along an imaginary line representing a continuum of either inviting or avoiding conflict (most participants choose the middle). A role play involved listening well or poorly. Then Marks drew circles on a board for participants to fill in elements they believe are necessary for peace, and to note where these elements overlap.

Peacebuilding requires two principles, as outlined by noted professor of international peacebuilding at the University of Notre Dame, John Paul Lederach: (1) increasing the participation of people affected by the conflict, placing a high value on the local people to create momentum, and not relying on people in political positions; and (2) a notion of responsibility—that we are all responsible, not just leaders for the structure they create—and that all people need to see themselves as actors. The challenge, as he outlines it, is how to link these grassroots efforts to high level efforts, so one doesn't just end up with nice programs with no broad impact (Lederach, 2007). His favorite solution is to "bring together a confluence of improbable people—meaning sit down with people not like you and who do not think like you." The fact that people avoid associating and communicating with people who do not think like them is a roadblock that must be overcome for peacebuilding to be possible.

This tendency is one dynamic underlying a psychological principle called the "approach-avoidance conflict"—a dynamic which Harvard social psychologist Herbert Kelman notes operates in the Israeli-Palestinian peace process. In his analysis (2007), Kelman proposes that as agreement gets close between the two groups, positive expectations are aroused but accompanied—and even outweighed—by fears and other negative reactions to concessions (about land or other issues). Resulting existential anxiety, he says, can only be resolved by (1) acknowledging each other's humanity and nationhood, (2) affirming the meaning and logic of historic compromise, and (3) a positive vision of a common future for the two peoples.

Bright lights need to be focused on grassroots projects such as those described in this chapter, to bring them more world attention. The media has the power to do that. Sadly, as an old adage in journalism goes, "if it bleeds, it leads." But I, and other journalists, believe that it's crucial to promote good news about such positive collaborations between Israelis and Palestinians. One person doing this is Paul Sladkus, through his appropriately named *Good News Broadcast* (www. goodnewsbroadcast.com). Paul has interviewed me about *Terror in the Holy Land* and grassroots peacebuilding described in this book, and is equally committed to Israeli-Palestinian peace. A like-minded journalist, and long time friend, Jane Velez Mitchell, has even called for a governmental "Department of Peace." In my newspaper columns and other media occasions—as much as possible—I cover stories of such cooperative efforts and hope. And women I know have written books of personal stories of Israelis and Palestinians, or of their own experiences, to foster understanding between the people. These include Dianna Armbruster's *Tears in the Holy Land*, Carol Grosman's *Jerusalem Stories* project, and Cathy Sultan's *Israeli and Palestinian Voices: A Dialogue with Both Sides*—motivated by her journey raising her children in war-torn Lebanon.

Blogs are an increasingly popular modern media outlet that can be used to spread the word about all these valuable projects.

Any ambitious project like achieving peace in a conflict region requires partnership between stakeholders from all aspects of society, cultures and countries. Such partnerships are being encouraged by individual philanthropists, and by major networks like the Clinton Global Initiative (CGI). In the 2006 CGI meeting, Ron Pundak, the director general of the Peres Center for Peace, announced its support of Journeys for Peace, the NGO described above. Chair of the CGI focus area titled "Mitigating Religious and Ethnic Conflict," Robert Malley—former special assistant to President Clinton for Arab-Israeli Affairs and member of the U.S. peace team at the Camp David summit—highlighted the importance of such partnerships and exchange programs involving youth, as well as the importance of harnessing the media. Also, President Clinton announced a grant to Abraham's Vision, a nonprofit organization which took Jewish and Palestinian American university students from six campuses known for tensions between Arab, Jewish, and Muslim groups to the past-Olympic site of Sarajevo. The city—often called a "small Jerusalem" for its religious mix—was chosen so that students could learn to analyze religious conflict in that region and apply those lessons to the troubled Middle East. "We need more projects like this," Clinton said.

Hope springs eternal and is warranted despite an unstable political climate. It was warranted in the case of the story of Palestinian and Israeli fishermen in the documentary film, *Men on the Edge: Fishermen's Diary*—which was shown at the Israeli Film Festival that I hosted. The fishermen lived, laughed, fished, and ate together on the border of Gaza and Israel. Ali, a Palestinian, taught Motti, an Israeli, ancient fishing techniques, while Motti acted as his Arab brother's required Jewish "escort" to allow them access to the fish-rich Israeli-controlled sea. Their friendship flourished through years of tough weather and tough times, but came to an abrupt end when eruptions of the Al-Aqsa Intifada barred the Palestinians from that beach. Sadly, the men drift apart and their once-lively hut turned into a ghostly shell.

But a second viewing of the film two years later—at the 2006 Human Rights Watch International Film Festival—held out more promise. At the audience discussion after the screening, producer Macabit Abramzon announced that after four years of separation, the fishermen were reunited on the now-desolate beach where their hut once bustled with their teasing and eating crabs over bonfires after rough days on the sea. Today, they are traveling throughout Israel for screenings of the film and appear onstage after the film to tell their story. The documentary had not yet been allowed to be shown in Gaza, but the men said they hoped one day it would. The rekindling of their friendship inspires the possibility that such reconciliation and lasting bonding can happen between Arabs and Jews throughout the world.

> "This is the Citizens Century, in which history calls all earth's citizens to engage, and change, outside of but in parallel with, governments. It is the undeniable requirement of the 21st century to unleash the necessary and unprecedented compassion for all that governments alone cannot provide."

Len and Libby Traubman,
co-founders of Living Room Dialogue

Notes

1. In this chapter, the first-person *I* refers to Dr. Judy Kuriansky.
2. Sherif's paradigm works under various conditions, including equal status of the groups, sustained interactions, support from authority, and potential to develop friendships.

References

Adwan, S. (2007). "Bringing Israelis and Palestinians into Dialogue." Panel at the 6th Annual Global Understanding Convention. *Global Solutions: Sharing Resources, Shaping Peace.* April 9–14.

Allport, G. W. (1954). *The nature of prejudice.* Cambridge, MA: Addison-Wesley.

Ben-tal, D. (2005, May 15) Shooting for equality—on the soccer field and off. Retrieved July 8, 2006 from http://www.israel21c.org/bin/en.jsp?enZone=Culture&enDisplay= view&enPage=BlankPage&enDispWhat=object&enDispWho=Articles%5E1989.

Ben Itzhak, B. (March 2, 2006). Personal communication.

Blakeman, S. (April 21, 2006). Personal communication.

Brownstein, B. (2005, April 20). Partners in peace—And food. *Montreal Gazette,* Arts and Life Section, page 1.

Kelman, H. (2007). The Israeli-Palestinian peace process and its vicissitudes: Insights from attitude theory. *American Psychologist.* Vol. 62(4): 287–303.

Kuriansky, J. (Ed.). (2006). *Terror in the Holy Land: Inside the anguish of the Israeli-Palestinian conflict.* Westport, CT: Praeger Publishers.

Lederach, J.P. (2007). Plenary address at the conference on "Peacebuilding and Trauma Recovery: Integrated Strategies in Post-War Reconstruction." Denver, Colorado: Conflict Resolution Institute, University of Denver. February 22.

Marks, S. C. (2007). Search for Common Ground workshop on principles of reconciliation. New York: Marble Collegiate Church. February 15.

Reiss, G. (2006). Breaking the cycle of revenge in the Israeli-Palestinian conflict. In Kuriansky, J (Ed.) *Terror in the Holy Land: Inside the anguish of the Israeli-Palestinian conflict.* 107–116. Westport, CT: Praeger Publishers.

Sarsar, S. (2007). Moderator, "Bringing Israelis and Palestinians into Dialogue." Panel at the 6th Annual Global Understanding Convention. *Global Solutions: Sharing Resources, Shaping Peace.* April 9–14.

Sherif, M. (1966). *Group conflict and cooperation.* London: Routledge & Kegan Paul.

Tajfel, H. and Turner, J. C. (1986). The social identity theory of inter-group behavior. In S. Worchel and L. W. Austin (eds.), *Psychology of Intergroup Relations.* Chicago: Nelson-Hall.

Tal-Or, N., Boninger, D., & Gleicher, F. (2002). Understanding the conditions and processes necessary for intergroup contact to reduce prejudice. In G. Solomon & B. Nevo (Eds.), *Peace education: The concept, principles, and practices around the* world (pp. 89–108). Mahwah, NJ: Erlbaum.

Trumbell, L. (2006, June 6). Personal communication.

PART IV

EFFORTS IN EDUCATION, MEDIA, AND MENTAL HEALTH

If we are to reach real peace in this world, and if we are to carry on a real war against war, we shall have to begin with the children.

—*Mohandas Gandhi*

If we have no peace, it is because we have forgotten that we belong to each other.

—*Mother Teresa*

There are some things that only governments can do, such as negotiating binding agreements. But there are some things that only citizens outside government can do, such as changing human relationships.

—*Dr. Harold Saunders, former U.S. Assistant Secretary of State and negotiator of Camp David Accords*

Efforts for peacebuilding can take place in the schoolroom, counseling room, or through the media—all of which are described in chapters in this part. Since children are the hope for the future, educational efforts can break the cycles of fear, hate, and violence. For example, *Ein Bsutan* (Arabic for "a spring in the garden") is a kindergarten in a small Bedouin village where Jewish and Arab three-year-olds are climbing on jungle gyms, sewing, baking, planting, and building models of homes and inviting each other over. The Middle East Children's Association (MECA) is an educational nongovernmental organization that helps teachers instruct on sensitive topics regarding the Israeli-Palestinian conflict. The founders, Palestinian Dr. Ghassan Abdullah and Israeli Adina Shapiro from Jerusalem, believe that students should be taught to understand each other rather than to hate, and should learn necessary skills to listen to a threatening narrative of "the other" to understand each other's pain without engaging in a contest of who suffers more. Innovative education projects described in this part include an award-winning collaboration between an Israeli and a Palestinian who developed shared curricula and textbooks that respect each culture.

The School for Peace exists within a unique community. Called *Neve Shalom,*—the Hebrew word for "Oasis of Peace"—this community embodies the true principle of grassroots partnership since Jewish and Arab families live there side by side. One day's discussion among the residents was not about politics, but a possible summer concert by Roger Waters of the famous rock group Pink Floyd. The impact of such a community is described in this part.

Chapters in this part also address training programs about peace and reconciliation, which often use issues of the Israeli-Palestinian conflict as a good example. A valuable mental health program has also been ongoing for 10 years between Israeli and Palestinian mental health professionals. But these and many other valuable and creative programs are struggling to survive in the current political and economic climate and some have suspended some activities or cancelled some projects altogether. Thanks to an ambitious effort by a team of Israeli and Palestinian innovators—whose work is also represented in this part—an ongoing e-mail exchange among educators and others interested in peace has started up and is thriving—proving the value of communication, contact, and cooperation among individuals around the globe committed to peace not only in the Israeli-Palestinian region but worldwide.

The media is an important stakeholder in the peace process. As a psychologist who is also a journalist, I certainly know how true this is, and make every effort to write stories supporting programs like those presented in this book. Chapters in this part address how radio, television, and other communication technologies are being harnessed for partnerships, and how journalists in the region are being trained not only to be sensitive to issues in conflict resolution, but to embody partnerships by working well with colleagues on the "other side."

> We are called to assist the Earth to heal her wounds and in the process heal our own—indeed, to embrace the whole creation in all its diversity, beauty and wonder. This will happen if we see the need to revive our sense of belonging to a larger family of life.
>
> —*Wangari Maathai, Kenyan Nobel Peace Prize Laureate, in her 2004 Nobel lecture*

CHAPTER 28

Booking Peace for Pupils: The PRIME Peace Education Project for Israeli and Palestinian Youth

Sami Adwan and Dan Bar-On

Our personal histories reflect the projects we collaborate on. You might say "we walk our talk." Sami is a Palestinian and Muslim, and Dan is Israeli and Jewish. Dan is a professor of psychology at Ben Gurion University in the south of Israel, and Sami is a professor of education at Bethlehem University in the Palestinian National Authority. We bridge this distance and our respective cultures in our collaboration and in the work we do.

We care about building peace between Palestinians and Israelis. We both believe that doing this involves understanding one's own and the other's history. That starts with our own. Dan is a child of Holocaust survivors who spent a decade conducting encounters between German adult children of Holocaust survivors and Nazi perpetrators—helping them to resolve residual hostilities—work that led him to look for ways this process can be applied to Israelis and Palestinians. Sami was active as a student with the Palestinian Fatah movement—the PLO group led by Yasser Arafat—and was jailed in an Israeli prison where he discovered the different treatments and behaviors of the Israeli guards made him aware that "the enemy had more than one face." We have both faced prejudice and pain and could have held on to anger or bitterness to an "enemy," but decided to use our personal experiences and professional skills to do useful projects to resolve tensions between Palestinians and Israelis and between generations.

We both co-direct a nongovernmental nonprofit organization of Palestinian and Israeli researchers—the Peace Research Institute in the Middle East (PRIME). The purpose of the organization is to pursue joint projects and peace building through joint research and outreach activities.

Booking Peace for Pupils

One of our favored projects—that won the Goldberg Prize for outstanding collaboration between an Israeli and a Palestinian—is an educational booklet for schoolchildren. Our six-year-long research on "Learning Each Other's Historical Narrative" resulted in the booklet and a curriculum for 15- and 16-year-olds for Israeli and Palestinians schools The figure below shows the front cover of the booklet.

Critics claim history books in both cultures are biased; one man's murderous suicide bomber is another's revered martyr. This project presents each side of the story, with an empty place in the middle for students to write their own story. It encourages students not to hate—and came as a natural outgrowth of Dan's work leading dialogues with children of Holocaust survivors and the children of Nazis (where kids learned the value of hearing each other's stories), and also as an outgrowth of Sami's work on Israeli and Palestinian school textbooks and his experiences training teachers.

"The heroes of one side are the monsters of the other," we say. Palestinian texts barely mention the Holocaust and Israeli texts rarely address the suffering of the Palestinians. The booklet adresses situations seen in a different light by each side. For example, for the Israelis, 1948 means the year of the birth of their nation, but for the Palestinians, 1948 is the "Catastrophe" (*Al Naqbah*) of becom-

Cover of school booklet for Palestinian and Israeli narratives.

ing refugees, without a state. The 1967 Six-Day War between Israel and Egypt, Jordan, and Syria, is seen as aggression by Palestinians but self-defense by Israelis. Regarding the Al-Aqsa Intifada/violence that broke out in the year 2000, the Israelis consider the Palestinians responsible for not living up to the Oslo Accords while the Palestinians ascribe it to the Israeli settlements and continuous occupation.

Much deliberation went into the design of the cover. Palestinian students did not want us to put the Israeli flag on the cover because it reminds them of Israeli military armor and tanks, and therefore created negative feelings. As a result, we decided to take the flags of both sides off the cover. Instead, we chose to picture an Israeli and a Palestinian man, both cultivating a tree, as a sign of growth. This choice was acceptable to the students.

Teachers have said that the booklet opens kids' eyes to the other side. And the project has gone global with translations into Spanish, Catalan, Italian, and French. But some parents have disapproved. At this point, too, the governments haven't given a stamp of approval, nor can teachers teach the story of the other side in regular school classes. As a result, teachers in the project— about 20 of them—meet jointly with a small number of students informally off school premises.

The Importance of Narrative

When people and their nations are in conflict, they develop their own narratives that they consider the ultimate truth and that devaluate and even dehumanize their enemy's narrative. These one-sided views become part of everyday culture, showing up in national and religious festivals, the media, and even what children are taught. Textbooks reflect the values, goals, and myths that a society wants to instill into the new generation (Apple, 1979; Luke, 1988). As a result, children grow up knowing only this narrative, having a biased understanding, and developing negative attitudes toward "the other" (Levinas, 1990).

Research on textbooks shows how each side, Palestinian as well as Israeli, presents its own narratives. In an analysis of 1948 Palestinian refugee problems (Adwan & Firer, 1997, 1999) in Palestinian and Israeli textbooks since 1995, both sides failed to talk about the complexity of the refugees' problems. The Israeli texts put most of the blame on the Palestinians and the Arabs for the refugees' plight, while the Palestinian texts mainly blamed the Israelis and the British. Some of the texts even fail to agree on the facts; for example, the numbers of 1948 Palestinian refugees. Israelis write that there were between 600,000 to 700,000 Palestinians who became refugees as a result of the 1948 war, while Palestinians wrote that there were more than one million Palestinians who were expelled from their homes and lands and became refugees as a result of the 1948 fighting.

Another comprehensive analysis of narratives of the conflict/relation in Palestinian and Israeli history and civic education (Firer & Adwan, 2004) shows that the texts reflect a culture of enmity. The terminology used in the texts had different meanings. What was positive on one side was negative on the other side. For example, while Israeli texts refer to the first Jewish immigrants to Palestine as "the pioneers," the Palestinian texts refer to them as "gangs" and "terrorists." A martyr or freedom fighter for the Palestinians is a suicide bomber to the Israelis. Also, the maps in the texts eliminate the cities and towns of the other side. The texts show the delegitimization of each other's rights, history, and culture. The findings show also that both sides' textbooks fail to include the peaceful periods of coexistence between Jews and Palestinians.

Daniel Bar-Tal (1995) analyzed the content of 124 Israeli schoolbooks from 1975 to 1995. According to Bar-Tal in times of intractable conflict, each side develops beliefs about the justness of its own goals, beliefs about security, beliefs about delegitimizing the opponents, beliefs of positive self-image, beliefs about patriotism, beliefs about unity, and beliefs about peace. These beliefs constitute a kind of ethos that supports the continuation of the conflict. The study showed that beliefs about security were emphasized in the Israeli textbooks. There was rarely delegitimization of Arabs but most of the texts stereotype Arabs negatively.

It is clear that the way Palestinian and Israeli texts each present their historical narratives affects the views of the students reading them, and that in order to rid each side of delegitimization, hate, and violence, the historical narratives need to change. One way to do this is by changing the way the other is being portrayed. We argue that in order to do this, children should learn and respect the other's narratives, as they are presented from that side's perspective. This led to our developing the innovative school booklets that contain both the Israeli and Palestinian narratives around certain dates or milestones in the history of the conflict. This means that students learn the narrative of the other besides their own, as a step toward acknowledging and respecting the other.

We acknowledge that teachers matter, besides texts. Studies show that teachers have more power than written texts in forming children's understandings and value systems (Angvik & von Borris, 1997; Nave & Yogev, 2002). As a result, the teachers actually developed these narratives, trying them out with their classes. The team included six Palestinian history and geography teachers and six Jewish-Israeli history teachers led by two historians, Professor Adnan Massallam from Bethlehem University and Professor Eyal Naveh from Tel Aviv University. Most of the Palestinian teachers, who came from Hebron, Bethlehem, and East Jerusalem, had not participated in dialogue encounters with Israelis. Several of the Israeli teachers, who teach in high schools in the center and north of Israel, had participated in previous encounters with Palestinians.

When both Israeli and Palestinian teachers and students open a workbook in which the opposite side's narrative is given together with their own, they feel relatively secure and less threatened by the other side's story. We recognize that a joint narrative can emerge only after the clear change from war culture to peace culture that requires time and the ability to mourn and work through the painful results of the past.

The Process

The participants convened more than 26 times in 2001 to 2007, mostly for a two-day workshop held at the New Imperial Hotel in the Old City of Jerusalem or at Talitha Kumi School near Beit Jala. In the summers we held our seminars (of one week) at the Georg Eckert Institute in Braunschweig, Germany. As the political and the military situations were very fragile, it was unclear until the last minute whether the Palestinian teachers would get permits to enter Jerusalem, or would be able to reach the places where the permits were issued. The workshops were called off several times, but each time we found ways and the energy to call them on again, and finally we succeeded to make them happen.

As the project operated within the reality of the conflict, it is critical to note the contexts from which the participants came. First, while the situation on both sides was bleak, difference and asymmetry existed with respect to the intensity of the general realities on the ground. For Palestinians, the reality has an unrelenting effect on day-to-day life with experiences of occupation by the Israeli army, which translates into restricted freedom of movement; curfews; tens of checkpoints; and fear of shootings, killings, uprooting trees, and house demolitions. Because of Palestinian suicide attacks, the everyday reality for Israelis reflects itself mostly in fear of riding buses, going downtown, or anywhere with crowds. Many on both sides fear sending their kids to schools. Given the fact that faith and hope were difficult for both sides to hold on to, we were amazed at the commitment on both sides. One of the Israeli teachers mentioned during the fourth seminar, "This work over the last year was my only source of hope in the current desperate situation," while a Palestinian teachers said "This is how we create a better future for our children."

During the first workshop, we formed three mixed-task groups to create a list of all the events relevant to the Palestinian-Israeli conflict and on which they would like to work. They worked on the Balfour Declaration of 1917, the 1948 war, and the first Intifada of 1987. On evenings we would stroll in the Old City of Jerusalem, to disconnect from our hostile surroundings.

In the second workshop, teachers developed their narratives. We continued our personal acquaintance and joint walks. In the third seminar, the teachers read the narratives in their own native language, the way they will have to present these narratives to their pupils in the following year. We addressed questions such as: Was the translation precise? Who was the person you mentioned in 1908? Why did you try to describe this event so briefly, while the others are described at length? Interestingly, there were almost no attempts of delegitimization of the other's narrative. According to our interpretation, the fact that each side could feel safe with its own narrative made it easier to relate to the other's narrative, being so different from one's own. One teacher said: "When we started I felt frustrated and angry with their text. Later I learned to accept it rationally. Only lately I also can feel empathy for their way of portraying the past."

The teachers tried out the texts, and their reports of their classrooms were very interesting and diverse. For example, one Israeli teacher was very creative in visualizing for her pupils what these texts actually represented. Her students could quite easily accept the two narratives as legitimate as they lacked the emotional involvement and identification with "their" narrative. Another Israeli teacher reported that his students were suspicious ("Are these texts really translated into Arabic and taught there?"). Some students showed great interest and asked to take them home to study them further.

One of the Palestinian teachers had to ask the permission of his principal (who actually came to our workshop and showed great interest in our work). He gave his students the texts and invited them to his house to discuss them (as the school was closed because of the curfew). Another Palestinian teacher brought written reactions of her pupils. Some of them expressed an interest to meet Israeli pupils to discuss these texts together. Others wanted to know more about this date or that person, mentioned briefly in the texts. There were reports of students who right away started to deconstruct the other's narrative. In general there was a surprise effect by presenting the two narratives, a surprise that created interest and curiosity. We could feel a general feeling of ownership and accomplishment of the teachers from both sides, in spite of the deteriorating external situation. They felt that they are creating something new for the future, which no one tried to do before.

The conflict taking place around us often affected our interactions. Yet, we all continued to do the work and were rewarded with glimmers of hope and excitement about the implementation of this project in the schools. We acknowledged to each other that peace could only be a result of both sides winning; a "peace" in which only one side wins has no value. Someone said: "The disarmament of history can happen only after the disarmament of weapons. But one can prepare it now." Events of the last months have highlighted the fact that without an informal peace process, involving face-to-face encounters between Jewish-Israeli and Palestinian peoples, a real and long-lasting peace will not be achieved. Furthermore, the booklet these teachers are creating and their implementation of it will provide a concrete way to spread the effects outward of this face-to-face encounter between a small group of teachers.

As Margaret Mead once said, "Never doubt that a small group of thoughtful committed citizens can change the world." In this case, "Never doubt that a small group of committed teachers—Palestinian and Israeli—can change the world, or at least one part of it."

Our Award

Here are some excerpts from Dan's acceptance speech, when we accepted the Victor J. Goldberg Institute of International Education Prize for Peace in the Middle East, in 2005:

> This Prize is for us an important acknowledgement of what we are trying to change between our two peoples: Mutual recognition and respect for the historical narrative of the other. . . . I believe that Sami's and my feeling of responsibility and our joint pragmatic approach brought about this project: Instead of excluding the narrative of the other and de-legitimizing it, in acknowledging and learning to respect it,

thereby trying to disarm our histories. . . . We are yet at the beginning of the road. I am deeply grateful to all of you, and hope that this small effort will, together with other similar ones, penetrate slowly the walls of hatred and exclusion, and create a change on the ground and in the hearts and minds of our people.

I will end with two quotes from our teachers' seminars: In our 13th meeting in summer 2004 an Israeli teacher asked his Palestinian colleague: "When I will teach the 50th from your perspective, what would you like me to emphasize?" This was a spontaneous question, and it took 13 meetings of the teachers over 3 years to come up with this important question. The second quote is from . . . a Palestinian teacher [who] told how he was approached by Sami and deliberated if to join the project. It was the beginning of the second Intifada and he said to himself: "How can I defend my child now? I do not believe in blood or power, so perhaps through this project I will be able to defend him." These are our small milestones in this long and laborious process.

Here are some excerpts from Sami's acceptance speech, when accepting the same award:

We are much honored to be awarded such a prestigious Prize and we sure deserve it. We owe this Prize to the teachers who committed themselves to the project. The road for peace is worthwhile trying and it is not expected to be a linear one especially in the middle of the conflict. One day you move forward a step but the next day you go back [a] few steps. It is like walking on a mines' field. But, we decided to take this road with all its challenges especially after the outbreak of the second Intifada in September 2000. It was not an easy decision of course but our conviction and commitment to a peaceful solution to the conflict and our vision of the necessity to have a peaceful future to our children and a peaceful coexistence were our major drives.

We know our grassroots work (peace building bottom-up formula) needs a political agreement (peacemaking top-down formula), but we do not have to wait until the latter one takes place; we should create the situation for it to happen. It is a painful process and many times we lose our energy. We are proud to state that our teachers have developed a supportive working condition instead of a competing one. This was mainly due to the relaxing design of the seminars, the feeling that each side's narrative exist beside the other's narrative and finally the sense of ownership of the project that teachers developed. This is a process-oriented project intended to a post conflict situation but we are sure it will be used as a base in the future development of both side's schoolbooks and in the teachers' training.

We are very much convinced that a bridging narrative is not feasible at this stage and this has to grow from within each individual and cannot be imposed, but we give this opportunity to happen by keeping the empty spaces between the two sides' narratives.

References

Adwan, S., & Firer, R. (1997). *The narrative of Palestinian refugees during the war of 1948 in Israeli and Palestinian history and civic education textbooks.* Paris: UNESCO.

Adwan, S., & Firer, R. (1999). *The narrative of the 1967 war in the Israeli and Palestinian history and civics textbooks and curricula statement.* Braunschweig, Germany: Eckert Institute.

Angvik, M., & von Borries, B. (Eds.). (1997). *Youth and history: A comparative European survey on historical consciousness and political attitudes among adolescents.* Hamburg: Koerber Foundation.

Apple, M. W. (1979). *Ideology and curriculum.* London: Routledge & Kegan Paul.

Bar-Tal, D. (1995). *The rocky road toward peace: Societal beliefs in times of intractable conflict, the Israeli case.* Jerusalem: The Hebrew University, School of Education. (In Hebrew)

Luke, A. (1988). *Literacy, booklet, and ideology.* London: Falmer Press.

Nave, E., & Yogev, E. (2002). *Histories: Towards a dialogue with yesterday.* Dafna Danon (Ed.). Tel-Aviv: Bavel. (In Hebrew)

Ruth, F., & Adwan, S. (2004). *The Israeli-Palestinian Conflict in History and Civics Textbooks of Both Nations.* Hannover:Verlag Hahnsche Buchhandlung.

CHAPTER 29

TEEN TALK: A HOPE FOR PEACE BETWEEN PALESTINIANS AND ISRAELIS

Warren Spielberg

Ahmed spoke clearly with pain "soldiers barged into my house in Ramallah and searched for weapons and secret walls. They broke our family treasures and our CDs and hurt my uncle. The wall you build now will only further imprison us."

Ofir sat with eyes downward. Like the other Israeli youth, he found it hard to listen. "Yes we are sorry for these things but there is terror—the wall and other things we do are to protect—not to imprison you."

The other young Palestinian teens were with Ahmed. "Yes we look forward to disengagement in Gaza, but we are still faced with checkpoints and a wall that takes our land."

Josh, an 18-year-old Israeli student, clenched his hand and said, "You must also try to understand us—we have had three years of silence between us."

Ofir and Josh were two teens taking part in a Peace Now Youth Dialogue Program in the summer of 2005.

The tragic events of September 11, 2001, as well as the past years of violence in the Middle East make psychopolitical dialogue and people-to-people contacts more necessary than ever. The failures of traditional diplomacy to address intractable conflicts such as that between the Israelis and the Palestinians has launched a myriad of private Track II nongovernmental—nonpolitical civilian—efforts that have brought Israelis and Palestinians together for discussion and dialogue. At the very least, such efforts bring familiarity to the participants with "the other" who before then was only the object of fear. As Oslo negotiator Yossi Beilin said recently, "It is much harder to hate people you really know" than some abstract notion of an enemy.

But people-to-people exchanges do more than temper images of our adversaries. They also help illuminate those dynamics, often unconscious, which underlie the psychological origins of conflict and serve as impediments to their resolution. Such insights, for their part, can augment diplomatic and political initiatives in ways that are subtle, yet powerful. In this context, it has been shown that dialogues between adolescents—like Peace Now's Youth Dialogue Program in which I have participated—are often more candid and authentic than dialogues between adults. Dialogues that occur between youth are free of politics and defensive preoccupations and come more from the heart. They more clearly demonstrate cultural and psychological attitudes because the participants are more open and psychologically less defended than their adult counterparts.

Young people will often voice cultural attitudes their parents may feel, but are afraid to voice. As Amir remarks to the group, "You Jews think you are superior to us—but you had help from Jews around the world in order to form your state—we have had only betrayal." Lily, an Israeli girl of 15, remarks that she "still feels that at bottom, most Arabs want us dead." The group process is also suffused with animosity reflective of the culture of the conflict. Throughout the dialogue, there is a competition for attention from the leaders and from each other. Although they pretend not to care what the other says, they are keenly aware of their impact on each other. A one-upsmanship game thrives, as each group tries to outdo the other. One Arab boy cites the humiliation of the checkpoints. An Israeli girl talks about her fear of terrorism. An Arab girl counters with the injuries her cousin sustained during the bulldozing of her home by an Israeli tank. Another Israeli girl retorts with the death of her friend during a bus explosion, and so on. In these remarks and actions, we see the vicissitudes of a relationship between two peoples that is undermined by fear, competition, stereotyping, and anger.

Youth dialogues are also advantageous because they bring together future leaders and citizens, individuals who can eventually find a new way of handling this generational conflict. Mohammed, whose father sits in the Palestinian parliament, is 16 years old and associated with a Fatah youth group. He is one youth who has played an active role in many dialogues. Consequently, he has come to "know Israelis in a different way, a way that will help me as I fight for my people." As participants on both sides gain greater familiarity with each other and with the political issues involved in this intractable conflict, there is greater hope that the next generation can gain the insight and courage to challenge intergenerational messages of hatred and try to do things in a "different way." All of these factors have certainly been the case with Israelis and Palestinians youth, as I discovered when I helped conduct several Peace Now Youth Dialogue sessions between 1998 and 2005.

The Peace Now Youth Dialogue Program

The Peace Now Youth Dialogue Program was originally developed in the years after the Oslo Accords (when optimism was high for peace) to bring together groups of young people from both the Palestinian and Israeli sides. The goal of the program was to bring familiarity to past enemies but also to help young people think about the political issues behind the conflict. During the latter half of the 1990s, the program had its heyday. Eighteen groups from Israeli cities were linked with corresponding city and village groups in the West Bank and Gaza. For instance, youth from Ramallah were in contact consistently with those from Jerusalem, and youth from Haifa were linked with those from Nablus. Groups met every few months and were encouraged to stay in e-mail or phone contact with their acquaintances in the interim. Twice a year the program would sponsor a long weekend wherein many youth would come together to discuss the political issues underlying the conflict and try to forge agreements. Many of these agreements could have been the envy of career diplomats for their intricacy and creativity.

Unfortunately, the Al Aska Intifada of 2005 brought a halt to many of the activities of the program. Palestinians became unable to travel to Israel. Israeli parents would not allow their children to travel beyond the green line. But while it became very hard to continue the program to its full extent, dialogue efforts continued, often secretly between friends or on rare trips abroad when the groups were brought together outside the country for a weeklong or weekend dialogue. Another difficulty was that funding for the program dried up, as money for peace projects was deemed by many as a waste of time and money, given the events on the ground as a three-year war between Israelis and Palestinians took a life toll of more than 1,000 killed. Yet, as we have seen in intractable conflicts around the world from Ireland to South Africa, it is important that participants keep talking, no matter what.

The nature and the issues involved in the dialogue have changed a great deal over the year but many of the themes have remained the same. The land has remained at the core of the agenda in any dialogue. So, too, have dysfunctional psychological dynamics that plague relationships between Israelis and Palestinians.

How I Came to Be Involved

I lived in Israel in the early to mid-1970s. As a young student, I volunteered in the Yom Kippur War, serving as a guard on a kibbutz on the northern front. I saw firsthand the result of an identity-based geopolitical conflict. From my time in Israel as an adolescent, I vowed to try to make a difference. Since 1980, I have been involved with the Peace Now movement in Israel and here in the United States. When I became a psychologist, I began to work with the emerging Youth Dialogue project in the late 1990s. From 2001, after the attacks on the World Trade Center until recently, I worked closely with the Fire Department of New York, assisting them in the development of their trauma programs. I returned to Israel in 2005 after a five-year hiatus, and observed many of the unfortunate effects of trauma on citizens I had encountered after 9/11. I decided to continue my work with the dialogue project, since a window for peace now exists. We must seize this opportunity as our best way of defusing a global conflict between the West and the Arab world.

Dialogue in Ramallah

In 1998, in one of the youth dialogues we had in Ramallah, the main topic we covered was land—a powerful symbol and a vital reality for both sides. During a conversation on this subject, the Israeli kids expressed their feeling of entitlement to be where they are, and used the Holocaust to justify their place in the region. One youth, Ophir, remarked that, "We were almost wiped out. We came here to save ourselves and built the land through hard work. My grandparents went through Auschwitz. We built Israel. Maybe some Palestinians lost their lands, but we did not steal it. My kibbutz is built from the desert; no Palestinians were there. Still, I would give back a lot of land for real peace."

The Palestinian kids were unimpressed with this Holocaust justification. They felt they knew about it, but in reality they possessed few of the details. One Palestinian youth, Nasir, said, "That was a European problem, and it has little to do with us. We are living our own holocaust. We are hounded. We are poor. We have no state yet. We have to go through checkpoints."

What was very surprising to the Israelis was the degree to which the Palestinians were willing to sacrifice to win the land. Omar remarked, "We are willing to die to win the land. The young men I know are willing to lose their lives in order to win the land back. We will not submit to Israeli power." This was difficult for the Israelis to understand. Ophir lectured the Palestinians about how they needed to get smarter, negotiate better, or use nonviolence to be more effective because violence only causes Israelis to fight back.

There were many flashpoints like this in the sessions I observed. But I was less interested in the substantive discussions than seeing what types of group enactments were on display—enactments being self-perpetuating, dysfunctional tendencies that undermine relationships. Enactments are often unknown to the participants themselves, and they can prevent true dialogue. Enactments can occur not just between individuals but between groups, based on mutually antagonistic assumptions and anxieties.

In this case, the major enactment was that of victim/victimizer. In order to keep their superior status and self-justification, Israelis resorted to disparagement, gossip, and condescension as Palestinians brought up their concerns and aspirations. When the Palestinians discussed their need to stand up to oppression and achieve equality, they were often put down and dismissed with lectures, warnings, and corrections from the Israelis.

In response, the Palestinians often upped the ante through more radical and provocative statements, continuing to try to impress the Israelis with their worthiness and justifications. The Israelis, in turn, became more condescending and angry, with their own history of victimization. At this stage it was hard to see who was the real victim and who the victimizer. Both felt similarly, and both enact behavioral patterns that fit this dynamic. For those who see themselves as victims will in turn victimize others.

These sessions did more than just reveal some of the motivations for violence. They also provided an insight into how the Clinton peace negotiations of 2000–2001 between the sides may have been undermined by similar psychological phenomena. Certainly there have been suggestions in various deconstructions of what happened at Camp David that suggest that both Ehud Barak and Yasir Arafat entered those talks harboring such mutual suspicions and animosities that perhaps a positive result was never possible at that time. Although the major explanatory narrative of the failure was one of Arafat's recalcitrance, on a psychological level, both Clinton and Barak put great pressure on Arafat in a sometimes highly dismissive manner to accept terms that he felt unprepared in the short term to do, and which was done in a heavy-handed and shaming manner. Illustratively, there is one famous photo of Barak pushing Arafat through a doorway to continue a negotiation session. The domination and pressure of the Israelis and Americans backfired as Arafat, already lacking political cover, reacted negatively to the pressure and chose not to go forth with a historic deal.

Continuing dialogues in Taba and elsewhere during the winter of 2001 showed greater progress but were overtaken by the events set in motion by Ariel Sharon's "walk" into the Temple Mount in the fall of 2000, which ignited the Al Aska Intifada that has claimed thousands of lives over the last four years. At that time, Sharon had entered the Temple Mount, one of the holiest sites in Islam, without permission and with a large detachment of soldiers and bodyguards. Many analysts feel that this provocation helped to instigate the second Intifada.

An analysis of dialogue process can help to clarify unconscious dynamics that impede authentic discussions between interlocutors. At Camp David in 2000, Barak and Arafat perpetuated their own type of ethnic enactment, one tinged by a mutual victim/victimizer relationship and a process of mutual shaming and recalcitrance at Camp David, rather than rising above these dynamics to strike a deal. One could even argue that the lack of a psychological breakthrough to form new relationships in this case belied the lack of a political breakthrough. Many subsequent analyses of the negotiations at Camp David point to the lack of rapport and trust that Barak and Arafat demonstrated toward one another. These feelings and attitudes were never addressed. Reports of the negotiations indicate that Arafat felt Barak's disrespect and condescending attitudes toward Arabs in general. For his part, Arafat became increasingly intransigent as the negotiations progressed, partly perhaps to assert his independence and autonomy, which was often challenged.

What's Happening Now?

In 2004 and 2005, the Peace Now youth dialogues started up again, slowly. There were far fewer participants and dialogues, largely due to fear on both sides and the lack of travel opportunities between Israel proper and the West Bank.

Since the second Intifada it has become very difficult for Palestinians to travel to Israel proper or even between separate Palestinian cities in the West Bank. However, in the fall of 2004, a weekend dialogue supported by European Union money took place in Cyprus. After years of house-to-house violence, Palestinian participants expressed their pain and outrage while Israelis—many on the left side of political stance—listened with both guilt and anguish. Daniel, the coordinator of the event, reports that despite the pain and silence of the last few years, young Palestinians and Israelis are trying to reach out to one another. As the discussion intensified, the greater depth of the pain of the Israelis who also had lost many friends arose. Many Israelis were eyewitness to the aftermath of suicide bombings. Many Palestinians were witness to the effects of Israeli military incursions. Some were able to share their memories and perceptions. Omar remembers, "losing my CD collection when the Israelis soldiers trampled through my room as they searched my house for weapons—none were ever there." Aviva recalls her friends injured in a bus explosion. They all share their common trauma, but in a few days, they can only begin to access their traumas and try to share them with one another.

However, in contrast to previous dialogues, there existed what I have termed elsewhere as an initial period of a "rage of silence" between the two groups. In private, both groups could talk about their hurt and pain, but found it very difficult to confront one another. This emerged from the fact that both groups of participants appeared to be frightened to cause too much trouble, or to provoke the other. However, as the weekend progressed, they were more able to open up to one another. As a result, just the fact of meeting together, and hearing "the other" speak their truth, began to open up their hearts and minds. This alone was cause for some sense of achievement. More dialogues are necessary in order to continue the process.

In July 2005, before the Israeli disengagement from Gaza, a small group of young students from previous groups sat in a hotel room again in Jerusalem and became reacquainted. The same patterns that were evident in Cyprus were noted by me. They expressed how the trauma of the last three years had been indescribable. One student reports how her friend's family lost a wall of his house when an Israeli unit was searching for terrorists. She reports that she is still traumatized, shaking when she speaks—reminding me of the trauma of survivors of the 9/11 collapse with whom I have worked. The Israelis are again often silent, not feeling free yet to voice their own terror and rage, just trying to attune themselves to the Palestinians. Despite the one student's happiness over the disengagement, the students all report that the Palestinians remain depressed. An Israeli girl, who is close to a Palestinian girl, recounts her friend's hopelessness, "There is no hope under occupation, the fence, the checkpoints—there is no economy and I can't even get to school often." An Israeli girl who lost a friend on a bus will speak only in private to group leaders during dialogues. She is afraid to upset the flow during dialogues, afraid to be insensitive to the pain of the Palestinians. But we are only at the beginning. As the program continues, the kids will have more time to trust and share and, hopefully, to work themselves out of the fears, stereotypes, and racial enactments that imprison them like the conflict itself. As they discover the humanity of each other, they can discover themselves as well and bring some greater peace to this troubled land. Despite their fears and traumas, the youth I have met are eager to go beyond the pain. They wish to encounter the other as real human beings, shorn from stereotyping and from the horrible political facts of the conflict.

As the project looks for new funding, and the disengagement and current peace process gives way to greater stability, the young of the region—those who will inherit the land—hopefully can have their say, including in projects such as this one. Such dialogues between Palestinian and Israeli youth are one of the few positive things taking place on an otherwise difficult political scene. It takes extraordinary determination to continue with dialogues under these difficult circumstances, yet it is imperative for Peace Now to persevere with this important work.

Bibliography

Agha, H., & Malley, R. (2001, August 9). Camp David: The tragedy of errors. *The New York Review of Books*, 18–26.

Lifton, R. (1979). *The broken connection.* New York: Simon & Shuster.

Slater, J. (2001). What went wrong? The collapse of the Israeli-Palestinian peace process. *Political Science Quarterly, 116*(2) 30–45.

Spielberg, W. (2003, March). Youth dialogue and the psychology of peace. *The Newsletter of Americans for Peace Now*, No. 8. 4–6.

Volkan, V. (2000). *Blood Lines: From ethnic pride to ethnic terrorism.* New York: Farrar, Straus & Giroux.

Weiner, E. (1998). *The handbook of interethnic co-existence.* New York: Continuum.

CHAPTER 30

HAND IN HAND: A REVOLUTIONARY EDUCATION MODEL FOR ISRAELI ARAB AND JEWISH CHILDREN

Josie Mendelson

If we are to teach real peace in this world, and if we are to carry on a real war against war, we shall have to begin with the children.

—*Mohandas Gandhi*

The name of our education program conveys what our revolutionary idea about schooling for Israeli Arab and Jewish children is all about: Hand in Hand. The approach is a model for teaching recognition and acceptance of cultural differences in an atmosphere of mutual respect. Considering the conflict in the region, the need for this approach is greater than ever.

Everything about the Hand in Hand community is based on equality and respect. Teaching understanding and appreciation of each other's culture is at the core of the Hand in Hand philosophy. Magda from Bet Safafa, the mother of Azam, a 10-year-old who has been in the school for five years, sums it up in saying, "We are equal in this school. That is why I feel equal to the parents, an Arab teacher feels equal to a Jewish teacher, and my son feels equal to the Jewish child sitting next to him."

Hand in Hand—the Center for Jewish-Arab Education in Israel—was established in 1997 with the goal of initiating and fostering egalitarian, bilingual, multicultural education for Jewish and Arab children. In the midst of the Israeli-Palestinian conflict and against all odds, the two co-founders, American social activist Lee Gordon, now director of American Friends for Hand in Hand, and educator and activist Amin Khalaf, native of the Arab village of Muqibla in northern Israel, set about looking for places in Israel that would be prepared to begin this revolutionary experiment.

By 2005, 665 students from prekindergarten to grade 8 attended our three accredited public schools located in Jerusalem, the Galilee, and Wadi Ara. The Bilingual School in Jerusalem has 12 classes (prekindergarten up to seventh grade); in the Arab-Jewish School in the Galilee, the first graduates have completed primary school and are now completing their second year of junior high; and the Bridge on the Wadi School in the Arab village of Kfar Kara in Wadi Ara in the center of the country has nearly 200 children—and for the first time in Israel's history, Jewish children come into this Arab village to get their education.

In all three schools, Israeli, Arab, and Jewish children learn together year after year, and with their families and leaders in the surrounding communities, are building a new model for quality education, partnership, and coexistence between Arabs and Jews.

Equality at All Levels

In each school, there are two principals, one Arab and one Jewish. In each class there is a Jewish and an Arab teacher, and half the children are Arab and half Jewish. The two teachers in each class teach the children simultaneously in both languages; however, nothing is translated, instead the teachers interact with each other, elaborating and elucidating each other's sentences. Each teacher teaches in her native tongue, and the children are encouraged to answer in whichever language they feel comfortable.

The children learn about each other's culture, history, and experience while at the same time strengthening their own religious, cultural, and ethnic identity—whether Jewish, Christian, or Muslim. Emphasis is placed on self and national identity; the children are exposed to the different historical narratives, and the complexity of the situation.

Our children, like all the children in Israel, are exposed to the constant violence surrounding the conflict. In Hand in Hand schools, the children are encouraged to express their ideas and feelings, to question, to see, and to deal with this complicated reality. A visitor to the school asked 10-year-old Zaher why he thinks there is a conflict. "The Arabs and Jews don't agree how to share their land," he answered. To the question of what he thinks they should do about it, he replied, "They have to sit down together and discuss it, and if they asked me I would tell them that if they can't agree it doesn't belong to anyone, but if they agree it could be for everybody."

In addition to working with the children in the schools, intensive work is being done with the staff. In many instances, starting work at our schools is the first opportunity that the teachers have had for meeting someone from "the other" group. The challenge is double: first, they have to learn to teach as a team, sometimes with somebody with a very different teaching style and experience; and second, they have to begin learning about another culture, lifestyle, and occasionally a very different approach to recent and present events in Israel. To help teachers with this process, they are given intensive training, workshops, and seminars as well as numerous organized social events.

The parents also form a very important part of the equation. Parents are our partners, involved in all the decision making and running of the schools. They, too, need to go through a process of learning and understanding; therefore, we encourage them to take part in seminars and learn about each other's culture and history. We also provide Jewish parents with lessons to learn Arabic.

Na'ama Gruenwald-Kashani, the mother of two students at the Jerusalem School, says, "We believe that as citizens in a State with both Jews and Arabs, we must know our neighbors from up close. We decided that for our family, this challenge begins with our children—to expose them to a people and a culture that is so geographically close, but different in so many ways. Ironically, in its diversity, Hand in Hand gives us a sense of belonging."

Faisal Haikal, the father of a student at the Wadi Ara School, says, "Our hope for our daughter is that she will learn to accept difference and be compassionate towards the other, but also learn to think independently and have a strong identity. We are confident that the Hand in Hand Bridge over the Wadi School is the place where that will happen."

How the Schools Work

The schools are governed by a steering committee, made up of the co-directors of Hand in Hand, the principals, teachers, parents, Ministry of Education and municipal representatives, and members of the public. The project was originally possible through the positive reception of the city of Jerusalem and the Regional Council of Misgav who, together with the Arab town of Saknin and the village of Shaab, were prepared to form partnerships to open a school.

Hand in Hand's Success

Hand in Hand has succeeded together with the children, their parents, the rest of the community, the Ministry of Education, and local authorities to build a cooperative framework that allows all involved to study and develop together, sustaining and strengthening each group's language and cultural traditions while learning about the other group on the basis of equality and mutual respect. Although still a relatively small community, we believe that we offer a real alternative to segregated education, and that our graduates will bring a new perspective to Israeli society, which could lead to real change.

Hand in Hand has received teaching and peace awards, including from Ben Gurion University, the Peace Prize of the Israeli/German Friendship Society, Israeli Federation of Teachers, and the BMW Group award for Intercultural Learning. We have student waiting lists, and communities are interested in setting up schools in their areas; for example, we have been approached by the

Mayor of Haifa to help them open a school and there are also initiatives in Beer Sheva and the Northern Galilee.

Parents and staff all express appreciation and enthusiasm. Dalia Peretz, principal of the Jerusalem School, says, "Our children learn how to see the reality in a very complicated way, and how to understand and be critical of this reality, while asking hard questions."

Research has been carried out by Dr. Zvi Bekerman of the Hebrew University of Jerusalem and Dr. Mohammed Amara of Bar Elan University in Tel Aviv. Dr. Amara's research has included more than 100 hours of recorded observations and structured interviews with teachers and principals, questionnaires about culture and language filled out by parents, and an in-depth examination of existing learning materials in the schools. Findings showed that despite the fact that both languages are taught and used to a great deal equally, there still exists a preference for Hebrew in interactions between teachers and students. Arab students gained a greater mastery of Hebrew than the Jewish students of Arabic— consistent with the dominance of the Hebrew language in the culture (Arab parents wanted their children to learn Hebrew, and Jewish parents wanted their children to be open to Arab children and culture but don't see mastery of Arabic as essential for their children's success). As a result, efforts are being made to create a more complete bilingual environment in the schools inside and outside the classrooms, in the homes, and in the mentality of all of those connected to the schools. A committee of principals, teachers, parents, and outside specialists has reexamined how languages are taught and how a bilingual environment can be created, and each school has drawn up a plan to increase efforts in teaching Arabic to parents and Jewish teachers.

My Journey to the Program

I was born in Johannesburg, South Africa, and grew up in the Jewish community that was a small minority within the larger white minority. Like any other white South Africans of my generation, I grew up knowing all about stereotyping, hatred, and fear. Two aspects of my childhood—being part of a minority within a minority, and seeing so much blind anger and fear around me—had a profound affect, and have been the motivation and moving force behind many paths I have taken.

From the age of 10, I was a member of a Zionist youth movement, so it was a natural decision to leave my family and friends at the age of 19 to make my home in Israel. I came to Israel in 1967 as a volunteer during the Six-Day War. Coming from an idealistic background, I believed that Israel was indeed the perfect example of democracy. I could quote from the Israel's Declaration of Independence, which in 1948 called upon the Arab inhabitants of Israel to "participate in the up building of the State on the basis of full and equal citizenship and due representation in all its provisional and permanent institutions." The declaration also promised that Israel will "ensure complete equality of social and political rights to all its inhabitants irrespective of religion, race or sex," and guarantees "freedom of religion, conscience, language, education and culture."

The reality in Israel was quite different from what I had expected. In time, as I became acquainted with more and more Palestinian citizens of Israel, I realized that my background enabled me to have some insight and understanding of the complicated situation of this minority, and the relationship between them and the Jewish majority in the country.

I got my teaching certificates in early childhood education and special education from the David Yellin Institute of Higher Learning in Jerusalem. After graduating, I worked as a kindergarten teacher, until 1990 when I was appointed director of the kindergarten at the West Jerusalem YMCA, a kindergarten in an international Christian institution, in a multicultural, binational, multireligion city. The children in the kindergarten, however, were all Jewish. I realized that here was the opportunity to start something new, so in spite of much skepticism and objection from certain quarters, but with a great deal of support and enthusiasm from my staff, we established the first Arab-Jewish kindergarten in Jerusalem. During the worst days of the first Intifada (Palestinian uprising), the children, parents, and staff at the YMCA proved that it was possible to create an island of sanity in the midst of total chaos.

From this experience, it is not surprising that in 2003, I left my position as director of early childhood education in Jerusalem to join Hand in Hand. The kindergarten at the YMCA continues to flourish, and many of its graduates become pupils in our school.

My Philosophy

Being an educator, I believe that schools hold the key to the future. I believe that as educators we assume a twofold obligation: to the child and to society. We owe the child exposure to a wide range of experiences that provide opportunities to make optimal use of his or her inherent abilities and to function maximally in the physical and social environment. Cultivating the child as an active, independent, social being, as part of an expanding, diverse social environment facilitates integration as a child and eventually as an adult in society. In addition, this kind of education allows for understanding and tolerance of both immediate and more distant surroundings, and serves as the foundation for getting to know and accept the wide range of lifestyles, traditions, and customs in our society and in the world.

Furthermore we owe it to society to introduce the child to content that will provide a common cultural background with respect and tolerance for diversity and with values that will encourage a democratic egalitarian society. As emissaries of a society that has taken upon itself the responsibility for the education of its children, it is our privilege, as well as our duty, to pass on to our children the central ideas, heritage, traditions, and values of this society.

My co-director, Amin Khalaf. Amin has taught in both Arab and Jewish public schools throughout Jerusalem and, since 1997, has lectured on education at the

David Yellin College of Education in Jerusalem. Amin earned his master's degree in Islamic and Middle Eastern Studies from the Hebrew University of Jerusalem, where he also received his teaching certificate in 1990, and has been intensely involved in national coexistence projects, including serving as a group facilitator for a Jewish-Arab dialogue group.

Both Amin and I live in Jerusalem with our respective spouses and children. Two of Amin's three children study at the Jerusalem School. We both feel privileged to work for such an important project that promotes children's education and contributes to the growth and peace of the families and communities we serve, and we hope, will help bring about change in Israeli society.

CHAPTER 31

No "Mission Impossible": Teaching Israeli and Palestinian Teens Peace

Gershon Baskin and Hanna Siniora

As co-chief executive directors of the Israel/Palestine Center for Peace Education and Information (IPCRI), we feel we represent a good model of coexistence, cooperation, and equality: Hanna Siniora is Palestinian, born in East Jerusalem, and Dr. Gershon Baskin is an Israeli and Zionist.

Our organization is a fully joint Palestinian-Israeli organization based on equal partnership and ownership, with a board of directors comprised of equal numbers of Israelis and Palestinians. We are a public policy think tank and a "do tank" where we work shoulder to shoulder with Israelis and Palestinians, Arabs and Jews, and dedicated others, to aid in the development of Israeli-Palestinian peace based on the principles of self-determination, security, and prosperity for all Palestinians and Israelis. We also aim to create mechanisms for ongoing sustainable cooperation between both peoples.

Besides our efforts in various departments that are more political—including working groups on strategic affairs, water and the environment, and economic development—a program we are most proud of is our Peace Education Department (PED), which is described in this chapter.

Background

The attempt to convince Palestinians to join at the early stage proved to be a "mission impossible." Enlisting Israelis, while problematic, was easier since Israel was the dominant society, ruling the occupied Palestinian Territories, and in general, a less centralized society than the Palestinians'. Most Israelis were skeptical about the ability of such an idea to take hold and work, but even more right-wing Israelis were willing to take part if important Palestinian personalities could be enlisted. Most Palestinian personalities' response was, "This is a great idea, but its time has not yet come." After a year of trying to set up a board of directors, a crucial breakthrough occurred when a PLO leader, Faisel Husseini, was released from Israeli prison. Even though some agreement on their participation could not be reached, there was an agreement to allow us to work and to prove our intentions and our abilities. A major accomplishment was that while initially the Palestinians could not see and review the Israeli army's budget for the military government/civil administration that taxed the Palestinian public and provided services from those tax revenues, an IPCRI working group member wrote an article in a main Israeli newspaper about this issue, and subsequently, the journalist was given a copy of the budget by the army that he then made available to the working group.

We have always tried to shape the agenda of Israeli-Palestinian deliberations. When we have many times been told that we are ahead of our time, we have come to realize that this signals to us that we are doing the right thing. Taking on issues deemed "too sensitive" has also been a guide to us, instructing that we are moving the dialogue forward. Yet we also realize that this must be done with great caution, a lot of common sense, and always involving highly respected individuals from both communities. In a conflict situation, people are very cautious not to be perceived by their own societies of collaborating with the enemy. Each side of the conflict very carefully constructs its own intellectual boundaries of what is acceptable and what is too risky. Frequent consultations are necessary in order not to overstep acceptable intellectual boundaries, but even here, taking into account that our goal is to shape the agenda, cautious overstepping is recommended. It is also critically important not to be seen as being disloyal to one's own society and political establishment and culture.

Teaching Israeli and Palestinian Kids

Education is key to empower the next generation of Israelis and Palestinians with the skills, knowledge, and motivation to create a peaceful Middle East. Young people today live daily with terrorism; they must learn how to live with peace, mutual respect, and understanding to transform this region into one of cooperation, prosperity, and freedom.

Textbooks currently used in Palestinian and Israelis schools do not create a culture of peace. We decided to focus our efforts on training teachers to implement a peace education program for their students. We focused on 10th and 11th graders (15- to 16-year-olds) in high schools in Israel and Palestine because at this age students have the cognitive ability to confront the subject materials and are not yet under the pressure of matriculation exams. In the 2003–2004 school year, 32 schools in Israel—12 Arab Israeli and 20 Jewish—and 27 schools in Palestine started participating in our program. The Peace Education Curricula is called "Pathways into Reconciliation" (PIR) in Israeli schools and "Education for

Peace" in the Palestinian schools. The two curricula were written by separate teams (one Israeli and one Palestinian) based on an agreed-upon statement of values. Emphasis has been placed on schools in development towns and poorer communities.

The program presents an integrative, holistic approach and involves teachers, students, principals, and others in the educational system. The idea is to create peace as a state of mind, a chosen value, and a way of life; impart values of tolerance and acceptance of the other, recognition of the equal right to liberty and social justice; develop awareness and critical perception; teach nonviolent communication and conflict resolution skills; and create encounters between Palestinians and Jews (since the Intifada has interfered with such efforts).

The program includes a five-day encounter for teachers and principals, held abroad; five-day teacher trainings in the Pathways into Reconciliation/Education for Peace curricula; 16 meetings for teacher facilitation of the curriculum in class; ongoing guidance for the teachers (meeting once every two weeks or as needed); student encounters lasting two days; teaching intergroup negotiation skills for teachers, about 22 hours; and guidance with school staff. At times, virtual encounters of students through the Internet and delegations abroad have been organized.

The trainings in the curricula take place during the summer vacation. Schools make their own decision about how to implement the program—whether it is two weekly hours per semester or in concentrated days (five days for the entire program).

Another curriculum that we use, called "Workable Peace," was designed by the Consensus Building Institute in Cambridge, Massachusetts, working with professionals from the local communities. In another curriculum we used, students are trained in peer mediation and negotiation skills (Program for Young Negotiators, PYN), developed by Harvard University and implemented by us with cooperation of the faculty of law at Haifa University.

The uniqueness of our Peace Education curricula is that it is based on existing subjects taught in the classes, including sociology/social sciences, literature, history, and English, that were infused with new concepts, activities, and text relating to the concepts of peace education. In this way, the concepts of peace education are taught every day in the course of the regular classes. It includes simulation games of the conflict between Athens and Milos in the fifth century B.C. and the more contemporary conflict between the Republicans and the Loyalists in Northern Ireland. The program was tested on a sample of classes and first implemented in 1997.

The holistic approach means that we include cognitive components (curriculum) and emotional experiential activities (workshops and encounters). We focus on teaching skills in negotiation and conflict transformation. This is done through joint work with all parties in the education system, including school principals, teachers, facilitators, steering teams, and curriculum development teams.

The Workshops

The student encounters provide an opportunity for Palestinian and Israelis to meet "the other" and to challenge their assumptions. The idea is for the participants to have more questions about the situation, and to be able to identify similarities and differences between them. The workshops move from a personal, to a cultural, and finally, to a political level of discussion. Prior to the encounters, students meet with the project facilitators several times to prepare and to maximize the experience. Afterward, the facilitators and teachers meet to analyze and understand the experience.

During the encounter, the students address personal level activities, looking at the issue of names, family history, place of birth, influential people, and so on. Cultural activities include dealing with boy/girl relations, music, customs, parent/children relations, folklore, and values related to culture, as well as preparing and presenting skits. Political activities include an exercise designed to illustrate the different narratives of the conflict through making multimedia posters. This sparks debate on relevant and specific political issues. In the closing sessions, students share their experience.

Initial evaluations of attitudinal and behavioral changing and skills carried out on this program are encouraging (Salomon, 2004). The two-day workshops had equal numbers of Israeli and Palestinian students and discussion leaders. One research study of the Israeli-Palestinian Youth Encounter Workshops showed that both Israeli and Palestinian participants (80 percent) came to the meeting with little to no interpersonal and/or educational experience with the other nationality and with an abundance of negative images of their counterparts. Yet, both sides were eager to meet youth of the other nationality and engage in dialogue with them (Maoz, 1998). During the workshop, Palestinian students spoke about limitations to their movement, problems with the supply of water, and negative treatment by the Israeli authorities and army, and repeatedly commented on the Israeli participants' moderation and openness to dialogue; the Israelis repeatedly emphasized the dissimilarity between the Palestinians on television (as rock throwers and "terrorists") and those across from them in the room. After the workshop, both Israeli and Palestinian students reported appreciating learning about the life experiences of the other side in relation to the conflict. The results showed that 70 to 90 percent of the students reported "A better understanding of the positions and opinions of members of the other people"; appreciated "Discussions with the members of the other people about the relations between the two sides"; and agreed that "I learned more about the other nation." They both also had more "Familiarity with the culture of the other nation"; "Clarification and formation of my own positions regarding the Israeli-Palestinian conflict"; "Forming ties with the members of the other nation"; "Intensifying the common feeling between me and the members of the other nation"; and "Helping me personally, to deal with the Israeli-Palestinian conflict." Both were more willing to associate with the "other and to "receive a member of the other national group as a tenant in my apartment." However, only 43 percent of Palestinians and 37 percent of Israelis agreed to "Increasing my trust in the members of the other nation."

The most impressive effect of the workshop was the change in negative stereotypes each group had of the other. Israeli and Palestinian perceptions of each other improved significantly, in seeing each other as friendly, good-hearted, tolerant, polite, considerate, and willing to make sacrifices for peace. Palestinians came to view the Israelis as increasingly more modest, and the Israelis viewed the Palestinians as more trustworthy, reliable to keep promises, educated, intelligent, clean, and well-rounded.

Another study of 565 Jewish Israeli and Palestinian 10th-grade male and female students (aged 15–16), half who participated in our workshops and half who did not (controls), asked the teens to free associate to questions about peace (Biton & Salomon, 2004). These included a definition ("What is the first thing that comes to your mind when you think of peace?"); its explanation ("How would you explain peace to a five-year-old child?"); its utility ("If there will be peace, what would be its utility?"), and strategy ("If peace depended on you, what main thing would you do so there would be peace between Israelis and Palestinians?"). Initially, Israeli students saw peace as the absence of violence, and Palestinian students stressed independence and equality. After the workshops, more Israelis and Palestinian students mentioned cooperation and harmony. Those who did not participate in the workshop increasingly suggested war as a means to attain peace, and Palestinians expressed more hatred to Jews, whereas the students who participated in the workshop showed no such increases. The workshops provided a barrier against deterioration of perceptions and feelings toward "the other."

Funding and the Future

The government of the United States funded the major portion of the project in its first six years through the MERC—Middle East Regional Cooperation program of USAID. We were very fortunate because other applications fell through and our humble request for only $70,000 resulted in a grant of half a million dollars. Further funding came from Yad HaNadiv; Keren Bracha; People-to-People; the British Council; and the governments of Sweden, Norway, Denmark, Switzerland, Holland, Finland, and Japan; and the European Union.

It is worth mentioning that the project was developed, funded, and started during the time when the peace process had more hopeful signs and higher appraisal from both the Palestinians and Israelis. Now, at a time in which the peace process is in jeopardy given the political shifts, when both sides are not as optimistic, it is all the more important to continue the Education for Peace project. Youngsters are the future of each society and they should be motivated, through education for peace, to find the courage to live with and next to each other in a peaceful and cooperative way.

We have developed 200 peace lesson plans in Arabic for Palestinian schools that were submitted to the Palestinian Ministry of Education, and are scheduled to be adopted in the coming year. Given that the peace education textbooks for Israeli and Palestinian schools were successfully developed for Grade 11, we are currently developing them for Grades 1–12. The same textbooks will be produced for both Israel and Palestinian schools, in Hebrew and Arabic, with an English version available for teachers throughout the world.

At the end of last year, we reevaluated our direction. We already had three PhD dissertations and lots of positive articles written about our work. But we were dissatisfied that our work had not reached critical mass. Some of the Palestinian schools had dropped out of participating, and our textbooks were being only used in private, not public, schools. So we changed our focus from implementing programs in the schools to designing lesson plans and teacher training.

We have been contracted to evaluate Palestinian textbooks, and to produce supplementary lesson plans for Palestinian schools. The lesson plans have been produced and completed, but we do not have the funding or possibility at this time to implement the use of the lesson plans in the classroom. We are planning to invite Palestinian schools to receive copies of the lesson plans.

The Peace Education Conference

A major outgrowth of our education plan is the International Conference on Education for Peace and Democracy we convened in November 2006, in Antalya, Turkey, which focused on the Israeli-Palestinian region but included international involvement as well. The conference brought together peace educators, curricula writers, encounter facilitators, peace studies practitioners, human rights educators, conflict resolutions practitioners, mediators, and activists from academia, research, government, and community organizations. The 270 attendees included 85 Palestinians, 90 Israelis, and international participants from 20 countries, including Austria, Switzerland, France, England, Ireland, Norway, Spain, the United States, Canada, Turkey, South Africa, Bosnia, and Iran. This conference served as a tremendous opportunity for dialogue, debate, and visioning; built connections between the different disciplines and bridges between the two communities; examined peace education programs; evaluated existing curricula; and explored the use of multimedia, including the Internet and the arts, in peace education. This led to an ongoing and active e-mail group for continued exchange.

New Media Directions

Our education program relies on the power of the media as an education tool to achieve understanding and cooperation. Given Dr. Baskin's background in understanding newspapers, we launched *The New Jerusalem Times*, a weekly Internet-based Palestinian-Israeli newspaper magazine that is in English, Arabic, and Hebrew. We are searching for funding to advance this project as well. Our next project is to roll out *The New Jerusalem Times* as a regional newspaper including the entire Middle East. The paper is meant not to be a peacenik project, but a pluralities and progressive way to expose people in the region to each other and to encourage dialogue.

Our next dream is to evolve the newspaper effort into a television station—not a show but a station—to reach even more people to dialogue for peace.

Our Personal Stories

Hanna Siniora: My Story

In my role as Co-CEO of the Israel/Palestine Center for Research and Information, I am proud to work on behalf of peace between the two peoples. This is my life work and my commitment. I believe that each side—Palestinians and Israelis—is trying to find a better quality of life, and at the IPCRI we try to help this happen.

I was born and raised in Jerusalem and lived in East Jerusalem, in upper Baka. Now, I still live in East Jerusalem. My father had a pharmacy, so I was forced to study pharmacy. Until 1980, I worked as a pharmacist, though it did not suit me. Then, in 1973, a cousin who founded a newspaper was kidnapped and so I was the one who had to look after the newspaper. I didn't know anything about newspapers at that time! But through that experience of being editor and publisher, I had to learn how to write and do everything to put a newspaper out. The newspaper was one of the major dailies in Arabic—called *Al Fajr* and later renamed *The Jerusalem Times*. This was a formative experience, because it led to my being involved in the efforts of IPCRI to develop a new kind of media.

This is not the first joint media enterprise. One of our joint media projects is Radio All for Peace, a joint project of the Palestinian publishing company Biladi and the Israeli Givat Haviva. The programming broadcasts in English, Arabic, and Hebrew. This programming aims to change the understanding of the two peoples. The principle behind our programming is this: When you sign a paper, it is just an agreement, but when you reach the people, when you tell the Palestinians that the Israelis are not the army but people, and when you tell the Israelis that we, the Palestinians, are not all terrorists, then the greater part of both societies can start to work together.

We have to commit to disarm the militants, either by force, or by integrating them in the political system. Today those militants are more powerful than our security forces. We hope Hamas can transform from being a violent organization to a responsible political party. We want to calm the situation and stop the vicious cycle of act and retaliation.

Gershon Baskin: My Story

When I was eight years old, I told my parents I didn't want a bar mitzvah, I wanted to go to Israel. I don't know where the thought came to me. It just did.

As a youngster, when I was eight years old, I traveled with my family to Virginia. At that time, the seeds for my being interested in the issues of human rights were sown, especially when I saw a sign "whites only" that made me get involved in civil rights, and led to my being involved in the antiwar movement.

When I was 14 years old, I was living in Bellmore, Long Island, a heavily Jewish town. Then we moved to Smithtown, also on Long Island, that was 16 percent Jewish with only 2 percent of Jews in the school I attended. I met someone in school and we set up a Young Judaea chapter, and in 1973, I became the president of the Long Island region. Then I spent the summer as an 18-year-old wandering around Israel.

I had a map of Israel without the green line on it above my bunk in Camp Tel Yehuda in Barryville, New York, and someone drew a green line on the map, and looking at the map with the Occupied Territories clearly delineated, it suddenly hit me that I had spent a year in Israel and not spoken to one Palestinian. At that time, I started reading every book about the Israeli-Palestinian conflict that I found. I changed my major from psychology to politics and history of the Middle East. As I began to get more politically involved, I was continually confronted by Israelis who said to me, "You are just a naïve American. You don't know them [meaning the Arabs]."

I knew at that time that I would have to find a way to become credible in the eyes of Israelis. I then heard about a new program called Interns for Peace run by Reform Rabbi Bruce Cohen, who was looking for Jews to go live and work in Arab villages in Israel for two years. It was a formative experience for me. I learned much more than I was capable of giving. I learned about Palestinian culture, firsthand. I spent two years living with Palestinian citizens of Israel and was exposed to Palestinians in the Occupied Territories through their eyes. I approached the issue of equal rights in Israel for Jews and Arabs and to the Israeli-Palestinian conflict through Jewish-Zionist eyes, given my background, and came to the conclusion that there does not have to be a contradiction in my desire to see Israel as a Jewish, and as a democratic, state. I also came to understand that Israel had to resolve both problems—the Israeli-Palestinian conflict and the internal conflict between Jews and Arabs. From my many meetings with Palestinians in the Occupied Territories, I came to understand that it was still too early to open a dialogue with Palestinians based on mutual recognition—the Palestinians were not yet ready.

Upon finishing my work in Interns for Peace in 1981, I proposed to the Israeli government that the issue of Jewish-Arab relations had to be dealt with at the governmental level and not solely by nongovernmental organizations. My proposal was accepted and I became the first civil servant responsible for Jewish-Arab relations. I was placed in the Ministry of Education and was responsible for creating education programs between the Jewish and Arab school systems. Later, through the prime minister's office (under Begin) and the Ministry of Education, I founded and directed the Institute for Education for Arab-Jewish Coexistence.

I did that until the outbreak of the first Intifada. Then I left the institute and founded IPCRI.

References

Biton, Y., & Salomon, G. (2004, May). *"Peace" in the eyes of Israeli and Palestinian youths as a function of collective narratives and participation in a peace education program.* Retrieved from http://construct.haifa.ac.il/~cerpe/pub/papers/Biton%20&%20Salomon%20Paper%20-final.pdf.

Maoz, Y. (1998). *Israeli-Palestinian Youth Encounter Workshops in the framework of the IPCRI Educational Peace Project: Basic summary of research findings.* Retrieved from http://www.ipcri.org/files/maoz.html.

Salomon, G. (2004). Does peace education really make a difference? *Peace and Conflict: The Journal of Peace Psychology, 12*(1). Retrieved from http://construct.haifa.ac.il/~cerpe/pub/papers/Does%20PE%20REALLY%20make%20a%20difference1.pdf.

CHAPTER 32

SCHOOL FOR PEACE: BETWEEN HARD REALITY AND THE JEWISH-PALESTINIAN ENCOUNTERS

Rabah Halabi and Nava Sonnenschein

For more than two decades the School for Peace at Neve Shalom/Wahat al-Salam has been bringing together Jews and Arabs for dialogue workshops. This chapter examines the unique approach that the School for Peace has developed over the years in the light of existing theory and research in the field of social identity construction and majority-minority relations. It further explains the five stages of conflict between Jews and Palestinians and shows how these stages evident in our encounter workshops reflect the history of the Jewish-Palestinian conflict from 1948 until today. Understanding these processes is essential to any attempt at building a more humane society based on equality and justice between the two peoples.

The very concept of encounter work is undergoing a crisis especially for organizations conducting "coexistence" (or interpersonal) encounters and striving to advance peace by developing warmer relations between Jewish and Arab individuals (Abu Nimer, 1999; Halabi, 2002). In light of the new political reality and despite tremendous investment of time and energy over the years in coexistence projects in Israel, Jews and Arabs have not only failed to get closer to each other, but the rift between them is now the most serious that we have ever known (Rabinowitz & Abu Baker, 2002).

The October uprisings, or *Intifadat al-Aksa*, have exposed a very real conflict between the two peoples, making it more difficult than ever for those of us working in the field of Jewish-Arab encounters (Abu Nimer, 1999; Suleiman, 2000). Soon after the outbreak of the Intifada, we conducted a conference for practitioners in the field of dialogue work, attended by about 250 practitioners from 35 NGOs. It came as no surprise that more and more people cast serious doubts on the benefits of coexistence projects. Since the Intifada, Arabs have no longer been particularly enthusiastic about participating in encounter work.

The School for Peace has always challenged the interpersonal approach of coexistence projects, claiming that they sweep problems under the rug and preserve existing inequalities and discriminatory power relations between Jews and Arabs (Abu-Nimer, 1999; Maoz, 2000; Sonnenschein, Halabi, & Friedman, 1998; Suleiman, 2000). Even encounters done the right way—on the intergroup basis—cannot change reality created by economic and political forces that only those forces can change (Halabi, 2003; Rouhana & Kroper, 1997; Suleiman, 2000).

However, the intergroup encounter is a unique opportunity to improve understanding of Jewish-Palestinian relations. Interviews with participants after our workshops show that the most important contribution of intergroup encounter to society is that they can provide participants with tools that help them analyze the reality in which they live, and enable them to imagine what might be in store for Jewish-Palestinian relations in the future. Ideally, this understanding will motivate participants to promote social change in their immediate surroundings, which, in turn, can prepare the way for large-scale change over the long term.

This chapter shows how the processes that we witness in our Jewish-Palestinian encounter projects can be used to gain insight into the development of Jewish-Palestinian relations in general. It includes a brief review of some of the models commonly used in the field, a presentation of the educational approach we developed at the School for Peace, the main processes that occur during the course of the encounter, and lessons we can learn and apply to real life.

Theories of Encounter Work

Encounters have been initiated in various parts of the world over several decades. These include encounters between blacks and whites, Russians and Americans during the Cold War, Tamil and Sinhalese in Sri Lanka, Separatists and Federalists in Canada, Turks and Greeks in Cyprus, as well as between Arabs and Jews (Abu-Nimer, 1999; Burton, 1986; Fisher, 1997; Halabi, 2003; Katz & Kahanov, 1990; Tidwell, 1998).

The theoretical and practical approaches to work involving intergroup meetings between groups in conflict are characterized by two major axes (Halabi & Sonnenschein, 2003). The first axis is a continuum defined by workshops in human relations at one end and workshops in conflict resolution at the other. Human relations workshops emphasize psychological aspects of the encounter experience and what participants have in common, sidelining conflict-inducing subjects in contrast to conflict resolution workshops that downplay participants' inner psychological world and their interpersonal relations and instead see individuals as representatives of their respective groups and seek to build bridges between the disparate goals of the two groups (Abu-Nimer, 1994; Brewer & Miller, 1984; Katz & Kahanov, 1990).

The second major axis is a continuum defined by the contact hypothesis approach at one end and the intergroup encounter approach at the other (Nadler, 2000). The former assumes that the conflict is the result of a lack of information about each other and that personal connection and interaction between them on a personal basis can reduce their hatred for one another and preexisting stereotypes they have about one another (Amir, 1976; Brewer & Miller, 1984).

In contrast, the intergroup approach contends that the encounter will be useful and reduce stereotypes not when the group identity of the participants is minimized but, rather, when it is emphasized, and when the interactions are primarily of a group nature. This experience then gets generalized to real life outside the group (Nadler, 2000; Wilder, 1984).

The two axes are similar in that at one pole each approach relies on deconstructing the group dimension in favor of individual contact, while at the other pole, they rely on strengthening the group dimension and on intergroup interaction. The approach of the School for Peace in Neve Shalom/Wahat al-Salam is closer to the second pole at the two axes.

The School for Peace

The School for Peace (SFP) was founded in 1979 in the Jewish-Arab village of Neve Shalom/Wahat al-Salam, situated in the center of Israel between Jerusalem and Tel-Aviv. It is presently home to 50 Jewish and Arab families who came together to find ways to advance understanding between the two peoples. The School for Peace was established to conduct courses and workshops for Jews and Palestinians. More than 30,000 Jews and Palestinians have taken part in SFP projects, including Jewish and Arab high school and university students, teachers, women's groups, social workers, journalists, and a variety of other change agents, from all socioeconomic backgrounds and parts of the political spectrum. Funded by foundations and by friends' associations of Neve Shalom/Wahat al-Salam, the SFP remains the only organization of its kind that grew out of a joint Jewish-Palestinian initiative and that is answerable solely to a Jewish-Palestinian decision-making body.

The Development of School for Peace
Goals and Objectives

Our approach—imported from the United States and the only one available at that time in Israel—started from the human relations and contact hypothesis approach focused on the individual rather than on the group. Our goal was to help participants develop awareness of Jewish-Arab relations as individuals and as members of two groups, to develop empathy for each other and to reduce stereotyping. Participants had to speak for themselves and not in the name of a group, and direct what they said to someone specific. When a participant spoke in the first-person plural ("*We* . . ."), we noted that he or she was not the spokesperson of the group. Since encouraging good communication between participants was important, we employed various interpersonal communication techniques, for example, listening exercises and role playing.

Evaluations of our workshops revealed that facilitators and participants—particularly Arabs—were frustrated and dissatisfied, and felt that meetings run on this model were artificial, inauthentic, and served the interests of Jewish participants (Bar & Bargal, 1995). Efforts to improve our workshops took us from the interpersonal and contact hypothesis pole and brought us closer to the intergroup and conflict resolution pole. However, our approach is not identical to any other, but was developed over years through trial and error and formalized in a number of theories in hindsight.

Our work is guided by the vision of a humane, egalitarian, and just society, and the necessity of a clear and mature identity to enable us to build reciprocal and egalitarian relationships (Helmes, 1990; Phinney, 1990). The objectives of our encounters are to develop participants' awareness of the conflict and their own roles in it, and to enable them to explore their identities and choose a path according to our understanding and consciousness. The encounter enables participants to explore and construct their identities through interaction with "the other." In pursuit of this common goal, the task of each group is different, since the reality in which they live is asymmetrical: the Arabs, as the minority group, must deal with internalized oppression and the reality of being controlled, while the Jews, as the majority group, must deal with being the rulers. Both groups investigate the oppressive patterns in which they are caught, moving toward liberation from these patterns through the search for what is human in them (Freire, 1974).

Our main assumption is that the conflict between Arabs and Jews is between two national identities—not between individuals. Hence, we consider the goal of the encounter can only be achieved by sharpening these identities and facing the reality of the conflict between the two nationalities as reflected by the two groups engaged in the specific encounter workshop (Brown & Hewstone, 1986; Wilder, 1984).

The Structure of the Encounter

At the start of the encounter, we give the participants a written and oral explanation of the method and goals of the encounter. In the encounters, the participants are given freedom to explore the conflict in a very open structure; consequently, we do not suggest topics and do our best to enable the group to behave as naturally as possible.

Participants are divided into small groups of 14 to 16 participants, with an equal number of Jews and Arabs, and two facilitators, one Arab and one Jewish. Discussions within the group take place all together (in a binational setting) and also in separate groups (a uninational forum) where the Arab group sits with the Arab facilitator and the Jewish group sits with the Jewish facilitator. We encourage participants to speak in their own language (both Hebrew and Arabic are the official languages) with facilitators offering translation services—to convey the message that the encounter is between two groups, two peoples, and two identities, and to advance dialogue between two identities to address the most difficult and painful issues that stand between the two groups. In practice, however, participants tend to speak in Hebrew—which reflects the asymmetry between the two groups (Halabi & Zak, 2003).

Facilitation

The facilitators are eight Jews and eight Arabs with academic backgrounds in a variety of fields, who have completed our yearlong 160-hour facilitator-training course. The program begins with the trainees experiencing the workshop as participants. They are then taught about conflict groups, social and ethnic identity, and work on acquiring practical facilitation skills. Later, they observe encounter workshops through a one-way mirror, with training staff helping them identify and analyze group processes. Finally, they facilitate a three-day workshop with a senior staff member. Most trainees are 20 to 30 years old, female Jews and male Arabs. Most SFP staff reside at Neve Shalom/Wahat al-Salam. Their role is to help the participants identify and analyze the processes that take place between the two groups and to link these processes to the larger reality of Jewish-Arab relations.

Intervention are based on three basic assumptions.

1. A person's identity and behavior are constructed upon conceptions and beliefs that are stable, deep-seated, resistant to change, and generally unconscious. Since statements, opinions, and stereotypes are only the outward indications of these conceptions, we try to enable participants to behave freely, as closely as possible in line with reality, so that through this behavior they can confront, examine, and gain insight into their deeply held conceptions (Bion, 1961; Burton, 1986). One of the principal conceptions is a feeling of superiority or inferiority, which flows from the asymmetrical reality influencing thinking and behavior within the conflict (Libkind, 1992; Tajfel, 1978). For example, a Jewish participant may say that he started out identifying with the "left" but that the interaction with the Arabs has made him more nationalist and even extremist. We interpret this to mean that the encounter has caused him to confront his own feeling of superiority, when he has suppressed this feeling up to this point, in order to be seen as liberal and enlightened; and he is now angry with the Arab for serving as his mirror and making him discover this side of himself.

2. We see the group as more than the sum of the individuals who constitute it, and regard the encounter as between two national groups rather than between individuals where individuals, shaped by their national group affiliation, relate as representatives of these groups. Hence, we treat individuals as spokespersons for the national groups to which they belong, and we treat the group as representing the collective unconscious of its members (Bion, 1961; Brown & Hewstone, 1986; Tajfel & Turner, 1986). For example, when there is an argument between Jews and Arabs over a particular issue and only one participant from a group

takes a stand, we treat that as the position of his or her group. When someone in the group expresses an opinion and no one challenges it, the group sees that position as representing everyone.

3. The third assumption is that the encounter within the small group is a microcosm of the reality in society at large (Freud, 1921; Yalom, 1970). The phenomena of majority-minority relations outside continue to express themselves in our workshops regardless of the actual number of Arab and Jewish participants in the room at any given point (Maoz, 2000). At the outset of the meeting, the Jewish group often expresses a variety of opinions whereas the Arab group rallies around a united position—reflecting the sociopolitical structure of real life outside. As such, the Arab group, as the minority, tries to gain strength by maintaining group cohesion while the Jewish group, enjoying the strength of being the majority group, can allow themselves the luxury of pluralism, expressing diverse opinions freely and openly.

Thus, we use the processes that emerge from the encounter to learn about the broader reality of Jewish-Arab relations. These processes even offer a window into future relations. For example, power relations within the encounter change only when the Arab group becomes stronger and forces the Jewish group to change accordingly. We can therefore conclude that the asymmetrical relations on the outside will be prone to change only if and when the Arabs in Israel become stronger and force these changes to take place (Sonnenschein, Halabi, & Friedman, 1998).

Observations of the Encounters

While changes take place within each national group and between the two national groups, individuals also undergo change as a result of these processes (Halabi, 2003). Since the positions of the groups are not symmetrical, the change individuals of each group undergo will be very different. Through the encounter, the Jews confront the nature of their position as members of the dominant majority group, as their desire to be liberal, egalitarian, and humane suddenly clashes with their position of control (Halabi, Sonnenschein, & Friedman, 2003). In contrast, the Arabs aspire for equality and must face the degree to which they have internalized their oppression. Theirs is a struggle for empowerment and liberation from their own oppression. Though the nature of the change that each side undergoes is different, it is ultimately a mutual process that must be shared by both sides if they are to break free of the situation of oppression in which both are partners (Sonnenschein & Hijazi, 2003).

Generally, the Jews readily report changes, seeing this as a courageous act deserving recognition from the Arab group, and expecting the Arabs to change in the same way. The Arab group tends not to report changes, seeing change as a sign of weakness or feeling that it is up to the Jewish group—as the strong group—to change because they have power to influence the broader reality (Halabi & Sonnenschein, 2003). The facilitators must be aware of these processes, to direct participants to the different spaces occupied by the two groups, and to raise awareness of the connection between these different spaces and the differing responses.

Five Stages of an Encounter Workshop

While every experience is unique, there appear to be five stages that repeat themselves in each ongoing encounter (Halabi et al., 2003). The first is the searching stage, in which the Jews and Arabs start out conducting themselves as they would outside. The Arabs present their situation, stressing discrimination that they experience while the Jewish group takes a liberal and generous stand, regarding the encounter as an opportunity for Jews and Arabs to meet each other as individuals, accepting anything that the Arabs say about discrimination.

The second stage is characterized by the strengthening of the Arab group whereby Arab participants, being the weaker and oppressed group, focus on politics to give them the upper hand, and become more assertive in presenting their arguments. In discussions at this stage, the Arab group challenges Israel's definition as a Jewish state, calling instead for a state for all its citizens (since Intifadat al-Aksa, the Arab group has been reaching this stage much more quickly). The Jewish group generally experiences this confrontation and loss of control as threatening (even though the groups never reach a position of equality in the room), feel cornered and abandon their initial intention to meet the Arabs as individuals rather than as two collectives, and unite to meet the threat.

This brings us to the third stage that we refer to as the Jews' "restoration of power." Being put on the defensive, the Jewish group begins to "counterattack," to put the Arabs back in their place, looking for weak points in Arab society that they can criticize. Uncomfortable with the political agenda set by the Arabs, the Jews question the Arabs' degree of humanity, change the agenda to discuss values and morality, and argue that despite inequalities and discrimination, the Jewish *society* is more benevolent, proven by the fact that if the Arabs were in control, they would massacre the Jews and throw them into the sea (showing that Arab values and morals are beneath the level of Jewish values and morals).

Though the Jewish group may regain some power from this stage, the Palestinian participants never return to the point at which they started the workshop. A struggle ensues between the Jewish group, which refuses to forfeit its power, and the Palestinian group, which has been empowered and is no longer prepared to appeal to the Jews as "the good Arabs." This struggle brings the two groups to the fourth stage.

The fourth stage—called the deadlock—is the most aggressive and long-lasting part of the encounter. Both groups dig in their heels; the atmosphere is tense; there is anger and frustration on both sides; and the arguments can get loud. The Arab group will be frustrated and may fall into despair by the apparent futility of their attempts to change the attitude of the Jewish group. In the earlier stages, as long as the Arabs complied with the Jews' definition of them as "Israeli

Arabs," the Jews accepted the Arab group with open arms. But once the Arab participants refer to their more "threatening" Palestinian identity, defining their reality as that of a national group, the Jews stop accepting them. The deadlock breaks—and stage five of a deeper dialogue begins—only when the Jewish group accepts responsibility for injustices done to the Palestinians as a national group, both historically and reflected in the encounter group.

In stage five, the dialogue addresses all of the points raised in the beginning of the workshop, but now the discussion is far more open and based on mutual recognition and respect. The Palestinian group feels less of a need to present a united front against the Jews; they put their cards on the table and expose the tactics they used previously in their struggle with the Jewish group. (However, as long as the Jewish-Palestinian reality is not equal, the dialogue between the two groups will never truly be equal either.) We believe that this objective can only be achieved through a dialectical process requiring both parties in the conflict.

The Encounter as a Microcosm of Reality

In this way, the five stages of the encounter become a microcosm for what has gone on historically in the conflict. The years of 1948 until 1967 reflect a situation similar to stage one—the searching stage. In this period, Arabs who remained in Israel were very confused but low-key, living more or less according to dictates of the Jews, accepting their identity as Jewish society defined it (Habiby, 1974; Lustick, 1980; Rabinowitz & Abu Baker, 2002).

With Israel's occupation of the West Bank and Gaza in 1967, Palestinians on both sides of the border renewed their contact with each other and were empowered by a rehabilitation of the Palestinian national identity in general (Rouhana, 1993; Smooha, 1988; Suleiman & Beit-Hallahmi, 1997). Palestinian pride was progressively strengthened by an Arab strike in 1976, protesting expropriation of Arab land in the Galilee; the first Intifada, in 1987; HizbAllah's success in expelling the Israeli army from Lebanon; and the outbreak of Intifadat al-Aksa in October 2002 (Rouhana, 1997; Rabinowitz & Abu Baker, 2002).

While the growth of Palestinian empowerment in real life has been slow, the Jewish-Arab encounters that we conduct enable us to witness this process as it occurs before our eyes. While 10 years ago, the Palestinian group was hardly capable of expressing itself in front of the Jewish group—and making our main task as facilitators to encourage the Palestinian group to put their distress into words—today, the Palestinian group expresses itself clearly and with confidence in front of the Jewish group. In the encounters today, the Palestinians often appear even stronger than the Jewish group—often astonishing the Jewish participants.

We find a correlation between the latest period of Jewish-Palestinian relations and stage three of the encounter process in which the Jews try to restore their power and return the Palestinian Arabs to "their place." In our view, the Arab empowerment is, at first, perceived by the Jews as something that comes at their expense—a threat not only to their state but also to their very identity. The Jews as a whole will overlook differences within their own society and unite to meet the threat. Failed attempts to restore the previous status quo demonstrate the view that Palestinians are no longer the same nice and subservient Arabs that remained in Israel after the Nakba in 1948. Until the Jews change their basic perception of the political reality, acknowledge and take responsibility for the injustice caused the Palestinians, the latter will have to continue to struggle for their existence, identity, and equality (Halabi, 2002; Rabinowitz & Abu Baker, 2002).

Just as we see in the workshops, the processes of awareness cannot simply be reversed. Palestinians will endure further oppression until they reach "stage five," the stage of the different dialogue, based on the Jews' recognition of the Palestinians as a group with a national identity and as equal partners. Once that dialogue begins, the hardest part of the struggle for peace is behind us.

References

Abu-Nimer, M. (1999). *Dialogue, conflict resolution, and change: Arab-Jewish encounters in Israel.* Albany: State University of New York Press.

Bar, H., & Bar-Gal, D. (1995). *Living with the conflict.* Jerusalem: The Jerusalem Institute for Israel Studies. (In Hebrew)

Bion, W. R. (1961). *Experience in groups and other papers.* New York: Basic Books.

Brewer, M. B., & Miller, N. (1984). Beyond the contact hypothesis: Theoretical perspectives on desegregation. In N. Miller & M. B. Brewer (Eds.), *Groups in contact: The psychology of desegregation* (pp. 281–302). London: Academic Press.

Brown, R., & Hewstone, M. (1986). *Contact and conflict in intergroup encounters.* Basil: Blackwell Press.

Burton, J. (1986). *International conflict resolution: Theory and practice.* Sussex, England: Wheatsheaf.

Fisher, R. (1997). *Interactive conflict resolution.* New York: Syracuse University Press.

Freire, P. (1974). *Pedagogy of the oppressed.* New York: Continuum.

Freud, S. (1921). *Group psychology and the analysis of the ego.* London: Hogarth Press.

Habiby, E. (1974). *Almutashael.* Haifa: Arabic Press. (In Arabic)

Halabi, R. (2002). Exploration, empowerment, confrontation and dialogue (in Hebrew). *Panim, 20,* 39–48.

Halabi, R. (2003). *Israeli and Palestinian identities in dialogue: The School for Peace approach.* New Jersey: Rutgers University Press.

Halabi, R & Zak, M. (2003). Language as a bridge and an obstacale. The School for Peace approach. In R. Halabi (Ed.), *Israeli and Palestinian identities in dialogue: The School for Peace approach* (pp. 119–140). New Jersey: Rutgers University Press.

Halabi, R., & Sonnenschein, N. (2003). Awareness identity and reality: The School for Peace approach. In R. Halabi (Ed.), *Israeli and Palestinian identities in dialogue: The School for Peace approach* (pp. 67–83). New Jersey: Rutgers University Press.

Halabi, R., Sonnenschein, N., & Friedman, A. (2003). Liberate the oppressed and their oppressors: Encounters between university students. In R. Halabi (Ed.), *Israeli and*

Palestinian identities in dialogue: The School for Peace approach (pp. 84–115). New Jersey: Rutgers University Press.

Helmes, J. Y. (1990). *Black and white racial identity: Theory, research, and practice.* London: Greenwood Press.

Katz, Y., & Kahanov, M. (1990). A review of dilemmas in facilitating encounter groups between Jews and Arabs in Israel (in Hebrew). *Megamot, 33*(1), 29–47.

Libkind, K. (1992). Ethnic identity-challenging the boundaries of social psychology. In G. M. Breakwell (Ed.), *Social psychology of identity and the self-concept* (pp. 147–185). London: Sunny University Press.

Lustick, I. (1980). *Arabs in the Jewish state.* Austin, Texas University of Texas Press.

Maoz, I. (2000). Power relations in intergroup encounters: A case study of Jewish Arab encounters in Israel. *International Journal of Intercultural Relations, 24,* 259–277.

Nadler, A. (2000). Intergroup conflict: A social psychology perspective. In R. Halabi (Ed.), *Identities in dialogue: Arab-Jewish encounters in Wahat al-Salam/Neve Shalom* (pp. 29–49). Tel Aviv: Kibbutz Hameuchad.

Phinney , J. S. (1990). Ethnic identity in adolescents and adults: Review of research. *Psychological Bulletin, 108*(3), 499–514.

Rabinowitz, D., & Abu Baker, H. (2002). *The stand tall generation: The Palestinian citizens of Israel today.* Jerusalem: Keter. (In Hebrew).

Rouhana, N. (1993). Accentuated identities in protracted conflicts: The collective identity of the Palestinian citizens in Israel. *Asian and African Studies, 27,* 97–127.

Rouhana, N., & Korper, S. (1997). Power asymmetry and goals of unofficial third party: Intervention in protracted intergroup conflict. *Journal of Peace Psychology, 3*(1), 1–17.

Rouhana, N. N. (1997). *Palestinian citizens in an ethnic Jewish state: Identities in conflict.* New Haven, CT: Yale University Press.

Smooha, S. (1988). *Arabs and Jews in Israel* (Vol. 1). Boulder, CO: Westview Press.

Sonnenschein, N., & Hijazi, A. (2003). "Home group": The uninational framework. In R. Halabi (Ed.), *Israeli and Palestinian identities in dialogue: The School for Peace approach* (pp. 248–278). New Jersey: Rutgers University Press.

Sonnenschein, N., Halabi, R., & Friedman, A. (1998). The Israeli-Palestinian workshops: Legitimation of national identity and change in power relationships. In E. Weiner (Ed.), *The handbook of interethnic coexistence* (pp. 600–614). An Abraham Fund Publication. New York: Continuum.

Suleiman, R. (2000). The planned encounter as a microcosm. In R. Halabi (Ed.), *Identities in dialogue: Arab-Jewish encounters in Wahat al-Salam/Neve Shalom* (pp. 71–93). Tel Aviv: Kibbutz Hameuchad.

Suleiman, R., & Beit-Hallahmi, B. (1997). National and civil identities of Palestinians in Israel. *The Journal of Social Psychology, 132*(2), 219–228.

Tajfel, H. (1978). *The social psychology of minorities.* London: Minority Rights Group.

Tajfel, H., & Turner, J. (1986). An integrative theory of inter-group conflict. In W. G. Austen & S. Worchel (Eds.), *Psychology of inter-group relations* (pp. 7–24). Monterey, CA: Brooks/Cole.

Tidwell, A. (1996). *Conflict resolved.* Oxford: Broadman & Holman.

Wilder, D. (1984). Intergroup contact: The typical member and the rule. *Journal of Experimental Social Psychology, 20,* 177–194.

Yalom, I. (1970). *The theory and practice of group psychology.* New York: Basic Books.

CHAPTER 33

The Peace Candle and Beyond: Women as Partners in Innovative Projects for Peace in the Middle East

Dena Merriam

The group of Palestinian and Israeli women finally met at the Movenpick Hotel on the Dead Sea in Jordan in December 2004. They came to a conference of the Global Peace Initiative of Women (GPIW) to explore peace initiatives between the Israelis and Palestinians. No one was sure of the outcome, since volatility in the region—the occupation and ongoing Intifada—had made planning difficult. As is typical of such meetings between the "two sides" of the conflict, the Israelis showed enormous interest and enthusiasm (hundreds who wanted to come had to be turned away to maintain balance in the delegations) while many interested Palestinian women hesitated, either wanting to see what happened before participating in the future or fearful of repercussions from their community. Thankfully, Palestinian Lily Habash helped convince her colleagues the risk was worth it.

In the last days before the conference, violence broke out in Gaza, the border was closed, and permits were denied; but at the last moment, Israeli women pressured the government to give in and a busload of 14 Gazan women arrived at the border into Jordan. They hadn't left Gaza in four years, and women from the West Bank, as well as Israeli women, hugged them. Later one of the women from Gaza sat next to the wife of a prominent Israeli rabbi and discovered that she had taught Arabic to this women's husband several years ago. It was like a family reunion.

In all, 240 women from 20 countries came from Asia, Africa, Europe, and North America. The group included peace activists, but also women from government, business, media, education, religion, and the NGO community, and youth from Israel and Palestine, and also Egypt, Sudan, and Iran. Key reconciliation leaders included Nobel Peace Laureate Mairead Corrigan Maguire from

Northern Ireland; a founding member of the Truth and Reconciliation Commission Dudu Chili from South Africa; Terry Rockefeller from the September 11 Families for a Peaceful Tomorrow in the United States; and the Venerable Guo Kuang Shih from Taiwan with her delegation of Buddhist nuns. As one Palestinian woman remarked, "I haven't had contact with any Israelis for the last four years. At first I didn't want to come, but I decided it was time to begin dialogue again."

Setting the Tone

> The way forward is to hear what others are saying, listening to their experiences.
>
> —*Palestinian youth delegate*

Given the stress of getting there for the Palestinian sisters, we began the conference with a "Spiritual Forum"—a session of sharing cultural and spiritual traditions including reflections, readings from poetry and spiritual texts, Sufi and Jewish chants and songs, and meditation. The peace candle was lit by members of the Parents Circle-Families Forum—Israeli mothers who lost their sons fighting in the army, a Palestinian woman from East Jerusalem whose sister was shot in the conflict, and a 20-year-old Palestinian whose fiancé was just killed by Israeli gunfire. They stood together in a display of solidarity and spoke of how their personal loss has inspired them to move past hate and revenge and be devoted to reconciliation and peace.

Participants gave presentations about why peace efforts have failed thus far, the role of the international community, and what reconciliation requires. A dramatic slide presentation was shown with graphic images of suffering by the Palestinians due to the occupation; and an Israeli woman stood up and protested that there were no equivalent visuals of Israeli suffering from suicide bombings. Heated exchanges ensured—that served to release inevitable emotional tensions. But a recommitment was made not to repeat a "competition of woes"—debating whose suffering, the Palestinians or Israelis, was worse—that happened at the first meeting in Oslo, Norway, over a year ago, and instead to maintain neutrality, listen to both sides, and focus on the future, not the past.

How to Begin Reconciliation

> Youth have the power of forgiveness—we don't hold onto things and therefore can move forward.
>
> —*Youth delegate from the UN Pan-Asian Youth Leadership Summit*

Dr. Alex Boraine, Chair of the South African Truth and Reconciliation Commission, confirmed that dialogue must begin and continue even before political solutions are found. In South Africa, meetings took place privately toward reconciliation, long before the political turn of events, so that by the time the environment was ripe for real reconciliation, relationships were already in place. In dialogue sessions facilitated by experts in listening and communication skills, participants shared experiences. Mairead Corrigan Maguire told of reconciliation efforts in Northern Ireland and Tho Ha Vinh spoke of Vietnam, where he had family members in both the north and south.

Three things were clear: (1) reconciliation is not a political exercise, but a spiritual, emotional, and moral effort that encompasses forgiveness, compassion, and a will to leave behind the past and build for the future; (2) women must have a leading role in the peace process given their skills to sympathize with others' pain and listen with their heart; and (3) reconciliation is a people-to-people process, not just a political process, that begins at the grassroots level. Person-to-person sharing separates the conflict from being a political war between Israelis and Palestinians, as face-to-face meetings dispel negative images of the other side. Individuals have power to influence events, but the international community can also serve as a neutralizing force.

Steps to Peace

A number of areas and projects were identified as a "road map to peace" on many levels of society.

Circles of Reconciliation

Meetings of Palestinian and Israeli women to tell healing narratives, in the spirit of the Parents Circle-Families Forum.

Empowering Women and Peacebuilding through Business Initiatives

Despite border restrictions and the Wall, a solution to Palestinian poverty is to build Israeli and Palestinian business collaborations, using the example of Palestinian-made items of embroidery, crafts, and handmade goods that could be marketed and distributed by Israeli, U.S., or European women. Some protested that such products keep women in traditional professions. Palestinians were skeptical about joint business endeavors, given checkpoints, absence of electricity, and difficulty to produce and transport goods, and suggested that Israeli businesswomen use their influence to help Palestinians obtain permits, make sure that deliveries and travel could take place, and help develop marketing strategies. Palestinian women also need training to develop the high-tech skills (especially in computer technology) for business success. Plans include Web-based training programs in business and computer science, specific steps Israeli women can take to help Palestinian women take part in joint business ventures (one successful project has been the "Peace Candle," which was lit at the opening of the conference and is being marketed in the United States), and attracting investment and international companies to the area.

Working with the Media

The media is influential in shaping public opinion, and there are increasing debates whether to report objectively what happens or to assume moral responsibility to guide public discourse in a more positive direction. Peacebuilding efforts—and women-led initiatives—are not covered well enough, agreed both a *Jerusalem Post* reporter and a Bethlehem television anchor. Suggestions included a Journalists' Forum to explore how to promote coverage of peacebuilding initiatives, drafting a dictionary of phrases to explain both sides' narratives, educating the public, and promoting publication of Israeli journalists in Palestinian print media and Palestinian journalists in Israeli print media, to give the public new input that could alter its views.

Peace through Education

"How do we remove checkpoints and barriers, but feel safe that we won't be bombed?" asked one Israeli youth. The young Palestinian woman whose fiancé was shot replied, "Although my fiancé was killed, I channel my energy and depression into something positive. It's important to note the positive things, as I easily could have become the other violent face."

Education to overcome such fears must be a bigger part of the peace process. Good examples of groups that address education include the Hope Flowers School, Hand in Hand, the Middle East Children's Association, Neve Shalom/ Wahat al-Salam (One Peace) level, Palestinian Youth Association for Leadership And Rights Activation (PYALARA), Language Connections, the Geneva Initiative, and the Parents Circle-Families Forum, as well as faculty and students from Al Quds University and Beir Zeit University in Palestine, Hebrew University and Tel Aviv University in Israel.

Traditional education should help children think not only independently but compassionately, with an open mind and heart, and with respect for others. Children have to be taught to acknowledge the pain and the reality of "the other," how to deal with fear and trauma, and to share firsthand experiences with good listening skills. Peace education must include teachers and parents, young children, and college students—the leaders of tomorrow.

Four levels of education should include individual students (to deal with fear and trauma); schools (like Hope Flowers School, Hand in Hand); communities (like the Middle East Children's Program focusing on preparing Israeli and Palestinian teachers to develop positive relationships and new curriculum and materials); and political decision makers (with an international commission serving as a monitor).

Working in full Palestinian-Israeli partnerships is important—to develop products and curricula acceptable to both sides, such as the Parents Circle-Families Forum where Palestinian and Israeli bereaved parents visit schools together to show the humanity of victims on both sides.

For nonviolence to work, Israelis and Palestinians have to get to know each other. But Palestinian youth usually only encounter Israelis soldiers and see tanks in the streets and house demolitions, while Israeli children only experience Palestinians as suicide bombers. One Palestinian educator told of how she was walking with a group of school kids who passed a soldier and were frightened, but the soldier talked to them in a friendly manner, making the kids see the soldier not as an enemy to be feared or hated, but as a friendly human being. This model can be applied more widely.

Children can also do media projects to develop friendships—using nonverbal activities, such as art or ecological projects, to bypass language barriers. An Internet site devoted to nonviolence for sharing ideas between students, parents, and teachers would be valuable, and could channel negative feelings toward constructive communication, and include a directory of female experts to share resources and curricula. Virtual meetings on the Internet can connect Israeli and Palestinian classrooms, especially in isolated areas such as Gaza, but the infrastructure for Internet communications is not yet available.

Mobilizing Women as a Political Force

Women have the power to calm situations, speak as "we" instead of "I" and work collectively. Suggestions offered to deal with those who endorse violence included to understand their motives (a Gazan youth said that many "fighters" also want peace); encourage the public to support moderates on both sides and encourage the moderates and "voices of the silent majority" to speak out against violence and for human rights and reconciliation; to see how "the other side" lives (e.g., Israeli women should visit Ramallah); and encourage internal dialogue, for example, settlers should reconcile with the Israeli general public and Palestinians should reconcile with "freedom fighters." Palestinian and Israeli women should continue to meet, with participation by the international community.

Symposium of Women Theologians

Peace has to happen on a spiritual level, guided by respected spiritual leaders, as was the case in South Africa with Bishop Desmond Tutu.

Gaza Conference

After disengagement, the global community needs to invest in social, emotional, and spiritual rebuilding of the region. A meeting of Israeli and Palestinian women to take place in Gaza will be planned.

Going Forward: Developing the Moral and Spiritual Fiber for Reconciliation

All agreed that the vision of reconciliation has to establish a neutral platform, acknowledge equality of the two communities, accept "the other" with sincere respect, and honor the dignity of each individual, so there is no one stronger or controlling force and both societies develop their inner integrity and independent strength.

Taking Home the Commitment

With the spontaneous singing of "We Shall Overcome," Palestinians, Israelis, and women from the international community stood hand in hand, ending the conference.

Appreciation was expressed to financial supporters (the government of Sweden, Anne Rockefeller Roberts, Dharma Drum Mountain, Chautauqua Institution, the Middle East Peace Dialogue, and the Ruder Finn Group); to Israeli and Palestinian participants who created a new sense of hope; and to international delegates who support their efforts.

Ongoing Summits

In March 2006, we managed to bring 17 delegates from Iraq—despite challenges of obtaining visas—to a Summit of Iraqi and U.S. women. The meeting of 110 women was made possible through generous donations of individuals, without government or foundation money. More healing dialogues are planned to explore ways for women to network, and to alleviate suffering in the world.

Chapter 34

From the Trauma Vortex to the Healing Vortex: A New Paradigm for Healing the Israeli-Palestinian Crisis

Gina Ross

An orthodox Jew from Kfar Saba who lost his brother in a suicide bombing believed all Arabs were enemies. During a training that I developed for Israelis and Palestinians to learn to heal their trauma, this man sat next to an Israeli Arab man from Nazareth. When I asked the participants in the group to pair with their neighbor and look at each other silently for a few minutes, concentrating on the other's ability to heal, the Jewish participant shared that: "At first, I felt tension rise in my body, thinking I couldn't possibly imagine looking so closely at the face of an enemy and even less see his capacity to heal. But as I got into my 'felt sense,' and focused on the constricted sensation in my belly, I watched the tension dissipate and release; and the layers of enemy images slowly dropped from my eyes to be replaced by the eyes and face of the man in front of me who had a wife and children, and who loved and suffered just like me. At the end, all I could see was his humanness and vulnerability."

In another joint training for Israeli and Palestinians journalists that I led, a Palestinian from Ramallah disclosed how much he resented the Israeli settlements and how hard this made it to connect with Israelis in general and settlers in particular. After the first day, he was truly excited to "learn the 'ins and outs' of his autonomic nervous system and his innate ability to calm the restlessness and anxiety held in his body," and was able to connect with a settler journalist. He began to acknowledge the complexity of the situation, and recognize how the Palestinian/Arab media amplified his people's rage and exacerbated their helplessness, which made them extol a violence that oppressed them even more than it hurt their enemy.

This journalist embraced the idea that he could contribute to the healing between the two peoples by writing an article about how the conflict can be seen from another perspective. He wrote an article about the pregnancy of the mother of Dura—the first child killed in the Intifada—to elicit hope and compassion in his readers rather than exacerbating their rage.

The stories of both of these men demonstrate dramatically how Israelis and Palestinians have been caught in what I call a "trauma vortex" and how they can emerge into a "healing vortex" that in essence heals the pains that fuel the conflict.

This chapter describes the model that I have developed that explains the impact of trauma on conflicts between groups and nations—including the Israeli-Palestinian problem in particular—and its application with groups of Israelis and Palestinians. By adopting a paradigm shift from the trauma vortex to the healing vortex, governments, media, and international bodies can collaborate in identifying trauma as a root cause of violence, and contribute solutions to prevent its escalation and facilitate the prospect for peace.

After eight years of studying the Middle East conflict and doing workshops with Israelis and Palestinians, it has become clear to me that no lasting resolution of this conflict is possible until personal and collective traumas are better healed. The painful stories from Israeli and Palestinian participants in the trauma healing trainings I have conducted reveal how suffering pervades the national psyche of both peoples and leaves a tremendous impact in its wake. This impact distorts narratives and polarizes beliefs and emotions, perpetuating the conflict. Differences that normally could be dealt with become unacceptable and even intolerable, leading to dehumanizing and demonizing each other (Ross, 2003a).

The Ross Model, which I developed, works with what I call the "collective nervous system" and introduces the metaphors of the *trauma vortex* and the *healing vortex*, terms that differentiate between destructive and constructive ways of meeting collective needs and that present approaches to conflict resolution.

Trauma Vortex, Healing Vortex, and Collective Trauma Vortex

As described by Dr. Peter Levine, biophysicist, researcher on stress, and creator of Somatic Experiencing Theory (SE), the trauma vortex and healing vortex metaphors illustrate the "accelerating and amplifying devastation of trauma as well as the inherent ability to neutralize it"(Levine, 1992), while the collective trauma vortex and collective healing vortex illustrate its application at mass levels (Ross, 2003b, 2005).

The *trauma vortex* refers to the self-perpetuating, dynamic, and escalating spiral of trauma's pain and confusion. This whirlpool of intrusive traumatic memories creates hopelessness and helplessness due to traumatized people's inability to control their physiology, emotions, thoughts, and behavior, now dominated by fear or rage. When a person is stuck in the trauma vortex, the sense of normalcy evaporates; prior understanding of the world and one's place in it are shaken; the world itself becomes unpredictable, making it easier to give up on morality and responsibility. Ensuing polarized beliefs, principles, and feelings make intolerance, revenge, and violence seem the only viable responses.

The *healing vortex* refers to humankind's innate capacity to cope with and heal from tragedy, a capacity for resiliency extolled by all ancient mystical systems and recently confirmed by psychological research, which shows that approximately 75 percent of people exposed to trauma cope on their own, without developing PTSD (Van der Kolk, Bessel, MacFarlane, & Weisaeth, 1996). A percentage of the remainder were thought to have irreparable brain damage, but fortunately, research confirming the brain's flexibility and ability to form new regenerative neural connections suggests that our organism can be brought back into balance (Siegel, 1999).

Clinical findings in SE, gathered during treatments done after the tsunami in Thailand and South India (Selvam, 2005), have further validated a remarkable finding—that within the traumatic event is contained the seed of healing; that is, in most cases, basic survival responses and extreme states of deregulation do not endure, as human beings appear also to be hard-wired to self-regulate their survival physiology back to health. However, when traumatic events overwhelm our physiology or persist for whatever reason, they can become a source of trauma symptoms and we fixate in the trauma vortex. Awareness and resources reenergize the healing vortex.

The *collective trauma vortex* metaphor refers to the impulsive and self-destructive behavior of a group. The Ross Model, applying the trauma and healing vortices concepts to collective levels, uses "collective trauma" to describe trauma's impact on communities and nations (Ross, 2003a) and expands those concepts to the collective group or society. Nations caught in a collective trauma vortex have great difficulty focusing on long-term viable solutions for their problems and express suffering in ways destructive to themselves and to others. Unresolved trauma's most serious long-term consequence is violence among nations.

Traumatic Narratives

The trauma vortex is contagious and its pull is magnetic. When activated, it totally absorbs people's attention. Obsession with what happened to them contaminates a people's consciousness, amplifying their *traumatic narrative*, which becomes increasingly distorted. Shaped around their status as victims, their narrative creates a righteous and deep belief that they have been greatly wronged and only they are good. They develop paranoia and mistrust toward others and in others.

Traumatized nations relive traumatic memories through cultural narratives, stories, folklore, art, and history. They become vulnerable to manipulation by powerful or dysfunctional leaders who use government-run media to evoke old traumatic memories (Staub, 1989). Replayed incessantly, these images create a distressing hyperarousal difficult to reverse, leading to violence and war.

Trauma, which alters people's biological balance, spurs an inwardly driven sense of danger and threat, drawing people to violent reenactments, in the hope of finally mastering the deep wounds of trauma (Levine, 2000).

On the hopeful side, awareness and discharging of traumatic energy can break the destructive cycle of reenactment.

The Collective Trauma Vortex in Groups or Nations

Traumatized groups or nations, like traumatized individuals, organize their identities by focusing on a common enemy, seeking justice for perceived torts, and creating a pseudo-unity.

When nations are in the throes of a collective trauma vortex, their reasoning capacity is lost, and their emotions hijacked by the brain's amygdala; unfulfilled basic needs make them more vulnerable to violent behavior. Nations eventually pull out of the trauma vortex, but such a vortex may lie dormant, only to re-emerge years, decades, or centuries later, prompted by anniversary dates, danger, or events reminiscent of the original trauma.

The Palestinian-Israeli Trauma Vortex

The Israeli and Palestinian populations seem to have overwhelming traumatic histories. Both are in the clutches of a "multiple vortex," fed by different events and people (Ross, 2001).

The Palestinian Experience

The Palestinian collective memory holds traumatic images of defeat, occupation and economic dependence, settlements, fence and border closures, with the people's daily livelihood at the mercy of a political process controlled by their autocratic leaders.

They have lost homes and land; their pride and hopes were dashed; they live in neighboring Arab countries, not allowed to assimilate lest it mean tacit acceptance of the existence of Israel.

Their leaders gave them false hopes, diverting much of foreign aid into fighting the Israelis. Their children are impoverished and schooled in revolution and hatred through school curriculum and camp activities. At the United Nations, Arab nations have discouraged them from making concessions to further the peace process. They have also been killed or expelled from Arab countries.

Most significant, Arabs and Palestinians perceive the existence of Israel as a humiliation to the Arab world and an affront to Islam, and an injustice done to Palestinians, who were not responsible for the Holocaust.

The Jewish Experience

The Jews have been accused of deicide, oppressed, expelled, and massacred over the centuries. Victims of systematic genocide, and haunted by the Holocaust's unspeakable atrocities, the Jews still struggle against ever-present anti-Semitism worldwide, suicide bombings of civilians, lynching of soldiers, and massive Holocaust denial in the Arab world.

At the United Nations they face a polarized Euro-Arab geopolitical, cultural, and economical alliance. Violent anti-Jewish and anti-Israeli Arab and European propaganda has exacerbated their fears and mistrust regarding Arab intentions toward Israeli Jews. Jews believe the media have misrepresented Middle East events, supporting the Palestinian cause. Their social fabric has been torn by ago-nizing doubts and internal disagreements over the occupation, creating hatred and intolerance between groups inside of Israel and concerns over civil war.

Jews have been fighting for land they believe belongs to them. By returning to their biblical land, their presence awakened the Arab world, motivating renewed aspirations for Arab/Muslim hegemony. They constantly fight for survival, all the while creating a haven for Middle Eastern and Russian Jewish refugees.

Characteristics of the Ross Collective Trauma Vortex

Understanding the dynamics of collective trauma in general and its applica-tion to the Israeli-Palestinian vortex in particular may be critical. The duration of a collective vortex may depend on (1) the momentum behind it, (2) the depth of the unresolved trauma and the amount of present misunderstood and unmet needs of the populations, (3) its impact on the global community, and (4) the subsequent interventions of outside forces. For example, Sudan and Rwanda were not important for the international community and the killings were in the hundreds of thousands or in the millions, while the Serbian conflict was impor-tant for the Americans and they intervened to stop it.

A nation eventually escapes its trauma. The vortex runs out of steam when people are no longer willing to pay the price of its aftermath or when other pow-ers intervene. But it will return. We cannot afford to let active collective trauma vortices keep spiraling, or to be ignorant of ones that can evolve. Seeing the signs is crucial.

Signs of Collective Trauma in Groups and Nations

The following checklist allows us to recognize a collective vortex in action. This is evident in the example of Nazi Germany, where the government was able to engage a significant part of its population in its programs (Staub, 1989).

- Elevating a group's ethnicity, race, religion, or economy over those of "the other"
- Promoting ethnic, racial, religious, and political "cleansing"
- Suspending critical thinking, and surrendering individuality to destructive pseudo higher causes
- Labeling and blaming "the other" for all one's suffering and problems
- Believing the destruction of "the other" will solve their problems
- Distrusting anything originating from "the other," even when positive
- Manifesting signs of xenophobia: forbidding, removing, or destroying all reli-gious, cultural, and artistic symbols of foreign influence
- Not accepting any responsibility in the origin or outcome of conflicts

- Demonizing and dehumanizing "the other"; portraying them as evil, incapable, and unworthy of compassion; generalizing the actions of some to the whole group
- Using belligerent language regarding other groups or nations
- Viewing violence as the only means to regain control and save face
- Instilling hatred in children, inciting them to violence and revenge against "the other"
- Repressing the media in all forms
- Encouraging killing and genocide.

Factors That Contribute to a Collective Trauma Vortex

Similar to health risk factors, there are collective trauma risk factors. These include:

- Difficult life circumstances
- Threat to physical and emotional well-being; humiliation
- Vulnerable and distorted societal self-concept
- Major changes in the political system in less than 10 years
- Anxiety
- Disruption of values, traditions, and lifestyle
- Economic stagnation
- Military defeat.

Cultural Influences That Contribute to a Collective Trauma Vortex

These include:

- A strong cultural tradition for authority and respect for leaders that overrides dissent and the need for checks and balances
- A history of violence in which aggression is a respected and idealized way of handling conflict as opposed to a necessary evil
- Built-in systematic devaluation of another group in the culture or religious dogmas, inciting the longing for "purity" and "cleansing"
- Cultural tendency to impose religious or racial values over others; mandate to enlarge the group's territory; lack of cultural flexibility.

Universal Basic Needs

Groups and nations, like individuals, have universal basic needs. Understanding these basic needs can help conflict resolution experts design and adopt measures to help satisfy those needs. These include safety, sovereignty, identity, respect, positive self-image, competence, connection, having a place/role in the world, validation of one's experience and reality, and trust in others and being trustworthy.

Examples of Needs Distorted by Trauma

An ex-radical Palestinian supported the implementation of my trainings when I explained that Palestinian suicide bombers are an example of attempts to fulfill basic needs in destructive ways—to regain self-esteem and control at the expense of the safety of their own children, the lives of Israeli children, and their own economy.

Many Israelis have now recognized that labeling, blame, and retaliation (instead of defensive force) for Palestinian suicide bombings and killings were attempts to implement security measures (intensified by escalating suicide bombings) that backfired. They exacerbated the Palestinian vortex, triggering their pride and further support for suicide bombings, and shocked public opinion.

Both these strategies can be seen as miscalculations brought upon by the intensity of the trauma vortex, in which victims become victimizers and again victims. If both cultures could bring themselves to understand their own trauma vortex and that of the other, through their philosophers, media, leading clergy members, and through joint projects, they would be able to invest their energies recovering from trauma instead of escalating it.

What Each Side Can Do to Engage the Healing Vortex

Israelis and Palestinians perhaps are being called to serve as examples of the development of new and different understandings of conflict resolution between nations.

If Arabs could understand that Jews came to Palestine not to colonize them but in search of their sacred land, it may reduce their trauma vortex. Many remember that in the past, and even today, in some places peoples of these cultures lived well together. Jews lived mostly peacefully in Arab countries before Israel existed. While Arabs nations still refuse to accept a Jewish state in the Holy Land, some of them are indeed accepting this fact. The international community must encourage them to accept Israel and make it beneficial to them. It needs to validate Arab outrage that foreign powers carved up the Middle East. Israel, in due course, may remind the Arabs that the Torah acknowledges the greatness of the Muslim nation, and invite them to be an example to the world of how to overcome anti-Semitism. With the help of the West, they can appeal to moderate and orthodox Islam's more peaceful orientation, which could counteract the Islamists, the radical Islamic fundamentalists.

Both Israelis and Palestinians want the issue of refugees to be addressed. Israelis know they have to be able to absorb Jewish diaspora in distress. Similarly, Palestinians who become confident that there is enough land to provide for their population growth and for the exiled brothers wanting to return to Palestinian territories may give up wanting the whole land.

If each side were to continue succumbing to their traumatic reactions, it will be an incalculable cost in loss of humanity and integrity for both populations and for the world. The international community must understand and address all the components involved in this ongoing trauma vortex if it wants to succeed in stopping its devastation, and facilitate Middle East and world healing.

Guidelines for Fulfilling Collective Needs within the Healing Vortex

Understanding the interrelated dynamics of trauma and violence allows us to recognize when nations are under the influence of the trauma vortex, and alter or slow it down. Early detection and warning are important. Once a collective vortex is in full swing, consciousness fades, and the vortex's insidious growth becomes difficult to halt. It may take forceful and severe diplomatic sanctions or military action—like the Serbian/Kosovan war—or a technological discovery to stop its destructive path. We encourage the healing vortex by offering safe forums for venting anger and seeking justice, such as the South African Truth and Reconciliation Commissions, facilitating reparations, mediation, and helping nations in trauma reconnect with their natural resources.

We have developed guiding principles that help steer nations out of the trauma vortex and help them meet their needs in healthy ways:

- The measures adopted to help resolve conflicts need to work for both parties involved
- The healing vortex must promote the fulfillment of most of the groups' needs without sacrificing the needs of others
- It is essential to validate negative feelings without condoning destructive actions. Traumatized groups are often convinced their actions are the only possible choice and believe their costs are inevitable. The following questions can help them evaluate the efficiency of their actions:
  - Are groups or nations meeting all or most of their basic needs?
  - Are they achieving a real or pseudo safety and autonomy? Is their sense of military power enhanced at the expense of their economy and infrastructure?
  - Do their actions bring them self-esteem and the respect of an unbiased international community? Do they help them receive validation for their suffering, or do they make them feel more isolated?
  - Are their goals informed by the trauma or the healing vortex?
  - Are they being efficient and constructive in meeting their needs?
  - Are their actions making them trust others and earning them the trust of others?
  - Is their behavior giving them a meaningful role in the world? Does it give meaning to their nation, religion, or culture in a way that is respected by all?
  - Ultimately, do the actions taken fulfill *all or most of the basic needs* without adversely affecting the needs of others?

The Ross Model: Healing the Vortices Involved in the Middle East Conflict

Working with the Collective Nervous System

The International Trauma-Healing Institute sponsors the development and application of the Ross Model, a practical program designed to bring awareness to the role trauma plays in conflicts between nations and helps resolve them by healing collective trauma, which will also bring relief to individuals caught in long-term conflict.

The model encourages governmental bodies to analyze trauma's role in regional or international conflicts (if a defenseless group is being massacred while not engaging in any kind of violence themselves, the international community needs to use immediate force to protect them). The model addresses collective traumas by engaging all social sectors that can help activate collective healing. These include the media, clergy, military, diplomats, NGOs, and peace workers, educators, mental and medical health workers, and the justice system.

Workshops for these groups promote shared understanding by introducing a universal language to help all these sectors recognize and address the consequences of collective trauma, develop measures to stop its effects, and provide care for traumatized nations. A positive side effect is to help the public develop resiliency against trauma. The model cautions that, today, no part of humanity can think of obliterating another part without risking obliterating itself. If enough moderate voices resist the pull of the vortex, and declare to the world their understanding of what's happening, they can raise the collective consciousness. The Ross Model recommends that nations in the trauma vortex be helped to reconnect with their collective resources—beliefs, traditions, myths, heroes, and art—which help their people feel calmer, safer, and more in control of their destiny.

People will transform their trauma vortex into a healing one more readily if they are respected, their identity is recognized, and their dignity restored. Nations engaged in collective healing are more likely to come together, for example, Japan and the United States after World War II.

The Ross Model Activities

For the past five years, ITI has offered trainings to Israelis and Palestinians to help them cope with their ongoing traumatization.

The workshops, designed for 25 to 35 professionals at a time and consisting of two nine-hour sessions, are didactic and experiential. They are led by trained professionals with several assistants, and have been held in hotels, trauma centers, the Center for Journalism, and at both Ministries of Education, in Jerusalem, Haifa, Tel Aviv, and Ramallah.

The participants are taught Somatic Experiencing tools, such as "tracking" and "titrating" sensations, "resourcing," "pendulating," and discharging traumatic energy, to practice coping skills.

On day one, participants learn to recognize signs of traumatic stress in others and in their own physiology, emotions, thoughts, and behavior. They learn to build their resilience by identifying their strengths and resources. They also learn that focusing for a short period of time on uncomfortable inner constricted sensations generated by a traumatic experience actually allows those sensations to shift and move through this body, relaxing the body, and reestablishing its natural balance—the foundation for self-esteem. Noticing sensations with neutral curiosity, observing them without dissociating, labeling, judging, or criticizing, can release and heal traumatic experiences.

Working in pairs, they look for innate and involuntary sensations of release that come up organically when reviewing trauma, such as vibrations, trembling, and shaking, thereby recuperating their instinctual survival processes. Participants are often amazed at how the plain awareness of their inner landscapes of sensations and reconnecting with their resources helps them not only release old and fixated traumatic energies, but also change negative beliefs and feel more empowered.

On day two, they use situations appropriate to their field to practice identifying signs of individual or collective trauma and applying their sector's skills to engage healing. They share without blame and criticism, and explore the peaceful advantages of understanding their own and their adversary's vortex, and ways to help reduce it instead of amplifying it.

Participants tell us how much they appreciate "having a clear structure that allows them to track when they are activated and in the 'trauma vortex'" and that shows them how to discharge and engage their healing vortex. They welcome having a choice to serve the healing vortex, and to become positive influences for conflict resolution.

Addressing the Different Sectors

Booklets in support of the training help the participants recognize how they may unwittingly trigger trauma—either individual or collective—in the course of their specific field of work, and offer precise guidelines to ease the effects of collective trauma.

The Role of Diplomats and NGOs

Diplomatic personnel and all individuals exposed but not directly involved in a conflict have the opportunity to reduce trauma by recommending policies and measures that help diminish collective trauma (Ross, 2003a, 2005b). These "active outsiders" must follow the model that trauma also naturally triggers a healing vortex. The Marshall Plan is an excellent example of transformative healing naturally following trauma. Remembering these possibilities can help reframe seemingly unsolvable situations and offer new options.

The Role of the International Community

What interventions would an international community, intent on helping transcend the trauma vortex, carry out? It would be aware that taking sides is harmful to peace, that it would simply deepen the sense of victimization, inflexibility, alienation, and violence of the parties involved (Ross, 2005a, 2005b). In the Israeli-Palestinian case, it would send unequivocal messages. It will not stand for the destruction of Israel or the occupation of a Palestinian population. It would encourage Israel to use only defensive/protective and not retaliatory force, ensuring Israel's right to defend its citizens from harm, while supporting sparing Palestinian civil lives. It would help Israel reassure the Palestinians of its intent to facilitate an independent Palestinian state if Israel's security needs are met and help Israel integrate culturally in the Middle East by supporting joint projects.

The international community can alert the Palestinians that their media's violent rhetoric and their support of suicide bombers rekindle the Jewish trauma of genocide and perpetuate the Israelis' mistrust, pushing them to strengthen their security. It can encourage all Arabs to curtail anti-Jewish/Israeli propaganda, to compromise and see a shared future. It can enlist the international media to report stories of common efforts to encourage the healing vortex.

The international community would help contain the shared grief carried in the bodies, experiences, stories, and cultures of both populations. True resolution and peace in the Middle East can only come from this level of intention and commitment and from the international community. The international community needs to explore the measures it needs to take to do all of these things.

The Role of the Media

Informed political analysts, broadcasters, and foreign correspondents can alert the public about the impact of traumatic responses on political developments, and shed light on how to mitigated or neutralize it. If uninformed about the trauma vortex, they can trigger it or unwittingly exacerbate an existing vortex (Ross, 2003b). Anything adding fear, helplessness, passivity, panic, or exaggeration of threat amplifies the trauma vortex. Anything promoting understanding, tolerance, creativity, hope, and kindness encourages the healing vortex.

The media can report on attempts at restraint and reason on both sides. They must avoid exploiting and flashing traumatic images repeatedly on the screen, which escalate the conflict. They must avoid being used for distorting facts to gain world sympathy by people who create violent scenes just for the media lenses. They can:

- Provide reliable and factual information and avoid speculation
- Evaluate whether their words and images feed or diminish trauma
- Humanize both sides of a conflict
- Validate suffering while still making people aware they are using destructive means of meeting needs
- Actively engage both parties' healing vortex, helping them construct a narrative not distorted by trauma
- Report healing and justice rituals
- Create radio shows, television programs, and films supporting the healing vortex, encouraging hope and trust, and showing people's capacity to care.

The Role of Other Social Sectors

The other social sectors can support collective healing by identifying trauma among their constituency, recognizing how they may unintentionally amplify trauma, and helping heal traumatized individuals.

Doctors participating in my trainings have realized that updated knowledge about trauma could help them identify (and refer for trauma treatment) up to 70 percent of the presenting medical complaints they see and cannot heal, as they are often-baffling symptoms of trauma, not clearly connected to the original event.

A clergy member in one of the trainings, seeing adversaries connecting with each others' suffering during the training, said: "I am amazed to see that people from many opposing factions, all nod in agreement at your presentation of collective trauma. I can now recognize how trauma disconnects people from their spirituality, and how it is now possible for me to identify my traumatized congregants and help them overcome the shame and despair that comes with trauma" (Ross, 2005b).

After the training, teachers, educational psychologists, and counselors felt capable of identifying unrecognized child traumas labeled as "learning disorders" or "behavioral problems" (Ross, 2005).

A military, aware of trauma's impact on its decisions, can attempt to make more rational war decisions along ethical guidelines. Palestinians requested a program for their police, and we are presently exploring the possibility of helping strengthen Israeli Border Police resiliency to war trauma, during battle and after (Ross, 2005b).

Summary and Conclusion

In joint trainings offered to journalists, psychotherapists, doctors, or educators, Israelis, Palestinians, and Israeli Arabs have worked together by helping one another with their fears. In all groups, participants welcomed the choices that the experiences gave them to free themselves from the trauma vortex and engage their healing vortex after traumatic events. This helped them recognize they could live together, demonstrating that workshops that focused on discharging people's trauma and engaging their healing vortex allowed them to reconnect to their desire for peace and normalcy.

References

Levine, P. (2000). *Trauma—The vortex of violence.* Retrieved on December 1, 2005, from www.traumahealing.com/resources.html.

Levine, P. (2001). *We are all neighbors.* Retrieved on December 1, 2005, from www.traumahealing.com/resources.html.

Levine, P. A. (1992). *Waking the tiger: Healing trauma.* Berkeley, CA: North Atlantic Books.

Ross, G. (2001). *The trauma vortex in action again in the Middle East.* Retrieved August 30, 2003 from www.traumainstitute.org/articles.php.

Ross, G. (2003a). *The political trauma vortex.* Retrieved from www.traumainstitute.org/articles.php.

Ross, G. (2003b). *Beyond the trauma vortex: The media's role in healing fear, terror and violence.* Berkeley, CA: North Atlantic Books.

Ross, G. (2003c). *Beyond the trauma vortex: Guidelines from trauma to healing for the media.* [Self-published].

Ross, G. (2005a). *Multiple vortexes affecting the Palestinian-Israeli conflict.* Retrieved from www.traumainstitute.org/articles.php.

Ross, G. (2005b, Fall). The political trauma vortex. *Viewpoint Magazine.* 49–57.

Ross, G. *Series Booklets: Beyond the trauma vortex: Guidelines from trauma to healing for (1) diplomats and NGOs, (2) the educational field, (3) the medical field, (4) the mental health field, (5) the military, (6) the clergy.* (In progress)

Selvam, R. (2005, November). Treating tsunami survivors for trauma. *Journal of Holistic Healthcare, 2*(4), 36–39.

Siegel, D. J. (1999). *The developing mind.* New York: Guilford Press.

Staub, E. (1989). *The roots of evil.* Cambridge, UK: Cambridge University Press.

Van der Kolk, B. A., MacFarlane, A. C., & Weisaeth, L. (1996). *Traumatic stress: A psychological and research perspective on trauma.* New York: Guilford Press.

CHAPTER 35

PALESTINIAN-ISRAELI COOPERATION ON MENTAL HEALTH TRAINING: GAZA COMMUNITY MENTAL HEALTH PROGRAM AND TEL AVIV UNIVERSITY, 1993–2007

Tamar Zelniker, Eyad El Sarraj, and
Rachel Hertz-Lazarowitz

This chapter is about a long-term, 14-year partnership between mental health professionals from Gaza and mental health professionals from Israel and what we learned from this endeavor. While the content of the project is mental health training, the project is evidently also about psychology and peace in the Middle East. This chapter describes the background of the partnership and its different phases spanning 14 years, points out some of the difficulties encountered, and proposes an assessment of its sustainability.

The Palestinian partners included 10 psychologists, social workers, and psychiatrists who work at the Gaza Community Mental Health Program (GCMHP). The clinic is an NGO, with several branches in the Gaza Strip and total staff of almost 200. The Israeli partners included 10 psychologists and psychiatrists, most of them from Tel Aviv University.

The background of the project was the increasing need for mental health services in Gaza, with the needs augmented by the protracted Palestinian-Israeli conflict. The Gaza clinic specializes in posttraumatic stress disorder (PTSD), working with children, families, and with adults.

The main goal of the partnership was to enable training and specialization of psychologists, social workers, and psychiatrists in order to establish a cadre of Palestinian professionals needed to provide mental health services in Gaza. Another goal was to develop professional projects that would advance and expand the Israeli and Palestinian partners' knowledge and understanding of background conditions and how these inform professional needs within the different social and cultural milieus.

For several years prior to 1993, the group from Gaza experienced a great variety of training courses and workshops provided by volunteer mental health professionals from around the world. While enjoying the multitude, the Gaza group decided that the diversified menu provided by the occasional visitors did not add up to a comprehensive plan, and set out to pursue a coherent program that would provide the knowledge and skills they wished to acquire.

Following a meeting of a group of Palestinian and Israeli mental health professionals in the summer of 1992 in Lisbon under the auspices of the European Union, participants from the Gaza clinic and from the group of the Israeli mental health professionals conducted a series of meetings in Tel Aviv. In these meetings the Gaza group expressed concern about their scant, disjointed training experiences and their quest for a coherent training program in psychotherapy. Subsequently, together, we planned our professional cooperation, which began in April 1993.

The Different Phases

The activities can be divided into three phases.

Phase 1: 1993–1997

We began the project in April 1993, which was at the peak of the first Intifada. In this phase, nine Palestinians, who constituted the main group of therapists in the Gaza clinic, came one day each week to Tel Aviv University to attend a three-year program of Continuing Studies in Psychotherapy. The program became a formal, integral part of Tel Aviv University's curriculum and included courses in psychopathology, psychotherapy, child psychotherapy, psychodrama, comparative theory of self and object, short-term therapy, group therapy, and group clinical supervision. While the three-year program extended over a period of four and a half years due to delays caused by the political situation and frequent closures imposed on Gaza, all nine Gaza participants completed the program successfully and obtained the program certificates.

Phase 2: 1997–2007 and Continuing

In the second phase, the Gaza clinic embarked on the establishment of a program of psychotherapy training in Gaza. Its goal was to offer a program of studies in community mental health. For this purpose, the Gaza clinic engaged international partners from universities around the world, including Tel Aviv University. The international partners are mental health professionals and social scientists from universities in Australia, Tunis, the United States, Holland, Norway, England, Israel, and Gaza. The structure and content of the program was designed by all participants with special attention to the specific conditions and needs in Gaza. The curriculum includes courses in human rights, developmental psychology, social psychology, communication, community mental health, clinical psychology, psychotherapy, and practical training in clinics and hospitals. Tel Aviv University provided the clinical psychology course as well as clinical supervision one day each week.

The international representatives constituted the initial teaching resources in the program and were accompanied by local Gaza clinic teachers who have been gradually taking over increasing portions of the teaching load. The international partners serve also as the academic board of the program, meeting once a year to evaluate the program and draft necessary modifications. The program has been operative since 1997 and in November 1999, we celebrated, in Gaza, the graduation of the first group of students. Program graduates assume jobs at GCMHP or other clinics and hospitals in Gaza. During the past six years, with the growing political conflict and increasing military and violent actions, it has become difficult to carry out the full program, and modifications are performed as necessary.

Phase 3: 2000–2001

The third phase, conducted in parallel with the second phase, constituted a research and training project. The research was on the psychological effects and resilience of elementary school children exposed to trauma on their psychological well-being as adolescents. Interviews and the administration of questionnaires and tests took place in Gaza. Training at Tel Aviv University entailed a course in qualitative analyses techniques, which were needed for processing the interview and questionnaire materials collected in this research project, as well as for future research materials to be collected and analyzed. The research program in Gaza progressed as planned and was completed in 2001, but the teaching activities at Tel Aviv University were disrupted in October 2000 due to the outbreak of the second Intifada.

Presently, we are trying to set up video-conference equipment in both Gaza and Tel Aviv University in order to resume the third phase of the project via distance learning. We also plan to use this equipment for teaching the clinical psychology course at the Community Mental Health Program of studies in Gaza, and to resume clinical supervision on a regular basis.

Difficulties Encountered

Along the way we faced considerable difficulty due to the incessant and escalating political strife. Political difficulties were manifested in administrative-organizational hurdles and in professional-personal strain. Administrative obstacles caused by the Israeli government included the refusal of entry permits to the Gaza group, and difficulties while crossing the checkpoint from Gaza to Israel even when such permits were granted. Another organizational obstacle was imposed by the Gaza clinic administrative board. As a response to severe measures taken by the Israeli government and in line with a decision taken by the Palestinian Authority at that time, the board boycotted all cooperation with Israelis. Consequently, our cooperation work in the latter part of the 1990s stopped once, for three months, and a second time, for almost six months.

Professional and personal manifestations of the political conflict pertain to contents raised and to the Israeli partners' role. The content of clinical cases discussed in training and in clinical supervision, as well as the content of issues raised at our academic board meetings, was often related to the political conflict. Emotion-laden examples were the Palestinian trauma cases resulting from actions taken by Israeli soldiers. The cases were presented by the Gaza partners to the Israeli partners, who proceeded to discuss the cases and advance the treatment of these patients. Other instances were inherently paradoxical, when the Palestinian partners who experienced at times extreme frustration with the conflict, depicted the Israeli partners as representing the Israeli government. At the same time, the Israeli partners' role as mental health professionals was to soothe the mental and emotional strain by containing the anger and by alleviating the frustration.

Although we encountered frequent physical difficulties and emotional strain, we maintained our partnership for more than 14 years.

Sustainability—An Assessment

According to the contact hypothesis (Amir, 1969), various conditions should be met in order for contact between groups that are parties to a conflict to be successful. Mutuality and equality of status and power are among the most crucial conditions required, as is the condition of achieving a common goal (Sherif, Harvey, White, Hood, & Sherif, 1961). In line with these principles, failure of interactions between conflicting groups is often attributed to their absence (Ben-Ari, 2004). In most Palestinian-Israeli cooperation projects, participants take particular care to foster mutuality, equality, and shared common goals. Yet, reality renders the two groups unequal, and under such conditions, true mutuality and common goals are difficult, if not impossible, to achieve. Even when conditions of specific projects permit meaningful mutuality, this does not change the political reality and the inequality in reality remains (Nadler & Liviatan, 2004). It is against the background of this reality as well as the generally accepted criticisms of the contact hypothesis that we assess our partnership.

We believe that our staying power is based on a number of significant factors:

1. The focus of our relationship is *professional* (psychotherapy training), rather than political, or on group dynamics and coexistence. The latter have been common pitfalls of numerous cooperation projects. Our coexistence is a positive outcome of our professional undertaking.

2. We share *common professional goals*. While the groups differ in basic interests and goals, we share a common end product as our paramount goal. The Palestinians expressed practical needs in terms of psychotherapy training and a concrete objective in the form of professional certificates. The Israelis expressed the desire for cooperation that would lead to future accord and harmony and operated on the basis of personal needs to do what they considered to be humane and moral in face of their government policies and actions. The end goal, which consisted of the completion of the Continuing Studies in Psychotherapy at Tel Aviv

University and the establishment of the Community Mental Health Program of Studies in Gaza, enabled partners in both groups to attain feelings of accomplishment and provided an opportunity for further developments.

3. Our communication and discussions of the form and the content of our partnership are based on *mutuality and equality*. While mutuality has been a solid principle of all phases of decision making, the issue of equality was more complex. The groups were not equal: the Israelis had many years of professional experience that enabled them to acquire substantial professional knowledge. Yet, the Palestinians' firm conviction in what they conceived to be their professional needs rendered them an equally powerful partner in the dialogue. Thus, while the two groups drew their strength from different sources, we perceive the power of the two groups to be ultimately balanced.

4. Partners on both sides shared a sense of *personal commitment* and resolve as well as faith in, and vision of, peaceful coexistence. In face of the ever-worsening political realities that produced, at times, insurmountable obstacles, personal commitment, persistence, and even stubbornness of partners in both groups enabled us to overcome the obstacles, and hence, enabled the continuation of the project.

5. Our prolonged *interaction promoted mutual trust and friendship*. Our interaction led to trust and friendship among participants. It also led participants from each group to accept heterogeneity in the other national group, which prior to this partnership represented the "enemy."

6. Partners to the project who were not partners to the regional conflict served as meaningful *external agents that mediated the alliance* in its different phases:

   a. Our initial acquaintance, 14 years ago, took place in Lisbon, under the auspices of the European Union. This setting enabled communication with the external agents, mitigating the complex, and at times, flaring, conflict between the parties.

   b. The first phase of the partnership was supported by Canadian and U.S. cooperation programs. These external agents were able to intervene in ways that alleviated stress and apprehension.

   c. The mental health program of studies established in Gaza by partners from eight universities around the world set the Palestinian-Israeli partnership within a wider context, attenuating the conflict by providing a safe space, and espousing the use of English as the common and neutral language.

Conclusions

We have maintained our partnership for more than 14 years, even though we did not escape the political context that has been looming large, and at times, cast a dark shadow on all of us. In fact, much of the content that came up in the training and supervision as well as at our academic board meetings had to do with the occupation and required a high level of tolerance and containment. Indeed, this ongoing challenge was met by the participating mental health professionals of both groups.

We learned that even when the political situation gets extremely difficult, we can maintain our strength and hope. The factors that appear to be most significant for maintaining our partnership are mutuality, personal commitment, and the professional framework that enabled the development of personal relationships, trust, and friendship.

Recent advances at GCMHP include a significant increase in the size of programs and services provided, and in the number of mental health personnel. Professional development of the primary GCMHP group of psychotherapists culminated in their formal completion of the continuation studies program at Tel Aviv University in 1997. More recently, several GCMHP members attained advanced degrees, including PhDs.

Members of the academic board of the international program at GCMHP continue to hold annual meetings evaluating the international program's structure and operations, as well as its academic contents and teaching. Recommendations provided by the academic board introduce new ideas and constructive suggestions, which, at times, may present a challenge to GCMHP training management and operations, but in general, constitute a significant contribution to the enhancement of clinical training and research at GCMHP. Recently, GCMHP revised its structure and operations in order to enhance its clinical services as well as human rights training for various Palestinian Authority institutions and Palestinian NGOs.

The Israeli and Palestinian partners' long-term involvement in and commitment to this cooperation yielded mutual personal trust and professional appreciation and esteem. On this background, it has been particularly frustrating to experience recurring difficulties in our recent attempts to obtain support for equipment for distance learning. Such equipment could enable cooperation during the present political strife while we cannot cross the order between Gaza and Israel.

At present, our cooperation consists of developing new joint research projects and capacity-building programs, including advanced courses that we plan to conduct via video conference with periodic meetings in neighboring countries.

References

This chapter is based in part on a paper presented at the Middle East and North Africa Regional Conference of Psychology, December 13–18, 2003, Dubai, United Arab Emirates.

Amir, Y. (1969). Contact hypothesis in ethnic relations. *Psychological Bulletin, 71,* 319–342.

Ben-Ari, R. (2004). Coping with the Jewish-Arab conflict: A comparison among three models. *Journal of Social Issues, 60*(2), 307–322.

Hertz-Lazarowitz, R., & Zelniker, T. (2004). Can peace education be enhanced via participatory research? Three case studies at Haifa University 2001–2003. *Peace Research, 36*(1), 119–134.

Hertz-Lazarowitz, R., Zelniker, T., White-Stephan, C., & Stephan, W. G. (2004). (Eds.). Arab-Jewish coexistence programs. *Journal of Social Issues, 60*(2), 237–452.

Nadler, A., & Liviatan, I. (2004). Intergroup reconciliation processes in Israel: Theoretical analysis and empirical findings. In N. R. Branscombe & B. Doosje (Eds.), *Collective guilt: International perspectives* (pp. 216–236). New York: Cambridge University Press.

Sherif, M., Harvey, O. J., White, B. J., Hood, W. R., & Sherif, C. W. (1961). *Inter-group conflict and cooperation: The Robber's Cave Experiment.* Norman: University of Oklahoma Press.

Stephan, C. W., Hertz-Lazarowitz, R., Zelniker, T., & Stephan, W. G. (2004). Introduction to improving Arab-Jewish relationship in Israel: Theory and practice in coexistence educational programs. *Journal of Social Issues, 60*(2), 237–252.

Zelniker, T. (2003, June 18–19). *Transcending problems involved in joint activities by Israeli and Palestinian academics: Mental health training in Gaza.* Paper presented at the Faculty for Israeli-Palestinian Peace (FFIPP) Conference, Tel Aviv.

Zelniker, T., El Sarraj, E., & Hertz-Lazarowitz, R. (2003, December 13–18). *Mental health training in Gaza: The case of Palestinian-Israeli endeavor 1993–2003.* Paper presented at MENA Regional Conference of Psychology, Dubai.

Zelniker, T., & Hertz-Lazarowitz, R. (2004). School-family partnership for coexistence (SFPC) in the city of Acre: Promoting Arab and Jewish parent's role as facilitators of children's literacy development and as agents of coexistence. *Language, Culture and Curriculum, 18*(1), 114–138.

CHAPTER 36

HEALING AFTER A TERROR EVENT ON CAMPUS IN ISRAEL: UNIQUE WORKSHOPS AND ALLIED TECHNIQUES FOR INTERNATIONAL JEWISH, AND ARAB STUDENTS, STAFF, AND EXTENDED COMMUNITY

Judy Kuriansky

On Wednesday, July 31, 2002, students and staff crowded into the cafeteria at the Frank Sinatra International Student Center at Hebrew University's Mount Scopus campus in Jerusalem during the typical lunch time. As they ate and chatted, an Arab worker walked unnoticed into the room and detonated a bomb concealed in his backpack. The explosive killed seven people—including Americans and other foreign nationals—and injured more than 80 others. The attack, for which Islamic Hamas claimed responsibility, set off shock waves and insecurity throughout the academic community, the society at large, and parts of the world. The bombing was especially traumatic as it violated the sanctity of an institute of learning. The blast also targeted random students—considering that not only Jewish but also Arab Israeli students attend the university, and that about 100 students from the United States and other Western countries had just arrived to begin classes the next day for the fall semester of the Rothberg International School.[1]

This chapter presents healing experiences offered to the student body and extended university community, including a unique workshop for students led by the author. These techniques can serve as a model in the event of similar tragedy.

Increase in School Terror Events Worldwide

Violence—the use of physical force to injure or abuse others—occurs in schools around the world. In the United States, such violence is sadly prevalent in inner-city schools but has also occurred tragically in other urban as well as rural settings. In the deadliest school shooting in U.S. history, a student at Virginia Polytechnic and State University massacred 32 people and wounded many more before committing suicide. The April 2007 murderous rampage evoked memories of an earlier reign of terror by two students at Columbine High School in Colorado in 1999 and the execution-style killings of young schoolgirls by a 32-year-old milk-truck driver at the West Nickle Mines Amish School in Pennsylvania in 2006. Assaults on pupils have happened in other parts of the world. In southern Russia in September 2004, armed militants held over a thousand hostages in a school gymnasium, resulting in the death of over a hundred children. Other student murders have happened in Munich Germany, Osaka Japan, Dumblane Scotland, and Sanaa Yemen (CNN, 2002).

Many efforts are made to identify the motivations and profiles of perpetrators of such violence, especially youth (Heide, 1999; Verlinden, Hersen, & Thomas, 2000). Experts have blamed violent films, video games, or rock lyrics; loneliness and serious psychological problems; medications; and even gun laws.

Terrorism is a specific type of school violence, as it is usually aimed at achieving political goals. Attacks traumatize innocents, triggering in them a chronic sense of uncertainty, loss of control, and fear of repeat events that could occur anytime and anywhere. Schools and universities, once immune from direct targeting, have become viable targets as a result of changes in terrorists' motivations, methods, and objectives (Adams & Sinai, 2003). Incidences of terrorism on campus include terror threats in Jakarta, Indonesia, in November 2002, which caused international schools to close, and dozens of fundamentalist attacks on schools in Afghanistan between 2002–2003, including arson and bombings accompanied by warnings that it is un-Islamic to send girls to school

Campuses have also been targeted in the Middle East; for example, a bomb attack in January 2007 near a university in Baghdad killed 70 people and wounded 170 more (CNN, 2007).

University students in the Palestinian territories suffer school-related problems like inability to get to campus due to restrictions caused by the occupation and specifically by checkpoints. In Israel, students are at risk, as evidenced by the Hebrew University bombing and incidences like that of a Palestinian who attempted to detonate a bomb at an Israeli public school in December 2003—but was arrested before he could do so. Students in the region are also under persistent stress from violence in the community, and bombings of school buses and youth gathering places (such as the June 2001 bombing at the Dolphinarium disco on the Tel Aviv beach frequented by teens).

Healing from School Terror Events

Efforts at healing from instances of terrorism in general involve local and extended community action, with support from mental health professionals (Kuriansky, 2003a). But such events targeting the school community on or off school grounds require specific interventions. For example, in the United States, many individual communities, as well as state school systems and even the federal government have responded by developing programs to address prevention as well as recovery (Safe Youth; National Mental Health Information Center, 2006). In October 2006, the White House convened a Conference on School Safety where experts from education, social service, and law enforcement agencies shared ideas, emphasizing the important role of school staff, counseling, and memorial programs to help the healing process (American Federation of Teachers, 2006). In one exemplary self-designed recovery process from a school-related terror event, a wife—also a schoolteacher—used rational and emotional mental processes to recover from the murder of her husband in his university office (Nicholson, 2000). The widow suggests applying principles of nonviolence and conflict resolution, addressing both private and public selves, setting individual and community goals, and involving experts on issues like race relations and ethics.

Rationale

Terror events on campus are particularly traumatic—and require intervention—because students are at an age when they are exploring their political as well as social views, and are at a developmental stage when they are vulnerable to threats to feeling safe. Such stress factors were compounded in the present case of the Hebrew University bombing because the campus had been known for its compatible mix of Arabs and Jews despite being in a country—Israel—where tensions between Jews and Arabs were high.

A particularly worrisome outcome of such events is a rise in anti-Arab sentiment. This had been noted after the 2001 attacks on the World Trade Center in varied social contexts (Howell & Shryock, 2003), and reported by students in New York after that attack and by students on the Jerusalem campus after the bombing there. Several Arab males said girls refused dates because of their heritage. The importance of ensuring students' safety—and creating an atmosphere of freedom of expression—has been recognized by psychologists, discussed on the Jewish Faculty Roundtable website, and pointed out by activists as being important in the Arab-Israeli conflict (Rothstein, 2003).

The Peace Workshop for Students

A few days after the bombing at the university campus in July 2002, at the invitation of the administration, I conducted a group workshop for students attending the school. Participants were preselected by the faculty, and included students of mixed international backgrounds, for example, Arabs, Canadians, and Jewish Americans (some of whom were fans of my radio call-in advice show, therefore they knew and trusted me). The two-hour experiential workshop consisted of modules developed by the author that integrate Eastern techniques (meditation and movements) and Western techniques (cognitive-behavioral-emotive techniques). I have used this model in various settings around the world and with various age groups, including for youth AIDS prevention, self-esteem building, and trauma recovery (Kuriansky 2003b, 2004, 2005a).

The fundamental principle of the workshop is that inner peace leads to outer peace. This is supported by the opposite premise that desperation and deprivation (as an outgrowth of dire living conditions, a poor economy, and oppression) contribute to violence (Afana, 2006; Kuriansky, 2005b). Given that people in the region suffer from prevalent feelings of insecurity—exacerbated by the unpredictability of terror attacks—the workshop exercises aim at increasing a sense of personal safety (through grounding and centering) and interpersonal safety (through connecting and establishing trust).

Efforts at trauma recovery in cases of intractable conflict—such as that between Palestinians and Israelis—are increasingly employing a binational as opposed to uninational approach—bringing together members from opposing sides (Albeck, Adwan, & Bar-On, 2002). The workshop described in this chapter therefore intentionally included Arab as well as Jewish students. This was deemed important, not just because the perpetrator who claimed responsibility for the terror event was Arab, but because students of all nationalities—Jewish and Arab—reported emotional upset.

At the beginning of the workshop, I explained the nature of the workshop as interactive and experiential, and that intellectual and emotional processing would take place afterward. The exercises included some techniques adapted from Eastern practices that integrate mind, body, and spirit, with the specific intention of healing trauma, including by rebuilding trust and restoring inner security and self-control. A similar approach has been used with participants in Israel and Gaza, employing techniques like self-expression (through words, drawings, and movement), mind-body approaches (guided imagery, meditation), and respectful group support (Gordon, 2006). In these workshops, breathing and movement exercises allow relaxation to replace agitation; and meditation to ease nightmares and flashbacks. The supportive group provides a safe environment to reconnect with others and re-establish trust. These efforts showed a substantial decrease—from 88 to 34 percent—in posttraumatic symptoms.

The first exercise in the present workshop involves body activation. Participants are invited to move individual body parts (feet, hands) and progressively add more body parts, while moving around the room at an increasingly fast pace. This creates physiological arousal, through stimulation of the autonomic nervous system and the flow of body chemicals like adrenalin. Vocalizing increases the activation. The next step intends to create a stark contrast, asking participants to come to an abrupt stop and enter a meditative state, quieting the body and the mind. Being totally still invokes the parasympathetic nervous system, and allows the experience of energy flow through the body in the form of sensations like tingling, pulsing, quivering, and electrical pulsations. The resulting feelings of energy, empowerment, and aliveness serve as an antidote to the "deadened" or desensitized feelings which often accompany trauma. Participants are then guided to emerge from this quiet state by moving around the room while consciously becoming aware of their feet being rooted to the ground—connected to the earth—in order to facilitate the personal strength and security essential in trauma recovery. This state is intensified by instructing participants in several power building exercises—moving the arms in particular ways adapted from practices of Buddhist monks. Such movements create strong feelings of energy centered in the body. Participants are then asked to imagine moving this energy intentionally to the area around the heart in order to activate a sense of openness and compassion towards others.

Participants then form two concentric circles to work in pairs. They are asked to gently gaze at each other—silently—with the intention of looking beyond noticing physical characteristics (hair or eye color) to appreciate the person's inner being, acknowledging how challenging this can be especially in certain cultural contexts. This activity is intended to neutralize prejudices and encourage the experience of commonality of hurts, anger, and love. In the next step, they are guided to do synchronized breathing—breathing in and out at the same time—which achieves harmony on a deep level, counteracts feelings of separation, and prevents making judgments which underlie intolerance.

Building on this connection, an activity I use extensively in cross-cultural settings, especially post-disaster, enhances safety (essential for trauma recovery) by having participants place both hands on their heart while saying aloud "I am safe." They then turn to the person next to them, extend one hand while keeping the other on their heart and say, "You are safe." Then they turn to the group, hands extended outward and say, "We are safe."

To help rebuild a solid sense of self and prevent dissociation from the self (which can happen after trauma), participants introduce themselves to each other by using a word to describe themselves that makes them feel valued. The others in the group then repeat the word back to them, as a way of offering acknowledgment. Being recognized for characteristics valued in the self ("loving people," "making people happy," "being real," "being open minded," and "my individuality") raises self-esteem and feeling appreciated by others. This is reinforced by asking participants to share dreams. Students mentioned desires like "to teach kids," "to be a doctor and help people," "to have a wonderful family," and "to be who I want to be without letting anyone stand in my way."

During the postworkshop processing, several students reported feeling hot (a natural outgrowth of raising energy); one student expressed confusion— a normal reaction to the newness and intensity of emotions raised regarding personal feelings and interpersonal relating. Other students' comments revealed that they experienced and internalized the intention of the workshop: "The purpose was to feel what you feel when you are present with others"; "I laughed but I realize that it takes bravery . . . you normally keep relationships shallow but this brings you closer together and to see where your boundaries are"; "It's good to go out of your comfort zone"; "I know now that for there to be any peace between people in the world, we have to examine the walls we put up between people. . . . I am grateful that I now know I can connect with another human being on a deeper level that you cannot do with words, that has changed me forever."

Informal Student Encounters

With another psychologist of Middle East origin who now lives in California, I met with students informally after the bombing, talking with them in parks, at bus stops, and on benches. These encounters were similar to those of "compassionate listening," where peace activists listen to people's stories in public sites (Green, 2002, 2006) and to the "guerrilla therapy" techniques (onsite supportive counseling) I have developed to help people process the experiences of the attacks on the World Trade Center (Kuriansky, 2003a). Students expressed varied disparate views, as we psychologists mediated the discussion in order to facilitate understanding and acceptance (Hakimi, 2002). For example, a British student criticized the settlements and Israeli occupation as inciting Palestinian rage, while an American student defended Israeli security measures as a necessary reaction to Palestinian suicide bombings. In several encounters, Arab students of various nationalities (including French and Jewish American) were challenged as if they represented the terrorist perpetrators. In all situations, the students were assisted to explore their beliefs systems and emotions, and to listen compassionately to each other.

Some non-Arab students expressed initial acceptance of fellow Arab students on campus, but confessed to a dramatic change in perspective after the event. For example, one student said, "I liked them before but I can't talk to any of them now." Others questioned the Arab students as if they knew the motivation for such acts. These challenging encounters ultimately resulted in rapport and positive feelings replacing hostility. This was especially evident when Arab students expressed disapproval of suicide bombings, and post-traumtic reactions similar to that experienced by the non-Arab students. For example, several Arab students mentioned that they could not study since the attack, and one said he had wanted to stay on campus after graduation but now couldn't wait to leave.

Discussion groups also took place at the university synagogue, facilitated by the school rabbi. In one such event, students gathered on one of the building's terraces and shared feelings about the experience.

Staff Workshop

A workshop was also run for university staff at their invitation. The substance was based on theoretical models related to social systems, and cognitive-behavioral and humanistic psychology. Didactic elements included explanations of the expected stages and symptoms of stress reactions after a traumatic event (including intense emotions, neglected self-care, agoraphobia, sleep and eating disorders); cognitive appraisal of the ability to control events; and descriptions of how reactions to the trauma can cause stress between colleagues or in family relationships. Experiential elements included cognitive-behavioral techniques like thought-stopping to control disturbing repetitive recollections of the event, and listing social support systems. An exercise to which participants were particularly responsive involved making a list of pleasurable activities that could serve as an antidote to stress and provide distraction from troubling thoughts about the event.

Ceremonies, Memorials, and Rituals

Memorials and rituals are a common way of healing postdisaster. For example, community gatherings were especially prevalent after the terrorist attacks on the World Trade Center in New York, consisting of both organized and spontaneous walls of remembrance, group singing, and services that included people of all nationalities (Kuriansky, 2003a). After the Hebrew University bombing, a variety of formal and informal, modern and traditional, secular and religious events and experiences (many of which I attended) were held in various locations to help the extended university community heal. The administration organized several memorial services on campus for the entire student body after the terror event, with speakers, songs, poetry readings, and benedictions by student representatives and political figures. Spontaneous as well as organized candle lighting ceremonies and memorials with flowers and other mementos also took place at the site of the bombing outside the cafeteria—similar to those created by mourners after Princess Diana's death. Participants included foreign politicians (some from New York) who coincidentally happened to be visiting the country on a mission.

Rituals also took place off campus. At the Ben Gurion Airport, some students and community members sat with the bodies of victims throughout the night (an orthodox religious practice). On the evening that the bodies of the American victims were to be transported back to the United States for burial, a ceremony was held in the airport where mourners—students, staff, relatives, community members, religious leaders, and U.S. and local government officials—sang songs, recited psalms, and listened to words of the Torah recited by the victims' teachers. Formal religious mourning rituals were also held at the Pardes Institute of Jewish Studies, where several of the victims had been students.

Memorials were also held in the victims' hometowns, and on other campuses and religious institutions (many of which I also attended), including at Yeshiva College and the Fifth Avenue Synagogue in New York and the University of California in Berkeley. These events and concerts brought together thousands of people, young and old, secular and religious, Jewish and non-Jewish, Israeli and non-Israeli. Students and parents participated in honoring the dead, expressing their views, pledging participation in peace activities (either through donations or missions), and calling for tolerance and an end to violence. Concerts featured top Israeli bands and even rap artists who sang about peace and tolerance, interspersed with speeches by family members, students, friends, and rabbis.

Parent Networks

Parents play an important role in their children's college experience. Thus, recovery requires interaction between parents and staff as well as students. Such involvement is particularly important when students are attending schools in high-risk areas such as Israel. Hebrew University, like other youth-oriented institutions, maintains a parents network to keep parents apprised of events and student welfare. After this particular terrorist event, the university officials provided parental support through its established network. Some parents of foreign students, however, were insistent on their children returning home—though very few students actually did so. In a spontaneous effort, my mother—concerned about her own daughter's safety but reassured after talking to me on the phone—reached out to several families of the Hebrew University students, to share feelings. Such unplanned actions that extend connections among parents to provide extra support is helpful in the immediate aftermath of such disasters.

Technology-Assisted Healing

E-mailing and text messaging have become typical modes of communicating throughout the world but particularly in Israel where everyone has a cell phone—partly as a means of staying in touch as a result of terrorism threats. Such instant methods of communicating are particularly crucial when a disaster occurs.

Adding a visual dimension to communication has become easier with the advent and popularity of cell phone cameras, as well as internet access on cell phones, so photos can be instantly taken and transmitted. These were not as available at the time of the Hebrew University bombing. But to provide visual reassurance for parents, I videotaped students speaking directly into a hand-held video camera, addressing their parents, expressing their feelings, and reassuring them that they felt safe and intended to stay at the school. I then mailed the individual tapes to their parents—who expressed great appreciation for this type of contact with their children. "It was one thing to hear my daughter say that she felt safe on the telephone," one mother told me, "but to be able to see her smiling face was much more real; no matter what she says, I can tell by looking at her whether she is telling me the truth or whether is really worried."

The usefulness of technology as a tool for communication between Israeli and Palestinian youth, especially in peacebuilding projects, has been suggested and explored (Schaarschmidt, 2005; Seeds of Peace, 2005). After this university bombing, students, staff, and community members used e-mail, chat rooms, and instant messaging for communication, notification about events, and exchange of personal accounts and photographs to comfort each other. Many students initially stayed in constant e-mail contact with each other. However, the initial mutual emotional support occasionally shifted into political disagreements, leading to their abandoning communication. This unfortunate outcome—which has happened on other occasions, for example between Israeli and Palestinian youth attending camps together—suggests that having a professional host or monitor on a listserv (as is done by many associations) can help focus an e-mail group on emotional healing and tolerance.

Social Action

A student who was the boyfriend of one of the school bombing victims in Israel organized a major community-wide social action day in memory of the two victims from the religious school where they had studied. Students and community members volunteered at soup kitchens, dressed as clowns and visited hospitals and nursing homes, decorated a section of a peace quilt, and cleaned up the neighborhood. Another former student, then in rabbinical school, organized a project in which schoolchildren in the United States and Canada sent thousands of cards to offer support to Israelis. These cards were hung throughout the country at stores and bus stations. A reiki master in Israel started an organization to bring together Jewish, Arab Israeli, and Palestinian students and practitioners of the energy healing method—transmitting energy through the hands—to perform reiki on each other in order to facilitate more inner peacefulness.

Conclusion

The tragic bombing in 2002 on a university campus in Israel with an international student body in this troubled region, as well as other incidents involving students, including an attack at a Palestinian university, highlight the extent of emotional as well as physical danger affecting both Arab and Jewish students. While an increase in campus security is certainly essential, the psychological trauma triggered by such events suggests the need for more comprehensive and integrated efforts at trauma prevention as well as disaster recovery to ensure an environment which insures emotional as well as physical safety and protects students of all nationalities and ethnicities from prejudice. Such a program—which could potentially be called "Campus International Peace Environment"—should provide ongoing workshops to achieve stress reduction and to facilitate inner peace and tolerance. While such efforts cannot prevent terrorism from outside sources, they can encourage more individual confidence, and communication between different groups on campus to create a supportive educational environment and bridge cultural divides among students on a campus serving a culturally-mixed or international student body. Student groups and student-faculty task forces can devise appropriate methods for their respective campuses to achieve this rapport, and share their models with other universities.

Given the impact of violent acts and terrorism on school campuses, it is recommended that specific risk reduction, response and recovery processes be planned and implemented on all school campuses. These should take into account past experiences of individuals as well as institutions, and cultural and religious factors appropriate to the specific situation and student body. Furthermore, given the well-known principle of "collateral damage"—whereby a wider network of individuals and organizations are affected—such prevention and intervention efforts should address not only the immediate, but the extended collegiate community. This would include individuals in satellite offices for the school, trustees, and even graduates who may be in other countries and who—as in the case of the Hebrew University bombing—may have been friends or classmates of victims.

Since it is well known that grief recovery is an ongoing, long-term process, single-instance workshops need to form the basis of a more sustained effort.

Particular attention should be paid on anniversary dates of the incident, to address "anniversary reactions" that can revive traumatic memories and emotions. The techniques described in this chapter should be researched to evaluate their impact. Nevertheless, in the case of unexpected trauma (such as happened in the Hebrew University bombing), innovative approaches can be helpful in the immediate aftermath to bolster recovery and resilience.

Note

1. Subsequent terrorist attacks in Bali, Spain, and London also victimized more international populations, not just Israelis.

References

Adams, J. A., & Sinai, J. (2003). *Protecting schools and universities from terrorism: A guide for administrators and teachers.* Alexandria, VA: ASIS International.

Afana, A. (2006). The mental health situation for Palestinians. In J. Kuriansky (Ed.), *Terror in the Holy Land: Inside the anguish of the Israeli-Palestinian conflict.* Westport, CT: Praeger Publishers.

Albeck, J., Adwan, S., Bar-On, D. (2002). Dialogue groups: TRT's guidelines for working through intractable conflicts by personal storytelling. *Peace and Conflict: Journal of Peace Psychology, 8*(4), 301–322.

American Federation of Teachers. (2006). *White House School Safety Conference Looks at Prevention, Recovery.* Retrieved January 2, 2007, from http://www.aft.org/news/2006/whitehouse_schsafety.htm.

CNN. (2002). Other school killings. Retrieved May 22, 2007 from http://archives.cnn.com/2002/WORLD/europe/04/26/deadly.school.violence.

CNN. (2007) Deaths top 100 in Baghdad bombing, shootings. Retrieved January 17, 2007, http://www.cnn.com/2007/WORLD/meast/01/16/iraq.main/index.html.

Gordon, J. (2006). Healing the wounds of war in Gaza and Israel: A mind-body approach. In J. Kuriansky (Ed.), *Terror in the Promised Land: Inside the anguish of the Israeli-Palestinian conflict.* 203–216. Westport, CT: Praeger Publishers.

Green, L. (2002, Winter). Just listen. *Yes! A Journal of Positive Futures*, 20–25.

Green, L. (2006, December). Blessed are the peacemakers: Voices from our 20th training delegation in Israel and Palestine. *The Compassionate Listening Project Newsletter*, 1.

Hakimi, M. (2002, August 4). Personal communication.

Heide, K. M. (1999). *Young killers: The challenge of juvenile homicide.* Thousand Oaks, CA: Sage Publications.

Howell, S., & Shryock, A. (2003). Cracking down on Diaspora: Arab Detroit and America's "War on Terror." *Anthropological Quarterly, 76*(3), 443–462.

Kuriansky, J. (2003a). The 9/11 terrorist attack on the World Trade Center: A New York psychologist's personal experiences and professional perspective. [Special edition on terrorism and psychology]. *Psychotherapie-Forum, 11*(1), 37–47.

Kuriansky, J. (2003b, December 13–18). *Peace and healing in troubled regions and times of terrorism: Impact on relationships, what East and West can learn from each other about treating trauma and a new integrated therapy model.* Plenary address given to Middle East North Africa Regional Conference of Psychology, Dubai, United Arab Emirates.

Kuriansky, J. (2004, May 24). *Therapy in times of terrorism: International models, clinical skills and the effectiveness of a new therapeutic approach integrating East and West techniques.* Keynote address at the International Conference on Counseling Psychotherapy and Mental Health Education, Nanjing, China.

Kuriansky, J. (2005a, April 16). *The yin and yang of safer sex for youth: Innovative workshop integrating Eastern and Western techniques.* Speech given at Student Conference, Hunter College, New York.

Kuriansky, J. (2005b, December 15). *Psychosocial aspects of the Israeli/Palestinian conflict.* Address at the 2005 Workshop on Humiliation and Violent Conflict, the Sixth Annual Meeting of the Dignity and Humiliation Studies, Columbia University, Teachers College, New York.

National Mental Health Information Center, United State Department of Health and Human Services—Substance Abuse and Mental Health Service Administration. *A guide for intermediate and long-term mental health services after school-related violent events.* Retrieved November 12, 2006, from http://mentalhealth.samhsa.gov/schoolviolence/part1chp11.asp.

Nicholson, J. (2000). Reconciliations: Prevention of and recovery from school violence. *The Annuals of the American Academy of Political and Social Science, 567*(1), 186–197.

Rothstein, R. (2003). Personal communication and retrieved January 29, 2007 from www.standwithus.org.

Safe Youth.(2006) *School violence.* Retrieved January 29, 2007 from http://www.safeyouth.org/scripts/topics/school.asp.

Schaarschmidt, S. (2005, December 15–16). *Cognitive and emotional in-group identification of youth in Israel and Palestine.* Presentation at the 2005 Workshop on Humiliation and Violent Conflict, the Sixth Annual Meeting of the Human Dignity and Humiliation Studies, Columbia University, Teachers College, New York.

Seeds of Peace. (2005). *Newsletters.* Retrieved January 24, 2007 from www.seedsofpeace.org.

Verlinden, S., Hersen, M., & Thomas, J. (2000). Risk factors in school shootings. *Clinical Psychology Review, 20*(1), 3–56.

CHAPTER 37

MEDIA AND SEARCH FOR COMMON GROUND IN THE MIDDLE EAST

John Bell

Zein, a young Palestinian girl living in Bethlehem, is only 15 years old, but her parents accept a young man's proposal to marry her. But Zein says no. But does her family let her make up her own mind?

You have to watch the next segment of the television show to find out.

Welcome to the "Friends" of Palestine—the groundbreaking new television soap opera series airing on Palestinian television stations throughout the Palestinian territories of Gaza and the West Bank. Called *Mazah fi Jad* ("Seriously Joking"), it is the first independently produced Palestinian television drama series. The 13-part series features three families, two Muslim and one Christian, who deal with a wide range of issues that affects their family and their community. More than a soap opera that entices viewers to escape dreary daily life into a world of fantasy, the shows are meant to impart serious educational and social messages while reflecting ordinary life. The shows do address "heavy" issues like corruption, high unemployment, individual rights, changing society by participating in elections, even leaving the country in search of a "better life"; and they do focus heavily on social issues about their relationships, their kids and neighbors, and even women's rights, the double standard applied to men and women, reconciling traditional and modern values, generation gaps, problems communicating, and alternatives to early marriage. But the series' main aim is to show that Palestinian life is not all about occupation but about ordinary people facing the same problems as everybody else. Some characters are even uncharacteristic of Palestinians, such as a divorced mom who runs a hair salon.

All ages like the show, but it's geared especially to young people—with story lines about their needs, challenges, and ambitions, and with young people falling in and out of love—since young people make up more than half of the Palestinian population.

The series ran on the West Bank's Ma'an Network of 10 local television stations, reaching the Palestinian territories during the month of Ramadan in 2005. This television soap opera, co-produced by Bethlehem television (Ma'an Network) and a Washington, D.C.–based organization called Search for Common Ground, with $170,000 in funding received from USAID and other support from the British Foreign Consulate Office, is breaking new ground in its approach to entertain as well as to educate.

The show has been so popular that not only did it attract viewers, but also necessary funding so that another 20 episodes could be produced, aired during Ramadan 2006. Monitoring and evaluation is planned to assess changes in knowledge/attitudes before and after the next round of programming.

Radio Soap Opera in Palestine: *Al-Dar Dar Abuna* (*Home Is Our Home*)

The soap opera concept extends to radio, bringing issues of life in Palestine to light aurally, in a radio drama called *Al-Dar Dar Abuna* ("Home Is Our Home").

In this story, you meet Amal, a young divorced Palestinian woman with no children; her brother, who mistreats her and blames her for her divorce; and Marian, a 25-year-old Palestinian single woman who helps Amal to continue her education and find work in order to support herself and her family. Amal's brother wants her to quit her job and stay at home. The question is raised whether Amal should stand up for her rights and tell her brother to help her put her life back on track. Meanwhile, Marian is a beautiful, well-educated woman who devotes herself to her people and family. In the end, she is heard saying, "When will I find someone I love who loves me back?" It shows that despite her successes, she still feels inadequate without finding love.

Other characters include young Palestinian friends Nadis, Lamees, Sally, Samer, Nadine, and Ameer, all students at Birzeit University—just outside of the city of Ramallah—who like to get together and discuss various issues. They talk about a broad range of topics, from personal stories about love, problems with parents, seeking a job, and watching favorite television programs, to serious political issues concerning the construction of the Separation Barrier/the Wall and the strategy of the Intifada.

As with the Palestinian television soap opera, this radio drama presents issues relevant to Palestinian daily life. The 26-part series, broadcast by nine stations in the West Bank and Gaza, is produced by Search for Common Ground together with MEND (Middle East Non-Violence & Democracy), a Palestinian NGO based in East Jerusalem. The series is in its third season.

The radio show is a highly effective way to reach the Palestinian population because virtually every household in the Palestinian territories listens extensively to radio (at home, in public and private transportation, etc.). Radio offers a broad-based, comparatively inexpensive means to spread awareness, particularly among young people, about important social messages such as promoting analytical skills and emphasizing the effectiveness of nonviolence as a strategy for social change. The radio soap opera series advisory board decided to focus on the 16 to 25 age group both because of its demographic size and because of its relative openness to new ideas.

Every episode stresses the principles of democracy and nonviolent techniques of resolution of conflicts. Examples of the type of messages of *Al-Dar Dar Abuna* include listening to others helps one understand others and realize that people are different; debate within the family helps keep the family together and encourage confidence and responsibility; respect for the opposite sex and equality in duties and responsibilities between the sexes is a prerequisite for a society that is cooperative; diversity and integration are necessary components of a healthy society; freedom of thought goes beyond religion and ideology.

My Personal Journey to Search for Common Ground

As someone who has spent his life working toward peace in the Middle East, I appreciated Search for Common Ground's efforts in this region over the years. When I was looking for an organization that resonates with my own personal approach to conflict resolution, one that emphasizes the deeply human elements of need, and that emphasizes transforming mindsets, I was happy to join Search as the director of its Middle East program. In addition to this commonly valued approach, I chose Search because it is well established in the region and has credibility with both sides of the conflict. It is also well equipped with an extensive conflict resolution toolbox, and is connected to influential representatives of all the main decision-making parties in Israel and Palestine, as well as in the Arab world, Europe, and the United States. Finally, I am proud to work with the dedicated staff and participants that make Search's programs so successful.

Search for Common Ground (SFCG) is a Washington, D.C., and Brussels–based nongovernmental organization (NGO) whose mission is to transform the way the world deals with conflict—away from adversarial confrontation and toward cooperative solutions. The Middle East program at SFCG started in 1991 before the Oslo Accords, at a time when the Israeli and Palestinian civil societies and governments did not communicate with each other. But Search felt that the time was right for more constructive interaction between the two parties and brought together key community leaders, academics, politicians, and others who were willing to talk in private.

As was to be expected, in the beginning, the parties spent most of the time vehemently criticizing each other. But after a while, they started talking about what could be done. SFCG took this opportunity to create a core working group, which allowed the participants to meet regularly to analyze the situation and come up with ideas for projects. It was very important that the parties to the conflict formulated the agenda. In a region like the Middle East, it's important for a third party not to be seen as imposing an agenda, because that would create suspicion of ulterior motives not necessarily in the best interests of the people of the region.

The core working group came up with four areas for projects that helped prepare the ground for more constructive interactions between the parties before
Oslo. These areas included civil society, security, media, and conflict resolution.
For each issue area, we made sure to find participants who would have influence
over decision makers and/or public opinion in their own nations. As time went
on, people who were initially hesitant to participate began to slowly lose their
reluctance, and the programs grew in number and in scope.

Besides applying conflict resolution tools to the Israeli-Palestinian conflict, we
were also able to introduce the use of conflict resolution tools in general, which
we helped to institutionalize in the region. We were also introduced to new conflict resolution tools that suit the local cultures, which we have added to our organizational toolbox. One example is that in the Middle East we learned that
polling can be a powerful tool in conflict resolution, so that was added to our
collection of conflict resolution tools. We are also sensitive to the human dimension of the roots of a conflict, and we therefore use strategies where we purposefully humanize the other side in our programming.

Since the inception of the program in 1991, Search for Common Ground in the
Middle East continued to grow. Our staff includes both locals and internationals
and has continued to conduct a multitrack program to promote peace, cooperation, and security in the Middle East. We also sponsor activities among Israelis
and Palestinians and promote regional cooperation. Recently, our emphasis has
been in the field of media, since Search for Common Ground has distinctive
strength in this area from projects in other regions around the world, and since
media activities are a powerful instrument for affecting public perceptions and
the policy environment because of their outreach and mediating role between
leaders and citizens in each society. In this regard, we actively support the development of independent media in the West Bank and Gaza.

Besides the television and radio soap operas described earlier, other current
media projects include a multipart television documentary series called *The
Shape of the Future*.

The Shape of the Future series portrays on a human level what an eventual
Palestinian-Israeli peace settlement could look like. While the Middle East
abounds with skepticism, numerous observers—Palestinian, Israeli, and international—believe that Israeli-Palestinian peace is possible. A frequently heard
maxim is that both sides can see the light at the end of the tunnel; they simply
cannot find the tunnel. We have made a television series about the light—not
how to find the tunnel.

Real people also have their say. Riki Amedi is an Arab mother living with her
husband and children in West Jerusalem, and is fearful for her children's lives
because of many of the attacks. "When my son goes to school, I hope he will
come back home," she says. Palestinian Sameeh Abu Rameikeh is also fearful
for his child. His son is ill, and he was worried about delays at the checkpoints
at Qalandia. Fortunately, he made it to the hospital in time, and his son was
safe.

The emphasis is on the future, not on the past—which makes this a unique documentary effort. But looking to the future is not easy, as distinguished Palestinian journalist and commentator Nabil Khatib says, "It's a difficult transformation from being prisoners of pain and suffering in the past to looking towards the future." But many in the film express dreams for peace. There are no scenes of violence and no historical footage. The core idea is to examine, in an even-handed way, the aspirations of both Israelis and Palestinians and to show that agreements are possible that do not threaten the national existence of either party. The series explores the background, the various positions, and the options for settlement in each of the disputed final status issues. Programs look at issues regarding settlements, refugees, Jerusalem, security, and the quest for a normal life.

Palestinians and Israelis alike say in the series that they want "a normal life." Zuhair Menasra, who headed the Palestinian Preventive Security Agency of the West Bank, said, "A Palestinian wants to wake up, drink his coffee, look at his calendar and see whether the weather will be nice or not. He goes to work, listens to music, goes for a walk, does sports, or maybe reads a book or poetry." For Neveen Abu Rumiller, a normal life means that every woman, her husband, and their children are able to live in a home where they do not need to lock the doors, "where you do not fear there are military raids outside."

A Jewish mother echoes her sentiment. Says Riki, "A normal life in this country, here in Jerusalem, is the kind of life where you really do not have to be afraid." In her husband Uri's view, a normal life is one where, "I do not have to look for a radio every hour to hear what happened . . . one where I have some inner quiet, knowing that when I leave in the morning that I will come home safely."

First aired in July 2005, the series has been produced in Hebrew-, Arabic-, and English-language versions and was the first program to be shown simultaneously on Israeli, Palestinian, and Arab (Abu Dhabi) television. Background music for the series is by David Broza and Said Murad, two of the most popular Israeli and Palestinian performers. The theme song, *In My Heart*, was released as a music video.

Ramzi Abu Radwan is known throughout Palestine as the poster child for the first Intifada. He was eight years old and walking home from school with his friend, who was shot by Israeli soldiers. "I was in shock. I picked up some stones and started running towards the soldiers," he describes in the documentary, "I got hit three times by bullets. From that time on, I kept throwing stones. Sometimes my grandfather used to tie me down with ropes to stop me from going out of the house."

Ramzi now has a new idea. "I would like, God willing, to work on a project that will bring music to a large number of children in refugee camps in the West Bank and Gaza. When children have hope, they will think more about living. If there is no hope, people will pick stones up and throw them."

Brigidier General Dov Sedaka, retired from the Civil Administration for the West Bank, empathizes with Palestinian frustration. "It can cause severe hatred to wake up every morning and to have to pass through roadblocks and barricades in order to reach school; or to be cut off from essential health care; or to be denied access to basic education," he says. But "hatred increases terror and hatred creates a lack of security for the state of Israel." Tzipi Livni, Israel's foreign minister and a member of the Kadima Party, thinks education offers a solution, "I think that what is really important is to teach the next generation, and I hope it happens among the Palestinians as well, to teach them how we can live together."

Former U.S. President Jimmy Carter said about *The Shape of the Future:*

> This documentary series examines the fears and aspirations of Israelis and Palestinians in an even-handed way. It shows how a negotiated agreement could address those fears and aspirations and do so without threatening the national existence of either side. Israel and Egypt were able to accomplish this task at Camp David more than 25 years ago and this series supports the belief that Israelis and Palestinians can do the same.

In another exciting project, we have been able to assist the Israeli and Palestinian co-directors of the Middle East Children's Association (MECA) to develop a teaching curriculum around the messages in *The Shape of the Future* documentaries. Related to this effort, we have also helped the Israel Palestine Center for Research and Information (IPCRI) to develop curricula around the renowned television series *A Force More Powerful,* and to train teachers in principles of nonviolence while building hope for peace.

Partnership with Palestinian Television Stations

Over the years, we have developed a solid partnership with the Ma'an Network of independent Palestinian television stations, covering the West Bank and Gaza. In 2003, production included a series of 26 roundtable political programs on nonviolent alternatives to spiraling violence. In 2004, we produced and broadcast a 15-part series titled *Reframing Incitement.* We also work to strengthen the member stations of the Ma'an Network through training and equipment upgrades, and support them in producing a biweekly television magazine series on cultural issues that is broadcast in the West Bank. The magazine series highlights positive aspects of Palestinian society and culture as a way to instill a sense of community among the disparate West Bank towns and to develop a relationship between independent media and the community. Further, broadcasting stories of a successful women's society in Tulkarem has the potential to instill hope in Palestinians, as it showcases instances of ambition, community togetherness, and civil society development. Examples of past shows include:

- The life of an artist in Nablus who draws wall paintings, and the ideas she explores within her paintings.
- Palestinian secondary educational stage and how important it is to the student, as it determines the student's future, skills, and entrance into university.

- The dangers and challenges that fishermen face in Gaza, the fishing season, the maximum amounts of fish that the market can sustain.
- A 10-year-old child in Hebron who memorizes large parts of the Holy Qura'an.
- The history of fencing and how is it practiced; segment covered the third-place win by the Union team from Bethlehem in the last championship in Jordan, and the impact of the winning on Palestinians.
- The role of the Alraja' Center for Special Education in Hebron in rehabilitation and integration of the handicapped into the society, which enables them to live a normal life.

Common Ground News Service

The Common Ground News Service (CGNews) publishes balanced and solution-oriented articles by local and international experts to promote constructive perspectives and encourage dialogue about current Middle East issues and the relationship between the West and the Arab/Muslim world. To spread the word, CGNews targets media outlets for further republications in the Middle East regional and international press, and has succeeded in securing more than 1,840 republications of our articles in media outlets as key as Al-Hayat, Ha'aretz, Al-Jazeera.net, Al-Quds, the *Daily Star*, the *Middle East Times*, the *Jewish Comment*, the *Lebanon Wire*, and the *Jordan Times*. CGNews also targets policymakers, scholars, think tanks, and interested readers worldwide, and today, has more than 13,370 subscribers, an active network of contributing authors, and major media partners. CGNews is one of comparatively few transmission mechanisms for continuing media interaction over the Middle East conflict and between the Arab world and the West. In the current atmosphere of distrust, this bridging role is more important than ever.

The CGNews board of editors comprises individuals in Jerusalem, Amman, Beirut, and Washington, with extensive knowledge of the Middle East and a "common ground" orientation. The editors monitor local and regional media daily, looking for articles that provide constructive, balanced, solution-oriented perspectives; promote dialogue and cooperation; encourage peaceful and nonviolent means to resolve conflicts and ease tension; express constructive self-criticism; highlight positive experiences between communities and nations that humanize "the other" and offer hope; highlight organizations and people working for a better regional environment; and interpret information, events, polls, and analyses in ways that encourage rational, moderate, and positive thinking.

Each week the editors select five articles to distribute in CGNews in Arabic, Hebrew, and English. As copyright permission is obtained for all articles, media outlets are free to republish them as desired. CGNews is distributed at no cost, and back copies can be found in the archive on its website: www.commongroundnews.org.

In addition to its weekly distribution, CGNews commissions special series of 6 to 10 original articles each on important topics, such as "Non-Violence"; "The

Arab Peace Initiative"; "The Geneva Accords"; "The Greater Middle East Initiative"; "The Relationship between the Arab/Islamic World and the US/West"; "Enlarging the Window of Opportunity"; "The Dynamics of Public Opinion"; and "The Role of Religion in the Middle East Conflict."

CGNews provides a touching example of how SFCG has specifically helped individuals. After the outbreak of the second Intifada, a time of serious political collapse in the region, participants in our programs stopped meeting, and direct communication ceased. During this time, CGNews became a powerful tool to make sure the program survived for the participants, since participants in our programs could not meet but could still read CGNews and share information. When they would see something written by someone they knew on the other side, it often encouraged them to get in touch with that person, and even to write an article themselves. In this way, the news service became a valuable channel for constructive articles during this period of extreme tension, maintaining moderate voices by commissioning some authors to write constructive articles and by acknowledging others who already did so.

Two participants who had created a relationship through SFCG—one Palestinian and one Israeli—did not communicate during the Intifada. When the Palestinian participant's house was hit by Israeli tank fire, he wrote an article about the experience, saying that he still believed in peace and that we need to keep working toward this goal. The Israeli with whom he had lost touch read the article and called him. He then wrote an article of his own, and a couple of months later, they co-authored a piece. To this day, CGNews remains a bridge of hope in times of despair.

Eliav-Sartawi Awards for Common Ground Journalism

Search for Common Ground holds annual Awards for Journalism in the Middle East. Known since 2003 as the Eliav-Sartawi Awards for Middle Eastern Journalism, the awards recognize and encourage journalism that contributes to better understanding between people and maintaining political dialogue in the Middle East. We honor articles that try to open windows of understanding on the people in the region, and the issues that divide them, provide insight into regional issues and debates, contribute to political dialogue, expose readers to new perspectives, and help to lay the groundwork for peaceful solutions. Winners have included Eetta Prince-Gibson who writes for *The Jerusalem Post*, Khaled Duzdar and Gershon Baskin who are published on the Arabic Media Internet Network, and Steven Erlanger of the *New York Times*.

Regional Media Working Group

At the end of 2004, we convened a meeting of our Media Working Group—the seventh since 1994—that brought together 20 key Arab and Israeli editors, publishers, producers, and columnists. Participants discussed the current role of the media—and how the media can contribute to the peace process. The highly productive workshop provided an opportunity to brainstorm on potential projects to be implemented in the future.

Based on the success of this working group, another meeting involving Middle Eastern and Western high-level television professionals was held in February 2006. This meeting was a workshop of key Middle Eastern and Western television professionals who focused on shared problems and exchanged experiences in order to identify and lay the groundwork for concrete actions and cooperative projects based on common goals.

An Israeli anchorman commented on the challenges he faces with respect to the Israeli-Palestinian conflict, saying, "The problem we have before us is not language or reporting; it is the problem of conflicting narratives. . . . We don't listen to each other; we don't absorb each other's story. . . . We have to meet somewhere on the road and strike a compromise."

Another dilemma faced is how to remain, as a journalist, outside of the conflict when reporting. "We as journalists are part of this conflict. We try not to be. . . . We try for objectivity, but I don't think we've been successful," remarked a correspondent for an Arab satellite station. The first day was spent drawing out these challenges and the end of the meeting concluded with brainstorming concrete, cooperative actions that, in part, respond to these challenges. Several interesting initiatives came out of the meeting and are currently being pursued.

Assistance to Palestinian NGOs

We assist several Palestinian NGOs in strengthening their capacity to encourage nonviolence and to promote moderation, dialogue, tolerance, and nonviolent methods of conflict resolution, and to reduce incitement. Many efforts have focused on youth; for example, through the Palestinian Center for Democracy and Conflict Resolution (PCDCR), our partner in Gaza and Nablus, we trained students as peer group mediators and now find many of those mediators active in elected student governments. PCDCR is established in 16 schools in Gaza and the West Bank. These student governments assist students to develop independent mindsets and methods of inquiry. By dealing with issues of real and immediate concern, they also learn to deal with authority figures in their society in the pursuit of answers.

Holy Sites Initiative

Holy sites are of crucial religious significance for millions of adherents of the Abrahamic faiths worldwide and are inextricably bound up in the religious, cultural, and political identities of the parties in conflict. Therefore, visible interreligious respect and cooperation concerning them might diffuse religious and political tension, both locally and internationally, as well as provide a model for further cooperative efforts. A Search regional initiative helps find common ground among key Muslim, Jewish, and Christian leaders in the Holy Land. In the belief that more can be done to empower and mobilize Middle Eastern religious leaders as peacemakers, we are facilitating a process that we hope will lead to a declaration by the religious leaders that recognizes and respects the attachments of the three monotheistic faiths to their respective holy sites in Jerusalem.

Funders

The activities of Search for Ground in the Middle East are funded by the European Union and the Canadian, Dutch, German, Spanish, Swedish, UK, and U.S. governments. We have also received support from the Nuclear Threat Initiative, the Compton Foundation, the Sagner Family Fund, Rational Games, Gordon McCormick, Rawander Singh, and other friends of Search for Common Ground.

A Holistic View

Conflict resolution requires a multidimensional approach. As such, besides approaching psychosocial issues, Search's Middle East program also includes security programs (with forums for influential experts in security and groups to brainstorm new initiatives for the region, such as linking the territorial disengagement to the Israeli-Palestinian political process and exploring ways to build bridges between Islamic political parties in the Middle East and their counterparts in the West); joint Israeli-Palestinian dialogue on economic issues stemming from the Israeli disengagement from Gaza; a Cooperative Disease Monitoring System (with public health experts and Ministry of Health officials from Israel, Jordan, Egypt, and Palestine, and advisors from the World Health Organization and other American and European organizations); and a Regional Chemical Risks Consortium.

CHAPTER 38

A Different Future: Raising the Voice of the Moderates in the Israeli-Palestinian Conflict

Bruce E. Wexler

The Palestinian-American poet Naomi Shihab-Nye said: "Moderate voices have to speak more loudly. We have to shout as moderates, even though it is not our style." I founded A Different Future (ADF, www.adifferentfuture.org) in 2002 for the purpose of amplifying the moderating voices of Israelis and Palestinians, and of Arabs and Jews in Israeli, who work together in mutual respect. ADF is an NGO of American Jewish, Christian, and Muslim religious leaders, scholars, business leaders, and communications experts. We believe that the way moderates should shout is through a professionally developed strategic communications program.

The Israeli-Palestinian conflict is in large part a conflict between extremists and moderates; extremist Israelis and extremist Palestinians against moderate Israelis and moderate Palestinians. The majorities of both Palestinians and Israelis are moderates; repeated polls show that roughly 75 percent of Palestinians and 75 percent of Israelis endorse the same general peace plan. However, the majority of the moderates on both sides say they do not believe the other side would accept the plan. The extremist minorities are winning the war by filling the public idea space with images of hatred and violence. These images deny the humanity of "the other" and create a sense of hopelessness and irreconcilable difference that paralyzes our imaginations and obstructs the work of diplomats. By controlling the public idea space, the extremists set the agenda and control the terms of discussion, thinking, and relating.

In February 2003, the Rockefeller Foundation recently hosted a meeting for ADF on the *Message and the Media: Why Is the Third Voice of Cooperation Not More Newsworthy?* A former president of NBC News and PBS and a member of the editorial board of *The New York Times* both explained that the "definition of news is when bad things happen to people." As a result, the actions and threats of extremists fill the news while the daily examples of cooperation and images of shared humanity rarely find their way even to the back pages or off-hours television reports. ADF resists this formulation of the news as a dangerous misrepresentation. Senior Palestinian and Israeli negotiators have said—"we could solve the problems that divide us if we trusted each other." In other words, a major barrier to peace is mistrust. If the definition of news is when bad things happen to people, then the media is inadvertently aggravating the fundamental underlying problem of mistrust. This point was expanded upon in an invited article for the May–June 2004 issue of the *Columbia Journalism Review.*

If moderates have the ability in other situations to convince people to make a different choice than they would ordinarily make—as advertisers do when they convince people to choose Coke over Pepsi, eat McDonalds rather than Burger King, or drive Chevrolets instead of Fords, then why can't moderates convince more people to more actively support the positions of moderates rather than extremists in the current Middle East crisis, or even convince extremists to change their position (i.e., from terrorism to peace or to more moderation)? The answer is in part that we have not applied our communications expertise or resources to the critically important task of reclaiming the public idea space from extremists. And it is not as if we have an inferior "product" to "sell." We are talking about the commonsense views of the majorities, the basic premise that even people different from us are human, and the shared teachings of the Abrahamic religions of the communities in conflict.

The mission of ADF is to:

- Amplify the voices of Arabs and Israelis who work together in mutual respect, but are seldom noticed by the media and little known to the general public.
- Create and sustain professionally developed strategic communications programs to increase awareness of these voices of reconciliation and cooperation.
- Bring together prominent religious, business, and civic leaders, scholars, and communications experts to craft and deliver messages based on shared religious principles, economic realities, and moral leadership. Use the full and creative range of communication vehicles to put these messages in the public idea space and deliver them more narrowly to target audiences.
- Help moderate majorities reclaim the battlefield of ideas from extremists, both among policymakers and in the broad public idea space, and contain the violence that originates within their communities. We pursue this mission through three interrelated programs:
  - *Single Source Publicity Resource.* Working with the Ruder Finn Company (an international public relations firm), ADF provides free publicity services for organizations in which Israelis and Palestinians, or Arabs and Jews in Israel, are working together. By providing the actual communication services rather than funds for each organization to do its own publicity, we are able to create a strategic communication plan in which the whole is greater than the sum of the parts.
  - *National Interreligious Leadership Initiative for Peace in the Middle East.* ADF brought together the national leaders of Jewish, Christian, and Muslim

organizations, representing more than 100 million Americans. This new collective interreligious voice gained extensive national and international press coverage (e.g., Google cited the press conference last January 2005 as the top news story in the world that day). The group met with then Secretary Powell in June 2004, Under Secretary of State Karen Hughes in February 2006, and then with Secretary Rice in January 2007 shortly before her renewed diplomatic efforts in the region in February and March 2007.

- *National Network of Local Interreligious Leadership Groups.* ADF has brought together senior religious leaders in cities across the country to build the constituency to support the United States taking a leadership role in the peace process. The initial event bringing the groups together was a transnational video conference, "Speaking for Peace from Jerusalem and Washington," which was viewed and discussed by interreligious audiences in 50 cities. Representative Hyde, head of the International Relations Committee in the House of Representatives, and Senator Lugar, head of the Foreign Relations Committee in the Senate, sent letters to all members of the Congress pointing to this event and acknowledging the expressions of urgency and resolve from constituents that the United States provide active and sustained leadership of the peace process.

Although we have a good "product" to sell, we are up against the fact that people in different cultures and with different belief systems have difficulty seeing each other as equally human. Furthermore, people are very uncomfortable when symbols of other peoples' belief system and culture appear in their environment. In my book *Brain and Culture: Neurobiology, Ideology and Social Change* (MIT Press, 2006), I refer to this as a "neurobiological antagonism to difference." In the book, I review the scientific research showing how the structure and function of our brains is shaped by the environments in which we live as children, how when we are adults the ability of our brain to reconfigure itself is much reduced and established structures are self-maintaining, and how difficult it is for us when the environment changes and no longer matches the established internal structures. These latter situations include bereavement, immigration, and the intermixing of cultures. These ideas led me to found ADF.

Extremists agitate and frighten the moderates within their communities by depicting "the other side" as aggressive, inflexible, and inhuman. They highlight the foreignness or difference of the other and appeal to their compatriots to defend their shared culture and interests. It is very difficult for someone outside of the community to combat this appeal and the associated fear. However, there are many organizations within the Israeli and Palestinian communities that interpret their own cultural and religious values as consistent with the view that even people different from oneself are equally human, and as inconsistent with the use of violence as the primary tool of conflict resolution. In addition to attempting to reclaim the public idea space from extremists, ADF aims to increase the stature of these organizations. We believe that if strengthened, these organizations within Israeli and Palestinian society can more effectively contain the violence that arises from their communities.

The Parents Circle, for example, is composed of Palestinians and Israelis who have lost close family members to the violence, but instead of calling for revenge, call for an end to the cycle of attacks and counterattacks. They send speaker pairs into schools and community meetings. Hand in Hand is an organization that has created school curricula that tell both the story of the Israelis and the story of the Palestinians. Neve Shalom is a community in which Arabs and Jews live together in peace and with mutual respect. Givat Haviva sponsors educational programs for Jewish and Arabic businessmen, students, and others. The Children's March for Peace brought hundreds of Arab and Jewish children together and sent them home wearing T-shirts and carrying messages for their parents about paths to peace. There are many other such efforts.

ADF has provided free publicity services to many of these organizations and to the National Interreligious Leadership Initiative, generating hundreds of news stories in papers and on television across the United States, in Europe, and throughout the Middle East. The BBC and Al-Jazeera interviewed the rabbis, imams, cardinals, and bishops in the Interreligious Leadership Initiative, and *The New York Times*, *The Washington Post*, Associated Press, and Reuters carried reports of their news conferences. When two women from the Parents Circle spoke on Long Island at the time of the presidential campaign in 2004, the local newspaper, *Newsday*, had their pictures on the front page along with pictures of President Bush and Senator Kerry. A full story with more photos filled page 3, and more than 1 million people saw the repeated news broadcasts about their visit on local news shows.

Still, we moderates are losing the battle. We have not yet decided to shout long enough and loud enough. We have not yet realized the full seriousness of the threat we face and begun to devote appropriate resources in response. I have heard commentators say that if we change our lifestyles in response to extremists' threats, it will be a victory for the extremists. ADF believes that if we do not acknowledge the danger we face, and change our lives accordingly, we will hand the future to the extremists.

CHAPTER 39

TRAINING PEACEMAKERS FOR ISRAELI-PALESTINIAN CONFLICT RESOLUTION

Julia DiGangi

A number of training programs for conflict resolution operate around the world. While diverse in their geographic locations and precise methodology, these programs share many similarities. All of these programs cultivate cross-cultural bonds; focus on shared humanity as a strategy for mitigating conflict; and are conducted as group meetings and seek to foster open dialogue as a means of developing best practices as well as empathy and understanding among participants. Participants come from diverse countries, many of which are conflict-ridden environments. Most important, all of these programs recognize that peace is a process that must be adopted by people and not just politicians.

Costs for these programs range in price from $600 to $2,000 and include food, lodging, and training. Fortunately for many students, the fees are usually funded by grants, endowments, and private gifts. Trainers are faculty members or program graduates, trained in conflict analysis, intervention, and dialogue facilitation, as well as invited diplomats, professors, or negotiators. Courses are often taught in English, but may very depending on the location of the training and language requirements of participants.

Unfortunately, many training programs specifically focused on Israeli-Palestinian relations were interrupted after the outbreak of the second Intifada, due to lack of funding and the charged political environment. But Israeli and Palestinian individuals still participate in conflict resolution programs all over the world that focus on the general principles of conflict resolution and involve case studies and can include issues related to Arab-Jewish conflicts. This chapter gives examples of several such international training programs.

International relations practitioners have classified diplomatic efforts into a track system. Most programs—like the ones presented here—operate on Track II

diplomacy, which refers to diplomatic efforts that involve nongovernmental initiatives, which are aimed at civilians, students, and community activists. In the
context of the Israeli-Palestinian conflict, many argue that too much emphasis
has been placed on Track I diplomacy, which refers to government-to-government
interactions.

The International School of International Training (SIT)

Located in Brattleboro, Vermont, the School of International Training hosts
several conflict resolution programs, including the CONTACT program and the
Youth Peacebuilding Camp described later.

Conflict Transformation Across Cultures (CONTACT) Summer Institute

After two years of unsuccessfully trying to obtain a U.S. visa, two Palestinians
from Gaza—a psychiatrist and a social worker—were able to participate in the
three-week CONTACT Summer 2005 institute (part of a three-year training
series). The director, Paula Green—who also directs the Karuna Center—
describes them as "very strong participants and very influential in their
communities." Despite being traditionally close-vested about their reactions, they
appeared to experience a "big impact" from interaction with others facing similar
challenges in different parts of the world, lessening their feelings of isolation.
Since Gazans have a difficult time accessing the media, the setting gave them a
forum to express their views and feelings to an international group.

Since its inception in 1997, 447 people have attended; of those, 15 have been
Israeli and 4 have been Palestinian. The CONTACT Summer Institute, hosted
on SIT's campus in the hills of southeastern Vermont overlooking the Connecticut River Valley, provides participants an opportunity to get to know each other
over the course of three weeks in a fairly neutral context they would be unable
to find at home (www.sit.edu/contact). The teachers, experts in peacebuilding,
often come from conflict-ridden homelands as well, like Bosnia, Rwanda, and the
Philippines. One Palestinian was on staff from 2003–2004.

The curriculum consists of group work, simulations of conflict situations, tolerance education, and role-plays. While the goal is to provide participants with
skills and techniques to reduce conflict in general and as such does not focus directly on one conflict—for example, between Palestinians and Israelis—the
well-known nature of the Palestinian-Israeli conflict makes it one of the case
studies that the participants dissect during each program cycle.

Participants stay in touch through listservs, which provide an outlet to remind
them that they are not isolated in their own conflicts and are part of an international community committed to peace.

Youth Peacebuilding Camp

The Youth Peacebuilding Camp, sponsored by the School of International
Training, is similar to CONTACT in bringing people from conflict hotspots to a

Vermont retreat, but caters to younger participants, aged 15 to 18 years old (www.sit.edu/youth).

In 2000 and 2001, the SIT operated a program specifically for Israeli Jewish and Arab youths, but—as with other Jewish-Arab mediation programs—had to suspend activities after the beginning of the first Intifada because of political tensions in the region and in the United States. It hoped to reopen the Middle East program in the summer of 2006—depending on the political context, finances, and the U.S. visa process for foreigners—but Israeli and Palestinian youths can still join other adolescents from conflict zones around the globe at the camp.

The program is designed for small groups of approximately a dozen youth, with an equal balance of Arabs and Jews, and gender. Activities include dialogue, skills training, and recreational activities and group discussion. The structured dialogue sessions progress from low-risk themes in the beginning of the week (e.g., definitions of conflict) to high-risk topics later in the week (e.g., personal experiences related to the conflict). Sessions are also held on comparative history to help each group understand the other's perspective. Sharing personal narratives is considered an effective way to help people see the "human face" of conflict and to begin building relationships that extend past stereotypes.

Participants are encouraged to express themselves in writing and to share personal narratives in various verbal or literary formats. This excerpt is from a poem written by an Arab youth during a 2001 session with Jewish and Arab teens:

> "The situation here is terrible" people say
> "Let's hope some day we'll have a new situation" people pray . . .
> "What's wrong with your present situation?" they wondered
> "He needs a shrink. He's so crazy!" I angrily answered
> "Well" they murmured "you must have patience"
> And then one asked "did you give him his medications?"
> "Medications?" I jumped "he is under medications?"
> "Well" they said, "only one. Give him each day a piece."
> "Which medication is that?" I asked
> "daaah, [sic] don't you know?" they shouted, "It's the medication of peace. . . . "

After hours in the classroom, participants go outdoors for problem-solving and trust-building activities—rope tugs, trust-circles, and sports like hiking and canoeing—to give the teens a chance to "blow off steam" and a reprieve from confronting the conflict. "At that age, you can't just talk all day without being able to get some of the tension out," Ungerleider explains. "Kids need to build relationships as human beings and just as representatives of their conflicts."

Jewish and Arab Israeli teens formed friendships that led to visiting each other's homes after the camp was over. Many stayed in touch on a 2000 and 2001 listserv, until the discussions became increasingly nationalistic and were abandoned by the majority of users.

After one camp, Israeli youths were filmed by a television station (aired on Israeli television). When one of the Jewish boys expressed his disappointment over not being accepted as a paratrooper in the Israeli military, an Arab girl told him that she was "happy he would not become a serious soldier." The camp director was moved by this interaction, perceiving genuine concern on the part of an Arab for her Jewish friend, for herself, and for peace.

While Ungerleider acknowledges that young people cannot single-handedly change the conflict, he hopes that more teens will go through programs like the Youth Peacebuilding Camp, and as a result, will grow into more formative roles in their respective societies to effect change.

The Karuna Center for Peacebuilding

The Karuna Center for Peacebuilding in Amherst, Massachusetts, offers international training programs in conflict transformation, dialogue, and reconciliation. Participants are typically mid-career NGO workers, educators, and mental health employees, who often live in conflict zones. Run by a social psychologist, the program emphasizes the importance of psychological drivers in resolving conflict, including individual needs, communication skills, and the role of identity in conflicts.

"Peacebuilding is a top down, bottom up and middle out process that requires participation for all sectors of society," explains executive director Paula Green.

The Karuna Center (www.karunacenter.org) suspended its Israeli and Palestinian programs after the outbreak of the 2000 Intifada, but resumed in July 2005, after receiving two independent invitations—one from a consortium of NGOs based in Ramallah and the West Bank, and another from a group of Israeli peace advocates and mental health professionals.

The Palestinian training lasted two weeks. The first week was devoted to developing strategies for conflict management, including tools for conflict analysis and intervention that can mitigate conflicts within the Palestinian society; basic mediation and conflict resolution skills; and methods for mapping the root causes of conflict and addressing underlying needs and fears of conflicting groups. The second week involved change management techniques, which were techniques that would enable Palestinian communities and organizations to better adapt to their changing environments and difficult circumstances.

After the training, one female participant from Nablus independently hosted and organized Israeli-Palestinian dialogue workshops both in her home and in the center where she treated children with hearing and learning impediments, which were often the result of war-related trauma. Previously, this individual had spent eight years imprisoned by Israelis for activities relating to Palestinian rights. Despite her personal anguish, she was committed to achieving peace through understanding and mutual concern for a joint future. Even when the Karuna Center program was forced to halt its dialogue programs, she maintained her contacts with Israelis via phone and e-mail.

The weekend training for Israeli peace activists and mental health professionals was held on the premises of a unique community called the Oasis of Peace where 45 families, half of which are Arab and the other half Jewish, live together.

The training examined the causes and cycles of intolerance and revenge between Israeli Jews and Arabs and taught techniques for interrupting these cycles to increase empathy, mutual respect, and social change.

The International Center for Cooperation and Conflict Resolution (ICCCR)

The ICCCR at Columbia University Teachers College—based on the scholar-practitioner model—offers research projects (e.g., on intractable conflicts) and trainings to professionals and members of the public who are interested in learning conflict deescalation methods (www.tc.columbia.edu/icccr). The Teachers College network hosts related conferences, including the 2005 Human Dignity and Humiliation Studies project of the Columbia University Conflict Resolution Network. At this conference, a wide array of international practitioners and academics was brought together to discuss broad themes related to conflicts around the world. Several participants presented issues specifically related to the Israeli-Palestinian conflict (www.humiliationstudies.org). Presenters on the Israeli-Palestinian conflict included the editor of this volume, Dr. Judy Kuriansky, who spoke on "Psychosocial Aspects of the Israeli-Palestinian Conflict"; and several authors, including Kjell Skyllstad, who discussed music initiatives in "From Humiliation to Empowerment: Creative Conflict Management in the Multi-ethnic School"; Sophie Schaarschmidt who presented her research on "Cognitive and Emotional In-group Identification of Youth in Israel and Palestine"; as well as peace activists who have lived and worked in Israel (e.g., individuals from the Israeli-Palestinian communal living community Neve Shalom).

The Institute for International Mediation and Conflict Resolution (IIMCR)

In 1993, former President Clinton sent Cody Shearer, a Washington, D.C.–based journalist, as an unofficial envoy to the Middle East in an attempt to broker a peace deal between the Syrians and Israelis. During this mission, Shearer recognized the need for an organization to teach people how to communicate, negotiate, and reconcile in complex and contentious environments and was inspired to create the Institute for International Mediation and Conflict Resolution (IIMCR).

Shearer's vision was to bring together adults at the beginning of their careers from around the world to learn relevant skills they could apply to their communities to promote peace, security, and understanding between conflicting factions (www.iimcr.org).

The Middle East division was formed in 2004 and hosts a yearly four-week Middle East Symposium in Cyprus (chosen for its general "neutrality" and central access to the Middle East countries), bringing together young adults from across the globe to discuss the conflicts in the Middle East. The curriculum consists of case studies, simulations, conflict analysis, and stakeholder analysis exercises, with the goal of teaching participants the how-tos of negotiation and mediation: how to set up a negotiation, how to get buy-in from the community, and how to prevent peace from being derailed.

During the first week, participants set up simple simulations of negotiations, for example, between two neighbors. As the weeks progress, the practice negotiations and mediations become increasingly complex. In the final week, a mediation of the Israeli-Palestinian conflict is often presented as the final simulation, where participants apply their newly acquired negotiation and mediation skills to see if they can successfully broker a deal.

Case studies usually deal with some aspect of the Israeli-Palestinian conflict, the conflict in Iraq, Lebanon, and Iran's nuclear standoff with the European Union and the United States, and some general theme like terrorism, or the role of religion or women in conflict.

The faculty includes negotiators and mediators, UN special envoys, staff at government or nongovernmental organizations; for example, 2005 speakers included Saeb Erakat, the chief negotiator for the PLO; Amre Moussa, Secretary General of the Arab League; and Dr. Ron Pundak from the Peres Center for Peace. The $4,500 cost of the training is awarded on a need basis and provided by the U.S. and Finnish governments and companies like Hewlett-Packard.

Students have applied the skills they learned to establish NGOs; mobilize constituents and monitor elections in Afghanistan and Iraq; organize peaceful student protests; serve as elected officials or advisors to elected officials in Kosovo and Lebanon; and act as Disarmament, Demobilization and Reintegration (DDR) observers.

The Institute for Multi-Track Diplomacy (IMTD)

"It's hard to raise money for peace," says Ambassador John W. McDonald, director of the Institute for Multi-Track Diplomacy (IMTD) to explain why the Arlington, Virginia–based training institute to help grassroots community leaders effect social change had to halt its Israeli-Palestinian programs in 2000 (www.imtd.org). However, unlike other organizations, it was not the Intifada that led to the suspension of activities, but rather the lack of funds, which IMTD primarily receives from dues-paying members, friends of IMTD, the Canadian, Dutch, and German governments, the United States Institute for Peace, and the National Endowment for Democracy.

In 1993, an Israeli group, made up entirely of Israeli Jews, called "Psychologists of the Left and Psychologists of the Right" invited IMTD to host a dialogue. With a neutral American psychologist as the chief of training, the program focused primarily on teaching listening skills. The program was so successful that IMTD received contract offers from the Israeli Ministry of Education and the U.S. governments—both of which were turned down so as not to compromise IMTD's neutrality.

The more relaxed mood in the region after the Oslo Accords allowed IMTD to resume programs with participants from both sides of the conflict. As a result, IMTD hosted a meeting with 30 women—7 Israeli Arabs, 8 Palestinians, and 15 Israeli Jews who had never met an Arab. During one of the discussion sessions,

Ambassador McDonald, who sat outside the circles and "just listened," heard two Palestinian women say that months earlier they had been asleep when Israeli soldiers raided their homes at 3 A.M. and took the women to jail where they were held for months without being told why and or being able to communicate with their families. After six months of detention, they were released without explanation or apology.

The Israeli women were shocked, saying that they had never heard anything like this before, spontaneously telling their Palestinian counterparts that they believed them, empathized with them, and offered an apology. The Palestinian women responded very positively to these expressions, demonstrating that expressions of remorse are a highly effective tool in conflict reconciliation, especially when one group feels humiliated or wronged by the other.

The trainings are not without setbacks. During a one-week program for 30 teachers, three communities in the region (Palestinian, Israeli Jews, and Israeli Arabs) encountered obstacles; the teachers—meeting in a neutral location in southern Turkey—were unable to reach agreement on a joint history of the region that would then be incorporated into the curriculum of 11th graders and money ran out before follow-up meetings could be held.

IMTD trainings typically last a week because the director believes that is all the material that participants can absorb at a time. But McDonald also feels that "one-shot deals" are not enough, preferring several one-week meetings over a five-year period. "The money's not there for the Middle East programs," he says, "but long-term commitments have been possible in Bosnia and Cyprus."

As for proof of effectiveness, McDonald says, "You can't prove peace. It's only the anecdotal evidence that works." While many such programs fail to achieve concrete gains related to the Israeli-Palestinian conflict, he explains that compelling stories from other regions provide hope and inspiration for what is possible in the Middle East with proper resources and attention. For example, after several week-long trainings between 20 Turkish and Greek Cypriots in England, participants started to eat meals together. On their final evening together, a group of Greek guitarists began playing Turkish folk tunes, which they had learned while living in close, albeit contentious, proximity to each other. The Turks then moved to sit next to the Greeks, and started strumming Greek folk dances. Finally, the entire group of Greeks and Turks began dancing Greek folk dances, arm-in-arm together. An 18-year-old boy expressed disbelief, "If my mother told me this, I wouldn't believe it. I had to see it with my own eyes."

In another success story, years after participating in the program, the deputy prime minister of Turkish Cyprus played a major role in removing the green line—a 180-km border that divides Cyprus into Greek and Turkish zones—which 5,000 people crossed the first day. Gains persist to date, in that some high school students in Cyprus, who live on one side of the line, go to school on the other.

"This is beyond an anecdote," says McDonald. "This is peace."

IMTD is seeking funds to renew its work with Israelis and Palestinians, and met with Prince Hassan of Jordan in October 2005, who agreed to sponsor a

Center in Peace and Conflict Resolution in Amman if enough money can be raised to build it.

Related Sources of Training

There are innumerable training and educational programs around the world that offer courses covering topics related to conflict resolution, and in the field of trauma recovery, which can be helpful even if not directly related to the Israeli-Palestinian conflict. For example, the Center for Justice and Peacebuilding (www. emu.edu/ctp) holds year-long and summer institutes. Two trainers, Odelya Gertel and her colleague, Jeffery From, have developed a unique model using theatre and arts as a medium to learn skills and techniques for recovery from trauma, for example, to image personal stories to break the cycle of violence and victimhood. The ICCCR at Columbia University Teachers College offers practical trainings locally and abroad for professionals and the public about methods to deescalate conflict as well as oversees research projects on topics like intractable conflicts (www.tc.columbia.edu/icccr). The Department of International and Transcultural Studies at Teachers College offers a degree concentration in Peace Education and the Peace Education Center offers many trainings and workshops (www. tc.columbia.edu/PeaceEd) where participation in various courses and intensive institutes can aid valuable skills in peacebuilding.

Any such program can enhance skills for healing individuals, families, and communities.

CHAPTER 40

PRIZES FOR PEACE: WINNING COOPERATIVE PROJECTS BETWEEN ISRAELIS AND PALESTINIANS

Judy Kuriansky

Maybe you can do something, by honoring those who do something.

—*Sandra Bullock in the movie Miss America*

An excellent way to build peace is to recognize and reward people who are good examples of cooperation in their lives or in their work. This is consistent with one of my favorite psychological principles: "Reward what you want repeated." That's the spirit behind giving prizes to people working for peace. Several organizations are doing just that, by formally recognizing individuals or partners for their outstanding contributions to Israeli-Palestinian cooperation and peace.

The Victor J. Goldberg Institute of International Education Prize for Peace in the Middle East

The Goldberg Institute of International Education (IIE) Prize for Peace in the Middle East is a $10,000 award to be shared by one Arab and one Israeli, working together to advance the cause of peace in the Middle East. It is meant to reward those who are courageous and committed enough to work together to overcome the religious, cultural, ethnic, and political issues that divide the Middle East. It is given annually, and can be used in any way the winners choose.

It is named for Victor Goldberg, a member of the board of trustees and former vice chairman of IIE, based on his belief that "the more you know someone, the less you demonize."

Goldberg, who also serves on a number of other nonprofit boards, says, "Political leaders and governments have so far been unable to bring lasting peace to this troubled area. Hatred and fear of "the other" abound. While there is no magic solution, one positive force is to encourage people to live and work together at the grassroots level, learning to trust and depend on one another for their common good."

The award is granted by the Institute of International Education. An independent nonprofit founded in 1919, IIE is among the world's largest and most experienced international education and training organizations, running over 200 different programs including the noted Fulbright Scholarships.

In 2005, the Goldberg Prize honored psychology professor Dan Bar-On, head of the behavioral sciences department at Ben Gurion University of the Negev in southern Israel, and his collaborator, educator Sami Adwan at Bethlehem University in the West Bank. Their four-year-long research on "Learning Each Other's Historical Narrative" led to a booklet and a curriculum for 15- and 16-year-olds in the Israeli and Palestinian schools. The booklet gives a history of major events in both cultures from each individual perspective, in Arabic, Hebrew, and English. This format is meant to help young people to read, understand, and compare the historical narratives of each side. This is especially important at a time when there has been much controversy over what Palestinian texts teach—particularly about hostility to Jews—and when Israeli texts also have their own bias, explains Goldberg. "The heroes of one side are the monsters of the other," say the two professors, who maintain a website for their Peace Research Institute on the Middle East (PRIME). They note that Palestinian texts barely mention the Holocaust, and Israeli texts rarely address the suffering of the Palestinians. In the first chapter, for example, 1948 is discussed as the year of the birth of their nation for the Israelis; but for the Palestinians, 1948 is the beginning of becoming refugees, without a state. The 1967 Six-Day War between Israel and Egypt, Jordan, and Syria, dealt with in the second chapter, is seen as aggressive by Palestinians but protective by Israelis. The third chapter addresses the violence that broke out in the year 2000, which the Israelis consider the Palestinians' fault for not living up to the Oslo Accords, and which the Palestinians ascribe to the Israeli settlements and occupation.

Both professors have their own compelling personal stories. Dan lost a close friend in the Six-Day War, and Sami was jailed by the Israelis but tempered his feelings by meeting a respectful prison guard. With some risk, and great effort given the political situation, the two professors brought together Israeli and Palestinian historians and teachers to develop the curriculum about those important moments of shared history of both cultures.

Teachers who have used the booklet say it opens students' eyes to the situation and to feelings of the "other side." Another success is that the project has become more global, with translations into Spanish, Italian, French and other languages. But, the scholars faced challenges along the way. For example, some parents have disapproved of the project, and Palestinian students' protests led to taking an image of both flags off the front covers. Also, the Israeli and Palestinian governments have not given a stamp of approval, nor can teachers teach the story of the other side in regular school classes. As a result teachers participating in the project—about 20 of them—currently meet with a small number of students informally off school premises.

Critics claim that history books in both cultures are biased; one man's murderous suicide bomber is another's revered martyr. To overcome that criticism, this project presents each side of the story, with a place in the middle for students to write their own story. It encourages students to think, and not to hate. The approach came as a natural outgrowth of Dan Bar-On's work leading dialogues with children of Holocaust survivors and the children of Nazis, where young people learned the value of hearing each other's stories.

Goldberg had been to Israel a few times on missions and tours, where he came to realize that the Middle East was very important to world peace. "I set up an endowment to support the annual prize because I was finishing 25 years as a trustee of the IIE and wanted to do something to express my appreciation for the opportunity to work in that wonderful organization." he says. Allan Goodman, IIE's president had offered, "We can name a room for you, but is that really what you want?" Goldberg proposed this prize instead.

Goldberg couldn't be happier to sponsor a prize that focuses on young people. "If you keep teaching kids in school to hate, there will never be peace," he says, "Changing the textbooks can make a big difference." The prize is meant to advance the cause of peace in the Middle East; to bring people together across religious, cultural, ethnic, and political divides; to break down barriers of hate toward "the other"; to recognize innovation; and to reward those who are courageous and committed enough to work to overcome the religious, cultural, ethnic, and political issues that divide the region. To that end, the award is meant to inspire others in the United States and the Middle East, and to motivate current and future IIE grantees to work toward peace in the Middle East. For nominations, see www.IIE.org/goldbergprize; e-mail: goldbergprize@iie. org; or phone: +1(212)984–5515.

The prize selection committee is made up of accomplished men and women from academic, NGO, and governmental backgrounds: the president of American University in Cairo, a former president of the American Jewish Committee, the president of the Ford Foundation, a former U.S. ambassador to United Arab Emirates and Syria, an Iraqi writer, a former U.S. Cabinet member, and the chairman of IIE.

The King Hussein Prize

The King Hussein Humanitarian Leadership Prize—started in 2000—is awarded to people or groups doing exceptional work to promote peace, equality, human rights, cross-cultural understanding, and tolerance between cultures. The medical humanitarian movement, Médecins Sans Frontières (Doctors Without Borders)—which sends volunteer medical staff around the world, including to Israel and the Palestinian territories—won the prize in 2004. In 2005, One Voice was the first joint Arab-Israeli organization to win the prize, and consistent with this, the award was accepted by two female youth—a Palestinian and an Israeli. One Voice—founded by an American Jewish businessman to promote peace in the Middle East—is a grassroots nonpartisan organization of ordinary citizens who want to end the conflict. The organization helps people "take back the agenda from extremists on both sides" by arranging town hall meetings, forums of top industrialists and businesspeople in the region, a youth leadership program, and meetings between Israeli and Palestinian youth interested in peace.

Queen Noor, who presented the prize to the representative of One Voice, said, "Eleven years ago, King Hussein and Prime Minister Rabin worked historically to overcome centuries of division to build a future of peace. . . . How do we create understanding and peace in a world where people look, sound and live so differently? [We must] create opportunities for communities to engage in cross-cultural dialogue."

Other Humanitarian Awards

There are many other humanitarian prizes given to people working on behalf of peace, though not necessarily specifically earmarked to be given to those working in the region. These include notably the Humanitarian Awards given by the Simon Wiesenthal Center and by the Eli Wiesel Foundation for Humanity. These awards are relevant to mention in this context given that their mission is aligned with the spirit of those working toward peace specifically in the Middle East. For example, the mission of the Wiesel Foundation is "to combat indifference, intolerance and injustice through international dialogue and youth-focused programs that promote acceptance, understanding and equality."

"The opposite of hate is not love," said Wiesel at the 2007 gala when TV star Oprah Winfrey was the awardee. "It is indifference."

The Eliav-Sartawi Awards for Middle Eastern Journalism

Another prize honoring cooperation efforts in the region, the Eliav-Sartawi Awards for Middle Eastern Journalism, is given by the esteemed Search for Common Ground organization. Search maintains projects in Israel and many countries on different continents around the world, particularly using media as a means to achieve conflict transformation. Journalists are recognized for their articles that facilitate understanding about the people in the region and the issues that divide them, provide insight into regional issues and debates, contribute to political dialogue, expose readers to new perspectives, and help to lay the groundwork for peaceful solutions.

These awards were started by a veteran American journalist, Zel Lurie, who began reporting on the Middle East during the British Mandate in Palestine before 1948. They are now named after two courageous pioneers of Israeli-Palestinian dialogue. Dr Issam Sartawi (1936–1983)—for whom the Centre for the Advancement of Peace and Democracy at Al-Quds University in Jerusalem is named—was assassinated in April 1983 in a hotel lobby in Lisbon, Portugal, while participating in the peacebuilding process. Lova Eliav has been active in Israeli politics and diplomacy since the founding of the state and in his role as secretary-general of the Labor Party in the early 1970s—a position he lost after calling for negotiations with the Palestinians.

Articles that win the award have appeared in a recognized Arab, Israeli, or Western newspaper, magazine, or other periodical, in Arabic, Hebrew, or English. The winner receives a monetary award of 1,000 Euros. A 2005 winner was Steven Erlanger for his *New York Times* piece, "Palestinians and Israelis Give Peace a Chance at Children's Clinic," about a pediatric oncology unit in a hospital in East Jerusalem. The article covered controversy over the hospital project, including concerns from some Palestinians that Israel's Hadassah Hospital—a partner in the venture, along with Italy and the Peres Centre for Peace—might take too much credit for the cross-border project. Despite the protests, the hospital's director, Dr. Twafiq Nasser—a Christian who maintains his Palestinian nationalism—persisted, believing that projects like this make people aware of "peace through health—trying to address fear on the Israeli side and anger on the Palestinian side." Nasser adds that such projects are "good for the Israelis to see the professional and caring side of the Palestinians and for Palestinians to see that not all Israelis are at checkpoints."

A 2004 prize went to a writer for her *Christian Science Monitor* piece, "One Year Later, Middle East Teens Still Cling to Ideals." The article followed teens participating in the Seeds of Peace camp in Maine: Adar, an Israeli, had a friend, Tom, who was killed when a suicide bomber blew up the bus he was riding in, and her bunkmate Saja, a Palestinian, had a friend who stopped talking to her because she made friends with "the enemy." The 2003 prize went to a journalist who wrote an article entitled, "Like a Bridge over (Very Troubled) Waters," about the Neve Shalom communal village where Israelis and Palestinians live together. Another winner was "Meeting Mohammed: Beginning Israeli-Palestinian Dialogue" by Libby and Len Traubman, about how living room dialogue between the two peoples dispels prejudice and encourages understanding and friendships. Their work is covered in another chapter in this book.

Not all journalism is about bad news; these prizes prove it.

A Winning Honor

Giving awards and prizes hardly makes lasting peace, but makes a valuable contribution by acknowledging and honoring the efforts of people who are making a difference, providing them with some funding, and sending a message to others about the value of such work. Their efforts and their recognition need to be more widely recognized and rewarded.

Afterword

Judy Kuriansky

As this book was going to press, tensions in the region were escalating. Civil war in Palestine was raging between competing militant factions in Gaza. More violence had broken out, and more deaths were suffered by both sides. Then in May, 2007, the already unstable situation in Lebanon was deteriorating, as the Lebanese troops battled Al-Queda-inspired militants. The situation got so dire, that it required intervention by the United Nations. I was in the UN building the day the Security Council met to decide on recommendations to calm the situation. Many of us—NGO representatives, journalists and some UN officials—were in a nearby room at a press conference about our upcoming non-governmental organization conference about climate change. That discussion focused on the impending dire consequences of global warming and greenhouse gas emissions, and the need for awareness and action including simple acts (change a lightbulb, use less water). Then, the attention of those of us in the room turned to the even more immediate dire circumstances of the Middle East situation being determined down the hall.

One pessimist said, "This conflict will never be solved. It will go on forever and ever." An optimist disagreed. "When I was growing up, we lived with the threat of nuclear war between Russia and the U.S.—two cultures that couldn't seem more divergent," he said. "In those days when we were ducking under our school desks as part of nuclear war drills, we never dreamed that things would ever get better. But they did. Nuclear war never broke out. The leaders came to agreement. The countries reached a détente. The world was at peace."

I remember those days well, and was glad to be reminded about perestroika, and how it can serve as a model that peace in the Middle East is also possible.

My personal optimism and faith that we will find a solution to the current crisis is continually renewed by my ongoing contact with individuals and projects like those described in this book: people who are actively doing something to make peace happen. I know those courageous souls will never cease in their efforts to find a common ground and forge a better understanding between the diverse cultures that comprise the region, and that they will continue to develop new projects to accomplish that. In 1992, the Abraham Fund published a 661-page directory of almost 300 projects and institutions divided into 22 broad categories—social, medical, educational and cultural services. While today some are not as active, others are new, adding more to such a volume, in a testimony to the persistent efforts and energy that is being devoted to Jewish-Arab coexistence and cooperation. While the directory focuses on factual accounts, this book is the first of its kind that presents the *feeling* about what these amazing people are doing, and the extent of their commitment and creativity about how to integrate coexistence into their everyday lives. This extends to business ventures, health efforts or even having fun. For example, just the other day I heard about teens selling t-shirts in the name of Israeli-Palestinian peace and also about a circus being produced by Israelis and Palestinians.

To expand this network, and help Jews and Arabs live together in safety, enhanced professional productivity and even personal interpersonal fulfillment through friendships—as I myself have found with so many people in the region—I invite you to join this effort and to get in touch with me.

The programs presented in this book—and the courageous people who run them—do so often at great risk, given the unstable political situation in the region. They deserve worldwide attention for their efforts, as well as economic and emotional support. Help spread the word about their contributions, to help work such as theirs reach enough of a "critical mass" that will provide the tipping point for peace. I continually think about the courageous men, women and teens who are bringing Palestinians and Israelis together to share their experiences for better mutual understanding, and all the young people who are camping, climbing, and cleaning up the environment together in efforts to learn about and care for each other despite their differences.

Contributing to people living in peace is not a vague, philosophically reputable thing to do. It actually changes your own self. Research on volunteerism and do-gooders has shown that brain chemicals shift, leading to more pleasurable, peaceful states of mind and within the body. I've experienced this first hand. On my last trip to Jordan, I felt exhilarated by meeting Jordanians and other Middle Easteners anxious to work together with others of all cultures, offering respect, extending hospitality, and enthusiastically brainstorming research ideas. But we also found some time to have fun together—taking an evening trip to the Dead Sea and a day-long trek at the archeological wonder-of-the-world, Petra. It was psychological research come to life: working and enjoying activities with others brings rapport, and also exhilaration. Such connection is the real purpose of life.

We especially have to reach, and support, young people involved in these efforts. I was especially heartened when I heard my friend Warren Spielberg speak recently at the New School's Wolfson Center for National Affairs about teens' experiences in the Peace Now program which brings Palestinian and Israeli youth together. When a Palestinian told of his home being bulldozed, and an Israeli youth said, "I am sorry," the compassionate response made a difference. Despite the conflict, Warren has found that it is not difficult to recruit youth from both sides to come together. Why? The wise psychological explanation is that in all of us, there can be a fear, but also a yearning, for the "other." Though as little children we may suffer from "stranger anxiety," as we mature, we come to see the "enemy" like ourselves, recognizing our common humanity. As one Palestinian youth told Warren, "I came [to the Peace Now program] to see the compassion of the other, and I was not disappointed." If young people grow up in a culture of hate, they will only unwittingly perpetuate conflict. The opposite can be true. For example, there is a school in Bethlehem—the Hope Flowers School—where Israeli students once studied alongside Palestinian peers, until the present political situation interrupted that. According to the administrator, not one of the school's graduates has engaged in violent or socially-polarising activities. Projects like these are the hope for the future and the people who participate in them are the real heroes for peace.

Here are some things you can do:

- Contact me about grassroots projects you are doing or that you hear about.
- Contact me about panels, workshops, or other events you would like to have for your campus, organization or group, to highlight the psychosocial aspects of the conflict as presented in *Terror in the Holy Land*, and to feature the real people on the ground doing people-to-people projects, working together for peace.
- See the description of this book and of *Terror in the Holy Land* at http://www.greenwood.com/catalog/C9041.aspx. Copies can be ordered directly from there.
- Circulate this message to colleagues and friends.
- Review this book or do a story about the issues and the people profiled here for a publication, electronic outlet, radio or TV show, special event, or blog.
- Use this book as required reading for a class, or recommend it to classes and professors.
- Tell your local library, school library, organization library or even museum store, to get a copy of both books for their collection.
- Recommend these actions to others you know.
- Follow the models in these chapters (for example, the techniques of dialogue groups and compassionate listening) in your personal and interpersonal life and in your work.

Be a part of the growing numbers of concerned and courageous citizens working for peace between the Israelis and Palestinians, and the world.

For all these contributions and participation email: BeyondBulletsAndBombs@gmail.com.

INDEX

About the Editor

JUDY KURIANSKY is a licensed clinical psychologist and adjunct faculty in the Department of Clinical Psychology at Columbia University Teachers College and the Department of Psychiatry at Columbia University College of Physicians and Surgeons. At the United Nations, she is the main representative for the International Association of Applied Psychology and the World Council for Psychotherapy, and an executive committee member of the NGO Committee on Mental Health. She has led workshops on peace, trauma recovery, crisis counseling, and her unique East/West intervention programs around the world, from Buenos Aires to Sagar, India; Singapore; Prague; Belgrade; Jerusalem; Dubai; and Tehran, Iran. Trained by the Red Cross and featured in its post–9/11 public service campaign, she has worked on disaster relief and helping survivors and families after earthquakes, floods, the 9/11 attacks on the World Trade Center, and hurricanes Hugo and Katrina in the United States, as well as around the world, including after SARS in China, bombings in Jerusalem, an earthquake in Australia, and the tsunami in Sri Lanka. A global advisory board member of the Human Dignity and Humiliation Studies Network, she is also a member of the executive committee of the section on Disaster Intervention of the World Psychiatric Association working with the Iberoamerican Ecobioethics Network for Education, Science and Technology. Elected as a Fellow of the American Psychological Association, she is a co-founder of the Media Psychology Division, active in the International Psychology Division, and on the executive board of the Peace Psychology Division (called the Society for the Study of Peace, Conflict, and Violence).

"Dr. Judy," as she is fondly called by millions of fans, is a pioneer of radio call-in advice and Internet advice and is well known for her decades of work as a media psychologist for her radio call-in advice programs, television appearances, and newspaper and magazine columns in print around the world. A former television reporter on WCBS-TV, WABC-TV, and other stations, and show host of "Money and Emotions" on CNBC-TV, she is a popular commentator on many news and talk shows, including on Fox News, MSNBC, Court TV, and CNN Headline News Showbiz Tonight. Currently a feature columnist for national and international print media, including *The New York Daily News* and *China Trends Health* magazine, and on the advisory board of *Bottom Line/Women's Health* magazine, she has written advice columns for publications including *Family Circle* and *Boardroom Reports* in America, *The Singapore Straits Times*, and *Hanako Magazine* and *Sankei Shinbun* newspaper in Japan. Her work has been featured in *The New York Times* and the *International Herald Tribune* as well as on CBS News, CNN, MSNBC, Japan's NHK-TV, and China's CCTV. She lectures extensively and collaborates with colleagues in Asia, and was appointed visiting professor of Peking University Health Science Center and honorary professor in the Department of Psychiatry at the University of Hong Kong. On the board of the Library of American Broadcasting, Kuriansky has received many awards, including the first International Outreach Award from the American Women in Radio and TV, an Olive Award from the Council of Churches, and a Freedoms Foundation Award.

An expert in relationships and many aspects of psychology, including about AIDS, teens, cross-cultural work, psycho-educational models, and disaster relief, Kuriansky has authored many scholarly papers in professional journals, including the *American Journal of Psychiatry*, the *Journal of Clinical Psychology*, and the *Journal of Drug Issues*, and has contributed to many books, including on psychological reactions in *Access: A Disaster Preparedness Manual* and on "Working Effectively with Mass Media in Disaster Mental Health" in *The Handbook of International Disaster Psychology* (4 vols.; Praeger, 2005). Her many books include the best-selling *The Complete Idiot's Guide to a Healthy Relationship*, *The Complete Idiot's Guide to Dating*, *The Complete Idiot's Guide to Tantric Sex*, *How to Love a Nice Guy*, and *Terror in the Holy Land: Inside the Anguish of the Israeli-Palestinian Conflict*. Her original foreign language books include *Goodbye My Troubles, Hello My Happiness* in Japanese and an advice book based on hotline services in China.

A graduate of Smith College, Kuriansky earned a master's degree from Boston University and a PhD in clinical psychology from New York University. She spent 10 years as a senior research scientist at the New York State Psychiatric Institute, doing cross-cultural work in England and the United States on the diagnosis and evaluation of psychiatric disorders and treatment. She also served as co-executive director of the Scientists Committee for Public Information and developed counseling programs for the Institutes for Religion and Health. She has a private practice and sees clients at the National Institute for the Psychotherapies, in New York.

Kuriansky has presented hundreds of addresses and plenaries around the world, including at the State of the World Forum, the World Federation of Mental Health conference in Cairo Egypt, and the Middle East/North Africa

Regional Conference of Psychology in Dubai, and in Amman, Jordan. She has given invited lectures to scores of health groups, women's and men's groups, and business organizations. Recently, her world music band performed at the International Peace Summit in Hiroshima, Japan attended by Nobel Peace Prize Laureates Archbishop Desmond Tutu, His Holiness the Dalai Lama and Betty Williams (noted for her work against violence in her native Northern Ireland). An advocate for mental health in Africa, she is on the Advisory Board of U.S. Doctors for Africa and director of their psychosocial health program.

Kuriansky has also organized and moderated panels at the United Nations Department of Public Information/NGO conferences on "Achieving Collective Security: Partnerships to Prevent Fear, Violence, Genocide, and Terrorism through Targeting the MDG Goals," on "Model Partnerships for Youth: Education, Business, and Technology Projects to Further Peace, Well-Being, Resilience, and Community Action," and on "Partnerships to Mobilize Community Health and Mental Health Resources for Recovery, Resilience and Risk Reduction of Climate Related Disasters." She also ran a workshop on "Integration of Mental Health and Psychosocial Issues into Disaster Risk Reduction and the Hyogo Framework for Action" at UN headquarters in Geneva, Switzerland. At the UN she also co-directs a student journalism program and hosts the UN NGO profiles aired on public television, which are also posted at www.lightmillenium. org. She lectures widely on the Israeli-Palestinian conflict, and has given addresses on "Helping Children Cope with the Israeli-Palestinian Conflict" at the World Congress of Psychotherapy conference in Buenos Aires, Argentina; on "Psychosocial Aspects of the Israeli/Palestinian Conflict and Grassroots Projects for Peace" at the 2006 Workshop on Humiliation and Violent Conflict held at Columbia University; and on "Peacebuilding between Muslims and Jews: A Gender-based View of Unique Projects" at the 2007 conference of Muslim Peacebuilding, Justice and Interfaith Dialogue, in coordination with American University's Center for Global Peace, the Islamic Society of North America, and Salam Institute for Peace and Justice. She has also participated in the leadership training on "Islamic Sources of Conflict Resolution."

About the Contributors

MOHAMMED ABU NIMER, PhD, is associate professor of peace and conflict resolution at American University's School of International Service in Washington, D.C., and co-editor of the *Journal of Peacebuilding and Development*. He has facilitated interfaith dialogue and conducted conflict resolution trainings around the world, particularly in Israel and Palestine, Sri Lanka, the Philippines, and the United States. He has authored books and articles on interfaith dialogue, nonviolence in Islam, and peacebuilding.

SAMI ADWAN, PhD, is a Palestinian teacher in the faculty of education of Bethlehem University and is co-director, with Professor Dan Bar-On of Ben-Gurion University, of the Peace Research Institute in the Middle East (PRIME, http://www.vispo.com/PRIME/). Together they received the 2001 Alexander Langer Prize in Bolzano, Italy; the 2005 Institute of International Education (IIE) Victor J. Goldberg Prize; and the 2005 European Association for the Education of Adults (EAEA) Third Grundtvig Award for their efforts in peacebuilding between Palestinians and Israelis. Adwan also received a Fulbright scholarship in 2007 and was a scholar-in-residence at Monmouth College in New Jersey, where he taught the class "Education: Interculturalism, Conflict and Peacebuilding." His articles are published in the *American Journal of Orthopsychiatry* and *Peace and Conflict: Journal of Peace Psychology*. He can be contacted via e-mail at sadwan@bethlehem.edu.

TOVA AVERBUCH, MSc, is co-founder of *Oganim*, an organization development consultant; breakthrough process designer, facilitator and teacher; and author of "Building Coalitions to Create a Community Planning Tool" in Bunker and Alban's *The Handbook of Large Group Methods* (Jossey-Bass, 2006). Having brought Open Space Technology to Israel, she is a pioneer in applying whole-system and large-group interventions for meaningful conversation and the emergence of collective new wisdom to business and sociopolitical life in Israel and in worldwide initiatives. She can be contacted via e-mail at averbuch@post.tau.ac.il.

RONIT AVNI is the founder and executive director of Just Vision, a nonprofit organization that informs local and international audiences about under-documented Palestinian and Israeli joint civilian efforts to resolve the conflict nonviolently (www.justvision.org). Using media and educational tools, Just Vision raises awareness to encourage civic participation in grassroots peacebuilding. She recently directed and produced the award-winning documentary film *Encounter Point* (www.encoutnerpoint.com) and formerly worked at Witness, a human rights organization, training human rights advocates world-wide to document, expose and prevent rights abuses using video.

DAN BAR-ON, PhD, is a professor of psychology at the Department of Behavioral Sciences at Ben-Gurion University, where he served as chair of the department between 1993–1995 and 2003–2005. He is the co-director of PRIME (Peace Research Institute in the Middle East) near Beit Jala, PNA, with Professor Sami Adwan of Bethlehem University. He was awarded the 2003 Remarque Peace Prize in Oesnabruck, Germany; and together with Professor Adwan, he received the 2001 Alexander Langer Prize in Bolzano, Italy; the 2005 Institute of International Education (IIE) Victor J. Goldberg Prize; and the 2005 European Association for the Education of Adults (EAEA) Third Grundtvig Award for their efforts in peacebuilding between Palestinians and Israelis. Bar-On received a Fulbright scholar-ship in 2007 and was a scholar-in-residence at Monmouth College in New Jersey where he taught the class "Education: Interculturalism, Conflict and Peacebuilding." His books include *Legacy of Silence: Encounters with Children of the Third Reich, Fear and Hope: Three Generations of Holocaust Survivors* and *The Indescribable and the Undiscussable.* An expert in the Holocaust, he co-developed TRT (To Reflect and Trust) intensive encounter groups.

DANIEL BAR-TAL, PhD, is professor of psychology at the School of Education at Tel Aviv University. Formerly co-editor of the *Palestine-Israel Journal* and president of the International Society of Political Psychology (1999–2000), his research interests in political and social psychology focus on psychological foundations of intractable conflicts and peacemaking. He has published 17 books in addition to more than 150 articles and chapters in major social and political psychological journals and books.

ABDUL BASIT, PhD, is a former assistant professor of psychiatry at the Feinberg Medical School, Northwestern University in Chicago, Illinois. He has served as director of the Multicultural Mental Health Services at the University of Chicago; as superintendent of a psychiatric hospital in Illinois; on the Action Planning Committee for Iraq Mental Health; and as a member of the US National Mental Health Advisory Council for four years. He was acknowledged by the U.S. government as a "Nationally Recognized Leader in the Field of Mental Health." A Fullbright scholar, Dr. Basit has written extensively on Muslim mental health, has authored the book *The Essence of the Quran: Commentary and Interpretation of Surah Al-Fatihah* (1997), and is currently editor-in-chief of the *Journal of Muslim Mental Health.*

GERSHON BASKIN is founder and one of the chief executive officers of the Israel/Palestine Center for Research and Information (IPCRI), a cutting-edge Israeli-Palestinian policy think-tank (http://www.ipcri.org/). He moved to Israel from the United States in the late 1970s and worked with Jews and Arabs within Israel until the first Intifada, when he began promoting dialogue and opportunities for cooperation between Israelis and Palestinians in the West Bank and Gaza.

ZVI BEKERMAN, PhD, teaches anthropology of education at the School of Education and the Melton Center, Hebrew University of Jerusalem. He is also a research fellow at the

Truman Institute for the Advancement of Peace, Hebrew University. His main interests are in the study of cultural, ethnic, and national identity, including identity processes and negotiation during intercultural encounters and in formal/informal learning contexts.

JOHN BELL is the program director for Search for Common Ground in their Middle East program, located in Jerusalem. He has extensive experience in diplomatic policy development and conflict resolution work, as well as writing and consulting on the Israeli-Palestinian conflict, Arab reform, and the role of culture in the Middle East. As a Canadian diplomat, he served in Cairo and as spokesperson of the Canadian Department of Foreign Affairs and International Trade. He also worked as special assistant with the Office of the United Nations Special Coordinator in the Occupied Territories, and most recently, as a core member of the "Jerusalem Old City Initiative," a project at the University of Toronto, Munk Centre for International Studies.

RACHEL BRANDENBURG received a BA from Tufts University in May 2005, with a double major in international relations and Middle Eastern studies. She has since worked in Brussels, Belgium; in Washington, DC; and in Jerusalem, Israel, where she spent 2006–2007 as a Fulbright Scholar. In 2003, she worked on a project examining the effects of the second Intifada on a number of Israeli-Palestinian coexistence-building initiatives that primarily work with youth. She intends to continue studying and exploring the Middle East, in pursuit of a career in international conflict resolution and intergovernmental negotiation related to the region.

CAROL DANIEL KASBARI, MA, earned her master's degree in nonprofit administration and public policy and a bachelor's degree in sociology and anthropology and French literature from the Hebrew University of Jerusalem, and holds numerous professional training certificates in organizational development methods. Born and raised in a Palestinian family from Nazareth, she works with local and international organizations on projects involving Israelis and Palestinians in areas ranging from project management and program coordination to conflict resolution and organizational development. She can be contacted via e-mail at carol@kasbari.net.

JULIA DIGANGI, MS, studied foreign service at Georgetown University and is currently a program officer for the American Center for the Washington, D.C.–based International Labor Solidarity. Her career focuses on international humanitarian issues, labor issues, and crisis management. In psychosocial work overseas with Catholic Relief Services, a U.S.–based international aid agency, DiGangi has helped develop programs for orphans and vulnerable children affected by the HIV/AIDS pandemic in southern Africa.

KAREN DOUBILET, PhD candidate in Bar-Ilan's Interdisciplinary Graduate Program on Conflict Management, is originally from Canada, and settled in Israel in 2003. She specializes in the social psychology of intergroup relations in the intractable conflict setting. Her research examines the impact of intergroup encounters as a method of peacebuilding in the context of the Palestinian-Israeli conflict. Karen is also the managing director of PeacePlayers International–Middle East, an organization that uses basketball as a tool to "bridge divides, change perceptions, and develop leaders" among Palestinian and Israeli youth.

EYAD EL SARRAJ, a psychiatrist, is a human rights and peace activist, founder and director general of the Gaza Community Mental Health Program, and secretary general of the Palestinian Independent Commission for Citizen's Rights. He won the Physicians for Human Rights Award in 1997 and the Martin Ennals Award for human rights defenders in 1998. He has published extensively on issues of peace, civil society, human rights, and psychopolitics.

TALI ELISHA, BA, graduated from Rutgers College with a bachelor's degree in psychology. She took leave from graduate studies at Ferkauf Graduate School of Psychology of Yeshiva University in order to make aliyah in June 2007 where she plans to finish her masters degree. Her areas of interest include the study of trauma, mental health, and PTSD among military personnel.

MEIR FENIGSTEIN is the founder and executive director of the Israel Film Festival. For more than 21 years, he has been dedicated to fostering cross-cultural awareness between the United States and Israel through the powerful medium of film (http://www. israelfilmfestival.com). Born and raised in Israel, he began his career as the drummer and beloved character "Poogy" in the band Kaveret, one of the most popular and influential rock groups in contemporary Israeli music. In 2001, he was honored with a Special Achievement Golden Satellite Award for outstanding devotion and commitment in promoting the best of Israeli films through film festivals in the United States.

RACHEL SUMMER CLAIRE FRIEDMAN received her BA from Harvard University and will graduate from Yale Medical School with her MD in May 2008. As student director for an NIH-funded grant for educational development in complementary and alternative medicine in 2005, she presented stress management workshops and organized a student leadership training program at the Omega Institute. She spent 2006 on an NIH-funded fellowship conducting research on the physiological effects of relaxation therapies. She met her father, Meir Fenigstein, for the first time in 1997, and has enjoyed deepening her relationship with him, Israel, and Israeli films ever since.

RICHARD C. GOODWIN was awarded an Honorary PhD from Drexel University which houses the Richard C. Goodwin College of Professional Studies. A real estate developer and major philanthropist, he is the benefactor of the Goodwin Holocaust Museum at the Jewish Community Center of Southern New Jersey, a member of the Ambassador's Circle of the World Jewish Congress, and on the board of directors of the American Friends of Neve Shalom/Wahat al-Salam from which he was awarded their Ambassador of Peace Award in April 2005. He is founder of the Middle East Peace Dialogue Network (www.mpdn.org) which supports over 55 Israeli and Palestinian groups to promote peace.

LEAH GREEN, MA, is founder and director of the Compassionate Listening Project (www.compassionatelistening.org). She holds a Masters degree in Public Policy from the University of Washington, where she also completed coursework for a Masters in Middle Eastern Studies. An internationally recognized leader in Jewish-Palestinian reconciliation, she has led 21 training delegations to Israel/Palestine, speaks and writes about Middle East peacebuilding, and has produced three documentaries about the conflict. Leah has led delegations to Jordan, Syria, and Lebanon, and in 2002, she co-founded the Jewish-German Compassionate Listening project. She teaches compassionate listening world-wide in public, private and academic settings and is a 2003 recipient of the Yoga Journal's Karma Yoga Award,.

RABAH HALABI, PhD, is currently director of the Research Center at the School for Peace. He was the director of the School for Peace for many years and is the editor of a book on the School for Peace approach, *Israeli and Palestinian Identities in Dialogue*. He researched the development of the identity of the Druze minority in Israel for his doctoral degree in the department of education at Hebrew University, where he now lectures.

SARI HANAFI, PhD, is a sociologist who earned his degree from the École des Hautes Études en Sciences Sociales in Paris and is associate professor at the American University of Beirut and former director of the Palestinian Refugee and Diaspora Centre in Shaml. Author of numerous journal articles and book chapters on economic sociology and network analysis of the Palestinian diaspora and international relations, his recent books are *The Emergence of a Palestinian Globalized Elite: Donors, International Organizations and Local NGOs, The Palestinians Sociology of Return*, and *NGOs and Governance in the Arab World*. For more information, see http://staff.aub.edu.lb/~websbs/Sociology/faculty/CVS/Hanafi_cv.htm.

AVNER HARAMATI, MA, has a master's degree in clinical and social psychology and a bachelor's degree in economics from Jerusalem's Hebrew University. A social entrepreneur and organizational consultant, he is co-founder of *Oganim* (supporting organizational and community effectiveness through promoting profit, spirit, and wellness); co-founder and former chairman of *Besod-Siach* (promoting dialogue between groups in conflict within Israeli society); and founding chairman of the Jerusalem Inter Cultural Center (promoting co-living for communities in Jerusalem). His work also focuses on educational and business projects joining Israeli, Palestinian, and international partners together to promote Jerusalem as an open, shared, equal, and prosperous city.

LISA HEFT is vice president of the Open Space Institute of the United States, poet laureate 2006 for the global Open Space community, and author of the *Open Space Idea Book* and numerous papers on facilitation and learning. An international facilitator and interactive learning specialist, she uses participative, dialogic, and interactive processes to help communities, organizations, and individuals work together creatively, communicate across differences, share interdisciplinary and intercultural knowledge, and identify emerging issues and opportunities. Ms. Heft works with businesses, organizations and communities, including Columbia University's Center for International Conflict Resolution, with whom she has consulted on the design and use of Open Space in Northern Iraq and East Timor.

RACHEL HERTZ-LAZAROWITZ, PhD, is a professor of social psychology and educational psychology in the faculty of education at the University of Haifa. She earned her PhD from the University of Texas in Austin in 1974. Her research focus is on intergroup relations between Arabs and Jews across gender and religion (http://construct.haifa.ac.il/~rachelhl/index.htm). In 2004, with Tamar Zelniker, Walter Stephan, and Cookie White Stephan, she edited a special issue of the Journal of Social Issues (Vol. 20, 2) on Arab-Jewish coexistence programs.

ARNINA KASHTAN, BA, is the founder of *Meitarim* ("Chords"), the Center for Non-Violent Transformation in Israel (www.meiterim.com). She conducts public workshops in Nonviolent Communication (NVC) and offers coaching, mediation, and training for individuals, families, groups, and organizations in Israel and the United States, the UK and El Salvador. She is a music graduate from the University of Tel Aviv, a poet and writer.

MIKI KASHTAN, PhD, conducts public workshops in Nonviolent Communication (NVC) and offers mediation, meeting facilitation, coaching, and training for organizations and businesses throughout the United States. In 2002, she co-founded Bay Area Nonviolent Communication (www.baynvc.org). She did her graduate work in sociology at the University of California in Berkeley.

BOAZ KITAIN, the Israeli general manager of Parents Circle-Families Forum, has a lifetime of experience in peacebuilding and coexistence education, specializing in mediation and conflict resolution. After army service as an Israel Defense Forces (IDF) officer, he served as co-director of Neve Shalom/Wahat al-Salam (One Peace) Regional School, general secretary of Neve Shalom, and co-director of the Educational Department of the Kibbutz Ha'artzi Movement in charge of schools across Israel. In 1985 he moved with his family to Neve Shalom/Wahat al-Salam—the only cooperative Jewish-Arab community in Israel, where he served as General Secretary (mayor) of the community, Co-Director of its Regional Primary School and General Director of the community's educational institutions. He and wife, Daniella, parents of four children, live in Neve Shalom/Wahat al-Salam. They lost their eldest son, Tom, in 1997 while he was on military duty.

JUDY KURIANSKY, PhD, is a clinical psychologist and adjunct faculty at Columbia University Teachers College and Columbia Medical School. She has done disaster relief and run unique trainings about recovery in countries from Australia to Iran, India, Israel, and Sri Lanka. At the United Nations, she is a representative for the International Association of Applied Psychology and the World Council for Psychotherapy, and on the executive committee of the NGO Committee on Mental Health. A veteran radio and television reporter and journalist, she writes for newspapers and magazines worldwide from *China Trends Health* magazine to *The New York Daily News*, and hundreds of professional journal articles. An author of many books on relationships translated in many languages, her latest book is *Terror in the Holy Land: Inside the Anguish of the Israeli-Palestinian Conflict*.

NED LAZARUS, PhD candidate in international relations at American University's School of International Service in Washington, D.C, served as program director of the Seeds of Peace Center for Coexistence in Jerusalem from 1996–2004. He is currently co-authoring a curriculum for teaching the Israeli/Palestinian conflict with Dr. Mohammed Abu Nimer, on behalf of the Just Vision and Abraham's Vision projects. Lazarus has published articles in *Haaretz*, *The Jerusalem Report*, *Slate*, *The Forum*, and the *Israel Studies Forum*.

HAGIT LIFSHITZ, MA, is a co-founder and director of *Mifgash* ("Encounter") *for Conflict Transformation*, a nongovernmental organization in Jerusalem. A graduate in educational counseling from Hebrew University, she is an organizational and educational consultant who conducts trainings in Nonviolent Communication (NVC), mediation and peacebuilding. She also facilitates dialogue groups in the context of diversity and conflicts, and mediates between individuals, families, groups, and organizations

EDIE MADDY-WEITZMAN, EdD, is a psychologist working at the Walworth Barbour American International School in Israel, where she is a counselor, coordinator of student services and head of the college counseling program. Her areas of interest include peace education, cross-cultural counseling, and crisis intervention in schools. The title of her dissertation from Boston University is "Waging Peace in the Holy Land: A Qualitative Study of Seeds of Peace, 1993–2004." She can be contacted via e-mail at eweitzman@wbais.org.

IFAT MAOZ, PhD, is a social psychologist, a senior lecturer in the communication department, and a research fellow at the Truman Institute for Advancement of Peace at the Hebrew University of Jerusalem. He can be contacted via e-mail at msifat@gmail.com.

JOSIE MENDELSON has diplomas in early childhood and special education from the David Yellin Institute of Higher Learning in Jerusalem and is former co-director of Hand in Hand, the Center for Jewish Arab Education in Israel. A veteran of education initiatives and Jewish-Arab coexistence programs, she founded Jerusalem's first Jewish-Arab kindergarten at the YMCA and facilitated people-to-people initiatives between Jews and Palestinians in the post-Oslo era. She also served as kindergarten coordinator for the Karev Foundation Educational Program and director of early childhood education for the City of Jerusalem. A volunteer for women's peace organizations, she was a founding member of Mothers and Women for Peace. She can be contacted via e-mail at josiemen@gmail.com.

DENA MERRIAM is founder and convener of the Global Initiative of Women Spiritual Leaders, an international interfaith organization that develops peacebuilding programs in areas of conflict and postconflict (www.gpiw.org). She has organized major interfaith summits around the world, including the Millennium Summit of Religious Leaders at the United Nations. Over the past few years she has worked extensively building dialogue between Israeli and Palestinian women, and has recently launched an initiative to build collaboration and good will between Iraqi and American women.

RAFI NETS-ZEHNGUT is a PhD candidate in the political science department at Tel Aviv University, and a Fellow at the MacMillan Center for International and Area Studies at Yale University. His research interests focus on conflicts, collective memory of conflicts, reconciliation, and healing. He is involved in various local and international activities and research projects that deal with peace and co-existence.

HARRISON OWEN is president of H. H. Owen and Company, the originator of Open Space Technology, and author of numerous books, including *Open Space Technology: A User's Guide, Expanding Our Now: The Story of Open Space Technology*, and *The Practice of Peace*. With an interest in the nature and function of myth, ritual, and culture in social systems, Owen has worked with organizations as diverse as small West African villages, the Peace Corps, and international health and governmental programs. Owen convened the First International Symposium on Organization Transformation. He explores the culture of organizations in transformation as a theorist and practicing consultant.

JODI SHAMS PRINZIVALLI, PhD, is president of the Alliance for Middle East Peace (www.allmep.org) and the U.S. coordinator for the Interfaith Encounter Association. A transpersonal psychotherapist and conflict resolution specialist, she is the founder/director of the Center for Conflict Resolution with programs in Manhattan, New Jersey, Chicago, and Jerusalem, and teaches a three-weekend workshop entitled "The School of Psychospiritual Healing" (www.energeticpsychology.com). Her recent book is *How to Be a Mystic in a Traffic Jam*.

YARON PRYWES is a PhD candidate in social-organizational psychology at Columbia University, and an organizational consultant with GHL Global Consulting, LLC. He recently co-authored *The Nature of Leadership*, a leadership self-help book published by the American Management Association. An adult sponsor for the New York City chapter of the Youth Peacebuilders Network—an offshoot of the International Educators for Peace Institute—he has led and assisted conflict resolution trainings at the United Nations

Secretariat New York Headquarters, Columbia University's International Center for Cooperation and Conflict Resolution, and the Washington International School. He has also facilitated and participated in interethnic peacebuilding programs at Bosnia & Herzegovina's International Educators for Peace Institute, New York City's Friends Seminary and Washington Irving high schools, and the School for International Training's Middle East Peace and Confict program in Jordan, Israel, and the Palestinian Territories.

GINA ROSS, MFCC, is a family therapist and international trauma expert specializing in cross-cultural therapy in seven languages. A featured presenter at international conferences who also appears on radio, television and in print, she is the founder and president of the International Trauma-Healing Institute, a non-profit organization with offices in the US and Israel (www.traumainstitute.org) Originator of the "Ross Model" for collective trauma, applied especially to Israeli and Palestinian societies, she is the author of *Beyond the Trauma Vortex: The Media's Role* in *Healing Fear, Terror, and Violence* (Berkeley, California: North Atlantic Books, 2003) many scholarly articles, and a series of booklets that promote social healing for relevant social sectors that interface with, influence and impact trauma. Born in Syria, she has lived in Brazil, Israel, and Canada and now resides in Los Angeles.

SOPHIE SCHAARSCHMIDT is a PhD candidate in psychology at the Open University (Fernuniversität) in Hagen, Germany; she earned her master's degree in the psychology of culture and religion from the University of Nijmegen, the Netherlands. Co-founder of the Dutch Con-Young-Tion association, which initiated the "Samen in Zee" summer camp with Belgian, Dutch, Israeli, and Palestinian youth, her current research focuses on the impact of emotional processes in Israeli and Palestinian youth peace encounters. She can be contacted via e-mail at sophie.schaarschmidt@gmail.com.

MARA GETZ SHEFTEL, BA, is a research team member at the Truman Institute for the Advancement of Peace at Hebrew University of Jerusalem, and the program coordinator for the Dorot Fellowship in Israel. She has a degree in international relations from Northwestern University and is currently pursuing a master's degree in public policy from Hebrew University.

RONNY A. SHTARKSHALL, PhD, BSW, is a tenured faculty member of the Braun School of Public Health (BSPH) and Community Medicine of the Hebrew University and Hadassah Medical Organization, where he teaches qualitative methodology, health behavior change, and sexual and reproductive health. He negotiated a four-lateral memorandum of understanding for collaboration in public health between Al-Quds University School of Public Health, The Centers for Disease Control and Prevention of the USA, Rollins School of Public Health, Emory University, and BSPH. He also teaches in the training program for sex therapists at Bar-Ilan University in Ramat-Gan, where he serves as the program's director of clinical internship.

HANNA SINIORA is a co-chief executive officer of the Israel/Palestine Center for Research and Information (http://www.ipcri.org/), a cutting-edge Israeli-Palestinian policy think-tank. The former chairperson of the American-Palestinian Chamber of Commerce, he is currently Chair of the European-Palestinian Chamber of Commerce and a member of the Palestine National Council. He is also the publisher of the Palestinian English weekly, The Jerusalem Times/Biladi.

KJELL SKYLLSTAD, professor emeritus at the Department of Musicology, University of Oslo, has done research in the areas of multicultural music education (the Resonant Community project) and music as a medium for conflict resolution and refugee rehabilitation (the AZRA project). He has initiated cooperation projects around the world, including with institutions in Thailand and Sri Lanka where he started the first Asian multicultural music festival in 1999 in the cities of Colombo and Kandy (www.intermusiccenter.com). He can be contacted via e-mail at kjell.muller.skyllstad@broadpark.no.

NAVA SONNENSCHEIN, PhD, is founder of the School for Peace (www.sfpeace.org) at Neve Shalom/Wahat al Salam and was its director for many years. She developed the facilitator training and courses that SFP conducts in universities in Israel, and has trained hundreds of Arab and Jewish facilitators in Israel and from areas of conflict around the world. She has taught the subject at Hebrew University and Tel Aviv University. She got her PhD from Hebrew University and did her thesis on "Processes of majority group identity formation during a Jewish–Palestinian encounter." She can be contacted via e-mail at naava.sfp@nswas.orgnaava.

WARREN SPIELBERG, PhD, teaches psychology and works with the Wolfson Center for National Affairs at the New School University. An authority on problems of men and boys, whose upcoming book *Black Boys* reports original research with African American boys, he was named a "Practitioner of the Year" by the American Psychological Association after 9/11 for his projects placing psychologists in firehouses. He has consulted to the Youth Dialogue Program of Peace Now in Israel for more than fifteen years.

SHOSHANA STEINBERG, PhD, is a senior lecturer in psychology at Kaye Academic College of Education in Beer-Sheva, where she served as the chair of the department between 1988–1996. A graduate of Ben Gurion University, she is actively involved in initiating and implementing projects aimed at promoting interaction and cooperation between Jewish and Palestinian Israeli citizens, and interested in the theoretical and practical aspects of intergroup relations, conflict resolution, peacebuilding, and peace education.

YEHUDA STOLOV, PhD, is the Executive Director of the Interfaith Encounter Association (www.interfaith-encounter.org), that works from Jerusalem for sustainable peace and coexistence by using interfaith encounter to foster respectful and friendly relations between people and communities in the Holy Land and the Middle East. He holds a Ph.D. from the Hebrew University in Jerusalem and is active in many international organizations and initiatives. He is an author of many publications, a public lecturer and was awarded the 2006 Prize for Humanity by the Immortal Chaplains Foundation. He can be contacted via e-mail at yehuda@interfaith-encounter.org.

LORENZO TOPPANO is a noted arranger/composer/singer/songwriter who has produced numerous gold and platinum albums in the world market. He is currently working on the IMAX film *Samsara/The Writings*, and a new musical with an Israeli-Palestinian theme, *The Kite Flyer*, for Brighton Productions. A native Australian, he now lives in California. His interest in world issues and peace has led him to participate in the Oseh Shalom-Sanea al-Salaam Family Peacemakers Camp in 2006.

ELIZABETH TRAUBMAN, MSW, is a retired clinical social worker. In 1982, in response to the threat of global nuclear war, she was a founding member of the Beyond War Movement. In 1992, she co-founded the Jewish-Palestinian Living Room Dialogue Group of San

Mateo, based on her earlier experience organizing the Beyond War conference for Israeli and Palestinian citizen-leaders that resulted in a historic signed document, *Framework for a Public Peace Process*. Libby is a trustee of the Foundation for Global Community, and in 1994 was inducted into the San Mateo County Women's Hall of Fame.

LIONEL TRAUBMAN, DDS, retired after 36 years from his practice of pediatric dentistry in San Francisco. He was regional alumni president of Alpha Omega Jewish dental fraternity, and received the 1998 Distinguished Alumnus Award of the University of California School of Dentistry. He wrote and published *The Oreckovsky Family: From Russia to America*, depicting his pioneer ancestors' immigration following the first pogroms of the early 1880s. For 25 years, Len has published on war and peace from personal experience with Russians and Americans, Armenians and Azerbaijanis, and Jews and Palestinians. With his wife, Libby, he runs the Jewish-Palestinian Living Room Dialogue Group. They initiated two new documentary films which model a new quality of communication: *Dialogue at Washington High*, and *Peacemakers: Palestinians and Jews Together at Camp* (http://traubman.igc.org/vids2007.htm).

CHERYL M. WALKER, MDiv, currently serves as the assistant minister at the Unitarian Church of All Souls in New York City. Previously, she served as intern minister at the Unitarian Church of Montclair, New Jersey, and as a chaplain at Columbia Presbyterian Hospital. She received her Master of Divinity degree from the Union Theological Seminary in New York, where she was awarded the prestigious Maxwell Fellowship for Excellence in Parish Ministry.

NEIL RYAN WALSH, MA, earned his master's degree in psychology from the New School for Social Research in New York City, and his BA in psychology and East Asian studies from St. John's University in New York. An alumnus of the Ronald E. McNair Scholars Program, the Freeman Asia Scholarship Program and the National Security Education Program's David L. Borin Scholars Program for Study at Japan's Sophia University, he was an intern with the United Nations Department of Public Information's Committee on Non-Governmental Organizations. Currently part of the Japan Exchange and Teaching Program, he is the director and coordinator of the Japan for Equal Dignity Program for the Human Dignity and Humiliation Studies Network.

BRUCE E. WEXLER, MD, a professor of psychiatry at Yale University School of Medicine, received his BA degree magna cum laude from Harvard College in 1969 with a concentration in government. His book *Brain and Culture: Neurobiology, Ideology and Social Change* (MIT Press, 2006) presents new ideas about the relationship between people and their environment, culture wars, and ethnic violence. These ideas formed the basis for his founding, with Ambassador Andrew Young, the nonprofit organization *A Different Future* (www.adifferentfuture.org), which uses professional communications expertise to amplify the voices of Israelis and Palestinians, and Arabs and Jews in Israel, who are working together in mutual respect.

TAMAR ZELNIKER, PhD, teaches cognitive development at the psychology department at Tel Aviv University, and is a member of the academic board of a psychotherapy and human rights program in Gaza (1996–2007). Her research is in the areas of cognitive development, theories of mind, and Jewish-Arab coexistence. She published an edited book with Tamar Globerson on cognitive style and cognitive development, and a special issue of the *Journal of Social Issues* with Rachel Hertz-Lazarowitz, Cookie White Stephan, and Walter G. Stephan, titled *Arab-Jewish Coexistence Programs*.